SELF-DETERMINATION AS VOICE

Self-Determination as Voice addresses the relationship between Indigenous peoples' participation in international governance and the law of self-determination. Many states and international organizations have put in place institutional mechanisms for the express purpose of including Indigenous representatives in international policy-making and decision-making processes, as well as in the negotiation and drafting of international legal instruments. Indigenous peoples' rights have a higher profile in the UN system than ever before. This book argues that the establishment and use of mechanisms and policies to enable a certain level of Indigenous peoples' participation in international governance has become a widespread practice, and perhaps even one that is accepted as law. In theory, the law of self-determination supports this move, and it is arguably emerging as a rule of customary international law. However, ultimately the achievement of the ideal of full and effective participation, in a manner that would fulfil Indigenous peoples' right to self-determination, remains deferred.

Natalie Jones is a policy advisor at the International Institute for Sustainable Development and a Research Affiliate at the Centre for the Study of Existential Risk, University of Cambridge. After graduating from the University of Canterbury, Jones completed an LLM and PhD at the University of Cambridge, where she won the Whewell Scholarship for International Law. She is an admitted barrister and solicitor in New Zealand.

Self-Determination as Voice

THE PARTICIPATION OF INDIGENOUS PEOPLES IN INTERNATIONAL GOVERNANCE

NATALIE JONES
University of Cambridge

CAMBRIDGE
UNIVERSITY PRESS

CAMBRIDGE
UNIVERSITY PRESS

Shaftesbury Road, Cambridge CB2 8EA, United Kingdom

One Liberty Plaza, 20th Floor, New York, NY 10006, USA

477 Williamstown Road, Port Melbourne, VIC 3207, Australia

314–321, 3rd Floor, Plot 3, Splendor Forum, Jasola District Centre, New Delhi – 110025, India

103 Penang Road, #05-06/07, Visioncrest Commercial, Singapore 238467

Cambridge University Press is part of Cambridge University Press & Assessment, a department of the University of Cambridge.

We share the University's mission to contribute to society through the pursuit of education, learning and research at the highest international levels of excellence.

www.cambridge.org
Information on this title: www.cambridge.org/9781009406314

DOI: 10.1017/9781009406321

First published 2024

A catalogue record for this publication is available from the British Library.

Library of Congress Cataloging-in-Publication Data
NAMES: Jones, Natalie (Writer on indigenous peoples), author.
TITLE: Self-determination as voice : the participation of indigenous peoples in international governance / Natalie Jones, University of Cambridge.
DESCRIPTION: Cambridge, United Kingdom ; New York, NY : Cambridge University Press, 2023. | Includes bibliographical references and index.
IDENTIFIERS: LCCN 2023027692 (print) | LCCN 2023027693 (ebook) | ISBN 9781009406314 (hardback) | ISBN 9781009406369 (paperback) | ISBN 9781009406321 (epub)
SUBJECTS: LCSH: Indigenous peoples (International law) | Indigenous peoples–Legal status, laws, etc. | Indigenous peoples–Government relations | Self-determination, National. | Indigenous peoples–Ethnic identity.
CLASSIFICATION: LCC KI280 .J66 2023 (print) | LCC KI280 (ebook) |
DDC 341.4/852–dc23/eng/20230616
LC record available at https://lccn.loc.gov/2023027692
LC ebook record available at https://lccn.loc.gov/2023027693

ISBN 978-1-009-40631-4 Hardback

For Samuel Jones

Contents

Acknowledgements

This book would not exist without the support and friendship of numerous people and institutions. It is based on my doctoral work, completed at the University of Cambridge with the material backing of the Commonwealth Scholarship from the UK Foreign, Commonwealth & Development Office, a fellowship from Graduate Women New Zealand, and the Whewell Scholarship for International Law from Trinity College, Cambridge. In Cambridge, I have deeply benefited from the support – in terms of both intellectual community and material conditions – of my colleges: Trinity College, and latterly Christ's College and Hughes Hall. Each exemplifies, in different ways, the best aspects of collegiate life. Special thanks are due to their respective gardeners. The Lauterpacht Centre for International Law and the Squire Law Library provided excellent working environments during my PhD.

I was extremely grateful for the supervision of Eyal Benvenisti and Kate Miles. Kate was the principal supervisor for this project in its early, evolutionary years, and without her encouragement, clarity of thought, and patience, it would not have come this far. Eyal at first co-supervised and later supervised the PhD thesis with characteristic acumen and care and continued to offer advice on the development of the manuscript. Doctoral examiners Surabhi Ranganathan and Mattias Åhren, and four anonymous peer reviewers for Cambridge University Press, gave generous and incisive advice as to how the thesis could be converted into a monograph, although I do not claim to have done their ideas justice.

Following the PhD, I was fortunate to undertake postdoctoral research at the Centre for the Study of Existential Risk at the University of Cambridge (CSER). CSER offered me not only the freedom, time, and moral support to write the book but also a highly stimulating academic environment. In particular, I am grateful to my line managers, S. J. Beard, Seán Ó hÉigeartaigh, and Jess Bland, the wonderful admin team led by Clare Arnstein, and the camaraderie of great researchers, including Alexa Hagerty, Ellen Quigley, Freya Jephcott, Mia Sannapureddy, Akaraseth Puranasamriddhi, Alex McLaughlin, Tom Hobson, Matthijs Maas, Lalitha Sundaram, and Lara Mani.

I owe thanks to several others who played important roles in guiding my thoughts on the book. The project benefited from conversations in particular with Lorand Bartels, Jamie Trinidad, Phillip Allott, Kiri Toki, John Adenitire, and Harum Mukhayer. I deeply appreciated the camaraderie of the Cambridge Public International Law PhD discussion group. Thanks to Ali Cole for insightful comments on specific chapters. I am of course to blame for any errors or shortcomings in the book. Sarah Nouwen, Julius Weitzdörfer, and Jorge Viñuales offered valuable advice on publishing. The Opening Lines writing group provided crucial camaraderie. I am forever grateful to Anna Sturman, Matt Scobie, and Max Harris for the conversations begun during lockdown. Parts of the book benefited from being presented at conferences and workshops. I am grateful to the participants and attendees at the 2018 Cambridge International Law Journal Conference, graduate talks at Trinity College, a talk given at the University of Canterbury in 2019, the 2021 European Society of International Law Conference, the 2021 Cambridge Zero Research Symposium, the 2021 Evidence for Action Symposium at the University of Sussex, and two successive work-in-progress seminars at CSER. A version of Chapter 1 has been published in the *British Yearbook of International Law*. I would also like to thank Tom Randall, Toby Ginsberg, and Gemma Smith at Cambridge University Press for their patience and help at all stages of the process. Thanks to Kate McIntosh for expert indexing assistance.

My academic interest would almost certainly not have developed in the way that it had if not for certain formative experiences. Specific thanks are due to the Aotearoa Youth Leadership Institute team at COP 19 and the New Zealand Youth Delegation to COP 21 for, to paraphrase Anna, being there when I discovered how international negotiations actually worked. Later, at the Earth Negotiations Bulletin, many amazing colleagues and friends – of whom there are really far too many to name – kept me not only close to the ground in various multilateral processes but also well stocked in inspiration and joy.

I have the deepest gratitude to my housemates, friends, and family, in Cambridge and afar. I particularly want to acknowledge Lydia Heinrichs, Mark Burrell, Max Wilkinson, Olivia Tidswell, Rory Little, Nick Gale, Cathy Mason, Anna Christie, Matilda Gillis, Olia Zadvorna, Duncan Wallis, Oliver Hailes, Emma Gattey, Annalise Higgins, Priya Devendran,

Ramya Rangan, Sven Wang, Beth Barnes, Tildy Stokes, and Àdria Garriga, all of whom met with good humour, and better advice, my considerable angst about the thesis/book. Dave, Courtlin, and Honey Allatt opened their door at just the right time. I'm not sure where I'd be without Kaitlin Naughten. All my friends at home would require another entire book to properly acknowledge. Thanks also to the Berkhamsted gang – Jules, Moira, and Jay. Andrew was forever encouraging, and I could not have written this book without him. The final word must go to Brent, Vicky, and Harry, for their endless love and belief. This book is dedicated to them.

Table of Cases

International Court of Justice

Accordance with International Law of the Unilateral Declaration of Independence in Respect of Kosovo (Advisory Opinion) [2010] ICJ Rep 403

Case Concerning Barcelona Traction, Light, and Power Company, Ltd (Belgium v. Spain) (Judgment) [1971] ICJ Rep 3

Case Concerning East Timor (Portugal v. Australia) (Judgment) [1995] ICJ Rep 90

Case Concerning Right of Passage over Indian Territory (Merits, Judgment of 12 April 1960) [1960] ICJ Rep 6

Case Concerning Rights of Nationals of the United States of America in Morocco [1952] ICJ Rep 176

Case of the Monetary Gold Removed from Rome in 1943 (Italy v. France, UK and USA) (Preliminary Question) [1954] ICJ Rep 19

Colombian-Peruvian Asylum Case (Judgment) [1950] ICJ Rep 266

Continental Shelf (Libyan Arab Jamahiriya/Malta) (Judgment) [1985] ICJ Rep 13

Dispute Regarding Navigational and Related Rights (Costa Rica v. Nicaragua) (Judgment) [2009] ICJ Rep 213

Fisheries Jurisdiction (United Kingdom v. Iceland) (Merits) [1974] ICJ Rep 3

Frontier Dispute (Burkina Faso v. Mali) (Judgment) [1986] ICJ Rep 554

Interpretation of the Agreement of 25 March 1951 between the WHO and Egypt [1980] ICJ Rep 73

Jurisdictional Immunities of the State (Germany v. Italy: Greece intervening) (Judgment) [2012] ICJ Rep 99

Legal Consequences for States for the Continued Presence of South Africa in Namibia (South West Africa) Notwithstanding Security Council Resolution 276 (1970) [1971] ICJ Rep 16

Legal Consequences of the Construction of a Wall in the Occupied Palestinian Territory (Advisory Opinion) [2004] ICJ Rep 136
Legal Consequences of the Separation of the Chagos Archipelago from Mauritius in 1965 (Advisory Opinion) [2019] ICJ Rep 95
Legality of the Threat or Use of Nuclear Weapons (Advisory Opinion) [1996] ICJ Rep 64
Military and Paramilitary Activities in and against Nicaragua (Nicaragua v. United States of America) (Merits, Judgment of 27 June 1986) [1986] ICJ Rep 14
Navigational and Related Rights (Costa Rica v. Nicaragua) (Judgment) [2009] ICJ Rep 213
North Sea Continental Shelf (Judgment) [1969] ICJ Rep 3
Reparations for Injuries Suffered in the Service of the United Nations (Advisory Opinion) [1948] ICJ Rep 174
Western Sahara (Advisory Opinion) [1975] ICJ Rep 12

Permanent Court of International Justice

"Lotus" (France v. Turkey), Judgment No. 9, [1927] PCIJ Series A, No. 10

African Commission on Human and Peoples' Rights

Centre for Minority Rights Development (Kenya) and Minority Rights Group International (on behalf of the Endorois Welfare Council) v. Kenya (Merits) (2010) Communication No. 276/03
Katangese Peoples' Congress v. Zaire (Merits) (1995) Communication No. 75/92
Kevin Mgwanga Gunme v. Cameroon (Merits) (2009) Communication No. 266/2003

Inter-American Court of Human and Peoples' Rights

Kichwa People of Sarayaku v. Ecuador, Judgment of 27 June 2012 (Judgments on Merits, Reparations, and Costs) IACtHR Series C No. 245
Saramaka People v. Suriname, Judgment of 28 November 2007 (Judgment on Preliminary Objections, Merits, Reparations, and Costs) IACtHR Series C No. 172
Saramaka People v. Suriname, Judgment of 12 August 2008 (Interpretation of the Judgment on Preliminary Objections, Merits, Reparations, and Costs) IACtHR Series G No. 185

Canada

Re Reference by the Governor in Council Concerning Certain Questions Relating to the Secession of Quebec from Canada, Supreme Court of Canada, 20 August 1998, 115 ILR 536

European Union

Case T-512/12 *Front Polisario v. Council of the European Union*, Judgment of the General Court, Eighth Chamber, ECLI:EU:T:2015:953

New Zealand

Waitangi Tribunal, *The Report on the Comprehensive and Progressive Agreement for Trans-Pacific Partnership – Pre-Publication Version*, WAI 2522 (Waitangi Tribunal, 2020) https://waitangitribunal.govt.nz/news/tribunal-releases-report-on-electronic-commerce-chapter-in-cptpp/

Table of Treaties

African Charter on Human and Peoples' Rights (adopted 27 June 1981, entered into force 21 October 1986) OAU Doc CABLEG/67/3 rev 5, 21 ILM 58

Agreement Establishing the Fund for the Development of the Indigenous Peoples of Latin America and the Caribbean (signed 24 July 1992, entered into force 4 August 1993) 1728 UNTS 380

Agreement Establishing the International Fund for Agricultural Development (opened for signature 20 December 1976, entered into force 30 November 1977) 1059 UNTS 191

Agreement on Andean Subregional Integration (Cartagena Agreement) (signed 26 May 1969, entered into force 16 October 1969) (1969) 8 ILM 910

Agreement on Cooperation on Aeronautical and Maritime Search and Rescue in the Arctic (signed 12 May 2011, entered into force 19 January 2013) 50 ILM 1119

Agreement on Cooperation on Marine Oil Pollution Preparedness and Response in the Arctic (signed 15 May 2013, entered into force 25 March 2016), https://oaarchive.arctic-council.org/handle/11374/529

Agreement to Prevent Unregulated High Seas Fisheries in the Central Arctic Ocean (signed 3 October 2018, entered into force 25 June 2021) OJ L 73, 3 March 2019, pp. 3–8

Charter of the United Nations (signed 26 June 1945, entered into force 24 October 1945) 1 UNTS 26

Constitution of the United Nations Educational, Scientific and Cultural Organisation (adopted 16 November 1945, entered into force 4 November 1946) 4 UNTS 52

Constitution of the United Nations Food and Agriculture Organization, reprinted in FAO, Basic Texts of the Food and Agriculture Organization of the United Nations (FAO 2017)
Constitutive Act of the African Union (adopted 11 July 2000; entered into force 26 May 2001) 2158 UNTS 3
Convention Concerning Indigenous and Tribal Peoples in Independent Countries (adopted 27 June 1989, entered into force 5 September 1991) 1650 UNTS 383
Convention Concerning the Protection of the World Cultural and Natural Heritage (adopted 16 November 1972; entered into force 17 December 1975) 1037 UNTS 151
Convention Establishing the World Intellectual Property Organization (adopted 15 July 1967, entered into force 26 April 1970) 828 UNTS 3
Convention on Access to Information, Public Participation in Decision-Making and Access to Justice in Environmental Matters (concluded 25 June 1998, entered into force 30 October 2001) 2161 UNTS 447
Convention on Biological Diversity (adopted 5 June 1993, entered into force 29 December 1993) 1760 UNTS 79
Draft Nordic Saami Convention, accessible at https://www.sametinget.se/105173
Euro-Mediterranean Agreement between the European Communities and their Member States and the Kingdom of Morocco (adopted 26 February 1996) OJ 2000 L 70
Framework Convention for the Protection of National Minorities (opened for signature 1 February 1995, entered into force 1 February 1998) CETS No 157
International Covenant on Civil and Political Rights 1966 (adopted 16 December 1966, entered into force 23 March 1976) 999 UNTS 171
International Covenant on Economic, Social and Cultural Rights 1966 (adopted 16 December 1966, entered into force 3 January 1976) 993 UNTS 3
Minamata Convention on Mercury (signed 10 October 2013, entered into force 16 August 2017) 3202 UNTS
Nagoya Protocol on Access to Genetic Resources and the Fair and Equitable Sharing of Benefits Arising from Their Utilization (concluded 29 October 2010, entered into force 12 October 2014) UN Doc UNEP/CBD/COP/DEC/X/1
Statute of the International Court of Justice (concluded 26 June 1945, entered into force 24 October 1945) 33 UNTS 993

Stockholm Convention on Persistent Organic Pollutants (adopted 22 May 2001, entered into force 17 May 2004) 2256 UNTS 119

Treaty between Australia and the Republic of Indonesia on the Zone of Cooperation in an area between the Indonesian Province of East Timor and northern Australia (signed 11 December 1989, entered into force 9 February 1991) 1001 Australian Treaty Series 9

Treaty of Lisbon amending the Treaty on European Union and the Treaty establishing the European Community (adopted 13 December 2007, entered into force 1 December 2009) 2702 UNTS

Treaty on European Union (adopted 7 February 1992, entered into force 1 November 1993) 1755 UNTS

UN Convention to Combat Desertification in Those Countries Experiencing Serious Drought and/or Desertification, Particularly in Africa (signed 14 October 1994, entered into force 26 December 1996) 1954 UNTS 3

UN Framework Convention on Climate Change (concluded 9 May 1992, entered into force 21 March 1994) 1771 UNTS 107

Vienna Convention on the Law of Treaties (adopted 22 May 1969, entered into force 27 January 1980) 1155 UNTS 331

Vienna Convention on the Law of Treaties between States and International Organizations or Between International Organizations (concluded 21 March 1986) 1155 UNTS 331

Abbreviations

AEPS	Arctic Environmental Protection Strategy
BEAC	Barents Euro-Arctic Council
BRC	Barents Regional Council
CAOFA	Central Arctic Ocean Fisheries Agreement
CBD	Convention on Biological Diversity
CCPICAN	Consultative Council of Indigenous Peoples of the Andean Community
CIF	Climate Investment Funds
COP	Conference of the Parties
CSO	Barents Committee of Senior Officials
DGM	Dedicated Grant Mechanism for Indigenous Peoples and Local Communities
ECOSOC	United Nations Economic and Social Council
EMRIP	Expert Mechanism on the Rights of Indigenous Peoples
ESF	Environmental and Social Framework
ESS	Environmental and Social Standard
EU	European Union
FAO	United Nations Food and Agriculture Organization
FCPF	Forest Carbon Partnership Facility
FILAC	Fund for the Development of the Indigenous Peoples of Latin America and the Caribbean
FPIC	free, prior and informed consent
GCF	Green Climate Fund
GEF	Global Environment Facility
ICC	Inuit Circumpolar Council

ICCPR	International Covenant on Civil and Political Rights
ICESCR	International Covenant on Economic, Social and Cultural Rights
ICJ	International Court of Justice
IFAD	International Fund for Agricultural Development
IGC	WIPO Intergovernmental Committee on Intellectual Property and Genetic Resources, Traditional Knowledge and Folklore
IIPFCC	International Indigenous Peoples' Forum on Climate Change
IIPFWH	International Indigenous Peoples' Forum on World Heritage
ILC	International Law Commission
ILO 169	International Labour Organization Convention No. 169 on Indigenous and Tribal Peoples
IPAF	IFAD Indigenous Peoples Assistance Facility
IPAG	GEF Indigenous Peoples Advisory Group
IPBES	Intergovernmental Science-Policy Platform on Biodiversity and Ecosystem Services
IPRIs	Indigenous peoples' representative institutions
IUCN	International Union for the Conservation of Nature
LCIPP	UNFCCC Local Communities and Indigenous Peoples Platform
OHCHR	Office of the UN High Commissioner on Human Rights
NGO	non-governmental organization
POPs	persistent organic pollutants
RAIPON	Russian Association of Indigenous Peoples of the North
SBI	Subsidiary Body for Implementation
SBSTA	Subsidiary Body for Scientific and Technological Advice
TWAIL	Third World Approaches to International Law
UN	United Nations
UN-REDD Programme	UN Programme on Reducing Emissions from Deforestation and Forest Degradation
UNCED	United Nations Conference on Environment and Development

UNDP	United Nations Development Programme
UNDRIP	United Nations Declaration on the Rights of Indigenous Peoples
UNESCO	United Nations Educational, Scientific and Cultural Organization
UNEP	United Nations Environment Programme
UNFCCC	United Nations Framework Convention on Climate Change
UNIPP	United Nations Indigenous Peoples' Partnership
UNPFII	United Nations Permanent Forum on Indigenous Issues
VCLT	Vienna Convention on the Law of Treaties
WCIP	World Conference on Indigenous Peoples
WGDD	Ad Hoc Working Group on the Draft Declaration
WGIP	Working Group on Indigenous Populations
WHC	UNESCO World Heritage Committee
WIPO	World Intellectual Property Organization

Introduction

Under the new sun an epoch is being staged!

Little peoples are to be granted the right of self-determination!

Small nations and remnants of nations are to sit beside their great allies at the Peace Table, and their just claims are to be duly incorporated in the terms of a righteous peace.

–Zitkala-Ša, 1919[1]

I am going to Geneva, and I suppose many stones have been placed in my path.

–Deskaheh, 1923[2]

In 1923, the Haudenosaunee leader Deskaheh undertook a long journey. From his homelands on the banks of the Grand River in the land colonially known as Canada, Deskaheh travelled to Geneva, under a mandate from the Haudenosaunee Confederacy,[3] to petition the League of Nations.[4]

[1] Gertrude Bonnin (Zitkala-Ša), 'Editorial Comment' (1919) 6(4) *American Indian Magazine*, 161–162, 161.

[2] Levi General (Deskaheh), 'I Am Going to Geneva' in Daniel M. Cobb (ed.) *Say We Are Nations: Documents of Politics and Protest in Indigenous America since 1887* (Chapel Hill: University of North Carolina Press, [1923] 2015) 45, 48.

[3] Often known as the Six Nations of the Iroquois Confederacy.

[4] Of interest is that Deskaheh's journey was facilitated not by a Canadian passport but rather by a passport issued by the Haudenosaunee Confederacy. This was not the first time Deskaheh had travelled on Haudenosaunee travel papers; two years earlier, he had appealed against Canada's treaty violations to the British Crown: Sheryl R. Lightfoot, 'Decolonizing Self-Determination: Haudenosaunee Passports and Negotiated Sovereignty' (2021) 27 *European Journal of International Relations*, 971–994, 981. Also see Sara Dehm, 'Passport' in Jessie Hohmann and Daniel Joyce (eds.), *International Law's Objects* (Oxford: Oxford University Press, 2018) 342, at 353. Haudenosaunee passports are still used today.

The Haudenosaunee sought membership of the League as an independent nation, on the basis of its treaties with Britain.[5] They further sought to appeal against Canada's violations of treaties and of the Haudenosaunee's right to self-determination.[6] Deskaheh was not without allies: several League members supported formal consideration of the application,[7] and as a result, Deskaheh's letter entitled 'The Redman's Appeal for Justice' was distributed to members of the Council of the League.[8] However, due to strong objections from Canada and Britain, the League did not hear Deskaheh's petition in person, and ultimately the issue fell off its agenda.[9]

This was by no means the first – or last – manifestation of Indigenous internationalism,[10] although it was among the first Indigenous attempts to seek justice via an international organization rather than appealing directly to

5 Richard Veatch, *Canada and the League of Nations* (Toronto: University of Toronto Press, 1975) 95: Deskaheh attempted to 'register with the League several strips of wampum representing treaties his ancestors had concluded [with the British]'.

6 Deskaheh, 'Geneva' 45; Deskaheh, 'To the League of Nations; The Redman's Appeal for Justice' (1923), accessed at www.docip.org. Ronald Niezen, *The Origins of Indigenism: Human Rights and the Politics of Identity* (Berkeley: University of California Press, 2003) 31–36; Douglas Sanders, 'The Legacy of Deskaheh: Indigenous Peoples as International Actors' in Cynthia Price Cohen (ed.), *Human Rights of Indigenous Peoples* (Ardsley, NY: Transnational Publishers, 1998) 73–88.

7 Before Deskaheh's journey to Geneva, he had travelled to Washington to successfully convince the Netherlands to sponsor the appeal to the League. Persia, Panama, Estonia, and the Republic of Ireland requested that the question be put to the Permanent Court of International Justice for an advisory opinion: Grace Li Xiu Woo, 'Canada's Forgotten Founders: The Modern Significance of the Haudenosaunee (Iroquois) Application for Membership in the League of Nations' (2003) 1 *Law, Social Justice & Global Development Journal*, 1; Amar Bhatia, 'The South of the North: Building on Critical Approaches to International Law with Lessons from the Fourth World' (2012) 14 *Oregon Review of International Law*, 131–175, 163–170.

8 Deskaheh, 'Redman's Appeal'. See Veatch, *Canada and the League of Nations*, 96–98.

9 Bhatia, 'The South of the North' 167–171. Canada retaliated against the Haudenosaunee by deposing its hereditary Council, and Deskaheh was never able to return home to the Grand River, dying in exile in New York in 1925.

10 Or, in other words, Indigenous peoples' expressions and assertions of external sovereignty. Witness, for example, the transnational confederations and treaties concluded among Indigenous peoples, such as the Mi'kmaw Nation, the Haudenosaunee themselves, and the 1701 treaty between the Haudenosaunee and the Anishinabek, and the many treaties concluded between imperial powers and Indigenous peoples in the 1700s and 1800s; for instance, the 1784 Haldimand Treaty between the British and the Six Nations, and the 1840 Treaty of Waitangi between Māori and the British Crown. For more examples of treaties and a classic treatment of the legal implications of such treaties, see Miguel Alfonso Martínez, 'Study on Treaties, Agreements and Other Constructive Arrangements between States and Indigenous Populations: Final Report' (22 June 1999) UN Doc E/CN.4/Sub.2/1999/20.

imperial powers.[11] The next year, Māori leaders Tahupōtiki Wiremu Rātana and Pita Moko sought a meeting with the secretary general of the League in order to appeal against British violations of the Treaty of Waitangi of 1840 but, like Deskaheh, were turned away without a hearing.[12] The hopes of Indigenous internationalists like Ihanktonwan leader Zitkala-Ša and other members of the Society of American Indians[13] – that the implementation of the principle of self-determination post-World War I might give Indigenous peoples representation in a world forum alongside other colonized peoples – were thereby dashed.[14] The structure of the international community ultimately functioned to exclude Indigenous peoples.[15]

A century on, the relationship between international institutions and Indigenous peoples is on its face starkly different to that prevailing in 1923. Far from excluding, ignoring, or rejecting Indigenous peoples, on the contrary, many states and international organizations have put in place institutional mechanisms for the express purpose of including Indigenous representatives in international policymaking and decision-making processes, as well as in the negotiation and drafting of international legal instruments. Indigenous peoples' rights have a higher profile in the UN system than ever before, following the creation of the Permanent Forum on Indigenous Issues (UNPFII) in 2000, the adoption of the UN Declaration on the Rights of Indigenous Peoples (UNDRIP) in 2007, and the creation of the Expert Mechanism on the Rights of Indigenous Peoples (EMRIP) later that same year, among other institutional innovations. Contrary to Deskaheh's experience of automatic exclusion in 1923, in 2023 an Indigenous leader can expect to be welcomed into many of the international forums relevant to the protection of Indigenous peoples' rights.

[11] A point made by Sophie Rigney, 'On Hearing Well and Being Well Heard: Indigenous International Law at the League of Nations' (2021) 34(2) *Third World Approaches to International Law Review*, 122–153, 140.

[12] Sheryl Lightfoot, *Global Indigenous Politics: A Subtle Revolution* (New York: Routledge, 2016) 36.

[13] Founded by Henry Standing Bear (Oglala), Charles Eastman (Mdewakantonwan), and others: Kiara M. Vigil, 'Who Was Henry Standing Bear? Remembering Lakota Activism from the Early Twentieth Century' (2017) 37(3) *Great Plains Quarterly*, 157–182, 174.

[14] Adom Getachew details how Woodrow Wilson and Jan Smuts 'excised the revolutionary implications of the Bolshevik right to self-determination and repurposed the principle to preserve racial hierarchy in the new international organization': Adom Getachew, *Worldmaking after Empire: The Rise and Fall of Self-Determination* (Princeton: Princeton University Press, 2019) 10 and chapter 2.

[15] Or, as Rigney puts it, 'a refusal to engage, a rejection, or a move to ignore': Rigney, 'On Hearing Well', 148.

Indeed, a process of discussion and negotiation has been underway in the past decade to consider whether and how to accord a separate status to Indigenous peoples to that of non-governmental organizations (NGOs) in the UN General Assembly, Economic and Social Council (ECOSOC), and related UN organs. Although these negotiations were initially expected to conclude in 2017, political setbacks have meant that as of writing these negotiations are in a holding pattern, with deep disagreements persisting – although the potential for resolution remains.

It is an opportune time to take stock of these developments. How did this extensive web of practice unfurl? What is the legal basis that underpins the participation of Indigenous peoples in policy-, decision-, and law-making at the international level? What does the practice of states and international organizations in respect of enabling and supporting Indigenous peoples' participation tell us about that legal basis? What insights can be gleaned from the multitude of past and ongoing practice to usefully inform ongoing and future negotiations towards greater inclusion of Indigenous peoples in the General Assembly and elsewhere? And does our initial observation – that international organizations and states now overwhelmingly include, rather than exclude or ignore Indigenous peoples in international governance processes – hold under close examination?

This book argues that the establishment and use of mechanisms and policies to enable a certain level of Indigenous peoples' participation in international governance has become a widespread practice among states and international organizations, and perhaps even one that is accepted as law. However, ultimately the achievement of the ideal of full and effective participation, in a manner that would fulfil Indigenous peoples' right to self-determination, remains deferred. Substantial barriers remain, raising the question of the extent to which an 'illusion of inclusion'[16] may function to bolster the legitimacy of the international processes under consideration – and, by extension, that of (Eurocentric) international law itself – while obscuring continued (neo)colonial economic and political relations that serve to facilitate further wealth extraction and dispossession of land from Indigenous peoples.

The book builds, and expands, on existing accounts of Indigenous peoples' participation in international organizations and international law-making processes to demonstrate how over the past four decades, international institutional forms that include Indigenous peoples have multiplied and expanded

[16] Jeff Corntassel, 'Toward Sustainable Self-Determination: Rethinking the Contemporary Indigenous-Rights Discourse' (2008) 33 *Alternatives*, 103–132, 111.

such that Indigenous peoples' participation in international governance is now a widespread phenomenon. This is the case both within and outside the UN, in regional organizations on several continents, in informal international institutions, as well as treaty bodies, and the most well-known international organizations. In theory, the law of self-determination supports such a move: from this body of law, we can derive a rule that peoples have a collective right to participate in international governance, accompanied by correlative obligations that are held by states and international organizations. In addition, from a doctrinal perspective, there is an argument to be made that the right of Indigenous peoples to participate in international governance is emerging as a rule of customary international law – regardless of whether we take a traditional, two-element approach, or an approach that focuses on one of the two elements to the exclusion of the other. Under such a rule, Indigenous peoples would have a legal right to be heard in international law-making, decision-making, policymaking, and other governance processes, and states have a corresponding duty to enable such participation.

Notwithstanding increasing international acceptance of Indigenous peoples' participation, the level of this participation is limited in key respects. Barriers to full and effective participation persist at systemic, institutional, and material levels. In tracing the rise of Indigenous peoples' participation, the book concurrently examines the level of participation established in the various organizations and bodies. In this sense, the book reveals how the level of Indigenous peoples' participation in a given body or process tends to be inversely proportional to the scope of that body's powers; how the structures of international organizations mean that the final say on a decision or policy tends to remain with states, no matter how equal the participation up until that moment; how the types of fora in which Indigenous peoples are heard commonly relate expressly to Indigenous peoples' rights, or environment and development matters, rather than international investment, trade, or other economic matters; and how financial and logistical barriers persist to Indigenous peoples' full and effective participation.

In this connection, the book also examines the publicly available evidence as to how state and international organization officials talk about practices and policies that enable Indigenous peoples' participation.[17] It demonstrates that many states express support, often in strong terms, for Indigenous peoples' participation. These officials primarily justify Indigenous peoples' participation by reference to the perceived usefulness of Indigenous peoples'

[17] In the form of written statements, submissions, oral interventions, speeches, press releases, policy documents, and verbatim and summary meeting records.

knowledge, practices, epistemologies, and ways of living for the achievement of the objectives, or fulfilment of the functions, of a given international organization or treaty-making or treaty implementation process. Such goals are generally framed as being universally held, or at least in the shared interests of both states and Indigenous peoples, in a universalizing move that obscures how these interests can be materially opposed. This rhetorical pattern is also instrumentalizing, in that it positions Indigenous participation as a means to an end held by the international organization or group of states concerned, rather than as necessarily a good in itself or as a means to fulfil Indigenous self-determination; as well as essentializing, in that it constructs an image of an "ideal" Indigenous participant that may or may not bear a resemblance to the vast, diverse array of Indigenous peoples globally.

I.1 SITUATING THIS BOOK IN THE FIELD

The law of self-determination has been a critical,[18] albeit contested,[19] component of the international legal order. Emerging as a political principle in the years leading up to Deskaheh and Rātana's respective attempts to seek justice via international organization, self-determination later proved instrumental as a legal framework for formal decolonization and even decades later remains much debated.[20] Scholarly work on self-determination has often

18 See, for example, Charter of the United Nations (adopted 26 June 1945 and entered into force 24 October 1945) 1 UNTS 26, arts 1(2) and 55. Self-determination is a rule of customary international law, and of *erga omnes* character: See, for example, *Legal Consequences for States of the Continued Presence of South Africa in Namibia (South West Africa) notwithstanding Security Council Resolution 276 (1970)* (Advisory Opinion) [1971] ICJ Rep 16, 31; *Western Sahara* (Advisory Opinion) [1975] ICJ Rep 12, 31–33; *Case Concerning East Timor (Portugal v. Australia)* (Merits) [1995] ICJ Rep 90, 102; *Legal Consequences of the Construction of a Wall in the Occupied Palestinian Territory* (Advisory Opinion) [2004] ICJ Rep 136, 171–172, 182–183.

19 The Åland Islands Commission of Rapporteurs' 1921 characterization of self-determination still resonates today: 'a principle . . . expressed by a vague and general formula which has given rise to the most varied interpretations and differences of opinion': Commission of Rapporteurs: 'The Aaland Islands Question: Report Submitted to the Council of the League of Nations by the Commission of Rapporteurs', League of Nations Doc B7 [C] 21/68/106, April 1921, 27.

20 Antonio Cassese, *Self-Determination of Peoples: A Legal Reappraisal* (Cambridge: Cambridge University Press, 1995); Andrés Rigo Sureda, *The Evolution of the Right of Self-Determination: A Study of United Nations Practice* (Leiden: AW Sijthoff 1973); James R. Crawford, *The Creation of States in International Law* (2nd ed., Oxford: Oxford University Press, 2007); Michla Pomerance, *Self-Determination in Law and Practice – The New Doctrine in the United Nations* (The Hague: Martinus Nijhoff, 1982); U.O. Umozurike, *Self-Determination in International Law* (Hamden, CT: Archon Books 1972); Hurst Hannum, *Autonomy, Sovereignty and Self-Determination: The Accommodation of Conflicting Rights* (rev. ed.,

considered its "internal" aspects, including the participation of peoples at the domestic political level.[21] However, it has devoted less attention to dimensions of external sovereignty aside from those pertaining to territorial status, including peoples' participation separately from the relevant state(s) at the international level. Meanwhile, Jan Klabbers argued in 2006 that self-determination had been transformed into a procedural norm that gave peoples the right to be heard and taken seriously in decision-making at the national level.[22] And several Indigenous advocates and scholars have suggested that Indigenous peoples have a right to a voice in the international realm – [23]

Philadelphia: University of Pennsylvania Press, 1996); Jamie Trinidad, *Self-Determination in Disputed Colonial Territories* (Cambridge: Cambridge University Press, 2018); Jane A. Hofbauer, *Sovereignty in the Exercise of the Right to Self-Determination* (Leiden; Boston: Brill 2017); Fernando R. Tesón (ed.), *The Theory of Self-Determination* (Cambridge: Cambridge University Press, 2016); James Summers, *Peoples and International Law* (2nd ed., Leiden: Martinus Nijhoff, 2014); Duncan French, *Statehood and Self-Determination: Reconciling Tradition and Modernity* (Cambridge: Cambridge University Press, 2013); Philip Alston (ed.), *Peoples' Rights* (Oxford: Oxford University Press, 2002); Karen Knop, *Diversity and Self-Determination in International Law* (Cambridge: Cambridge University Press, 2008); Joshua Castellino, *International Law and Self-Determination: The Interplay of the Politics of Territorial Possession with Formulations of Post-Colonial National Identity* (The Hague, Boston: Martinus Nijhoff, 2000).

[21] Michla Pomerance, *The New Doctrine in the United Nations*, 37; Cassese, A *Legal Reappraisal*, 101. On internal self-determination generally, see Allan Rosas, 'Internal Self-Determination', and J. Salmon, 'Internal Aspects of the Right to Self-Determination', in Christian Tomuschat (ed.), *Modern Law of Self-Determination* (Dordrecht: Martinus Nijhoff, 1993) 225 and 253.

[22] Jan Klabbers, 'The Right to Be Taken Seriously: Self-Determination in International Law' (2006) 28 *Human Rights Quarterly*, 186–206.

[23] S. James Anaya, 'A Contemporary Definition of the International Norm of Self-Determination' (1993) 3 *Transnational Law and Contemporary Problems* 131–164, 157; Iris Marion Young, *Inclusion and Democracy* (Oxford: Oxford University Press, 2000) 275; Karen Knop, *Diversity and Self-Determination*, 13; S. James Anaya, *Indigenous Peoples in International Law* (2nd ed., Oxford: Oxford University Press 2004), 153; S. James Anaya, 'International Human Rights and Indigenous Peoples: The Move toward the Multicultural State' (2004) 21 *Arizona Journal of International & Comparative Law*, 13–61, 14; Timo Koivurova and Leena Heinämäki, 'The Participation of Indigenous Peoples in International Norm-Making in the Arctic' (2006) 42 *Polar Record*,101–109, 101–102; Alan Boyle and Christine Chinkin, *The Making of International Law* (Oxford: Oxford University Press, 2007), 50; Natalia Loukacheva, '"Arctic Indigenous Peoples" Internationalism: In Search of a Legal Justification' (2009) 45 *Polar Record*, 51–58, 52–53; Claire Charters, 'A Self-Determination Approach to Justifying Indigenous Peoples' Participation in International Law and Policy Making' (2010) 17 *International Journal of Minority & Group Rights*, 215–240; Leena Heinämäki, 'Towards an Equal Partnership between Indigenous Peoples and States: Learning from Arctic Experiences' (2011) 3 *Yearbook of Polar Law*, 193–246, 223; Mattias Åhren, *Indigenous Peoples' Status in the International Legal System* (Oxford: Oxford University Press, 2016), 132; Dorotheé Cambou, 'Enhancing the Participation of Indigenous Peoples at the Intergovernmental Level to Strengthen Self-Determination: Lessons from the Arctic' (2018) 87 *Nordic Journal of*

although this proposition is often treated as 'self-evident'.[24] This book draws deeply on these works and builds on them to elaborate an account of how the participation of Indigenous peoples at the international level can form part of the international law of self-determination. It largely bypasses contemporary debates such as those regarding whose claims to self-determination are legitimate, whether self-determination can justify a right to secede,[25] and those on unresolved colonial cases.[26] It is intended, in part, as a contribution to theoretical and doctrinal thought on the law of self-determination, buttressed by an empirical account of state and international organization practice regarding Indigenous peoples' participation.

This book is also intended to contribute to the corpus of scholarship on Indigenous peoples' rights,[27] by analysing in close detail the right to participate in decision-making in an international context that is asserted by Indigenous scholars and activists alike. It draws upon a volume of secondary literature on specific institutions in which Indigenous peoples participate, such as the Arctic Council, the UN Framework Convention on Climate Change, and the World Intellectual Property Organization's Intergovernmental Committee on Intellectual Property and Genetic Resources, Traditional Knowledge and Folklore.[28] In addition to these

International Law, 26–55, 26; Tracey Whare, 'Reflective piece on Māori and the ILO' (2020) 24 *International Journal of Human Rights*, 303–306, 303–304.

24 See, for example, Koivurova and Heinämäki, 'The Participation of Indigenous Peoples', 102. The fullest explanation so far has been given by Charters, 'A Self-Determination Approach'.

25 See, for example, Stephen Macedo and Allen Buchanan (eds.), *Secession and Self-Determination* (New York: New York University Press, 2003); Thomas M. Franck, 'Post-Modern Tribalism and the Right to Secession' in Catherine Brölmann, René Lefeber, and Marjoleine Zieck (eds.), *Peoples and Minorities in International Law* (Leiden: Martinus Nijhoff, 1993), 3–27; Aleksandar Pavkovic and Peter Radan (eds.), *On the Way to Statehood: Secession and Globalisation* (Aldershot: Ashgate, 2008).

26 See, for example, Trinidad, *Disputed Colonial Territories*.

27 Relevant volumes include Åhren, *Indigenous Peoples' Status*; Mauro Barelli, *Seeking Justice in International Law: The Significance and Implications of the UN Declaration on the Rights of Indigenous Peoples* (London: Routledge, 2016); Stephen Allen and Alexandra Xanthaki (eds.), *Reflections on the UN Declaration on the Rights of Indigenous Peoples* (London: Hart, 2011); Elvira Pulitano, *Indigenous Rights in the Age of the UN Declaration* (Cambridge: Cambridge University Press, 2014); Alexandra Xanthaki, *Indigenous Rights and United Nations Standards* (Cambridge: Cambridge University Press, 2010); Claire Charters and Rodolfo Stavenhagen (eds.), *Making the Declaration Work: The United Nations Declaration on the Rights of Indigenous Peoples* (Copenhagen: IWGIA, 2009); James Anaya, 'Indigenous Peoples in International Law'; Pekka Aikio and Martin Scheinin (eds.), *Operationalizing the Right of Indigenous Peoples to Self-Determination* (Turko: Institute for Human Rights, Åbo Akademi University 2000).

28 See, for example, Koivurova and Heinämäki, 'The Participation of Indigenous Peoples'; Heinämäki, 'Towards an Equal Partnership'; Cambou, 'Lessons from the Arctic'; Sabaa

relatively well-studied cases, the book draws upon original research into several mechanisms for Indigenous peoples' participation in international organizations that have not yet been examined in the academic literature.

A key limitation of this book relates to epistemic positionality and representation. This is primarily a story about the practices of states and international organizations within a framework of European international law[29], rather than a story about practices of 'Indigenous international law',[30] that is, the distinct ways in which Indigenous communities use law to address their relationships with other entities. Indigenous people(s), organizations, and communities are an explicit part of this narrative only to the extent that they participate in negotiations and take up leadership positions. Although the driving force of transnational Indigenous movements as a key factor in the expansion of participatory mechanisms is assumed as a given and constitutes an undercurrent throughout the text,[31] this approach will still fall short of the kind of centring of non-European peoples' perspectives and agency in international law that is called for by those working in critical and Third World Approaches to International Law (TWAIL) traditions.[32] To borrow a turn of phrase from Cait Storr, this book 'makes no claim to represent [Indigenous] experiences of, engagements with, or modes of resistance to, [international organizations and international governance]'.[33] Rather, as a Pākeha[34] scholar trained in international law in Aotearoa New Zealand and now the United Kingdom, I take up the challenge set by Sophie Rigney to 'international lawyers trained in the European mode to consider how this legal order has disregarded Indigenous international law – and whether there are any alternatives'.[35] In the course of this quest, the book utilizes "textbook" tools and methodologies of (European) international law – a reliance on doctrinal

Ahmad Khan, 'Rebalancing State and Indigenous Sovereignties in International Law: An Arctic lens on Trajectories for Global Governance' (2019) 32 *Leiden Journal of International Law*, 675–693.

29 On plural international legal systems, see, for example, Rigney, 'On Hearing Well', 128; more generally Anthea Roberts, *Is International Law International?* (Oxford: Oxford University Press, 2018).

30 See Rigney, 'On Hearing Well'.

31 For more on this, see Lightfoot, *A Subtle Revolution*.

32 For just one example of an excellent study in this tradition that highlights the contributions and perspectives of Third World jurists, see Arnulf Becker Lorca, *Mestizo International Law: A Global Intellectual History 1842–1933* (Cambridge: Cambridge University Press, 2014).

33 Cait Storr, *International Status in the Shadow of Empire: Nauru and the Histories of International Law* (Cambridge: Cambridge University Press, 2020), 38.

34 European settlers and their descendants. Or *tangata tiriti*: all people who came to Aotearoa New Zealand under the authority of the Treaty of Waitangi.

35 Rigney, 'On Hearing Well', 126.

methods, an analysis of sources, and an interrogation of the existence of custom – in a manner that, in its orthodoxy, will be legible to practising international lawyers trained in this tradition. It does so in order to show how in great part the key institutions of international governance, and (European) international law itself, have to a large extent embraced the participation of Indigenous peoples – at least to a certain level – and to question what and who this serves, including to what extent *Indigenous* international law remains disregarded. Nevertheless, this book is both literally and figuratively a view from Cambridge, rather than reflecting a Fourth World approach to international law.[36] This book is as a drop compared with the ocean of Indigenous peoples' own accounts of Indigenous participation in international governance.

A second limitation in the approach turns on the empirical method. The chapters of this book that canvass the many and varied participatory forms and mechanisms rely on a corpus of primary sources that consists of organizational constitutions and rules, verbatim or summary records of meetings, oral interventions and written submissions by states or Indigenous peoples to international organizations or negotiation processes, resolutions and decisions of international organizations, speeches by state and international organization officials, press releases, web pages, and policy documents. Where available, this book also incorporates first-person accounts by Indigenous and other participants, and intergovernmental officials. However, the primary research did not involve interviewing Indigenous participants, nor did it include in-person ethnographic analysis of these processes. As such, the book will not satisfy socio-legal scholars. Suffice to say that much more research remains to be done by others.

I.2 SOME DEFINITIONAL MATTERS

The astute reader, by this point, might be wondering about the term 'international governance'. I use this term as a pragmatic shorthand for the wide variety of law-making, policymaking, and decision-making activities that are carried out at the international level, by international organizations and by states.[37]

36 On the Fourth World, see George Manuel and Michael Posluns, *The Fourth World: An Indian Reality* (Minneapolis: University of Minnesota Press, [1974] 2018).

37 As opposed to "global governance," which has been used to denote these as well as private and hybrid public-private forms of global regulation. See, for example, Nico Krisch and Benedict Kingsbury, 'Introduction: Global Governance and Global Administrative Law in the International Legal Order' (2006) 17(1) *European Journal of International Law*, 1–13.

A second term that requires a brief word is 'Indigenous peoples'. While Indigenous peoples themselves resist definition, the working definition first laid out in the 1980s by José Martínez Cobo, Special Rapporteur of the Sub-Commission on Prevention of Discrimination and Protection of Minorities, remains influential.[38] But ultimately, as McMillan and Rigney put it,

> it is up to Indigenous people to decide – and not for non-Indigenous people to place, define and confine within a definitional sense. Although it may be comforting to western scholars and institutions to assert a definition for indigeneity, it is important to recognise that Indigenous peoples do not exist for the comfort of others. It is the considerations of Indigenous peoples that should be paramount in any discussions on the need or otherwise for a definition of indigeneity.... Indigenous peoples know who we or they are. This is how we or they know the worlds that we or they inhabit and share.[39]

I.3 OUTLINE

The remainder of this work is structured as follows. Chapter 1, 'Participation in International Governance and the Logic of Self-Determination', makes a case for how a collective right of Indigenous peoples to participation in international governance relates to the law of self-determination. The chapter

38 'Indigenous communities, peoples and nations are those which, having a historical continuity with pre-invasion and pre-colonial societies that developed on their territories, consider themselves distinct from other sectors of the societies now prevailing on those territories, or parts of them. They form at present non-dominant sectors of society and are determined to preserve, develop and transmit to future generations their ancestral territories, and their ethnic identity, as the basis of their continued existence as peoples, in accordance with their own cultural patterns, social institutions and legal system. This historical continuity may consist of the continuation, for an extended period reaching into the present of one or more of the following factors: a) Occupation of ancestral lands, or at least of part of them; b) Common ancestry with the original occupants of these lands; c) Culture in general, or in specific manifestations (such as religion, living under a tribal system, membership of an Indigenous community, dress, means of livelihood, lifestyle, etc.); d) Language (whether used as the only language, as mother-tongue, as the habitual means of communication at home or in the family, or as the main, preferred, habitual, general or normal language); e) Residence on certain parts of the country, or in certain regions of the world; f) Other relevant factors': José R. Martínez Cobo, 'Study of the Problem of Discrimination against Indigenous Populations, Volume V, Conclusions, Proposals and Recommendations' (1986) UN Doc E/CN.4/Sub.2/1986/7, 29. See also Commission on Human Rights, 'Study of the Problem of Discrimination against Indigenous Populations', 'Final Report (Supplementary Part) submitted by the Special Rapporteur Mr. Jose R. Martinez Cobo' (20 June 1982) UN Doc E/CN.4/Sub.2/1982/2/Add.6.

39 Mark McMillan and Sophie Rigney, 'The Place of the First Peoples in the International Sphere: A Logical Starting Point for the Demand for Justice by Indigenous Peoples' (2016) 39 (3) *Melbourne University Law Review*, 981–1002, 990.

begins by examining the development of the law of self-determination in order to develop an account of its underlying logic. It isolates four, interconnected and overlapping characteristics that explain how self-determination has developed and inform us as to how it may develop in future. The chapter shows that self-determination is dynamic, multifaceted, relational, and remedial: that is, it is capable of multiple expressions that develop over time so as to remedy relationships of domination, subjugation, or exploitation. In other words, I argue that self-determination is a principle that, over time, has provided an umbrella for the development of various legal rules concerning the relations between peoples and states; those rules have tended to emerge in a remedial manner. The implication of this is that if new relationships of domination or subjugation emerge, or relations change, in a manner affecting the self-determination of peoples, this justifies a remedy in the form of a new rule attaching to the principle of self-determination.

Building on this account of self-determination, the chapter then contends that peoples' right to self-determination is not only opposable against states. It proposes that while other manifestations of the law of self-determination have focused on remedying domination of a people by a state, the book argues that in addition there is a structural relationship between Indigenous peoples on the one hand and international organizations and collectives of states on the other, a relationship of the kind the law of self-determination is concerned with remedying. It elaborates on this relationship, drawing on the literature on international organizations' accountability and international public authority. Exploring whether existing law can provide an appropriate remedy to this situation of domination, it refutes arguments that the law of internal self-determination, and individual rights to civil society participation in international law-making, respectively, already constitute an effective remedy. It argues that a right to participate in international governance could fill this gap in the law.

Chapter 2, 'Finding Support for Indigenous Peoples' Participation in the Sources of International Law', turns to a doctrinal analysis. It undertakes an examination of relevant sources of international law on self-determination and Indigenous peoples' rights, in treaties, declarations, and decisions of international judicial and quasi-judicial bodies. We see how the law of self-determination has been interpreted by the latter bodies as meaning – among other things – participation of peoples at the national (but not necessarily the international) level, and how participation is at the heart of the law on self-determination specific to Indigenous peoples. However, on the basis of these sources of law alone, we see how it is difficult to find that a right of Indigenous peoples to participate in international governance exists in positive law.

We then turn to customary international law. I review and contextualize various methodologies for the identification of customary international law, including a traditional, two-element approach, an approach that prioritizes *opinio juris* (often known as a "modern" approach), and an approach that prioritizes practice. I summarize how, using each of these lenses, we can interpret the evidence described in later chapters. Through these lenses, I discuss various methodological debates, including the legal status we should assign to the UNDRIP in and of itself, how a provision of the UNDRIP might later crystallize into a rule of custom, and how to regard international organizations in relation to the identification of custom. This discussion reveals limitations associated with each approach.

The next two chapters outline the proliferation of Indigenous peoples' participation in international governance. In Chapter 3, 'The Proliferation of Indigenous Peoples' Participation, 1982–2007', I trace how a pattern of state practice unfurled over a span of 25 years, beginning with the establishment of the Working Group on Indigenous Populations (WGIP) and spreading to numerous other UN organs, international organizations, and other international governance mechanisms. The aim of the chapter is threefold. Firstly, commencing with an account of the WGIP and its successor, the Ad Hoc Working Group on the Draft Declaration (WGDD),[40] the chapter aims to show that the WGIP and WGDD were both role models for, and platforms through which Indigenous peoples could advocate for, participation in other fora. The WGIP constituted a precedent that Indigenous peoples, their allies, and like-minded states and international organizations could present as "best practice" for adaptation to, and emulation in, other settings. It also served to amplify Indigenous peoples' visibility and demands, including those related to procedural rights, as a platform for contestation and struggle. As Indigenous participation spread into more and more intergovernmental spaces, these dynamics were reproduced and magnified.

Secondly, the chapter aims to demonstrate that by the time of the UNDRIP's adoption in 2007, a widespread practice had emerged, broadly characterized by procedural rules by which Indigenous peoples' representatives could submit inputs into and participate in discussions in international negotiations towards legal instruments as well as in policymaking, decision-making, and other regulatory processes, and in regional as well as multilateral institutions. These procedural possibilities for Indigenous peoples'

[40] The WGDD, established by Commission on Human Rights res 1995/32 of 3 March 1995 and ECOSOC res 1995/32 of 23 July 1995, operated from 1995 until 2006, when the draft UNDRIP was forwarded to the General Assembly for adoption.

participation tended to be backed up by mechanisms established to provide financial and other material support to Indigenous peoples' delegates – although, importantly, the effectiveness of these has depended on states' subsequent willingness to contribute to funding bodies. Alongside this, a pattern of practice emerged among states of including Indigenous peoples' representatives on their national delegations. However, the chapter demonstrates that Indigenous peoples' participation in many of these processes was ultimately limited by the state-centricity of international institutions.[41]

To map this widespread practice, the chapter at first takes a chronological approach, tracing relevant practice from 1988 to 1994 in processes such as the negotiations towards the International Labour Organization Convention No. 169 on Indigenous and Tribal Peoples,[42] UN conferences including the 1992 Rio Conference on Environment and Development and the 1993 World Conference on Human Rights, and several UN expert workshops. It then considers how momentum grew towards the establishment of the UN Permanent Forum on Indigenous Issues. The chapter next turns to consider several parallel trends. It turns to mechanisms for Indigenous peoples' participation in environment and development negotiations, specifically in the Convention on Biological Diversity, the UN Framework Convention on Climate Change, and the World Intellectual Property Organization. Then, the chapter traces Indigenous peoples' participation in decision-making in international development institutions, in particular the World Bank and the UN Development Programme. The chapter ends by examining three regional stories: the Arctic, specifically the Arctic Council, the Barents regional cooperation, and the Nordic Saami Convention; Latin America and the Caribbean, focusing on the Fund for the Development of the Indigenous Peoples of Latin America and the Caribbean, as well as the Andean Community; and the European Union.

Thirdly, the chapter aims to demonstrate that during this period, states' and international organizations' practices of enabling Indigenous peoples to be heard in governance processes were not accompanied by the belief that such a practice was required by law. Under the predominant two-element approach to identifying a rule of customary international law, therefore, we cannot conclude that a customary rule congruous with an entitlement of

[41] This point was made in relation to the WIPO IGC by Charles Lawson, Edwin Bikundo, and Kieran Tranter, 'The Perils of Parliamentarism: The World Intellectual Property Organization and Indigenous Peoples' (2019) 39(2) *Oxford Journal of Legal Studies*, 285–315, 307, 310.

[42] Convention concerning Indigenous and Tribal Peoples in Independent Countries (adopted 27 June 1989 and entered into force 5 September 1991) 1650 UNTS 383.

Indigenous peoples to participate in global governance processes affecting them had emerged by 2007.[43] On the contrary, when states and international organizations expressed motivations for establishing mechanisms and policies to support Indigenous peoples' participation, these tended to fall into three overlapping contexts. First, Indigenous participation was often justified in terms of the instrumental value of participation in terms of contributing to achieve the mandated objectives of the treaty or organization concerned, whether due to the perceived value of Indigenous peoples' knowledge or epistemologies – often in terms of Indigenous peoples' relationship with land and the environment – or due to a sense of the importance of their participation for the credibility and legitimacy of the process (for instance, a statement along the lines of "the participation of Indigenous peoples is vital to the success of our mission"). Second, a justice- or affectedness-oriented justification ("Indigenous peoples ought to be able to participate since they are affected by this process"). Third, a simple expression of the "importance" of Indigenous peoples' participation, without further elaboration. Often, all three of these motivations were at play in respect of a given organization.

Chapter 4, 'Emerging Status as Law? Participation of Indigenous Peoples in International Governance, 2007–2022', continues the narrative from the point of the adoption of the UNDRIP in September 2007. In this period, the general trend of proliferation of participatory policies and mechanisms identified in Chapter 3 only intensified. Organizations that had not previously attempted to include Indigenous peoples in a systematic way now adopted mechanisms and policies to do so, while those that had previously instituted such mechanisms or policies sought to enhance them. The first aim of this chapter is to map the contours of this continuing trend, showing how the participation zeitgeist spread through numerous UN organs and international organizations. As previously, this shift was spearheaded by Indigenous peoples, their organizations, and global movements, now assisted by institutional actors like the UNPFII and the EMRIP, which was established in 2010 in a process directly following on from the UNDRIP. The UNPFII and EMRIP proved to be institutional settings in which Indigenous peoples could present their demands and hear them amplified – including those related to participation rights in other fora – and engage in dialogue with states.

Second, this chapter again assesses the question of states' and international organizations' motivations for enabling Indigenous peoples to be heard in such fora. This chapter shows that, as previously, Indigenous peoples'

[43] For a discussion of the methodology for determining a rule of customary international law, see Chapter 2.

participation was often justified, by state and international organization officials alike, as (i) instrumentally useful; (ii) morally required due to Indigenous peoples' affectedness; and/or (iii) because of a general sense of the "importance" of Indigenous peoples' participation.

However, these three threads of logic were often joined by a fourth: states and international organizations now increasingly justified participation policies by reference to the UNDRIP itself, particularly Articles 18, 19, and 41. In other words, Indigenous peoples' participation was seen as desirable not just because it helped states and organizations achieve goals related to, for example, environmental protection, sustainable development, regional governance, or the protection of cultural heritage, nor solely because of a normative sense that Indigenous peoples ought to have a say in policymaking processes that affected their self-determination. Rather, it was viewed as required by international law. In the case of some mechanisms that began before 2007, in the post-UNDRIP period, states began to express sentiments linking these practices to the UNDRIP. Under a rules-based approach to international law, as discussed in Chapter 2, this could indicate the emergence of a rule of customary international law.

The third and final aim of this chapter is to demonstrate how, in nearly all cases, barriers to full and effective participation remain.

This chapter proceeds, like Chapter 3, by charting developments in parallel. It first examines Indigenous peoples' participation at the UN post-2007, mapping the rise of the EMRIP, the process leading up to the 2014 World Conference on Indigenous Peoples, and subsequent negotiations towards an enhanced status for Indigenous peoples at the General Assembly and other UN organs. Then, following the same logic as Chapter 3, it turns to mechanisms for Indigenous peoples' participation in environment and development negotiations and policymaking processes, specifically in the UN Framework Convention on Climate Change, the International Union for the Conservation of Nature, the Intergovernmental Science-Policy Platform on Biodiversity and Ecosystem Services, the UN Educational, Scientific and Cultural Organization, and the UN Food and Agriculture Organization. The chapter then considers Indigenous peoples' participation in decision-making in international development institutions, in particular the International Fund for Agricultural Development, the UN Food and Agriculture Organization, the Global Environment Facility, the UN Environment Programme, the UN-REDD Programme, the UN Development Programme, the World Bank, the Green Climate Fund, the Climate Investment Funds, and the UN Indigenous Peoples Partnership. Finally, the chapter revisits the regional stories: Latin America, focusing on the Andean Community's Consultative Council of

Indigenous Peoples; the Arctic, focusing on developments in the Barents regional cooperation, and negotiations towards the Central Arctic Ocean Fisheries Agreement; and the European Union, specifically the Arctic Dialogue and evolutions in Indigenous peoples' participation in EU development cooperation.

Chapter 5, 'New Epoch, Old Stones?', is the conclusion of the book. It first synthesizes the findings of the examination of practice conducted throughout Chapters 3 and 4, setting out a statement of the scope and content of the emerging rule in (European) international law. Then, by reference to the persistent limitations to participation, it raises questions about what and who the proliferation of mechanisms for Indigenous participation – and the emergence of a legal standard in custom – serves. The chapter engages with the work of Indigenous political theorists to question whether that current mechanisms for Indigenous participation in global governance may in part function to legitimize and protect (neo)colonial global economic and political structures. This does not invalidate the conclusion that the right is part of customary international law, nor is it to say that the project of Indigenous peoples' participation international governance is not necessarily worth pursuing. Rather, it serves to highlight the limitations of the right, the contingencies of its application, and ultimately to gesture at a space to develop alternative possibilities for Indigenous internationalism and sovereignty.

1

Participation in International Governance and the Logic of Self-Determination

Pursuant to the universal application of the right of self-determination . . . we call for, at a minimum, permanent observer status within the United Nations system, enabling our direct participation through our own Governments and parliaments. . .

–Alta Outcome Document, 2013[1]

1.1 THE NATURE OF SELF-DETERMINATION

The lack of clarity in the law of self-determination is irksome in many respects. But it can also be perceived as its greatest strength, for ambiguity permits scope for contestation, flexibility, and interpretation through which the law can accommodate unforeseen circumstances.[2] This does not imply, however, that the law can be interpreted to mean anything one likes, nor that it is hopelessly indeterminate. On the contrary, by tracing the development of the law of self-determination, we can isolate four, interconnected, and overlapping characteristics that inform us as to how self-determination may develop in future.[3]

1.1.1 *Self-Determination as Dynamic*

First, the law of self-determination is *dynamic*. This is evident in its transformations throughout the last hundred years and across several dimensions. The most basic evolution has been its shift in status from a political principle into

[1] Alta Outcome Document, in UN General Assembly, 'Letter dated 10 September 2013 from the Permanent Representatives of the Plurinational State of Bolivia, Denmark, Finland, Guatemala, Mexico, New Zealand, Nicaragua, Norway and Peru to the United Nations addressed to the Secretary-General' (13 September 2013) UN Doc A/67/994, Annex, 7, 9.

[2] James Summers, *Peoples and International Law* (2nd ed., Leiden: Martinus Nijhoff, 2014), 39.

[3] The intention here is to sketch the shape of the law, rather than to exhaustively recount it.

one of law. While from the eighteenth century onwards, self-determination was promulgated as a political principle with a variety of meanings,[4] it was not considered a principle of international law during the post-World War I settlements,[5] and its transformation into a principle of law occurred only with the adoption of the UN Charter.[6] Moreover, this legal principle was not initially accompanied by rights or obligations: it was an aspirational goal rather than an operative principle.[7] The Charter primarily envisaged self-determination as contributing to one aim of the UN and did not impose related obligations on member states.[8]

Self-determination came to be associated with a legal right – the right of peoples subjected to colonial rule to freely determine their international status – in the political and historical context of decolonization:[9] The 1960 Declaration on the Granting of Independence to Colonial Countries and Peoples (the Colonial Declaration)[10] framed self-determination in universalist language, as a right of 'all peoples', while specifying that the populations of trust and non-self-governing territories 'or all other territories which have not yet attained independence' were entitled to 'complete independence'.[11] The UN General Assembly soon afterwards clarified, in Resolution 1541, the nature of the basic colonial unit and the non-self-governing territory

4 Including by Woodrow Wilson and Vladimir Lenin: Antonio Cassese, *Self-Determination of Peoples: A Legal Reappraisal* (Cambridge: Cambridge University Press, 1995), 14–23.

5 *The Aaland Islands Question: Report Submitted to the Council of the League of Nations by the Commission of Rapporteurs* (April 1921) League of Nations Doc. B7 [C] 21/68/106, 27. However, the principle was 'crucial for the legitimacy of states and their boundaries' and thus 'shaped the content of the law': Summers, *Peoples and International Law*, 179.

6 Charter of the United Nations (signed 26 June 1945 and entered into force 24 October 1945) 1 UNTS 26, art 1(2).

7 Allan Rosas, 'Internal Self-Determination' in Christian Tomuschat (ed.), *Modern Law of Self-Determination* (Dordrecht: Martinus Nijhoff 1993), 225–252, 225.

8 Cassese, *Self-Determination of Peoples*, 43. Indeed, many states stressed that the inclusion of self-determination was not to be construed as a right to secession, independence, or democracy: Summers, *Peoples and International Law*, 198–199.

9 *Legal Consequences for States for the Continued Presence of South Africa in Namibia (South West Africa) notwithstanding Security Council Resolution 276 (1970)* [1971] ICJ Rep 16; *Western Sahara* (Advisory Opinion) [1975] ICJ Rep 12 paras. 55 and 59. Patrick Macklem, 'Self-Determination in Three Movements' in Fernando R. Tesón (ed.), *The Theory of Self-Determination* (Cambridge: Cambridge University Press, 2016), 94–119, 99–104.

10 UNGA Res 1514 (XV) (14 December 1960) UN Doc A/RES/1514(XV) ("Colonial Declaration").

11 Colonial Declaration, paras. 4–5.

entitled to independence, as well as the means by which they could attain self-government.[12]

A further shift has occurred from a legal right to a human right, marked by Common Article 1 of the International Covenant on Civil and Political Rights and the International Covenant on Economic and Social Rights.[13] Some even situate self-determination as a necessary precondition for, and means to, the realization of all other human rights.[14] Moreover, Common Article 1 provided for new dimensions of self-determination: the right to control natural wealth and resources;[15] non-interference between states in general;[16] and the right of a people of a state to freely choose their rulers.[17] Indeed, this latter development heralded the expansion to what many have called the internal dimension of self-determination, the migration of the right 'from the international to the domestic realm'.[18] Internal self-determination is the right of peoples to enjoy the freedom of authentic self-government, which may entail autonomy vis-à-vis other entities in the state.[19] The internal dimension encompasses a right to equitable representation in legislative, executive, and judicial institutions[20] and is also said to enable peoples to freely choose their political and economic regimes and enjoy related rights, such as the right to vote, the right of peaceful assembly, and the freedom of expression.[21] While the expansion from external to internal did not necessarily exclude the continued application of external aspects of self-determination, it evidences the flexibility and dynamism of the principle and its ability to adapt to respond to new situations as they occur.

12 UNGA Res 1541 (XV) (15 December 1960) UN Doc A/RES/1541(XV). Also see the 1970 Declaration on Principles of International Law Concerning Friendly Relations and Co-Operation among States UNGA Res 2625(XXV) (24 October 1970) UN Doc A/RES/2625 (XXV).

13 International Covenant on Civil and Political Rights 1966 (adopted 16 December 1966 and entered into force 23 March 1976) 999 UNTS 171; International Covenant on Economic, Social and Cultural Rights 1966 (adopted 16 December 1966 and entered into force 3 January 1976) 993 UNTS 3. See Robert McCorquodale, 'Self-Determination: A Human Rights Approach' (1994) 43(4) *International & Comparative Law Quarterly*, 857–885.

14 McCorquodale, 'A Human Rights Approach', 872.

15 See Cassese, *Self-Determination of Peoples*, 55–56.

16 Ibid., 55.

17 Ibid., 52–55.

18 Macklem, 'Three Movements', 108.

19 On internal self-determination, see, for example, Cassese, *Self-Determination of Peoples*, 101.

20 *Re Reference by the Governor in Council Concerning Certain Questions Relating to the Secession of Quebec from Canada* [1998] 2 SCR 217 (Supreme Court of Canada), para. 136.

21 James Crawford, *The Creation of States in International Law* (2nd ed., Oxford: Oxford University Press, 2007), 25.

Another broad shift in the law of self-determination has been the gradual expansion in the identity of the holders of the right: from the aggregate populations of states, to the peoples of colonized territories, to peoples under occupation and other forms of alien domination, to Indigenous peoples. The reference to the self-determination of "peoples" in the UN Charter was apparently not intended to be understood as conferring rights to minorities or peoples in any ethno-cultural meaning of the term, nor to colonized peoples: "peoples" were to be regarded as the entire populations of states rather than sub-segments of states, and as such, the principle pertained only to relationships between states.[22] In the decolonization period, as outlined above, territorial considerations proved paramount in limiting who could hold the right.[23] Self-determination attached to the entire populations of colonial territories, rather than peoples within a colonized territory, even though the externally imposed colonial boundaries tended to group together several cultural and ethnic groups.[24] Although states did not widely contemplate that peoples would continue to have a right to self-determination after the completion of decolonization, with references in the 1960 Colonial Declaration and the 1970 Friendly Relations Declaration to 'peoples under alien subjugation, domination and exploitation',[25] it became arguable that self-determination extended beyond the overseas colonialism of Western states to, for instance, peoples under racist regimes, occupied peoples, and the people of Palestine.[26]

With the adoption of the UNDRIP,[27] it became clear that Indigenous peoples were also "peoples" entitled to self-determination.[28] The 2007

[22] Mattias Åhren, *Indigenous Peoples' Status in the International Legal System* (Oxford: Oxford University Press, 2016), 28–29; Cassese, *Self-Determination of Peoples*, 39–43; Crawford, *Creation of States*, 112–114.

[23] There is a consensus that colonized peoples have the right to self-determination; see, for example, Summers, *Peoples and International Law*, 45–436; Cassese, *Self-Determination of Peoples*, 71; Crawford, *Creation of States*, 127. On territorial interpretations, see UNGA Res 1541, Principles IV and V.

[24] Åhren, *Indigenous Peoples' Status*, 31, 35; Karen Knop, *Diversity and Self-Determination in International Law* (Cambridge: Cambridge University Press, 2008), 56–57; Cassese, *Self-Determination of Peoples*, 141–146; Summers, *Peoples and International Law*, 305.

[25] Also see UNGA, Vienna Declaration and Programme of Action (25 June 1993) UN Doc A/CONF.157/23.

[26] On peoples under racist regimes, see UNSC Res 581 (13 February 1986) UN Doc S/RES/581, para. 7. On occupation, see, for example, *Case Concerning East Timor (Portugal v. Australia)* (Judgment) [1995] ICJ Rep 90, para. 90; UNGA Res 42/15 (10 November 1987) UN Doc A/RES/42/15. On Palestine, see, for example, *Wall Advisory Opinion*, para. 118; UNGA Res 3236 (XXIX) (22 November 1974) UN Doc A/RES/3236(XXIX).

[27] UNGA Res 61/295 (2 October 2007) UN Doc A/RES/61/295.

[28] See, for example, S. James Anaya, 'The Right of Indigenous Peoples to Self-Determination in the Post-Declaration Era' in Claire Charters and Rodolfo Stavenhagen (eds.), *Making the*

Declaration, as the first widespread recognition by states that self-determination was not confined to colonial peoples, was a significant development in the evolution of the law of self-determination. Although Indigenous peoples are inherently strongly connected to land and place, not all have a fixed or exclusive territory: they may be geographically dispersed in the manner of a minority group throughout a more diverse population.[29] Previously, peoples had been exclusively understood as aggregate populations of states or territories; the decolonization regime had bypassed Indigenous peoples, who merely 'became the subjects of new forms of colonization'.[30] That peoples can now 'in addition be defined in terms of common ethnicity and culture is at least arguably a new feature in international law'.[31]

Thus, while the core meaning of self-determination has become solidified and entrenched – that all peoples should be able to control their own destinies under conditions of equality[32] – the fluid nature of self-determination means that the principle has supported various specific legal rules over the course of its history. Nothing in this history suggests that the law of self-determination cannot continue evolving, as political circumstances develop, well into the future.

1.1.2 *Self-Determination as Multifaceted*

The second aspect of the law that I wish to highlight thus flows from the first. Self-determination is *multifaceted*: it has multiple expressions with different meanings in different situations.[33] It is not synonymous with colonial

Declaration Work: The United Nations Declaration on the Rights of Indigenous Peoples (Copenhagen: IWGIA, 2009), 184–199, 185; Marc Weller, 'Self-Determination of Indigenous Peoples: Articles 3, 4, 5, 18, 23, and 46(1)' in Jessie Hohmann and Marc Weller (eds.), *The UN Declaration on the Rights of Indigenous People: A Commentary* (Oxford: Oxford University Press, 2018), 115–149, 146.

29 Joshua Castellino and Cathal Doyle, 'Who Are 'Indigenous Peoples'? An Examination of Concepts Concerning Group Membership in the UNDRIP' in Jessie Hohmann and Marc Weller (eds.), *The UN Declaration on the Rights of Indigenous People: A Commentary* (Oxford: Oxford University Press, 2018), 7–37, 32–36.

30 Åhren, *Indigenous Peoples' Status*, 35.

31 Martin Scheinin and Mattias Åhren, 'Relationship to Human Rights, and Related International Instruments' in Jessie Hohmann and Marc Weller (eds.), *The UN Declaration on the Rights of Indigenous People: A Commentary* (Oxford: Oxford University Press, 2018), 63–86, 63.

32 Adopted from S. James Anaya, *Indigenous Peoples in International Law* (2nd ed., Oxford: Oxford University Press, 2004), 74. This was chosen from the multiplicity of (similar) formulations in the literature as it seems to accurately capture the intent and spirit of the law.

33 Caroline Foster, 'Articulating Self-determination in the Draft Declaration on the Rights of Indigenous Peoples' (2001) 12 *European Journal of International Law*, 141–157, 143;

independence, or with secession, or with what is known as "internal self-determination." So much is clear from the above account of its development. Helpful in this regard is Antonio Cassese's conceptualization of self-determination as consisting, firstly, of a general principle, which Cassese formulates as 'the need to pay regard to the freely expressed will of peoples' when their fates are at issue.[34] This principle, according to Cassese, 'sets out a general and fundamental standard of behaviour' that 'governments must not decide the life and future of peoples at their discretion'; rather, peoples 'must be enabled freely to express their wishes in matters concerning their condition'.[35] Like any principle, self-determination is 'general, loose and multifaceted', lending itself to 'various and even contradictory applications', and with 'great normative potential and dynamic force'.[36] From the broad principle, then, one can deduce specific customary rules where 'a broader measure of agreement has emerged among States as to ... proper conduct'.[37] The principle indicates the method of exercising self-determination, can act as a standard of interpretation where a customary rule is unclear or ambiguous, and can be useful in cases not covered by specific rules.[38] The specific manifestations of self-determination already mentioned here, such as the right of peoples to exercise control over natural resources or the external self-determination of colonized peoples, can be thought of as specific rules under the heading of this broader principle.

1.1.3 *Self-Determination as Relational*

So much, so clear. But if self-determination has multiple aspects that develop over time, what principles unite its disparate elements and explain its evolution? Going some way to answer this question is self-determination's *relational* nature. Self-determination fundamentally concerns the relationships between a people and others – states, empires, governments, and other peoples.[39] As evident from its development, it is a specific kind of relationship – one of dominance, subjugation, or exploitation of a people by a state or other

Alexandra Tomaselli, 'The Right to Political Participation of Indigenous Peoples: A Holistic Approach' (2014) 24 *International Journal on Minority and Group Rights*, 390–427, 403–404.

34 Cassese, *Self-Determination of Peoples*, 126–127. See also *Western Sahara*, para. 59.

35 Cassese, *Self-Determination of Peoples*, 128.

36 Ibid., 128–129.

37 Ibid., 129.

38 Ibid., 131.

39 Benedict Kingsbury, 'Reconciling Five Competing Conceptual Structures of Indigenous Claims in International and Comparative Law' (2001) 34 NYUJILP, 189–250, 223.

entity – that both give rise to exercises of self-determination and constitute such exercises. All peoples that exercise their right to self-determination do so in relation to another unit, typically a state, and that unit holds reciprocal obligations towards that people throughout the exercise. This is evident on the face of the language of the relevant instruments. For instance, the Colonial Declaration's condemnation of '[t]he subjection of peoples to alien subjugation, domination and exploitation'[40] immediately raises the question: subjugation *by who*? Domination *by who*? To speak of 'dependent peoples' fundamentally assumes a relationship between the people subjected to subjugation, domination and exploitation, and the entity that is doing the subjecting – in this case, colonizing states. The Declaration goes on to impose duties: it states that 'armed action or repressive measures of all kinds directed against dependent peoples shall cease',[41] again presupposing the existence of a certain relationship between a dependent people and the entity applying such measures. It prescribes the future nature of the relationship: '[i]mmediate steps shall be taken' by the colonial states 'to transfer all powers' to the dependent peoples 'in accordance with their freely expressed will and desire'.[42] Thus, in the Colonial Declaration, it is the colonial relationship of "alien subjugation, domination, and exploitation" between the colonial state and the colonized people that both give rise to an entitlement to self-determination and define the consequent obligations of the colonial state. The same lens can be applied to other relevant international instruments, as well as judicial decisions.[43]

1.1.4 *Self-Determination as Remedial*

The final aspect that helps to explain the law's logic is the *remedial* nature of the specific legal rules that have developed under the umbrella of self-determination: specific legal rules have emerged in a remedial manner so as to provide redress for ongoing situations of domination, subjugation, or exploitation. Self-determination is a continuous process whereby the law forms new remedies when so required. This can be illustrated by reference to the development of the rules on decolonization. The colonization process and the international law that accompanied and justified it denied countless non-European peoples recognition and the ability to determine their own

40 Colonial Declaration, para. 1.

41 Ibid., para. 4.

42 Ibid., para. 5.

43 For instance, judicial decisions on the *erga omnes* nature of self-determination assume a relation between a people and all other states.

futures.[44] The Colonial Declaration itself, adopted in large part due to the work of the then blooming decolonization movement,[45] recognized this and explicitly offered itself as a remedy. The preamble, recognizing 'the passionate yearning for freedom in all dependent peoples' and noting that 'the continued existence of colonialism . . . impedes the social, cultural and economic development of dependent peoples', proclaimed 'the necessity of bringing to a speedy and unconditional end colonialism in all its forms and manifestations'.[46] The Colonial Declaration thus 'treats the right of self-determination as an instrument that addresses international law's complicity with colonialism'.[47] The right of colonial peoples to determine their own territorial status did not emerge on its own; rather, it was the response of the expanding international community to the colonial relationship between colonial powers and colonized peoples that undermined self-determination. It would not make any sense isolated from that historical and political context. Therefore, we can say that while the principle of self-determination was the entry point and legal catalyst, although the right of colonized peoples and nations to independence was regarded at the time as synonymous with the right of self-determination[48] decolonization procedures 'did not of themselves embody the substance of the right . . . rather, they were measures to remedy a *sui generis* violation of the right that existed in the prior condition of colonialism'.[49]

Similarly, the international law on the rights of Indigenous peoples, including self-determination, can also be viewed as a remedy for a *sui generis* violation of self-determination. This stems from Indigenous peoples' exclusion from the decolonization processes of the mid-twentieth century. The "salt water" doctrine in Resolution 1541 formally linked the right of colonized peoples to independence to Western overseas colonial dominions, which implied 'the exclusion of Indigenous peoples clustered within independent States' boundaries from the scope of application of the principle of self-determination'.[50] In addition, the doctrine of *uti possidetis* preserved the

[44] On this, see Antony Anghie, *Imperialism, Sovereignty and the Making of International Law* (Cambridge: Cambridge University Press, 2004), 13–29, 32–33, 43, 48–49, 53, 61–62; Martti Koskenniemi, *The Gentle Civilizer of Nations: The Rise and Fall of International Law 1870–1960* (Cambridge: Cambridge University Press, 2001), 72–75, 113–115, 126–168.

[45] Summers, *Peoples and International Law*, 203, 209.

[46] Third, seventh, and twelfth recitals.

[47] Macklem, 'Three Movements', 100.

[48] Summers, *Peoples and International Law*, 205 n 64.

[49] Anaya, 'Post-Declaration Era', 189.

[50] S. James Anaya and Luis Rodríguez-Piñero, 'The Making of the UNDRIP' in Jessie Hohmann and Marc Weller (eds.), *The UN Declaration on the Rights of Indigenous People: A Commentary* (Oxford: Oxford University Press, 2018), 38–62, 40.

former colonial boundaries, meaning that Indigenous peoples within a former colony that had gained independence experienced only a change in ruler.[51] Thereby Indigenous peoples were continually excluded from determining their own destiny. This continued omission 'lies at the heart of Indigenous peoples' expression of their demands in terms of self-determination'.[52] Viewed in this light, the UNDRIP, adopted following decades of global Indigenous peoples' activism,[53] is 'essentially a remedial instrument' based on the identification of a long-standing *sui generis* violation of self-determination.[54] It was required to remedy the systemic inequality and injustice arising from international law's failure to recognize Indigenous peoples' sovereignty and self-determination over the course of centuries.[55] The Declaration represents a step towards rectifying 'the adverse consequences of how international law validate[d] morally suspect colonization projects that participated in the production of the existing distribution of sovereign power'.[56] This is, essentially, a different angle on the "historical sovereignty" argument made by some Indigenous scholars.[57]

Under a relational, remedial account, then, 'the law of self-determination is the law of remedies for serious deficiencies of freedom and equality'.[58] Self-determination is a continuous, ongoing process – a 'constant entitlement'[59] – in which new remedies come to be required by law.[60] Just as decolonization procedures were not the substance of the right, but rather measures to remedy what the international community had come to recognize as a violation of the rights of colonized peoples, the rules on the self-determination of Indigenous peoples reflected in the UNDRIP are also remedial measures for a *sui generis* situation of domination, subjugation, or exploitation.

51 Anaya, *Indigenous Peoples*, 54.

52 Anaya and Rodríguez-Piñero, 'The Making of the UNDRIP', 140.

53 See Sheryl R. Lightfoot, *Global Indigenous Politics: A Subtle Revolution* (New York: Routledge, 2016), 34–38, 43. See also UN Sub-Commission on Prevention of Discrimination and Protection of Minorities, 'Study of the Problem of Discrimination against Indigenous Populations' UN Doc E/CN.4/Sub.2/1986/7 & Adds.1–4, 1987 ("Martínez Cobo report").

54 Anaya, 'Post-Declaration Era', 190.

55 Charters, 'A Self-Determination Approach', 228.

56 Patrick Macklem, 'Indigenous Recognition in International Law: Theoretical Observations' (2008) 30 *Michigan Journal of International Law*, 177–210, 179.

57 See, for example, Claire Charters, 'A Self-Determination Approach to Justifying Indigenous Peoples' Participation in International Law and Policy Making' (2010) 17 *International Journal of Minority & Group Rights*, 215–240.

58 Kingsbury, 'Reconciling Five', 232.

59 Rosalyn Higgins, *Problems and Process: International Law and How We Use It* (Oxford: Oxford University Press, 1995), 120.

60 On self-determination as an ongoing process, see Higgins, 'Problems and Process', 120.

1.2 STRUCTURAL RELATIONS BETWEEN PEOPLES, STATES, AND INTERNATIONAL ORGANIZATIONS

Self-determination, then, rather than being synonymous with colonial independence, is a right capable of being realized in multiple ways and has evolved considerably over time to provide redress in circumstances where a particular kind of relationship is present. A people self-determines only in relation to others, who then tend to hold correlative obligations. Thus if novel or different arenas of domination, subjugation, or exploitation, or novel actors involved in perpetuating such a relationship, were to emerge, a new rule would be justified under the auspices of the principle of self-determination to remedy the situation. As James Anaya put it:[61]

> Other forms of violation of self-determination may be identified, and the remedies forthcoming need not necessarily entail the emergence of new states. Substantive self-determination may be achieved from a range of possibilities of institutional reordering other than the creation of new states. What is important is that the remedy be appropriate to the particular circumstances and that it genuinely reflect the will of the people, or peoples, concerned.

I propose that we should consider, in addition to the well-known position of domination, subjugation, or exploitation that a state may hold over a people, the less-considered relationship between a *group of states* collectively pursuing some objective, or an *intergovernmental organization*, and a people or peoples. I argue that a people's ability to self-determine can be adversely affected not only by a state that has colonized, occupied, or is otherwise dominating, subjugating, or exploiting it. Rather, a people's self-determination can also be undermined by groups of states that act collectively to make and implement international law and policy through international organizations or other intergovernmental fora, as well as by international organizations themselves insofar as they are autonomous actors capable of making law, policies, and decisions and carrying out activities.[62] I will make this case by, first, outlining how states and international organizations exercise public authority, before turning to specific ways in which collectives of states and international

[61] Anaya, 'Post-Declaration Era', 189.

[62] Armin von Bogdandy, Rüdiger Wolfrum, Jochen von Bernstorff, Philipp Dann, and Matthias Goldmann (eds.), *The Exercise of Public Authority by International Institutions: Advancing International Institutional Law* (Heidelberg: Springer, 2010); Sabino Cassese, Bruno Carotti, Lorenzo Casini, Eleonora Cavalieri, and Euan MacDonald, *Global Administrative Law: The Casebook* (3rd ed., Rome: Irpa, 2012).

organizations exercise public authority in ways capable of undermining the self-determination of peoples. I will argue that this relationship is one of domination, of the kind implicated by the law of self-determination.

1.2.1 *The Exercise of Public Authority through Treaty-Making and International Organizations*

It is trite to say that states collectively exercise broad powers through the making of treaties, pooling their sovereignty at the inter-state level in order to meet some shared objective, for instance, in the making of plurilateral or "megaregional" trade and investment agreements.[63] This can be seen as groups of states exercising public authority in a shared or collective manner. The making of megaregional trade agreements, for instance, is an act that may affect individuals and communities within the states parties (as well as outside the states parties), and this effect may be seen to stem from the joint act of the states parties rather than only from the state in which an individual finds themselves.

In addition to bilateral or plurilateral settings, states make international law, make policy and set standards through intergovernmental organizations, and at times assign such functions to those organizations themselves. But states are not always, or necessarily, the only agents. The growth of international organizations – and the expansion of their powers 'through informal processes of discourse, practice and (re)interpretation' – is well documented.[64] International organizations, enabled by the doctrine of implied powers,[65] among other factors, have come to exercise extensive powers with far-reaching impacts on individuals, communities, and domestic societies,[66] through their

[63] On 'megaregional' economic agreements, see Benedict Kingsbury, David M. Malone, Paul Mertenskötter, Richard B. Stewart, Thomas Streinz, and Atsushi Sunami, *Megaregulation Contested: Global Economic Ordering after TPP* (Oxford: Oxford University Press 2019).

[64] Guy Fiti Sinclair, 'State Formation, Liberal Reform and the Growth of International Organizations' (2015) 26 *European Journal of International Law*, 445–469, 446. See, for example, Eyal Benvenisti, *The Law of Global Governance* (Leiden: Brill Nijhoff 2014), 25–69.

[65] Under which IOs are held to have, in addition to the powers explicitly granted by member states, those necessary for their effective functioning. See generally Viljam Engström, *Understanding Powers of International Organizations: A Study of the Doctrines of Attributed Powers, Implied Powers and Constitutionalism* (Åbo: Åbo Akademi University Press, 2009).

[66] See, for example, Armin von Bogdandy, Matthias Goldmann, and Ingo Venzke, 'From Public International to International Public Law: Translating World Public Opinion into International Public Authority' (2017) 28(1) *European Journal of International Law*, 115–145, 116.

ability to make laws,[67] set standards,[68] make decisions and recommendations,[69] and disseminate information.[70] These activities can be viewed as the exercise of public authority.[71] To a certain extent, and in some cases, international organizations may be said to exercise these broad powers in their own right;[72] at the same time, in some circumstances, the exercise of public authority by an organization may be attributed to the collective member states of an organization.[73] The limitations of what had been the default response of international law to the rise of organizations – a functional approach that tended to shield international organizations themselves from external legal scrutiny or accountability and has regarded organizations as mere agents of their collective principal member states – have been widely recognized.[74] International organizations are now seen, at least under some approaches, as autonomous global actors in their own right: 'not … neutral arenas for the

[67] José E. Alvarez, *International Organizations as Law-Makers* (Oxford: Oxford University Press, 2006).

[68] See, for example, Kevin Davis, Angela Fisher, Benedict Kingsbury, and Sally Engle Merry (eds.), *Governance by Indicators: Global Power through Classification and Rankings* (Oxford: Oxford University Press, 2012); Jürgen Friedrich, 'Legal Challenges of Non-Binding Instruments: The Case of the FAO Code of Conduct for Responsible Fisheries' in von Bogdandy et al. (eds.), *Exercise of Public Authority*, 511–540.

[69] This is illustrated in, for example, Maja Smrkolj, 'International Institutions and Individualized Decision-Making: An Example of UNHCR's Refugee Status Determination' in von Bogdandy et al. (eds.), *Exercise of Public Authority*, 165–194.

[70] See, for example, Bettina Schöndorf-Haubold, 'The Administration of Information in International Administrative Law – The Example of Interpol', in von Bogdandy et al. (eds.), *Exercise of Public Authority*, 229–268.

[71] See, for example, Richard B. Stewart and Michelle Ratton Sanchez-Badin, 'The World Trade Organization: Multiple Dimensions of Global Administrative Law' (2011) 9(3–4) *International Journal of Constitutional Law*, 556–586, 557. One definition of an exercise of international public authority is 'the adoption of an act that affects the freedom of others in pursuance of a common interest': von Bogdandy, Goldmann, and Venzke, 'Public International to International Public', 117.

[72] Jan Klabbers, 'Sources of International Organizations Law: Reflections on Accountability' in Jean D'Aspremont and Samantha Besson (eds.), *The Oxford Handbook of the Sources of International Law* (Oxford: Oxford University Press 2017), 987–1006, 988.

[73] Also known as a "principal-agent" or "vertical approach": Jan Klabbers, 'International Organizations in the Formation of Customary International Law' in Enzo Cannizzaro and Paolo Palchetti (eds.), *Customary International Law on the Use of Force: A Methodological Approach* (Leiden: Martinus Nijhoff 2005), 179–195, 183.

[74] Eyal Benvenisti, 'Upholding Democracy Amid the Challenges of New Technology: What Role for the Law of Global Governance?' (2018) 29(1) *European Journal of International Law*, 9–82, at 10–12, 16–30. On functionalism and its limitations, see generally Jan Klabbers, 'The Transformation of International Organizations Law' (2015) 26(1) *European Journal of International Law*, 9–82.

solution of common problems but rather sites of power, even of dominance'.[75] This book is, in part, situated in the vein of international legal scholarship that has thus turned to critiquing international organizations' lack of accountability to those affected by their activities – those 'disempowered disparate domestic electorates, who could not benefit from the traditional constitutional checks and balances found in many democracies intended to limit executive discretion'[76] – and studying ways in which they can be held to account.[77]

1.2.2 A *Relationship of Domination*

Rather than further expound upon the ways in which the activities of international organizations and state collectives may affect vulnerable or marginalized groups in general, or the global public at large, I will here elaborate on the ways in which international organizations and collectives of states exert power over Indigenous peoples. I will suggest that this exhibits the qualities of a relationship of the kind self-determination is concerned with: that is, one of alien domination, subjugation, or exploitation. While different from the formally colonial relationship between a people and a state, this relationship is such as to justify the application of the law of self-determination.

Before moving to specific examples, it is helpful to understand the relationship between international organizations and collectives of states on the one hand, and Indigenous peoples on the other, as structural, arising from the public or regulatory authority situated in international organizations. In the language of self-determination, an international organization, or a group of states acting collectively, can "dominate" an Indigenous people, interfering with its ability to determine its own destiny. Under the definition of domination developed by Philip Pettit and Iris Marion Young, an agent dominates another 'when the agent has power over that other and is thus able to interfere with the other *arbitrarily*'; interference is when 'one agent blocks or redirects the action of another in a way that worsens that agent's choice situation by

[75] Andrew Hurrell, 'Power, Institutions, and the Production of Inequality' in Michael Barnett and Raymond Duvall (eds.), *Power in Global Governance* (Cambridge: Cambridge University Press 2005), 33–58, 56.

[76] Benvenisti, 'Upholding Democracy', 13.

[77] See, for example, August Reinisch, 'Securing the Accountability of International Organizations' (2001) 7(2) *Global Governance*, 131–149; Devika Hovell, 'Due Process in the United Nations' (2016) 110(2) *American Journal of International Law*, 1–48; Richard B. Stewart, 'Remedying Disregard in Global Regulatory Governance: Accountability, Participation, and Responsiveness' (2014) 108(2) *American Journal of International Law*, 211–270, 221.

changing the range of options', and it is "arbitrary" 'when it is chosen or rejected without consideration of the interests or opinions of those affected.[78] An entity may therefore dominate another without ever actually interfering with it; domination 'consists in standing in a set of relations which makes an agent *able* to interfere arbitrarily with the actions of others'.[79] International organizations and collectives of states acting together are manifestly able to interfere with other agents, including peoples; they wield public authority in a way that can directly or indirectly change the range of options available to peoples. It is this structural possibility of interference – which may be positive or negative – that constitutes domination.

The remainder of this section illustrates this point by reference to actual examples of domination and interference, in the sense meant by Pettit and Young, in the realm of state collectives and international organizations carrying out law-making, standard-setting, and policymaking activities that affect peoples. This is not the only field of activity that is relevant: decision-making, for instance, regarding development projects and finance, international territorial administration, and other activities of international organizations and state collectives are also pertinent. While not exhaustive, this section is intended to contain sufficient detail to demonstrate that international organizations, and states acting collectively, have exercised power through the making of standards and policies affecting peoples in myriad fields of activity.

International organizations and other intergovernmental bodies have on several occasions been fora for the setting of standards that have defined the rights and self-determination of Indigenous peoples in general. Examples of such instruments include the UNDRIP, which self-evidently goes to the heart of Indigenous peoples' affairs and concerns, and its development by states and UN organs clearly demonstrates the power the latter exercise over Indigenous peoples.[80] Similar instruments on Indigenous peoples' rights developed in international fora include the American Declaration on the Rights of Indigenous Peoples, the International Labour Organization (ILO) Convention No. 169, and the Draft Nordic Sámi Convention.[81]

78 Iris Marion Young, *Inclusion and Democracy* (Oxford: Oxford University Press, 2000), 258.

79 Young, *Inclusion*, 258–259.

80 Of course, the Declaration was developed with high levels of participation by Indigenous peoples themselves.

81 American Declaration on the Rights of Indigenous Peoples (15 June 2016) OAS Doc AG/RES.2888 (XLVI-O/16); Convention concerning Indigenous and Tribal Peoples in Independent Countries (adopted 27 June 1989 and entered into force 5 September 1991) 1650 UNTS 383; for the draft of the Nordic Saami Convention in English, see https://sametinget.se/105173.

Other international organizations have developed, or are in the process of developing, policies and standards on topics that by their nature affect or have the potential to affect Indigenous peoples' self-determination. For instance, WIPO develops laws and policies relating to intellectual property,[82] including standard-setting activities affecting Indigenous peoples in respect of their traditional knowledge. Recognition that the WIPO framework is unable to provide protection to many forms of traditional knowledge, which are left vulnerable to misappropriation and "biopiracy,"[83] led to the establishment in 2000 of the WIPO Intergovernmental Committee on Intellectual Property and Genetic Resources, Traditional Knowledge and Folklore (IGC).[84] Since then, the IGC has been undertaking textual negotiations on draft instruments related to traditional knowledge, traditional cultural expressions, and genetic resources.[85] It has produced Draft Articles on the Protection of Traditional Knowledge, the Protection of Traditional Cultural Expressions, and a consolidated document relating to intellectual property and genetic resources.[86] There is a great deal at stake for Indigenous peoples in these negotiations: '[f]or a people whose relationship of dependence with their ecosystem is first nature and a basis for their knowledge and socioeconomic and cultural life ... intellectual property's role in knowledge enclosure is a fundamental human rights issue bordering on life and survival'.[87] The IGC process has the potential to address Indigenous peoples' 'claims for cultural recognition' and 'significantly accommodat[e] an alternative indigenous understanding of knowledge'.[88] The conclusion of international agreements on genetic resources, traditional knowledge, and traditional cultural expressions 'would

[82] Convention Establishing the World Intellectual Property Organization (adopted 15 July 1967 and entered into force 26 April 1970) 828 UNTS 3, arts 3 and 4.

[83] On misappropriation, see, for example, Sumathi Subbiah, 'Reaping What They Sow: The Basmati Rice Controversy and Strategies for Protecting Traditional Knowledge' (2004) 27(2) *Boston College International & Comparative Law Review*, 529–559.

[84] Established in 2000 by the WIPO General Assembly: WIPO, 'WIPO General Assembly, Twenty-Sixth (12th Extraordinary) Session, Report' (3 October 2000) WIPO Doc WO/GA/26/10, para. 71.

[85] WIPO, 'Assemblies of the Member States of WIPO, Fifty-Seventh Series of Meetings, October 2 to 11, 2017, Summary Report, Addendum, Item 18 of the Consolidated Agenda', (11 October 2017) WIPO Doc A/57/11/Add.6.

[86] For the most up-to-date versions of these drafts, see www.wipo.int.

[87] Chidi Oguamanam, *Intellectual Property in Global Governance:* A Development Question (New York: Routledge 2012), 81.

[88] Franziska Boehme, Lindsay Burt, Patricia Goff, and Audie Klotz, 'Cultural Diversity and the Politics of Recognition in International Organizations' (2018) 9 *Journal of International Organizations Studies*, 27–41, 30.

be a landmark in international law and in IP law, and could potentially contribute to the prevention of their misappropriation'.[89]

The traditional knowledge and self-determination of Indigenous peoples are also implicated in activities under the Convention on Biological Diversity (CBD). The CBD itself recognizes 'the close and traditional dependence of many indigenous and local communities embodying traditional lifestyles on biological resources',[90] and its Article 8(j) obliges states parties to respect, maintain, and preserve this knowledge. However, the establishment of protected areas (under Article 8) has sometimes served as an instrument, intentionally or not, for the exclusion of Indigenous peoples from their traditional lands and territories.[91] The Nagoya Protocol on Access and Benefit-Sharing, developed under the CBD's auspices, has implications for the protection of Indigenous traditional knowledge, innovations, and practices associated with genetic resources.

Further examples of international organizations affecting Indigenous peoples include the FAO, which through its Committee on Food Security develops policy recommendations and guidance on food security and nutrition;[92] the UN Educational, Educational and Scientific Organization (UNESCO), which engages in standard-setting activity and in so doing 'addresses key concerns of indigenous peoples such as endangered languages, mother tongue education, education for sustainable development, indigenous knowledge in scientific and environmental decision-making, and building knowledge societies';[93] the International Maritime Organization, through which states set standards on topics, including, of particular relevance to Indigenous peoples, rules on heavy fuel oil, the avoidance of marine mammals, greenhouse gases and black carbon, underwater noise, sewage

89 Daniel F. Robinson, Pedro Roffe, and Ahmed Abdel-Latif, 'Introduction: Mapping the Evolution, State-of-play and Future of the WIPO IGC' in Daniel F. Robinson, Ahmed Abdel-Latif, and Pedro Roffe (eds.), *Protecting Traditional Knowledge: The WIPO Intergovernmental Committee on Intellectual Property and Genetic Resources, Traditional Knowledge and Folklore* (New York: Routledge, 2017), 3–9, 3.

90 Convention on Biological Diversity (adopted 5 June 1993 and entered into force 29 December 1993) 1760 UNTS 79, Preamble, twelfth recital.

91 Paige West, James Igoe, and Dan Brockington, 'Parks and Peoples: The Social Impact of Protected Areas' (2005) 35 *Annual Review of Anthropology*, 251–277, 258.

92 Constitution of the United Nations Food and Agriculture Organization, reprinted in FAO, Basic Texts of the Food and Agriculture Organization of the United Nations (FAO 2017), art IV.9.

93 UNESCO, Policy on Engaging with Indigenous Peoples (9 August 2017) UNESCO Doc 202 EX/9, para. 15.

and grey water discharge, and invasive species;[94] and the International Seabed Association, which makes rules, regulations, and procedures relating to prospecting, exploration, and mining of mineral resources in the seabed, ocean floor, and subsoil thereof beyond the limits of national jurisdiction[95] – rules that are likely to disproportionately affect Indigenous peoples living traditional lifestyles on coasts and islands.[96]

In addition to broad standard-setting affecting Indigenous peoples in general, international organizations may make policies that impinge on the self-determination of a specific people or peoples. One example of this are the decisions of the European Union (EU) to ratify agreements with Morocco on trade and fisheries and to implicitly accept their application to Western Sahara, which specifically affect the Sahrawi people.[97] Another is the effect of EU legislation on Arctic Indigenous peoples' communities.[98] European Directive 83/129/EEC of 1982 prohibited the importation into the European Economic Community of skins and other products derived from seal pups.[99] While the makers of the directive did not appear to expect any adverse effects on Indigenous peoples, and indeed the directive in its preamble recalled that traditionally practised hunting does not harm seal pups and is 'a natural and legitimate occupation, conducted with due respect for the balance of nature, and part of indigenous peoples' traditional way of life and economy', the ban in fact triggered the collapse of the EU market for seal furs.[100] In turn, this affected the Inuit economy, which depended on the cash income from the fur market. Although a later version of the directive made an exception for Inuit

[94] See International Maritime Organization, 'Marine Environment Protection Committee, 70th session, Agenda Item 17, Any other business, Arctic indigenous food security and shipping, submitted by FOEI, WWF and Pacific Environment' (19 August 2016) IMO Doc. MEPC 70/17/10, paras. 3–14.

[95] See, for example, International Seabed Association, Regulations on Prospecting and Exploration for Polymetallic Nodules in the Area (22 July 2013) ISA Doc. ISBA/19/C/17.

[96] Julie Hunter, Pradeep Singh, and Julian Aguon, 'Broadening Common Heritage: Addressing Gaps in the Deep Sea Mining Regulatory Regime' (2018) *Harvard Environmental Law Review* (online), https://harvardelr.com/2018/04/16/broadening-common-heritage/ (noting that deep sea exploration has already had adverse impacts on Indigenous peoples' livelihoods due to disturbances of fish populations and detriments to water quality).

[97] For example, Euro-Mediterranean Agreement between the European Communities and their Member States and the Kingdom of Morocco (adopted 26 February 1996) OJ 2000 L 70. See Case T-512/12 *Front Polisario v. Council of the European Union*, Judgment of the General Court, Eighth Chamber, ECLI:EU:T:2015:953.

[98] See generally Federica Scarpa, 'The EU, the Arctic, and Arctic Indigenous Peoples' (2014) 6 (1) *The Yearbook of Polar Law Online*, 427–465.

[99] Council Regulation (EC) No. 1007/2009 of the European Parliament and of the Council of 16 September 2009 on trade in seal products [2009] OJ L 286/36.

[100] Scarpa, 'The EU, the Arctic', 428.

hunting, Canadian Inuit were still disproportionately affected, and in any case, the market had long since collapsed.[101] This example shows that the regulatory acts of international organizations may affect not only peoples within their member states but also peoples who are "distant strangers" or "global others" due to being located in a state or states that are not members of the organization.[102]

The other side of this coin is that – as Indigenous peoples have known as long as international organizations have existed – international organizations can be vehicles for emancipation. The same power and international public authority that means that international organizations' activities can negatively impinge on the exercise of self-determination also means, at least in theory, that international organizations could be vehicles to hold states to account and that Indigenous peoples by becoming members of such organizations could shape and influence international governance.

1.3 EXISTING LAW DOES NOT ADEQUATELY REMEDY THE RELATIONSHIP

Because Indigenous peoples, and international organizations and groups of states, exist in a relationship of domination of the former by the latter – that is, the kind of relationship that the law of self-determination is concerned with – it can be argued that the law of self-determination is called on to evolve to provide a remedy. However, before jumping to such a conclusion, we must examine whether an adequate remedy is already found in existing law. I will assess the existing law on internal self-determination, as well as emergent norms and practice regarding civil society participation, particularly through NGOs.

1.3.1 *Internal Self-Determination and Domestic Political Participation*

It may be tempting to imagine that the self-determination of Indigenous peoples with respect to international organizations and groups of states can be realized simply via Indigenous peoples' political participation on the domestic plane. One element of the internal aspect of self-determination is the right of a people to participate in the political affairs of the state in which it

[101] Ibid., 429.

[102] On the accountability of states to "strangers," see Sivan Shlomo Agon and Eyal Benvenisti, 'The Law of Strangers: The Form and Substance of Other-Regarding International Adjudication' (2018) 68(4) *University of Toronto Law Journal*, 598–660.

is located. Thus if a people is well represented in the relevant domestic government(s), such an argument would run, additional rights at the international level are not necessary. Rather, it is for the state to balance competing domestic interests. Indeed, to enable Indigenous peoples' voice in both domestic and international fora – "two bites of the apple,"[103] so to speak – could give them *too* much influence over international regulation.[104]

It is true that in some cases a state may be able to represent an Indigenous people at the international level so as to protect the latter's right to self-determination – such as when the interests of the state and the people broadly overlap on a given issue and the Indigenous people have provided their free, prior, and informed consent, or where they hold a dominant, rather than marginal place in domestic society. In such situations, the Indigenous people would not require an additional voice on the global stage.

However, in most cases, participatory rights at the domestic level are not enough. Often the interests of a people do not align with those of the relevant state, meaning that the state's position in an international forum will necessarily be at odds with the interests of the Indigenous people, even taking into account the people's right to participate within the state.[105] Of course, for any position a government takes on the international stage, there will invariably be some group of people who do not agree. It is in the nature of a diverse democracy that competing domestic interests must be balanced.[106] But an Indigenous people, by virtue of its right to self-determination, is different from other domestic actors: it is not equivalent to a trade union, or an interest group, or a political party. Of course, it is not here suggested that such interest-based constituencies should not have a voice. The point is that the right to self-determination distinguishes Indigenous peoples from the (valid) reasons to participate possessed by other domestic constituencies.[107] To deny them a

103 The phrase "two bites of the apple" is borrowed from August Reinisch and Christina Irgel, writing in the context of NGO participation: 'The Participation of Non-Governmental Organisations (NGOs) in the WTO Dispute Settlement System' (2001) 1(2) *Non-State Actors & International Law*, 127–151, 132.

104 Erik B. Bluemel, 'Separating Instrumental from Intrinsic Rights: Towards an Understanding of Indigenous Participation in International Rule Making' (2005) 30(1) *American Indian Law Review*, 55–132, 75.

105 Navajo Nation Council, *Adopting and Recommending Position Statements Regarding the United Nations Recognition for the Navajo Nation* (22 July 2009) NNHRC/Report 03/2009, 22–23.

106 Jürgen Habermas, 'Three Normative Models of Democracy' (1994) 1 *Constellations* 1–10, at 5.

107 Timo Koivurova and Leena Heinämäki, 'The Participation of Indigenous Peoples in International Norm-Making in the Arctic' (2006) 42 *Polar Record*, 101–109, 102.

right to participate at the international level would be to, by default, crush their interests under the weight of majoritarian concerns.

Second, in many states, it is the executive branch of government, rather than the legislature, which determines foreign policy and represents a state in international organizations. Although the legislature may have input on decisions of considerable domestic importance, forms of internal self-determination that provide for participation in the electoral process or for a level of autonomous self-government will not provide for the accountability to peoples of the state's delegates who will take the political decisions in inter-governmental fora.[108] Although this executive-led approach could conceivably have advantages, including that executives are in principle able to protect minority interests since they are not bound to make majoritarian decisions,[109] in practice there are risks associated with the isolation of the conduct of international relations from accountability to minority groups.

Third, in practice, even in a democratic state, a people may not in fact be able to exercise its right to internal self-determination in the first place. And not all states are democratic. In these cases, internal political participation cannot assist a people to exercise voice in international organizations that affect them.

Fourth, some peoples exist across state boundaries. For instance, the Sámi extend across parts of Norway, Sweden, Finland, and Russia, and the territory of the Inuit encompasses part of Russia, the United States, Canada, and Denmark-Greenland.[110] In cases like these, it is unlikely that any one state can effectively represent the interests of the transnational Indigenous people at the international level. The Indigenous people may not be able to exercise its right to internal self-determination within all of the relevant states, and it is even less likely that the interests of the people and all of the relevant states will coincide.[111]

Relatedly, different Indigenous peoples located in different states often share common interests. In this situation, a domestic balancing of interests

[108] Anne Peters, 'International Organizations in International Law' in Jacob Katz Cogan, Ian Hurd, and Ian Johnstone (eds.), *The Oxford Handbook of International Organizations* (Oxford: Oxford University Press, 2016), 33–59, 46.

[109] Robert O. Keohane, Stephen Macedo, and Andrew Moravcsik, 'Democracy Enhancing Multilateralism' (2009) 63(1) *International Organization*, 1–31.

[110] Timo Koivurova, 'Sovereign States and Self-Determining Peoples: Carving Out a Place for Transnational Indigenous Peoples in a World of Sovereign States' (2010) 12(2) *International Community Law Review*, 191–212, 204.

[111] This point was made with respect to transnational interests generally in Reinisch and Irgel, 'Participation of Non-Governmental Organisations', 132.

within each state will tend to mean that the shared interest is systematically obscured from view at the international level.

Sixth, international organizations themselves delegate authority to organs, such as executive boards or secretariats, in which not all member states are included, so that even if a state is a member of an international organization, it does not necessarily have a voice in all activities carried out within that organization. While such a delegation of powers can be practical,[112] it means that these organs, which 'act on behalf of the international entity, and are not to be equated with the (collectivity of) states',[113] are less accountable to states and by extension those within them. Secretariats, generally speaking, are capable of exercising considerable bureaucratic power independently of their member states, for instance, by steering or manipulating the decision-making of states through the management and organization of information.[114] If a secretariat's activities affect an Indigenous people, a state may not necessarily be able to effectively represent that people, even if their positions align. A secretariat should, in theory, be accountable to member states, but in practice this may not happen.[115]

Similarly, boards can exercise executive functions, and even independent governing and legislative functions within an institution.[116] The activities of executive boards, such as those in charge of allocating financing, can impact on strangers to the organization.[117] In addition, while the boards of some organizations are constituted of the representatives of several member states, other boards, such as the European Commission and the Executive Council

112 Henry G. Schermers and Niels M. Blokker, *International Institutional Law: Unity within Diversity* (Leiden: Martinus Nijhoff 2011), 307–308.

113 Ramses A. Wessel, 'Executive Boards and Councils' in Jacob Katz Cogan, Ian Hurd, and Ian Johnstone (eds.), *The Oxford Handbook of International Organizations* (Oxford: Oxford University Press, 2016), 802–821, 804.

114 Touko Piiparinen, 'Secretariats' in Jacob Katz Cogan, Ian Hurd, and Ian Johnstone (eds.), *The Oxford Handbook of International Organizations* (Oxford: Oxford University Press, 2016), 839–858, 839–840, 843.

115 See, for example, J. Benton Heath, 'SARS, the "Swine Flu" Crisis and Emergency Procedures in the WHO' in Cassese et al., *Global Administrative Law*, chapter I.B.10.

116 Wessel, 'Executive Boards and Councils', 814–820.

117 See, for example, the Executive Board of the World Health Organization: Abigail C. Deshman, 'International Organizations and Horizontal Review: The World Health Organisation, the Parliamentary Council of Europe, and the H1N1 Pandemic' in Cassese et al., *Global Administrative Law*, chapter I.E.9, and the European Commission: Treaty of Lisbon amending the Treaty on European Union and the Treaty establishing the European Community (adopted 13 December 2007 and entered into force 1 December 2009) 2702 UNTS, arts 106(3) and 45(3)(d).

of the African Union, hold responsibility for specific policy areas;[118] still others, such as the Executive Board of UNESCO, sit as individual experts rather than state representatives.[119] For an Indigenous people affected by the activities of a board to have a voice only within its own state is manifestly inadequate.

For all these reasons, the so-called internal self-determination in the sense of the participation of Indigenous peoples in domestic public affairs is not an adequate remedy to the problem of the dominance of Indigenous peoples by international organizations.

1.3.1 *Civil Society Participation in Intergovernmental Fora*

Is civil society participation a potential remedy?[120] Since the 1990s, civil society participation in international organizations has proliferated.[121] The UN Economic and Social Council (ECOSOC) has provided for consultative status since its inception,[122] and in the late twentieth century, the number of NGOs taking up that status vastly increased.[123] NGOs have played influential roles in a number of international law-making processes.[124] The importance of public participation in, *inter alia*, decision-making relating to the environment has been progressively recognized.[125] A considerable bulk of literature

[118] Treaty on European Union (adopted 7 February 1992 and entered into force 1 November 1993) 1755 UNTS, art 17(3); Constitutive Act of the African Union (adopted 11 July 2000 and entered into force 26 May 2001) 2158 UNTS 3, art 14.

[119] Constitution of the United Nations Educational, Scientific and Cultural Organization (adopted 16 November 1945 and entered into force 4 November 1946) 4 UNTS 52, art V(2).

[120] Here the terms "civil society" and "NGO" are used interchangeably: For a fuller discussion of these terms and their differences, see Sabine Lang, *NGOs, Civil Society, and the Public Sphere* (Cambridge: Cambridge University Press, 2013) chapters 2 and 3.

[121] Holly Cullen and Karen Morrow, 'International Civil Society in International Law: The Growth of NGO Participation' (2001) 1(1) *Non-State Actors & International Law*, 7–39.

[122] UN Charter, art 71.

[123] Zoe Pearson, 'Non-Governmental Organizations and the International Criminal Court: Changing Landscapes of International Law' (2006) 39(2) *Cornell International Law Journal*, 243–284, 245.

[124] For accounts of such processes, see, for example, K. Anderson, 'The Ottawa Convention Banning Landmines, the Role of International Non-Governmental Organizations, and the Idea of International Civil Society' (2000) 11(1) *European Journal of International Law*, 91–120; Cynthia Price Cohen, 'The Role of Nongovernmental Organizations in the Drafting of the Convention on the Rights of the Child' (1990) 12(1) *Human Rights Quarterly*, 137–147.

[125] See, for example, World Commission on Environment and Development, *Our Common Future* (1987), para. 107; UNGA, Rio Declaration on Environment and Development (13 June 1992) UN Doc A/CONF.151/26, Principle 10; Convention on Access to

advances both intrinsic and instrumental justifications for NGO participation in global governance: civil society participation is said to combat the democratic deficit, improve international organizations' legitimacy,[126] provide unique technical and practical expertise and information not otherwise available, increase the variety of political options, improve the quality of outcomes, and build domestic public support for such policies.[127] Legally, it has been proposed that participation in international law-making is an individual human right, derived from Article 25 of the International Covenant on Civil and Political Rights – the right 'to take part in the conduct of public affairs, directly or through freely chosen representatives' – and that this right should in practice be exercised through NGO participation.[128] One could argue that NGO participation, then, solves the problem outlined above: Indigenous peoples may engage through NGOs, within existing NGO participation mechanisms, to have their voices heard at the intergovernmental level.

I suggest otherwise. Although NGO participation founded on an individual human right to participate in international organizations and other intergovernmental fora is certainly valuable as well as legally justifiable for the reasons referred to above, it is not sufficient to remedy the problem of the domination of peoples by international organizations and groups of states, nor to enable peoples the full exercise of self-determination. Beyond the obvious point that NGOs, unlike peoples, do not have the right to self-determination, this is so for two reasons, one theoretical and one practical: systems of participation founded solely on individual human rights tend to result in the disregard of (marginalized) groups, and in practice, Indigenous peoples' organizations and representative institutions are not necessarily compatible with international organization mechanisms for the accreditation of civil society, as Indigenous advocates have stressed. Let us expand on each of these in turn.

The first objection can be understood by reference to (liberal) political theory. In domestic societies, it has long been recognized that formally democratic arrangements tend to undermine the interests of non-dominant

Information, Public Participation in Decision-Making and Access to Justice in Environmental Matters (concluded 25 June 1998 and entered into force 30 October 2001) 2161 UNTS 447.

126 Steve Charnovitz, 'The Illegitimacy of Preventing NGO Participation' (2011) 36(3) *Brooklyn Journal of International Law*, 891–910, 894–895, 904ff.

127 Kal Raustiala, 'States, NGOs, and International Environmental Institutions' (1997) 41(4) *International Studies Quarterly*, 719–740; Peter Van den Bossche, 'NGO Involvement in the WTO: A Comparative Perspective' (2008) 11(4) *Journal of International Economic Law*, 717–749, 720.

128 Nahuel Maisley, 'The International Right of Rights? Article 25(a) of the ICCPR as a Human Right to Take Part in International Law-Making' (2017) 28(1) *European Journal on International Law*, 89–113.

societal groups.[129] Minority groups that have distinct interests from, but are numerically outweighed by, the rest of the population are persistently outvoted and hence under-represented. They are 'in a very real sense political captives of the majority', who may monopolize political power with barely more than half of the votes.[130] Where structural inequalities exist, 'formally democratic procedures are likely to reinforce them'.[131] While scholars initially conceived of this problem as relating to so-called classical ethnic, religious, and national minorities,[132] it is equally applicable to peoples such as Indigenous peoples. In many states, Indigenous peoples constitute a numerical minority or are otherwise a non-dominant societal group. In other words, individual civil and political rights do not suffice to protect the interests of Indigenous peoples, nor those of other marginalized groups. To correct for this problem, many states have instituted minority rights and Indigenous peoples' rights in national and international law,[133] including minority rights and Indigenous peoples' rights to participation in domestic public affairs, as well as mechanisms such as weighted voting,[134] political and associational institutions designed specifically to increase the representation of minorities or Indigenous peoples,[135] seats in parliaments designated for members of minorities or peoples,[136] and other types of 'political consociationalism'.[137] In this way, the universal, individual human right to take part in the conduct of public affairs,[138] which on its

[129] See generally, Vernon Van Dyke, 'Human Rights and the Rights of Groups' (1974) 28(4) *American Journal of Political Science*, 725–741; Will Kymlicka, *Multicultural Citizenship: A Liberal Theory of Minority Rights* (Oxford: Clarendon, 1995).

[130] Eyal Benvenisti, 'Margin of Appreciation, Consensus, and Universal Standards' (1999) 31(4) *New York University Journal of International Law and Politics*, 843–854, 848–849.

[131] Young, *Inclusion*, 34. An important caveat is that a group that is in the numerical minority is not always powerless; indeed, a powerful minority may be the dominant societal group: See, for example, Eric Kaufmann and Oded Haklai, 'Dominant Ethnicity: From Minority to Majority' (2008) 14 *Nations and Nationalism*, 743–767, 747–753.

[132] Van Dyke, 'Human Rights' 32; Kymlicka, *Multicultural Citizenship*, 52.

[133] See, for example, Framework Convention for the Protection of National Minorities (opened for signature 1 February 1995 and entered into force 1 February 1998) CETS No. 157; Article 27, International Covenant on Civil and Political Rights (adopted 16 December 1966 and entered into force 23 March 1976) UNTS 171.

[134] Montserrat Guibernau, 'Nations without States: Political Communities in the Global Age' (2004) 25(4) *Michigan Journal of International Law*, 1251–1282.

[135] Young, *Inclusion*, 141.

[136] Andrew Reynolds, 'Reserved Seats in National Legislatures: A Research Note' (2005) 30(2) *Legislative Studies Quarterly*, 301–310.

[137] Arend Lijphart, *Democracy in Plural Societies: A Comparative Exploration* (New Haven: Yale University Press, 1977). Examples of consociational states include Belgium and Burundi: René Lemarchand, 'Consociationalism and Power Sharing in Africa: Rwanda, Burundi, and the Democratic Republic of the Congo' (2006) 106(422) *African Affairs*, 1–20.

[138] International Covenant on Civil and Political Rights, art 25.

own would tend to reinforce structural inequalities, is supplemented by group rights.

Returning to the international realm, an analogous argument can be made. An individual human right to participation in international organizations, on its own, tends to reproduce existing structural global inequalities. Such inequalities in access and participation are well documented. Individuals and groups who are already marginalized globally find themselves disregarded in the intergovernmental sphere.[139] This is observable, for example, in relation to civil society observer participation in international organizations, where many more NGOs from the Global North participate than NGOs from the Global South.[140] An individual right to participation in IOs, exercisable through NGO participation, must be supplemented by an equivalent right of peoples – just as individual political participation rights on the domestic plane need to be complemented by minority rights to political participation and the so-called internal aspects of self-determination of peoples.[141] The argument here is not that participation is unimportant or undesirable in itself. Rather it is that, in a system characterized by NGO participation and lacking recognition of the procedural rights of groups, the voices and interests of peoples who occupy marginalized positions in the global order, including Indigenous peoples, tend to get lost.

At a more practical level, there is a mismatch between the structure and organization of NGOs and that of Indigenous peoples, which limits the extent to which Indigenous peoples are able to fit within existing procedures for the accreditation of NGOs to participate in international organizations. Indigenous peoples' organizations may have been constitutionally, legally, or politically recognized by the relevant state.[142] Many Indigenous peoples' organizations exercise self-governance functions over peoples and territories; hence they are loath to identify themselves as "non-governmental" organizations in order to seek accreditation.[143] Moreover, taking the criteria for consultative status with the ECOSOC as an example, NGOs are required to

[139] Stewart, 'Remedying Disregard'.

[140] Jackie Smith and Dawn West, 'The Uneven Geography of Global Civil Society: National and Global Influences on Transnational Association' (2005) 84(2) *Social Forces*, 621–652.

[141] Of course, this raises the question of whether a right of national minorities to participate in international law-making exists. Due to the so-called firewall between the law applicable to "minorities" and that applying to "peoples," this question is not appropriate for further consideration here.

[142] Human Rights Council, 'Ways and means of promoting participation at the United Nations of indigenous peoples' representatives on issues affecting them: Report of the Secretary-General' (2012) UN Doc A/HRC/21/24, para. 8.

[143] Ibid., para. 9.

have an established headquarters with an executive officer and provide a copy of its constitution, charter, or statutes, as well as a certificate of registration, and a financial statement.[144] An NGO must also have 'recognized standing'.[145] In addition, NGOs in consultative status with ECOSOC must be broadly representative of major segments of society in a large number of countries in different regions of the world.[146] By contrast, many Indigenous peoples' organizations are not recognized by the state in question. They may not have a headquarters, nor an "executive officer," and may function on the basis of oral traditions rather than written documentation; moreover, they rarely represent a major segment of society.[147] While there are limited exceptions,[148] in general these accreditation requirements limit civil society participation from being a remedy to the relationship of domination.

Might NGOs that fit the accreditation requirements – regardless of whether or not they are Indigenous peoples' representative institutions[149] – be able to effectively represent the voices of peoples regardless? Scholars have documented how "affected persons' organizations" and NGOs may fruitfully form alliances, whereby an NGO provides its expertise and organizational, operational, and financial support to an affected persons' organization that may be less experienced and resourced, while centering the concerns of the affected group.[150] Hence one can imagine that in individual cases an Indigenous people might partner with an NGO to, for instance, send its representatives to international meetings using the NGO's existing accreditation, funding, and advocacy support networks. However, this cannot be viewed as a general solution.

1.4 TOWARDS A RIGHT OF PEOPLES TO PARTICIPATE

We have seen that existing law does not adequately remedy the issue of international organizations' and state collectives' domination over

144 ECOSOC res 1996/31, principle 10.

145 Ibid., principle 9.

146 Ibid., principle 22.

147 Human Rights Council, 'Ways and Means', para. 10.

148 For instance, several Indigenous peoples' organizations have ECOSOC status, including the Saami Council, the Association of Indigenous Peoples of the North, Siberia and Far East of the Russian Federation (RAIPON), the Asia Indigenous Peoples Pact (AIPP), the Assembly of First Nations, and the International Indian Treaty Council (IITC).

149 Noting that some ECOSOC-accredited Indigenous peoples' organizations are not necessarily representative.

150 Annette Schramm and Jan Sändig, 'Affectedness Alliances: Affected People at the Centre of Transnational Advocacy' (2018) 3(5–6) *Third World Thematics*, 664–683.

Indigenous peoples. Civil society participation, underpinned by an individual human rights-based approach, does not account for group interests; nor is it well suited in practice for Indigenous peoples' organizational forms. Meanwhile, Indigenous peoples' participation on the domestic level, even where this occurs, is not necessarily enough to protect their right to self-determination.

Under the logic of self-determination, a remedy is warranted to fill the gap: a right of Indigenous peoples to participate in intergovernmental and international organizations' activities that concern their self-determination, including law-making, policymaking, decision-making, and standard-setting. This remedy, this rule, would co-exist with other rules of the law of self-determination and would not preclude, in appropriate circumstances, their application.[151]

We have identified a gap in the law of self-determination within which a right of Indigenous peoples to participation in global governance could fit. But this necessarily leads to the question of where is the rule located, and how can it be justified, within the positive sources of international law.

[151] As Xanthaki notes, states are 'eager to 'fill' the meaning of the right to self-determination with democracy and participation, as an attempt to set the external aspect of the right – and secession – aside': Alexandra Xanthaki, *Indigenous Rights and United Nations Standards* (Cambridge: Cambridge University Press, 2010), 162.

2

Finding Support for Indigenous Peoples' Participation in the Sources of International Law

This chapter aims to establish a doctrinal framework within which the following chapters may be understood. It undertakes an examination of relevant sources of international law[1] to show how, although the case for the existence of a right of Indigenous peoples to participation in international governance finds only limited support in treaty law and declaratory "soft" law such as the UN Declaration on the Rights of Indigenous Peoples (UNDRIP), it is in principle possible that the right could emerge as a rule of customary international law. It discusses various approaches to identifying a rule of custom.

[1] This chapter largely relies on the classical sources of international law as contained in the Statute of the International Court of Justice (concluded 26 June 1945 and entered into force 24 October 1945) 33 UNTS 993 ("ICJ Statute"), Article 38. I regard as unlikely the argument that the right to self-determination in all its manifestations is a peremptory norm (Vienna Convention on the Law of Treaties (adopted 22 May 1969 and entered into force 27 January 1980) 1155 UNTS 331 (VCLT), Article 53, Article 64). For that argument, see Alexander Orakhelashvili, *Peremptory Norms in International Law* (Oxford: Oxford University Press, 2006) 51, and Antonio Cassese, *Self-Determination of Peoples: A Legal Reappraisal* (Cambridge: Cambridge University Press, 1995) 140, relying on *Case Concerning Barcelona Traction, Light, and Power Company, Ltd (Belgium v. Spain)* (Judgment) [1971] ICJ Rep 3, Separate Opinion of Judge Ammoun, 304; International Law Commission, 'Draft Articles on the Law of Treaties with Commentaries' (1966) Yearbook of the International Law Commission, vol. II, 187, 248. Some states also suggested this during deliberations on the VCLT, on the Friendly Relations Declaration, and in submissions to the ICJ: see Cassese, *Self-Determination of Peoples*, 137–140, 170–172. For the opposing view, with which I agree, see, for example, Matthew Saul, 'The Normative Status of Self-Determination in International Law: A Formula for Uncertainty in the Scope and Content of the Right' (2011) 11(4) *Human Rights Law Review*, 609–644, 636.

2.1 SELF-DETERMINATION AS PARTICIPATION OF PEOPLES AT THE NATIONAL LEVEL

Classic statements on self-determination contain open formulations of the right.[2] While not precluding a participatory aspect, on their face they merely offer an umbrella under which, in the words of Caroline Foster, a 'broad range of international legal understandings about self-determination take shelter'.[3] But to the extent that they can be interpreted to provide for internal self-determination – that is, representative government – they can therefore be said to support a right to participation at the domestic level. Representative government 'by definition requires effective avenues for political participation by all individuals and groups subject to a particular government'.[4] In relation to Common Article 1, as Foster highlights, an examination of negotiators' discussions in the development of the Covenants reveals an interpretation of the article concerned with internal governance.[5] The Human Rights Committee and the Committee on Economic, Social and Cultural Rights have on several occasions interpreted self-determination in Common Article 1 as requiring participation of peoples in decision-making on matters affecting them at the national level.[6] The Committee on the Elimination of Racial Discrimination, in its general recommendation on the right to self-

2 Charter of the United Nations (signed 26 June 1945 and entered into force 24 October 1945) 1 UNTS 26, Articles 1(2) and 55; Common Article 1 of the International Covenant on Civil and Political Rights 1966 (adopted 16 December 1966 and entered into force 23 March 1976) 999 UNTS 171 (ICCPR) and the International Covenant on Economic, Social and Cultural Rights 1966 (adopted 16 December 1966 and entered into force 3 January 1976) 993 UNTS 3 (ICESCR); Article 20(1) of the African Charter on Human and Peoples' Rights (adopted 27 June 1981 and entered into force 21 October 1986) OAU Doc CABLEG/67/3 rev 5, 21 ILM 58; Helsinki Final Act (1975) 14 ILM 1293–1325, Principle VIII.

3 Caroline E. Foster, 'Articulating Self-Determination in the Draft Declaration on the Rights of Indigenous Peoples' (2001) 12(1) *European Journal of International Law*, 141–157, 144.

4 Foster, 'Articulating Self-Determination', 151. See also Gregory H. Fox, 'The Right to Political Participation in International Law' (1992) 17 *Yale Journal of International Law*, 539–607, 606.

5 Foster, 'Articulating Self-Determination', 146. Several countries, including the USA, Greece, Denmark, New Zealand, and a number of developing countries, proposed that self-determination should include a right to be free from an authoritarian regime, and Western states also argued for rights of political participation and representative government.

6 Human Rights Committee, 'Report of the Human Rights Committee, Volume I' (2000) UN Doc A/55/40, 498–528 (in which the HRC called on Australia to allow Indigenous peoples a stronger role in decision-making over their traditional lands and natural resources); Human Rights Committee, 'Concluding Observations: Sweden' (24 April 2002) UN Doc CCPR/CO/74/SWE, 15 (expressing concern that Sweden does not allow the Sámi people a significant role in decision-making processes that affect their traditional lands and economic activities); Human Rights Committee, 'Concluding Observations on the Sixth Periodic Report of Morocco' (1 December 2016) UN Doc CCPR/C/MAR/CO/6, para. 10 (Morocco was

determination, considered that the right has an internal aspect linked with the right of every citizen to take part in the conduct of public affairs.[7]

Decisions of the ICJ lend support to the idea that self-determination can be construed as a participatory right of peoples.[8] In the *Western Sahara* advisory opinion, the Court defined self-determination as 'the need to pay regard to the freely expressed will of peoples'.[9] Judge Yusuf, in his separate opinion in the *Kosovo* proceedings, considered that self-determination chiefly operates internally to entitle the population of a state 'to determine its own political, economic and social destiny and to choose a representative government' and also to entitle 'a defined part of the population . . . to participate in the political life of the State, to be represented in its government and not to be

recommended to enhance meaningful consultation with the people of Western Sahara with a view to securing their FPIC for development projects and resource extraction operations affecting them); Human Rights Committee, 'Concluding Observations: Mexico' (27 July 1999) UN Doc CCPR/C/79/Add.109, para. 19 (urging Mexico to take appropriate measures to ensure Indigenous communities' participation in the country's institutions); Human Rights Committee, 'Concluding Observations: Norway' (1 November 1999) UN Doc CCPR/C/79/Add.112, para. 10 (welcoming developments in Norway to ensure 'full consultation' with the Sámi in matters affecting their traditional livelihoods); Human Rights Committee, 'Concluding Observations: Norway' (25 April 2006) UN Doc CCPR/C/NOR/CO/5, para. 5 (welcoming an agreement between Norway and the Norwegian Sámi Parliament setting out procedures for consultation between the central government and the Sámi Parliament, which it noted was in furtherance of Article 1 of the Covenant); Human Rights Committee, 'Concluding Observations on the Seventh Periodic Report of Norway' (25 April 2018) UN Doc CCPR/C/NOR/CO/7, para. 37(b) (calling on Norway to ensure meaningful consultation with the Sámi in practice); and Human Rights Committee, 'Concluding Observations on the Second Periodic Report of Honduras' (24 July 2017) UN Doc CCPR/C/HND/CO/2, para. 46 (expressing concern that a draft law on Indigenous peoples' rights had not been developed with the participation of Indigenous peoples). Committee on Economic, Social and Cultural Rights (CESCR), 'Concluding Observations on the Fifth Periodic Report of Costa Rica' (21 October 2016) UN Doc E/C.12/CRI/CO/5, para. 8 (expressing concern about the failure by Costa Rica to consistently consult Indigenous peoples with a view to obtaining their FPIC in respect of decision-making processes affecting their ability to exercise their rights); and CESCR, 'Concluding Observations on the Second Periodic Report of Honduras' (11 July 2016) UN Doc E/C.12/HND/CO/2, para. 12 (recommending that Honduras involve Indigenous peoples in the preparation of its draft law on Indigenous peoples' rights).

7 Committee on the Elimination of Racial Discrimination, General Recommendation 21: The Right to Self-Determination (1996) UN Doc A/52/18, Annex VIII, 125, para. 4.

8 Jan Klabbers, 'The Right to Be Taken Seriously: Self-Determination in International Law' (2006) 28 *Human Rights Quarterly*, 186–206, 194–195.

9 *Western Sahara* (Advisory Opinion) [1975] ICJ Rep 12, paras. 59 and 162. The Court leaves undefined the entity – presumably, a state – that needs to 'pay regard to' a people's freely expressed will.

discriminated against'.[10] In separate opinions in the *Chagos* advisory proceedings, participation was framed as key to a lawful exercise of external self-determination. Judge Gaja's separate opinion in the *Chagos* advisory proceedings pointed out that the Chagossians 'were never consulted or even represented' in the process that led to the separation of the Chagos Archipelago from Mauritius, nor were the people of Mauritius 'given an opportunity to express their views'. In part because '[t]he will of the peoples belonging to the non-self-governing territory did not play any significant role in the process', the decolonization process had not been lawfully completed.[11] Similarly, Judge Abraham implicitly recognized that the Chagossians ought to have been consulted. He declared that if the British authorities had consulted the Chagossian people, and if the Chagossians 'had expressed their free and informed will' not to be integrated into Mauritius, the 'parameters of the question submitted to the Court would ... have been substantially different', and self-determination may require the freely expressed will of the different components of a population of a territory to be taken into account 'even if that leads to partition as a solution'.[12]

The African Commission on Human and Peoples' Rights has also supported the idea of self-determination as participation:[13]

> [i]n the absence of concrete evidence of violations of human rights ... and in the absence of evidence that the people of Katanga are *denied the right to participation in government* ... the Commission holds the view that Katanga is obliged to exercise a variant of self-determination that is compatible with the sovereignty and territorial integrity of Zaire.

The separate opinions in the *East Timor* case evidence judges' awareness of the need to hear affected peoples in both ICJ proceedings and

[10] *Accordance with International Law of the Unilateral Declaration of Independence in Respect of Kosovo* (Advisory Opinion) [2010] ICJ Rep 403, Separate Opinion of Judge Yusuf, para. 9.

[11] *Legal Consequences of the Separation of the Chagos Archipelago from Mauritius in 1965* (Advisory Opinion), 25 February 2019, General List No. 169, Separate Opinion of Judge Gaja, paras. 1–2. Further, the compensation that the Chagossians received for their displacement did not 'make their will insignificant' under the perspective of self-determination: para. 6.

[12] *Chagos Advisory Opinion*, Declaration of Judge Abraham, 2.

[13] *Katangese Peoples' Congress v. Zaire* (Merits), ACHPR (1995) Communication No. 75/92, 1. Further, in *Mgwanga Gunme*, the Commission held that the people of southern Cameroon were not entitled to secede from the state in part because they were represented in the national assembly: *Kevin Mgwanga Gunme v. Cameroon* (Merits), ACHPR (2009) Communication No. 266/2003, para. 190.

intergovernmental negotiations.[14] The Timor Gap Treaty[15] between Australia and Indonesia delimited the continental shelf between East Timor and northern Australia and established a joint regime for exploiting the area's oil reserves. Portugal claimed that Australia, by entering into negotiations and concluding and implementing the Treaty, had infringed the right of the people of East Timor to self-determination, to territorial integrity and unity, and to permanent sovereignty over its national wealth and resources, by signalling its recognition of the Indonesian incorporation of East Timor.[16] The interests of the East Timorese people were vitally affected by the dispute at hand. As Judge Weeramantry noted, the oil and gas potential of the area formed 'in all probability the principal economic asset of the East Timorese people, awaiting them at such time as they achieve self-determination'.[17] If a substantial time were to elapse before East Timor achieved independence, with the Timor Gap Treaty regime fully operational in the meantime, 'a substantial segment' of these resources might well be lost to East Timor 'for all time'.[18] The Treaty, by dividing these resources between Australia and Indonesia without the consent of the East Timorese people, with no indication that the benefits of resource exploitation would be channelled back to East Timor, thus substantially impacted the fulfilment of their right to self-determination.

[14] *Case Concerning East Timor (Portugal v. Australia)* (Judgment) [1995] ICJ Rep 90. The context was that East Timor had been a colony of Portugal from the sixteenth century until 1975, when the Portuguese administration withdrew. Three months later, a local group declared independence. Indonesia promptly staged a military intervention. Since 1975, East Timor had remained under Indonesia's occupation and effective control. East Timor was on the list of non-self-governing territories within the meaning of Chapter XI of the UN Charter, although Portugal remained its administering Power: *East Timor* paras. 11–13 and 16; Dissenting Opinion of Judge Weeramantry, 144. Several GA and SC resolutions had denounced the military intervention and called upon states to respect East Timor's territorial integrity and the right of its people to self-determination: See, for example, UNGA Res 3485 (12 December 1975) UN Doc A/RES/3485; UNSC Res 384 (22 December 1975) UN Doc S/RES/384; UNSC Res 389 (22 April 1976) UN Doc S/RES/389. Indonesia had not accepted the ICJ's compulsory jurisdiction and therefore could not be subject to proceedings.

[15] Treaty between Australia and the Republic of Indonesia on the Zone of Cooperation in an area between the Indonesian Province of East Timor and northern Australia (signed 11 December 1989 and entered into force 9 February 1991) 1001 Australian Treaty Series 9, preamble. The oil reserves were estimated at between 500 million and 5,000 million barrels: Dissenting Opinion of Judge Weeramantry, 147.

[16] *East Timor*, paras. 10, 17, and 19.

[17] Dissenting Opinion of Judge Weeramantry, 151.

[18] Ibid., 198.

In separate and dissenting opinions,[19] three judges explicated the link between self-determination of peoples and participation in matters affecting them, in both international negotiations and international courts. Judge Vereshchetin held that Indonesia's lack of consent was only one reason for the finding of lack of jurisdiction. The other, 'no less important' in his view, was 'the lack of any evidence as to the views of the people of East Timor', on whose behalf the application was filed.[20] The people of East Timor were 'another "third party"' in this case, but their consent 'was sought neither by Portugal before filing the Application with the Court, nor by Australia before concluding the Timor Gap Treaty'.[21] Neither Portugal nor Australia had provided reliable evidence of the wishes and views of the people of East Timor.[22] But Judge Vereshchetin explicitly ruled out the possibility that the ICJ could place the people of East Timor on the same procedural level as the states parties to the case – a position clearly excluded by Article 34 of the ICJ Statute – and stopped short of suggesting any procedural reform. He said, merely, that 'the right of a people to self-determination, by definition, requires that the wishes of the people concerned at least be ascertained and taken into account by the Court'. As such, Portugal had a duty 'to consult the leaders or representatives of the people before submitting the case to the Court on their behalf'.[23] Judge Vereshchetin thus 'created the possibility of a colonial people's indirect participation before the court in a case concerning their right to self-determination'.[24]

Judge Skubiszewski's and Judge Weeramantry's respective dissenting opinions, while not going as far as that of Judge Vereshchetin, also reveal an awareness that an affected party was going unheard and indicate that

[19] Following the *Monetary Gold* rule, the majority held that the ICJ lacked jurisdiction to consider the claim, as to do so would require ruling upon the lawfulness of Indonesia's entry into and continued presence in East Timor: *East Timor*, paras. 33–34. Compare Dissenting Opinion of Judge Skubiszewski and Dissenting Opinion of Judge Weeramantry. See *Case of the Monetary Gold Removed from Rome in 1943 (Italy v. France, UK and USA)* (Preliminary Question) [1954] ICJ Rep 19, 32–33.

[20] Separate Opinion of Judge Vereshchetin, 138.

[21] Ibid., 135.

[22] Ibid., 136.

[23] Indeed, the Secretary-General had been holding consultations on the future of East Timor with a broad cross section of East Timorese people representing various trends of opinion, as well as the governments of Indonesia and Portugal: UNGA Res 37/30 (23 November 1982) UN Doc A/RES/37/30. Judge Vereshchetin considered that in these consultations 'the East Timorese people [was] considered as a distinct party "directly concerned," which [could] speak for itself through its representatives', 137.

[24] Karen Knop, *Diversity and Self-Determination in International Law* (Cambridge: Cambridge University Press, 2002), 207.

self-determination has a participatory element. Judge Skubiszewski, like Judge Vereshchetin, noted that while 'both Parties invoked the interests of the East Timorese people', neither presented evidence of the actual wishes of the people.[25] He went on to make 'certain elementary assumptions', including that the people's interests would be best served 'when the active participation of the people is guaranteed', rather than when their interests were negotiated by other states alone.[26] Judge Weeramantry, too, recognized that the people of East Timor were not themselves participants in proceedings, characterizing East Timor as 'a territory not in a position to speak for itself'.[27] In considering the *locus standi* of Portugal, however, he came to a different view to that of Judge Vereshchetin: Portugal could represent the people of East Timor, as any other view 'would result in the anomalous situation of the current international system leaving a territory and a people, who admittedly have important rights opposable to all the world, defenceless and voiceless precisely when those rights are sought to be threatened or violated'.[28] Indeed, he considered the fact that Portugal had a 'direct nexus' with East Timor and was the administering Power recognized by the UN strengthened Portugal's claim to speak on behalf of East Timor.

2.2 SELF-DETERMINATION AND PARTICIPATION OF INDIGENOUS PEOPLES

Moving from the general to the specific, in the case of Indigenous peoples' participation, is central to the right to self-determination. The right of Indigenous peoples to participate in matters affecting them is found in the earliest international legal instrument on Indigenous peoples' rights: it is a pillar of ILO Convention No. 169.[29] Article 6.1 of that Convention imposes an obligation on states to establish means by which Indigenous peoples can freely participate 'at all levels of decision-making in elective institutions and

[25] Dissenting Opinion of Judge Skubiszewski, 136.

[26] Ibid., para. 52.

[27] Dissenting Opinion of Judge Weeramantry, 181.

[28] Ibid.

[29] Convention Concerning Indigenous and Tribal Peoples in Independent Countries (adopted 27 June 1989 and entered into force 5 September 1991) 1650 UNTS 383 (ILO 169). Albeit only ratified by twenty-three countries, ILO 169 has had an outsize influence on subsequent international legal instruments and standards. For the status of ratifications, see ILO, 'Ratifications of C169 – Indigenous and Tribal Peoples Convention, 1989 (No. 169)' www.ilo.org/dyn/normlex/en/f?p=NORMLEXPUB:11300:0::NO:11300:P11300_INSTRUMENT_ID:312314:NO.

administrative and other bodies responsible for policies and programmes which concern them'.[30]

Under the architecture of the UNDRIP,[31] self-determination is regarded as a 'foundational right'[32] that grounds many of the other rights in the Declaration. Article 3 of the UNDRIP mirrors Common Article 1 of the Covenants. The condition on which states were able to agree to this provision, which entailed considerable difficulty for some,[33] was the inclusion of Article 46(1), which stipulates that nothing in the Declaration can be interpreted as implying 'any right to engage in any activity or to perform any act contrary to the Charter of the United Nations or construed as authorizing or encouraging any action which would dismember or impair, totally or in part, the territorial integrity or political unity of sovereign and independent States'. Hence Article 3 does not bestow a right to territorial independence. Rather, it is generally interpreted as entailing internal self-determination in the sense of self-government, autonomy, and political participation in state affairs.[34] The drafting history of Article 3 shows that for several states, self-determination included the right of Indigenous peoples to participate fully in decisions affecting them.[35] For instance, Australia 'recognize[d] that the intention of Article 3 is to enunciate ... the legitimate aspirations of indigenous peoples to enjoy more direct and meaningful participation in decision-making and political processes and greater autonomy over their own affairs'.[36] Canada, similarly, stated that 'self-determination is now seen by many as a right which

30 ILO 169, Article 6.1(b).

31 The question of the legal status of the UNDRIP will be discussed below. For now, suffice to say that here I regard UNDRIP as "soft law" that is, while highly influential, not formally legally binding.

32 Marc Weller, 'Self-Determination of Indigenous Peoples: Articles 3, 4, 5, 18, 23, and 46(1)' in Jessie Hohmann and Marc Weller (eds.), *The UN Declaration on the Rights of Indigenous People: A Commentary* (Oxford: Oxford University Press, 2018), 115–149, 115, 124.

33 John B. Henriksen, 'The UN Declaration on the Rights of Indigenous Peoples: Some Key Issues and Events in the Process' in Claire Charters and Rodolfo Stavenhagen (eds.), *Making the Declaration Work: The United Nations Declaration on the Rights of Indigenous Peoples* (Copenhagen: IWGIA, 2009), 78, 79–80; Joshua Castellino and Cathal Doyle, 'Who Are 'Indigenous Peoples'? An Examination of Concepts Concerning Group Membership in the UNDRIP' in Jessie Hohmann and Marc Weller (eds.), *The UN Declaration on the Rights of Indigenous People: A Commentary* (Oxford: Oxford University Press, 2018), 7–37, 26–29.

34 Helen Quane, 'The United Nations and the Evolving Right to Self-Determination' (1998) 47 (3) *International & Comparative Law Quarterly*, 537–572, 571; Dorotheé Cambou, 'Enhancing the Participation of Indigenous Peoples at the Intergovernmental Level to Strengthen Self-Determination: Lessons from the Arctic' (2018) 87 *Nordic Journal of International Law*, 26–55, 32.

35 Quane, 'Evolving Right', 271.

36 Referred to in Foster, 'Articulating Self-Determination', 152.

can continue to be enjoyed in a functioning democracy in which citizens participate in the political system and have the opportunity to have input in the political processes that affect them'.[37] Norway opined that 'the right to self-determination includes the right of indigenous peoples to participate at all levels of decision-making in legislative and administrative matters and the maintenance and development of their political and economic systems'.[38]

Article 4 reinforces the notion that self-determination for Indigenous peoples is to be exercised by "internal" rather than external, territorial means, providing that Indigenous peoples, 'in exercising their right to self-determination, have the right to autonomy or self-government in matters relating to their internal and local affairs, as well as ways and means for financing their autonomous functions'. Autonomy is also related to participation: it 'may be seen as a way of increasing participation in public life in much the same way as devolution or other autonomy arrangements have tried to do so in non-indigenous contexts'.[39] Moreover, Article 5 provides that Indigenous peoples have the right to maintain and strengthen their own distinct institutions while retaining their right to participate fully in the life of the State. It can thus be seen that self-determination for Indigenous peoples, under the Declaration, manifests in 'on the one hand, autonomous governance and, on the other, participatory engagement'.[40]

Against this background, the provisions of the UNDRIP on participation, as well as those on free, prior, and informed consent (FPIC), have been viewed by some states,[41] as well as scholars,[42] as an expression of, or part of the substance of, the right to self-determination.

In particular, Article 18 of the UNDRIP contains a right 'to participate in decision-making in matters which would affect their rights, through representatives chosen by themselves in accordance with their own procedures, as well as to maintain and develop their own indigenous decision-making institutions'. While Article 6.1 of ILO 169 specifies that participation must be 'at all levels of decision-making', implying that an international dimension could be read in, Article 18 of the UNDRIP is silent on this matter. On its face, the text

37 Ibid.,151.

38 Ibid., 151.

39 Quane, 'Evolving Right', 273. See also Article 20 UNDRIP.

40 S. James Anaya, 'The Right of Indigenous Peoples to Self-Determination in the Post-Declaration Era' in Claire Charters and Rodolfo Stavenhagen (eds.), *Making the Declaration Work: The United Nations Declaration on the Rights of Indigenous Peoples* (Copenhagen: IWGIA, 2009), 184–199, 193.

41 Quane, 'Evolving Right', 271.

42 Ibid., 263, 276–277. See also Foster, 'Articulating Self-Determination', 151.

could be read broadly to include participation in all levels of governance.[43] However, an earlier version of this article in the 1994 Draft Declaration originally included the phrase 'at all levels of decision-making',[44] indicating that agreement could not ultimately be reached on this.[45] Further, Article 23 of the UNDRIP provides for the right of Indigenous peoples to decide their own priorities for development and participate in the formulation and implementation of development plans and programmes – in a similarly openly worded provision.[46]

Further relevant to participation and self-determination is the law on FPIC. FPIC is 'premised on and essential for the operationalisation of the right to self-determination', as it allows a people to exercise control over their destiny.[47] The UNDRIP requires the FPIC of Indigenous peoples in a decision-making process that could result in their relocation, or the disposal or storage of hazardous materials in Indigenous peoples' lands and territories.[48] In addition, states are required to 'consult and cooperate in good faith' with Indigenous peoples 'in order to obtain' FPIC before adopting and implementing legislative or administrative measures that may affect them or approving any project affecting their lands, territories, and other resources.[49] While some argue that these latter articles impose an absolute obligation to obtain consent, the statements of a number of states following the adoption of the Declaration, as well as a comparison with previous drafts of the articles, suggest a more restrictive interpretation.[50] The FPIC requirements in the UNDRIP should

[43] Cambou, 'Lessons from the Arctic', 34; S. James Anaya, 'International Human Rights and Indigenous Peoples: The Move toward the Multicultural State' (2004) 21 *Arizona Journal of International & Comparative Law*, 13–61, 53.

[44] Working Group on Indigenous Populations, Draft Declaration on the Rights of Indigenous Peoples (1994) UN Doc E/CN.4/Sub.2/1994/2/Add.1 ("1994 Draft Declaration"), Article 19.

[45] Compare Cambou, 'Lessons from the Arctic', 35.

[46] ILO 169, Article 7; UNDRIP, Article 23. See also ILO 169, Articles 2, 5, 27, and 28.

[47] Jérémie Gilbert and Cathal Doyle, 'A New Dawn over the Land: Shedding Light on Collective Ownership and Consent' in Stephen Allen and Alexandra Xanthaki (eds.), *Reflections on the UN Declaration on the Rights of Indigenous Peoples* (London: Hart, 2011), 290, 310. See also Tara Ward, 'The Right to Free, Prior, and Informed Consent: Indigenous Peoples' Participation Rights within International Law' (2011) 10 *Northwestern University Journal of International Human Rights*, 54–84, 55, 58; Bartolomé Clavero, 'The Indigenous Rights of Participation and International Development Policies' (2005) 22 *Arizona Journal of International & Comparative Law*, 41–51, 42.

[48] Articles 10 and 29(2). Compare ILO 169, Articles 6, 15, 16, and 17.

[49] Articles 19 and 32(2).

[50] See the 1994 Draft Declaration. Mauro Barelli, *Seeking Justice in International Law: The Significance and Implications of the UN Declaration on the Rights of Indigenous Peoples* (London: Routledge, 2016), 253–254 suggests that the expression 'consult in order to obtain consent' still requires more than mere consultation and should be approached with a degree of

not be read as conferring a general right to veto, merely that consultations must be held in good faith and with the objective of reaching agreement.[51] However, the importance of reaching consent varies according to the strength of the Indigenous interests and the impact of the decision involved: according to the UN Special Rapporteur on the rights of Indigenous peoples, in cases of a 'direct impact on indigenous peoples' lives or territories', there is a 'strong presumption' that consent is required, and 'in certain contexts, that presumption may harden into a prohibition of the measure or project in the absence of indigenous consent'.[52] Effective participation requires that the state must consult with the Indigenous peoples concerned in good faith, provide them with sufficient information, and respect their customs and traditions; the objective of the consultation should be the reaching of an agreement among the parties.[53] The information provided must be in clear and accessible language and be complete enough to guarantee that if consent is given, it

flexibility in such a way that guarantees the effective protection of Indigenous peoples' fundamental rights.

51 Human Rights Council, 'Report of the Special Rapporteur on the Situation of Human Rights and Fundamental Freedoms of Indigenous People, James Anaya' (15 July 2009) UN Doc A/HRC/12/34, para. 47.

52 Ibid. See also EMRIP, 'Final Report of the Study on Indigenous Peoples and the Right to Participate in Decision-Making' (17 August 2011) UN Doc A/HRC/18/42, Annex: Expert Mechanism Advice No. 2 (2011): Peoples and the Right to Participate in Decision-Making, para. 22; *Länsman et al. v. Finland*, Communication No. 511/1992, UN Doc CCPR/C/52/D/511/1992 (1994), paras. 9.5– 9.8 (Finnish decision to allow stone quarrying in a reindeer-herding area did not violate the right of the Sámi in the area to enjoy their culture, because the relevant communities had been consulted and the quarrying activities had only a limited impact on their way of life and did not amount to a denial of their rights); *Angela Poma Poma v. Peru*, Communication No. 1457/2006, UN Doc CCPR/C/95/D/1457/2006 (2009), para. 7.6 (measures that substantially compromise or interfere with Indigenous peoples' culture required FPIC, not merely consultation); CESCR, 'General Comment no. 21, Right of everyone to take part in cultural life' (21 December 2009) UN Doc E/C.12/GC/21, para. 37 (when the preservation of Indigenous peoples' cultural resources is at risk, the state should obtain FPIC); *Centre for Minority Rights Development (Kenya) and Minority Rights Group International (on behalf of the Endorois Welfare Council) v. Kenya* (Merits), (2010) Communication No. 276/03, para. 291 (state required to obtain FPIC, not merely consult, on development or investment projects that would have a major impact within the territories of Indigenous peoples); *Saramaka People v. Suriname*, Judgment of 28 November 2007 (Judgment on Preliminary Objections, Merits, Reparations, and Costs), IACtHR Series C No. 172, para. 134 (for small-scale development projects, mere consultation suffices, but FPIC is required for large-scale development projects or investments that would have a major impact within Indigenous peoples' territories, or where the cumulative effects of a number of small-scale projects would resemble that of a large-scale project); *Saramaka People v. Suriname*, Judgment of 12 August 2008 (Interpretation of the Judgment on Preliminary Objections, Merits, Reparations, and Costs) IACtHR Series G No. 185, para. 41.

53 *Saramaka*, para. 133; *Kichwa People of Sarayaku v. Ecuador*, Judgment of 27 June 2012 (Judgments on Merits, Reparations, and Costs) IACtHR Series C No. 245, paras. 180–211.

has been given free from manipulation, and that consultation entails the right to play a real role in the decision-making process.[54]

Article 41 of the Declaration sheds some light on the interpretation of Articles 18 and 23:

> The organs and specialized agencies of the United Nations system and other intergovernmental organizations shall contribute to the full realization of the provisions of this Declaration through the mobilization, inter alia, of financial cooperation and technical assistance. *Ways and means of ensuring participation of indigenous peoples on issues affecting them shall be established* (emphasis added).

On its own, the latter sentence is ambiguous as to who is to establish the ways and means of ensuring Indigenous peoples participation. Nor is it clear as to whether participation should be at the domestic or international level. But by reading the second sentence in the light of the first, we understand that UN agencies and organs and other intergovernmental organizations are required to establish ways and means of ensuring participation of Indigenous peoples in their processes on issues affecting them.

Read in the light of Article 41, Articles 18 and 23, which were on their face ambiguous as to international participation, arguably apply to the participation of peoples in international organizations.[55] Article 41 creates a strong expectation that Indigenous peoples will be enabled to participate on issues affecting them in UN and other intergovernmental processes. The Human Rights Council and the Expert Mechanism on the Rights of Indigenous Peoples (EMRIP) have both taken the view that Articles 18 and 41 constitute a basis for the promotion of the participation of Indigenous peoples at the UN level.[56]

2.3 OBLIGATIONS OF INTERNATIONAL ORGANIZATIONS?

In Chapter 1, we saw how, in theory, international organizations themselves – not only states – should hold obligations in relation to Indigenous peoples' participation. However, it is difficult to identify a basis in the positive law for such obligations. For states, Common Article 1(3) creates a broad duty to

[54] *Kichwa*, para. 167.

[55] Notable too is Article 36, providing for the right of Indigenous peoples to maintain and develop contacts, relations, and cooperation with other peoples across borders.

[56] 'Ways and means of promoting participation at the United Nations of indigenous peoples' representatives on issues affecting them' (2012) UN Doc A/HRC/21/24, paras. 2–3. Human Rights Council, 'Report of the Expert Mechanism on the Rights of Indigenous Peoples on its fourth session' (19 August 2011) A/HRC/18/43, proposal 3.

'promote the realization of' and respect the right of self-determination, under which the specific duties outlined in Chapter 1 could fit:

> The States Parties to the present Covenant, including those having responsibility for the administration of Non-Self-Governing and Trust Territories, shall promote the realization of the right of self-determination, and shall respect that right, in conformity with the provisions of the Charter of the United Nations.

However, neither the Covenants nor any of the other international instruments or decisions discussed above establish equivalent obligations for international organizations. The ICCPR and ICESCR limit membership to states, restricting international organizations from becoming parties,[57] and even where membership is not *prima facie* constrained, it can be difficult in practice for international organizations to become members of treaties.[58] Indeed, the question of under what circumstances international organizations hold obligations is notoriously uncertain.[59] Falling logically prior to the issue of responsibility, as the existence of an obligation is a precondition for responsibility for breach,[60] the matter of obligations of international organizations is much less developed than that of their responsibility. According to the advisory opinion of the ICJ in *WHO-Egypt*, in theory, international organizations can hold obligations under treaties to which they are parties:[61]

57 ICCPR, Article 48(1); ICESCR, Article 26(1).

58 See, for example, the EU's proposed accession to the ECHR: European Commission, 'Communication from the Commission to the European Parliament, the Council, the European Economic and Social Committee and the Committee of the Regions: 2016 Report on the Application of the EU Charter of Fundamental Rights' (18 May 2017), SWD(2017) 162 final, 8.

59 Jan Klabbers, 'Sources of International Organizations Law: Reflections on Accountability' in Jean D'Aspremont and Samantha Besson (eds.), *The Oxford Handbook of the Sources of International Law* (Oxford: Oxford University Press, 2017), 987–1006, 989; Kristina Daugirdas, 'How and Why International Law Binds International Organizations' (2016) 57(2) *Harvard International Law Journal*, 325–381.

60 International Law Commission, 'Draft Articles on the Responsibility of International Organizations' (3 June 2011) UN Doc A/CN.4/L.778, Draft Articles 3, 4, and 10(1). The Draft Articles are thus largely unhelpful for the purposes of the present study, as they do not address the basis, sources, or scope of international organizations' obligations. See further Dina Shelton, *Remedies in International Human Rights Law*, 3rd ed. (Oxford: Oxford University Press, 2015), 46–50.

61 *Interpretation of the Agreement of 25 March 1951 between the WHO and Egypt* (1980) ICJ Rep 73, para. 37. On the international legal personality of international organizations, see *Reparations for Injuries Suffered in the Service of the United Nations* (Advisory Opinion) [1948] ICJ Rep 174 and178.

> International organizations are subjects of international law and, as such, are bound by any obligations incumbent upon them under general rules of international law, under their constitutions or under international agreements to which they are parties.

As a corollary, international organizations are *not* bound by treaties to which they are *not* parties.[62] While some argue that, to the contrary, international organizations can be bound by treaties to which they are not parties, as to hold otherwise would allow member states to frustrate or avoid their obligations by acting through an international organization,[63] this argument encounters significant obstacles: there may not be much overlap in the obligations held by all member states of an organization; to hold an international organization to an obligation held by not all member states would violate the *pacta tertiis* rule, and if the common treaty obligations were to automatically bind an international organization upon its establishment, this would diminish the wide discretion of member states to modify their treaty obligations under the VCLT.[64]

A possible exception is Article 41 of the UNDRIP, but this argument encounters difficulties, since while this provision certainly holds substantial legal weight, it is not formally binding.[65]

2.4 CUSTOMARY INTERNATIONAL LAW

Where, then, does this leave us? One remaining source of positive law that we have not yet discussed is customary international law. The existence of a general practice accepted as law could provide an alternate route to establishing the duties of states, and international organizations, to enable Indigenous peoples to participate in international governance that affects them.

[62] Vienna Convention on the Law of Treaties between States and International Organizations or Between International Organizations (concluded 21 March 1986) 1155 UNTS 331 (VCLT-IO), art 34. The VCLT-IO remains contested and has not attracted enough ratifications to enter into force, so while it may be treated as persuasive on this point, it is not definitive.

[63] See, for example, Frédéric Mégret and Florian F. Hoffman, 'The UN as a Human Rights Violator? Some Reflections on the United Nations Changing Human Rights Responsibilities' (2003) 23 *Human Rights Quarterly*, 314–342, 318.

[64] Daugirdas, 'How and Why', 350–351.

[65] See Section 2.4.3.

2.4.1 "Traditional" and "Modern" Customary International Law

It is difficult to think of a more fraught source of law than 'international custom, as evidence of a general practice accepted as law'.[66] Its formation is 'a complex psychological and sociological process'.[67] Problems and paradoxes abound. Hence it is unsurprising that some have argued custom is completely indeterminate and malleable, simply a "matter of taste."[68]

At least three broad schools of thought have sought to theorize custom. These can be characterized as "traditional," "modern," and "practice-oriented."[69] The *two-element* or "traditional" approach to customary international law holds that the two classic elements, practice and *opinio juris*, are both necessary to establish a rule of custom.[70] Under this view, an 'extensive and virtually uniform' practice,[71] 'in the form of interstate interaction and

[66] ICJ Statute, Article 38. Customary international law has been the subject of many studies; see, for example, Michael Byers, *Custom, Power and the Power of Rules: International Relations and Customary International Law* (Cambridge: Cambridge University Press, 1999); David J. Bederman, *Custom as a Source of Law* (Cambridge: Cambridge University Press, 2010); Brian D. Lepard, *Customary International Law: A New Theory with Practical Applications* (Cambridge: Cambridge University Press, 2010); see also the work of the International Law Commission (ILC), especially ILC, 'Formation and Evidence of Customary International Law, First Report on Formation and Evidence of Customary International Law, by Sir Michael Wood, Special Rapporteur' (17 May 2013) UN Doc A/CN.4/663; ILC, 'Identification of Customary International Law, Second Report on Identification of Customary International Law, by Sir Michael Wood, Special Rapporteur' (22 May 2014) UN Doc A/CN.4/672; and ILC, 'Identification of Customary International Law, Third Report on Identification of Customary International Law, by Sir Michael Wood, Special Rapporteur' (27 March 2015) UN Doc A/CN.4/682.

[67] *North Sea Continental Shelf* (Judgment) [1969] ICJ Rep 3, Dissenting Opinion of Judge Tanaka, 176.

[68] J. Patrick Kelly, 'The Twilight of Customary International Law' (2000) 40 *Virginia Journal of International Law*, 449–543, 451.

[69] The first two of these labels follow Anthea Roberts, 'Traditional and Modern Approaches to Customary International Law: A Reconciliation' (2001) 95(4) *American Journal of International Law*, 757–791; the third draws on the ILC, 'First report'.

[70] See Art 38(1)(b) ICJ Statute. See, for example, Gerald Fitzmaurice, 'The Law and Procedure of the International Court of Justice, 1951–1954: General Principles and Sources of Law' (1953) 30 *British Yearbook of International Law*, 1–70, 68; Anthony D'Amato, 'Trashing Customary International Law' (1987) 81(1) *American Journal of International Law*, 101–105, 102; Michael Akehurst, 'Custom as a Source of International Law' (1974–1975) 47(1) *British Yearbook of International Law* 1–53, 53; Gennady M. Danilenko, 'The Theory of Customary International Law', (1988) 31 *German Yearbook of International Law*, 9–47, 19–20; Grigory I. Tunkin, 'Remarks on the Juridical Nature of Customary Norms of International Law' (1961) 49(3) *California Law Review*, 419–430, 421.

[71] *North Sea Continental Shelf*. Also see *Colombian-Peruvian Ssylum Case* (Judgment) [1950] ICJ Rep 266 ("constant and uniform usage").

acquiescence',[72] is the bedrock of a customary rule, supported by the belief that such practice is required by law.[73] The second element, *opinio juris*, is what distinguishes a practice followed out of a sense of legal obligation from one followed due to 'considerations of convenience or simple political expediency'.[74] The temporal order of these elements is not determinative, but they must both exist.[75] The identification of a customary rule is carried out 'through an inductive process in which a general custom is derived from specific instances of state practice'.[76]

In the 1980s and 1990s, it became fashionable in some circles to argue that traditional custom was anachronistic, no longer an appropriate means for developing law in the light of the increasing number and diversity of states, the acceleration of social, economic, and technological changes, the emergence of new global challenges calling for urgent legal regulation, and the need to respond to pressing moral concerns such as human rights abuses.[77] The proposed solution to such concerns was an *opinio-oriented*, or "modern" approach to custom that focused on *opinio juris* rather than state practice.[78] This kind of custom, it was said, could develop more rapidly and flexibly than

72 Roberts, 'Traditional and Modern Approaches', 758.

73 The ILC treats opinio juris as secondary to state practice: 'First Report', para. 96. See *"Lotus"(France v. Turkey), Judgment No. 9*, [1927] PCIJ Series A, No. 10, 18 ('only if [the practice in question] were based on their being conscious of having a duty [to do so], would it be possible to speak of an international custom').

74 *Asylum*.

75 ILC, 'Draft Conclusions', Commentary to Conclusion 3, para. 9.

76 Roberts, 'Traditional and Modern Approaches', 758. On induction, see further Stefan Talmon, 'Determining Customary International Law: The ICJ's Methodology between Induction, Deduction and Assertion' (2015) 26 *European Journal of International Law*, 417–443, 421–422.

77 See, for example, Bin Cheng, 'Epilogue' in Bin Cheng (ed.), *International Law: Teaching Practice* (London: Stevens & Sons, 1982), 203–233, 223; Andrew T. Guzman, 'Saving Customary International Law' (2005) 27(1) *Michigan Journal of International Law*, 115–176; Michael P. Scharf, 'Seizing the 'Grotian Moment': Accelerated Formation of Customary International Law in Times of Fundamental Change' (2010) 43(3) *Cornell International Law Journal*, 439–469, 467–468; Oscar Schachter, 'New Custom: Power, *Opinio Juris* and Contrary Practice' in Jerzy Makarczyk (ed.), *Theory of International Law at the Threshold of the Twenty-first Century: Essays in Honour of Krzysztof Skubiszewski* (The Hague: Kluwer, 1996), 531–540, 533. Also see Lepard, A *New Theory* (proposing to view customary international norms as having their sources in a belief on the part of states in the desirability of having certain international norms, which are then subsequently interpreted utilizing universally recognized ethical principles). See also *North Sea Continental Shelf*, Dissenting Opinion of Judge Sorenson at 245, Dissenting Opinion of Judge Lachs, 231.

78 See the authors mentioned in the previous note, as well as Brian D. Lepard, 'Toward a New Theory of Customary International Human Rights Law', in Brian D. Lepard (ed.), *Reexamining Customary International Law* (Cambridge: Cambridge University Press, 2017), 233–265, 252.

traditional custom, 'because it is deduced from multilateral treaties and declarations by international fora such as the General Assembly, which can declare existing customs, crystallize emerging customs, and generate new customs'.[79] Similarly, some authors supported permitting transnational actors and NGOs to have a voice in the creation of custom.[80] While a modern approach is supported by some – albeit a fraction of – judicial practice,[81] it is also criticized by many for being highly normative in nature, reflecting aspirations (or *lex ferenda*) rather than set standards (or *lex lata*).[82] Indeed, the ICJ in *South West Africa* rejected the deduction of rules of law from 'humanitarian considerations' and 'moral principles'.[83]

Taking the inverse approach, others have argued that it is not practice, but *opinio juris*, that can be largely unnecessary.[84] This *practice-oriented* approach

79 Roberts, 'Traditional and Modern Approaches', 758. Relatedly – though coming from a more critical perspective – B.S. Chimni argues for the formation of custom on the basis of deliberative reasoning, rather than mere coordination: B.S. Chimni, 'Customary International Law: A Third World Perspective' (2018) 112(1) *American Journal of International Law*, 1–46, 38.

80 For example, Isabelle R. Gunning, 'Modernizing Customary International Law: The Challenge of Human Rights' (1991) 31 *Virginia Journal of International Law*, 211–247; Noora Arajärvi, 'From State-Centricism to Where? The Formation of Customary International Law and Non-State Actors' (3 May 2010), available at http://ssrn.com/abstract=1599679 23; also see Chimni, ibid.

81 See, for example, *Military and Paramilitary Activities in and against Nicaragua (Nicaragua v. United States of America)* (Merits, Judgment of 27 June 1986) [1986] ICJ Rep 14. Roberts, 'Traditional and Modern Approaches', 758–759: 'The Court paid lip service to the traditional test for custom but derived customs of non-use of force and nonintervention from statements such as General Assembly resolutions. The Court did not make a serious inquiry into state practice, holding that it was sufficient for conduct to be generally consistent with statements of rules, provided that instances of inconsistent practice had been treated as breaches of the rule concerned rather than as generating a new rule'.

82 See, for example, Noora Arajärvi, 'From the "Demands of Humanity": The Formulation of *Opinio Juris* in Decisions of International Criminal Tribunals and the Need for a Renewed Emphasis on State Practice' in Lepard (ed.), *Reexamining Customary International Law*, 189–230, 190; D'Amato, 'Trashing' (the modern approach trashes the theoretical foundations of custom by inverting the traditional priority of state practice over opinio juris); Bruno Simma and Philip Alston, 'The Sources of Human Rights Law: Custom, *Jus Cogens* and General Principles' (1989) 12 *Australian Year Book of International Law*, 82–108, 83; Robert Y. Jennings, 'The Identification of International Law' in Bin Cheng (ed.), *International Law, Teaching and Practice* (London: Stevens & Sons, 1982), 3–9, 5; Daniel Bodansky, 'Customary (And Not So Customary) International Environmental Law' (1995) 3(1) *Indiana Journal of Global Legal Studies*, 105–119, 110–112.

83 Referred to in Talmon, 'Induction, Deduction and Assertion', 430.

84 Anthony D'Amato, 'Customary International Law: A Reformulation' (1998) 4 *International Legal Theory*, 1–6; Hans Kelsen, 'Théorie du droit international coutumier' (1939) 1(4) *Revue international de la théorie du droit*, 253–274, at 264–266 (although noting that Kelsen subsequently changed his view); Torsten Gihl, 'The Legal Character of Sources of

began as an attempt to bypass the logical paradox inherent in the formation of custom: that the requirement of *opinio* juris at a time before a rule of custom has been established inherently requires states to commit an error of law.[85] Several ICJ judges have supported such a view. Judge Azevedo, in *Asylum*, opined that in the case at hand, 'concordant cases, by their number, would clearly reveal an *opinio juris*'.[86] In *North Sea Continental Shelf*, Judge Tanaka, lamenting the extreme difficulty of obtaining evidence of the existence of *opinio juris*, said there is no other way to ascertain it 'apart from the fact of the external existence of a certain custom and its necessity felt in the international community, rather than to seek evidence as to the subjective motives for each example of State practice'.[87] Rather, he said the 'appraisal of factors must be relative to the circumstances and therefore elastic'.[88] Similarly, Judge Lachs held that it was 'surely over-exacting' to require consciousness of an obligation in the case of every state that had applied a given rule; rather, 'the general practice of States should be recognized as prima facie evidence that it is accepted as law'.[89] Judge Sorenson found it unnecessary to go into the question of *opinio juris*, citing the problem of proof. According to Judge Sorenson, the widespread and representative practice of states in the case at hand 'may be taken as sufficient evidence of the existence of any necessary *opinio juris*'.[90] In order to avoid the problem of distinguishing 'usages which give rise to legally binding custom' from those 'which remain in the sphere of mere courtesy or convenience', Hugh Thirlway proposes that the view that 'the custom *should* be law' suffices to fulfil the subjective requirement.[91] Similarly, Taki proposes that practice becomes customary international law 'when its content is related to "a matter of international law"', or in other

International Law' (1957) 1 *Scandinavian Studies in Law*, 53–92, 84; Lazare Kopelmanas, 'Custom as a Means of the Creation of International Law' (1937) *British Yearbook of International Law*, 127–151, 129–130; Hersch Lauterpacht, *The Development of International Law by the International Court* (London: Stevens & Sons, 1957), 149 n 29; Hiroshi Taki, 'Opinio Juris and the Formation of Customary International Law: A Theoretical Analysis' (2008) 51 *German Yearbook of International Law*, 447–466.

85 See Kelsen, 'Théorie du droit', explained in Taki, 'Opinio Juris', 448.

86 *Asylum*, Dissenting Opinion of Judge Azevedo, 336.

87 *North Sea Continental Shelf*, Dissenting Opinion of Judge Tanaka, 177.

88 Ibid.

89 *North Sea Continental Shelf*, Dissenting Opinion of Judge Lachs, 232.

90 *North Sea Continental Shelf*, Dissenting Opinion of Judge Sorenson, 247.

91 Hugh Thirlway, *International Customary Law and Codification: An Examination of the Continuing Role of Custom in the Present Period of Codification of International Law* (Leiden: Sijthoff, 1972), 53.

words 'a matter for legal regulation', accompanied by a consciousness of a norm (not necessary a legal norm).[92]

The work of the International Law Commission (ILC) on the identification of customary international law, carried out between 2013 and 2018,[93] has demonstrated the general consensus of states on the continuing relevance of the traditional, two-element approach.[94] Far from being anachronistic in the light of contemporary challenges, it is clear that the two-element approach to the identification of customary law is still relevant for states. However, in what follows, I will take each of the three approaches seriously.

2.4.2 *The Relevance of General Assembly Declarations in Identifying Custom*

Contrary to early views as to the irrelevance of General Assembly resolutions to the identification of custom,[95] there is now a general consensus that resolutions of the General Assembly can be relevant to establishing the existence of custom.[96] Divergent views exist, however, as to how.[97]

Opinio-oriented approaches hold that resolutions of international bodies, most prominently those of the General Assembly, can be norm-generating acts in and of themselves. Critics of this view often point to the implication that such resolutions would have 'instant quasi-legislative effect, which finds no explicit support in the Charter' and would give the General Assembly 'an exorbitant power that was never intended'.[98] This approach has also been criticized for being too utopian and 'ignoring how states behave in reality'.[99]

92 Taki, 'Opinio Juris', 465–466.

93 See ILC, 'Draft Conclusions on Identification of Customary International Law, with commentaries' (2018) UN Doc A/73/10.

94 Arajärvi, 'From the "Demands of Humanity"'.

95 As noted in Arajärvi, 'From the "Demands of Humanity"'.

96 Rosalyn Higgins, *The Development of International Law by the Political Organs of the United Nations* (Oxford: Oxford University Press, 1963), 5: General Assembly resolutions can be a rich source of evidence about the development of customary international law.

97 For an overview of debates, see, for example, Krzysztof Skubiszewski, 'Resolutions of the U.N. General Assembly and Evidence of Custom', in *Le droit international à l'heure de sa codification – Études en l'honneur de Roberto Ago* (vol. I) (1987) 503, at 506–507. See also Grigory I. Tunkin, 'The Role of Resolutions of International Organizations in Creating Norms of International Law' (1987) 230 *Coexistence*, 5, at 12–15.

98 Marko Divac Öberg, 'The Legal Effects of Resolutions of the UN Security Council and General Assembly in the Jurisprudence of the ICJ' (2015) 16(5) *European Journal of International Law*, 879–906, 898.

99 Öberg, 'Legal Effects of Resolutions', 898; Gaetano Arangio Ruiz, 'The Normative Role of the General Assembly of the United Nations and the Declaration of Principles of Friendly Relations' (1972) 137 *Recueil des cours*, 419–742, 476; Rosalyn Higgins, 'The United Nations and Lawmaking: The Political Organs' (1970) 64 ASIL, 37–47, 47.

On the other hand, traditional approaches to custom have held that General Assembly resolutions do not generate rules of custom in and of themselves, but rather are possible starting points in the development of international custom,[100] being particularly relevant to establishing *opinio juris*.[101] As the ILC has held, a resolution 'may provide evidence for determining the existence and content of a rule of customary international law, or contribute to its development'.[102] Alternatively, it might reflect a rule of custom if it is already 'established that the provision corresponds to a general practice that is accepted as law'.[103] But resolutions 'cannot be a substitute for the task of ascertaining whether there is in fact a general practice that is accepted as law'.[104]

The leading cases on the matter are *Nicaragua* and the *Nuclear Weapons* advisory opinion. In *Nicaragua*, the ICJ held that an *opinio juris* concerning the rule of prohibition of the threat or use of force against the territorial integrity or political independence of other states could be 'deduced from, inter alia, the attitude of the Parties and the attitude of States towards certain General Assembly resolutions', consent to the text of which could be understood as 'an acceptance of the validity of the rule or set of rules declared by the resolution by themselves'.[105] In the *Nuclear Weapons* advisory opinion, the Court noted that General Assembly resolutions, 'even if they are not binding, may sometimes have normative value', as they could, 'in certain circumstances, provide evidence important for establishing the existence of a rule or the emergence of an *opinio juris*'.[106]

In *Nuclear Weapons*, the court substantiated how *opinio juris* may be deduced from one or more General Assembly resolutions. According to the court, in a passage cited approvingly by the ILC,[107] it was necessary to examine 'its content and the conditions of its adoption', as well as 'whether an *opinio juris* exists as to its normative character'.[108] In addition, 'a series of

[100] Simma and Alston, 'Sources of Human Rights Law', 89–90; ILC, 'Draft Conclusions', Conclusion 12(1).

[101] On whether resolutions may also constitute state practice, the ICJ is unclear. Some authors think they can, but others reject this view: see the overview in Öberg, 'Legal Effects of Resolutions', 898.

[102] ILC, 'Draft Conclusions', Conclusion 12(2).

[103] ILC, 'Draft Conclusions', Conclusion 12(3).

[104] ILC, 'Draft Conclusions', Conclusion 12, commentary para. 3.

[105] *Nicaragua*, paras. 188 and 191. See Öberg, 'Legal Effects of Resolutions', 897.

[106] *Legality of the Threat or Use of Nuclear Weapons* (Advisory Opinion) [1996] ICJ Rep 64, para. 70. ILC, 'Draft Conclusions', Conclusion 22, commentary para. 5.

[107] ILC, 'Draft Conclusions', Conclusion 12, commentary para. 6.

[108] *Nuclear Weapons*, para. 70.

resolutions may show the gradual evolution of the *opinio juris* required for the establishment of a new rule'.[109] As Öberg has discussed, the court thereby identifies three criteria for how *opinio juris* may be established from a General Assembly resolution: conditions of the adoption, content, and reality of the *opinio juris*.[110] In addition, as Öberg notes, all General Assembly resolutions to which the ICJ has arguably attributed an impact on customary international law are in the form of declarations. Therefore, although this may not be necessary or sufficient, the form is seen to carry some weight.[111]

The key question is as follows: 'Does a large majority of (the most concerned) states intend the resolution to express the current *opinio juris*?'[112] As to the factors identified in *Nuclear Weapons*, content means 'whether the resolution has normative content and, if so, whether it is couched in legally binding terms'.[113] According to the ILC, the 'precise wording' is the starting point, with significance potentially to be accorded to 'reference to international law, and the choice (or avoidance) of particular terms' in the preambular or operative text.[114] Relevant conditions of adoption might include the number of votes in favour, against, and abstaining;[115] whether and to what extent the states voting for or against the resolution are broadly representative; whether the mode of adoption of the resolution 'permits a fair expression of each state's point of view';[116] and 'the debates and negotiations leading up to the adoption of the resolution and especially explanations of vote and similar statements given immediately before or after adoption'.[117] Large majorities appear crucial.[118] In the *Nuclear Weapons* case, several of the resolutions

[109] Ibid.

[110] Öberg, 'Legal Effects of Resolutions', 900. The following paragraph draws heavily on Oberg's analysis. Relatedly, see Maurice H. Mendelson, *The Formation of Customary International Law* (Brill, 1998): whether GA resolutions should be treated as evidence of the *opinio juris* of states (or at least those voting in favour) depends on the terms of the resolution and the context.

[111] Öberg, 'Legal Effects of Resolutions', 903.

[112] Ibid. See also ILC, 'Draft Conclusions', Conclusion 12, commentary para. 6: 'a careful assessment of various factors is required in order to verify whether indeed the States concerned intended to acknowledge the existence of a rule of customary international law'.

[113] Öberg, 'Legal Effects of Resolutions', 901.

[114] ILC, 'Draft Conclusions', Conclusion 12, commentary para. 6.

[115] ILC, 'Draft Conclusions', Conclusion 12, commentary para. 5: 'negative votes, abstentions or disassociations from a consensus, along with general statements and explanations of positions, may be evidence that there is no acceptance as law'.

[116] Öberg, 'Legal Effects of Resolutions', 900.

[117] ILC, 'Draft Conclusions', Conclusion 12, commentary para. 6.

[118] ILC, 'Draft Conclusions', Conclusion 12, commentary para. 6 ('The degree of support for the resolution (as may be observed in the size of the majority and where there are negative votes or abstentions) is critical'). Differences of opinion expressed on aspects of a resolution may indicate that no general acceptance as law (*opinio juris*) exists, at least on those aspects, and

under consideration were adopted with substantial numbers of negative votes and abstentions, and the Court held that they therefore fell short of establishing *opinio juris*.[119] Regarding the reality of the *opinio juris*, this is 'the key criterion', since, firstly, the General Assembly is a political organ, and states may have moral, political, or pragmatic reasons for voting in a given way,[120] and, secondly, the state representatives who vote in the Assembly do not normally have authority to commit their states to legal obligations.[121]

Even if a General Assembly resolution does not by itself generate the requisite *opinio juris* for a rule of customary international law to be identified, it can still be relevant for the establishment of a rule of custom. As Arajärvi puts it:[122]

> General Assembly resolutions can provide a well-articulated normative touchstone for the future evolution of state practice and *opinio juris*. On the one hand, General Assembly resolutions may reflect some of the existing or developing elements of customary international law, and reinforce them. On the other, General Assembly resolutions may act as a catalyst for a more formalized legal rule in the form of a treaty, or direct subsequent state practice, strengthening the basis for the development of customary international law on a given topic.

The question is therefore one of iteration, rather than a binary issue.

2.4.3 *The UNDRIP and Customary International Law*

We are now equipped to enquire into the status of the UNDRIP in relation to customary international law. Five possibilities exist:

(1) The Declaration is customary international law in and of itself;[123]

resolutions that attract negative votes or abstentions are unlikely to be regarded as reflecting customary international law'.

119 *Nuclear Weapons*, para. 71.

120 ILC, 'Draft Conclusions', Conclusion 12, commentary para. 6.

121 Öberg, 'Legal Effects of Resolutions', 902.

122 Arajärvi, 'From the "Demands of Humanity"', 198. See also ILC, 'Draft Conclusions', Conclusion 12, commentary para 7: resolutions 'may sometimes play an important role in the development of customary international law', for example when 'a resolution (or a series of resolutions) provides inspiration and impetus for the growth of a general practice accepted as law (accompanied by *opinio juris*) conforming to its terms, or when it crystallizes an emerging rule'.

123 This view is taken by Siegfried Wiessner, 'Rights and Status of Indigenous Peoples: A Global Comparative and International Legal Analysis' (1999) 12 *Harvard Human Rights Journal*, 58–128; Siegfried Wiessner, 'Indigenous Sovereignty: A Reassessment in Light of the UN Declaration on the Rights of Indigenous Peoples' (2008) 41 *Vanderbilt Journal of*

(2) The Declaration provides evidence for determining the existence of a rule of customary international law, according to the test laid out in *Nuclear Weapons*;

(3) The Declaration reflects an existing rule or crystallizes an emerging rule, of customary international law;

(4) The Declaration provides inspiration and impetus for the growth of a general practice accepted as law;[124] or

(5) The Declaration is of no significance whatsoever to customary international law, but is only "soft law,"[125] though it may still hold significant persuasive weight.

An *opinio*-oriented approach, as discussed above, would regard (1) as the correct answer. But under a two-element approach, we can discard the possibility immediately. Let us then turn to possibility (2).

The UNDRIP is self-evidently a declaration, a format restricted to 'formal and solemn' instruments on 'rare occasions when principles of great and lasting importance are being enunciated', creating 'a strong expectation that members of the international community will abide by' the UNDRIP.[126] In content, it is highly normative. The articles of the Declaration are couched

Transnational Law, 1141–1176; S. James Anaya, *Indigenous Peoples in International Law* (2nd ed., Oxford: Oxford University Press, 2004), 65–71; Javaid Rehman, 'Between the Devil and the Deep Blue Sea: Indigenous Peoples as the Pawns in the US "War on Terror" and the Jihad of Osama Bin Laden' in Stephen Allen and Alexandra Xanthaki (eds.), *Reflections on the UN Declaration on the Rights of Indigenous Peoples* (Oxford: Hart 2011), 561–584; Anaya, S. James and Luis Rodríguez-Piñero, 'The Making of the UNDRIP' in Jessie Hohmann and Marc Weller (eds.), *The UN Declaration on the Rights of Indigenous People: A Commentary* (Oxford: Oxford University Press, 2018), 38–62, 62; Mattias Åhren, *Indigenous Peoples' Status in the International Legal System* (Oxford: Oxford University Press, 2016), 106–107.

124 Rodolfo Stavenhagen, 'Making the Declaration on the Rights of Indigenous Peoples Work: The Challenge Ahead', in Stephen Allen and Alexandra Xanthaki (eds.), *Reflections on the UN Declaration on the Rights of Indigenous Peoples* (London: Hart, 2011), 147–170, 152, and Mauro Barelli, 'The Role of Soft Law in the International Legal System: The Case of the United Nations Declaration on the Rights of Indigenous Peoples' (2009) 58(4) *International & Comparative Law Quarterly*, 957–983, 967, express the view that the UNDRIP may become CIL over time.

125 On soft law generally, see Christine Chinkin, 'The Challenge of Soft Law: Development and Change in International Law' (1989) 28 *International and Comparative Law Quarterly*, 850–866; Alan Boyle, 'Soft Law in International Law-Making' in Malcolm D. Evans (ed.), *International Law* (4th ed., Oxford: Oxford University Press, 2014), 118–135; Stephanie Lagoutte, Thomas Gammeltoft-Hansen, and John Cerone (eds.), *Tracing the Roles of Soft Law in Human Rights* (Cambridge: Cambridge University Press, 2016).

126 Commission on Human Rights, 'Report of the Eighteenth Session' (1962) UN Doc E/CN.4/832/Rev.1, para. 105. See Barelli, 'The Role of Soft Law', 971; Åhren, *Indigenous Peoples' Status*, 103.

in terms indistinguishable from those used in major human rights treaties, like the ICCPR and ICESCR. They declare that Indigenous peoples 'have the right to' various things. Article 3 mirrors almost exactly Common Article 1 of the ICCPR and ICESCR, and others mirror provisions of ILO 169.[127] In several places, it mandates that 'states shall' undertake certain actions, language that suggests a legal obligation.[128] Some argue that its provisions refer to rights and principles that were either already recognized or were emerging, in international human rights law.[129] It aligns in some respects with the practice of human rights treaty bodies.[130] In this way, it can be said to constitute an agreed interpretation of pre-existing international legal sources.[131]

Regarding conditions of adoption, the Declaration was adopted with overwhelming support from every corner of the globe. Some writers argue that this evidences general acceptance of its principles and bestows it with a 'special legitimacy and authoritativeness'.[132] It was adopted by a large majority of

[127] Barelli, 'The Role of Soft Law', 972–977.

[128] See, for example, Article 8(2) (prevention of and redress for forced assimilation); Article 11(2) (redress for taking of cultural property); Article 12(2) (access and repatriation of ceremonial objects and human remains); Article 13(2) (protection of right to histories and languages); Article 14(3) (education in own culture and language); Article 15(2) (combatting prejudice and eliminating discrimination); Article 16(2) (state-owned media); Article 17(2) (protecting Indigenous children); Article 19 (free, prior, and informed consent); Article 21(2) (economic and social conditions); Article 22(2) (protection of Indigenous women and children); Article 26(3) (legal recognition and protection to lands, territories, and resources); Article 27 (recognition to Indigenous peoples' laws); Article 29(2) and (3) (storage and disposal of hazardous materials); Article 30(2) (usage of lands for military activities); Article 31(2) (cultural heritage); Article 32(2) and (3) (development projects); Article 36(2) (right to contacts across borders); Article 38 (states shall take appropriate measures to achieve the ends of the Declaration).

[129] Barelli, 'The Role of Soft Law', 972–977, and *Seeking Justice*, 53–55.

[130] Barelli, 'The Role of Soft Law', 972–977.

[131] Alexandra Xanthaki, 'Indigenous Rights in International Law over the Last Ten Years and Future Developments' (2009) 10 *Melbourne Journal of International Law*, 27–37, 36; Anaya and Rodríguez-Piñero, 'Making of the UNDRIP', 62.

[132] Barelli, 'The Role of Soft Law', 969–970. See also Anaya and Rodríguez-Piñero, 'Making of the UNDRIP', 62; Åhren, *Indigenous Peoples' Status*, 103–104; Christopher J. Fromherz, '"Indigenous Peoples" Courts: Egalitarian Juridical Pluralism, Self-Determination, and the United Nations Declaration on the Rights of Indigenous Peoples' (2008) 156(5) *University of Pennsylvania Law Review*, 1341–1381, 1355, 1367; Clive Baldwin and Cynthia Morel, 'Using the United Nations Declaration on the Rights of Indigenous Peoples in Litigation', in Stephen Allen and Alexandra Xanthaki (eds.), *Reflections on the UN Declaration on the Rights of Indigenous Peoples* (London: Hart, 2011) 121–144, 123–124. A total of 143 states voted in favour, with four (Australia, the United States, Canada, and New Zealand) opposed, 11 abstaining, and 34 absent; the opposers have all subsequently reversed their position to support the Declaration.

144 states in favour, four votes against, and eleven abstentions.[133] All four states that initially voted against, and three of the abstaining states, later reversed their positions and expressed support for the Declaration.[134] The negotiation and drafting history of the Declaration was extensive, dating back 25 years to 1982,[135] but as Malgosia Fitzmaurice notes, this was a 'tortuous process' and it does not seem that there was a strong convergence on the underlying principles of the Declaration.[136]

The reality of the *opinio juris* is the most difficult factor to establish. During explanations of vote in the General Assembly, eleven states emphasized that they did not perceive the Declaration as legally binding.[137] Three additional

[133] Australia, Canada, New Zealand, and the United States voted against. Azerbaijan, Bangladesh, Bhutan, Burundi, Colombia, Georgia, Kenya, Nigeria, Russian Federation, Samoa, and Ukraine abstained. See UNGAOR, 61st session, 107th plenary meeting, UN Doc A/61/PV.107, 19.

[134] Colombia, Samoa, and Ukraine.

[135] As discussed in Chapter 3, Baldwin and Morel, 'Using the United Nations Declaration', 124, and Barelli, *Seeking Justice*, 47–49, say this supports the view that the Declaration holds special legal weight.

[136] Malgosia Fitzmaurice, 'The 2007 United Nations Declaration on the Rights of Indigenous Peoples' (2012) 17 *Austrian Review of International and European Law*, 139–266, 146; Russel Lawrence Barsh, 'Indigenous Peoples and the UN Commission on Human Rights: A Case of the Immovable Object and the Irresistible Force' (1996) 18(4) *Human Rights Quarterly*, 782–813, 805.

[137] UNGAOR, 61st session, 107th plenary meeting, UN Doc A/61/PV.107, 10, 11, 15, 17, 22, 26, and 27; UNGAOR, 61st session, 108th plenary meeting, UN Doc A/61/PV.108, 3, 5, and 9. Australia ('with regard to the nature of the declaration, it is the clear intention of all States that it be an aspirational declaration with political and moral force but not legal force. It is not intended itself to be legally binding or reflective of international law. As this declaration does not describe current State practice or actions States consider themselves obliged to take as a matter of law, it cannot be cited as evidence of the evolution of customary international law'.), Canada ('we also underline our understanding that this Declaration is not a legally binding instrument. It has no legal effect in Canada, and its provisions do not represent customary international law'.), New Zealand ('we place on record our firm view that the history of the negotiations on the Declaration and the divided manner in which its text has been adopted demonstrate that this text . . . does not state propositions which are reflected in State practice or which are or will be recognized as general principles of law'.), Colombia ('the Declaration is not a legally binding norm for the State and in no way constitutes the establishment of conventional or customary provisions that are binding for Colombia'), the United Kingdom ('this Declaration is not legally binding and does not propose to have any retroactive application on historical episodes'.), Thailand ('Thailand understands that the Declaration does not create any new rights'), Guyana ('We also take note of the fact that the Declaration is political in character, as opposed to being a legally binding document, though not without potential legal implications'.), Suriname ('the Republic of Suriname recognizes this document as a political document to express and demonstrate the goodwill of the State regarding the promotion and protection of all human rights and fundamental freedoms, including those of indigenous peoples'.), Nepal ('It is Nepal's understanding that the

states expressed the view that the UNDRIP was an 'important tool' for the promotion and protection of the rights of Indigenous peoples, implying that they did not see it as a legally binding instrument.[138] Only one state expressed the view that the UNDRIP was legally binding.[139] It is impossible in these circumstances to argue that a large majority of states intended the Declaration to establish the then *opinio juris*. Some suggest that because the states who opposed its adoption 'appeared to do so through fear that by accepting, they would be accepting some form of legal commitment', the Declaration holds legal significance.[140] But these states, while rejecting the Declaration, simultaneously explicitly rejected any notion that it would be legally binding, making that suggestion a difficult one to sustain. When these states subsequently accepted the Declaration, they maintained their position that it was not legally binding.[141] Moreover, the Declaration's preamble '[s]olemnly proclaims ... [UNDRIP] as a standard of achievement to be pursued in a spirit of partnership and mutual respect'.[142] A "standard of achievement" is a different thing from a rule of customary international law.

Therefore it seems unlikely that proposition (2) holds. The UNDRIP, in and of itself, may hold substantial persuasive authority by reason of its format, support, drafting history, and the degree to which it aligns with previously existing law (proposition (5)). In Chapter 4, we will explore how proposition (4) could hold, in that the Declaration has provided inspiration and impetus

principles mentioned in this Declaration are collective reflections of the good intentions of the international community as guidelines for the protection and promotion of the rights of indigenous peoples and therefore do not create any binding legal or political obligations on the part of the States that voted in favour of it'.), Turkey ('The Declaration is not legally binding. However, it can constitute an important policy tool for those States that recognize indigenous peoples within their national territories'.), and Guatemala ('the Declaration is the expression of the political will of the international community to recognize, defend and respect those peoples'.).

138 Slovakia ('My country in principle welcomes the [UNDRIP] as an important tool for the promotion and protection of the rights of indigenous peoples'.), Montenegro ('We consider that it will be an important tool that will help enhance the promotion and protection of the rights of indigenous peoples'.), and Finland ('We view the Declaration as an important tool in underscoring the principle of full and effective participation by indigenous peoples in decision-making processes'.): UNGAOR, 61st session, 108th plenary meeting, UN Doc A/61/PV.108, 5, 7, and 9.

139 Namibia: 'The argument that the Declaration is not binding did not appeal to us. We take our obligations seriously. Once we adopt an instrument we want to promote, defend and protect it'. UNGAOR, 61st session, 108th plenary meeting, UN Doc A/61/PV.108, 3.

140 Baldwin and Morel, 'Using the United Nations Declaration', 124; Åhren, *Indigenous Peoples' Status*, 104.

141 See note 138, above.

142 Recital 24.

for the growth of a general practice accepted as law. And in Chapter 3, we will also see how the UNDRIP has reflected, and reinforced, some of the developing elements of custom, but that it seems unlikely to reflect an existing rule (proposition (3)).

2.4.4 *Is Subsequent Practice Justified by Reference to the UNDRIP Evidence of Customary International Law?*

Of crucial concern to us are the ways in which declaratory soft law may crystallize into customary rules. One necessary element is the development of practice subsequent to, and inspired by, the Declaration. As we will see in Chapter 4, there is a great deal of practice, subsequent to (and inspired by) the UNDRIP, regarding the participation of Indigenous peoples in international governance.

The other necessary element, as we know, is evidence of acceptance as law. As will be seen in Chapter 4, in many cases of practice subsequent to the adoption of the UNDRIP, the UNDRIP and its provisions, particularly Articles 18, 19, and 41, are referred to by states and international organizations in justifying their practice. Can such references evidence *opinio juris*? At face value, we might think that they surely can, since this means that the practice is being carried out not only for reasons of comity or courtesy but rather, or in addition, due to a sense of obligation.

This is not entirely a straightforward question. One might argue that the so-called Baxter paradox applies here by analogy. In relation to the problem of distinguishing whether a rule contained in a treaty provision had also emerged as a rule of custom, in 1970 Richard Baxter observed:[143]

> the proof of a consistent pattern of conduct by non-parties becomes more difficult as the number of parties to the instrument increases. The number of participants in the process of creating customary law may become so small that the evidence of their practice will be minimal or altogether lacking. Hence the paradox that as the number of parties to a treaty increases, it becomes more difficult to demonstrate what is the state of customary international law dehors the treaty.

In other words, it may prove difficult to demonstrate that in acting in a particular way, states believed and recognized that their duty to conform to a particular norm was required not only by their (soft) obligations under the

143 Robert R. Baxter, 'Treaties and Custom' (1970) 129 *Recueil des cours*, 25–106, 64; see also at 73, 96.

Declaration but also by customary international law. The number of states that still have not approved the UNDRIP is small. Therefore, one could argue that when states subsequently carry out a practice aligned with Articles 18, 19, and 41 of the UNDRIP, while explicitly justifying their practice by reference to those provisions, their actions are simply driven by the Declaration itself, rather than motivated by a rule of custom.

If taken to its logical conclusions, that argument results in difficulties. Consider the following scenario, which we will see repeatedly in Chapter 4. States, through the framework of an international organization, or an international organization acting largely in its own right, establish a mechanism by which Indigenous peoples have a voice in the decision-making, law-making, or policymaking processes of that organization. In the process of establishing that mechanism or policy, or subsequently during the mechanism's operation, officials of several of the states involved, and/or international organization officials, make speeches or submissions stating that they established the mechanism because they believed doing so was required by, or at least consistent with fulfilling, the UNDRIP, in particular Articles 18, 19, and/or 41.

In this scenario, clearly the UNDRIP is having some normative, legal effect. If officials are to be taken at their word – which, in the absence of mind-reading technology, one must assume – the Declaration is assigned legal significance. States perceive that they have to carry out this practice in order to comply with their obligations. The question is then, if this obligation is *not* found under customary international law, where is it located? Alternative options are lacking – unlike in the classic formulation of the Baxter paradox, which pertains to treaties.[144] In this case, as we have seen, this Declaration has no recognized legally binding status under a conservative approach to the sources of international law. It is difficult to conceptualize how else states could imagine themselves to be obliged to follow a given course of conduct, if not under a rule of custom.[145]

Another counterargument to the Baxter paradox arises from the fact that, as we will see in Chapter 4, much of the subsequent practice functions to populate the relatively general terms of Article 41 UNDRIP with substantive content. Articles 18 and 41, by their terms, leave open many questions. Most pressingly, what constitutes "participation"? What are "matters which would affect [indigenous peoples'] rights"? What does it mean to establish "ways and

[144] Though see Crawford, arguing that the paradox is more apparent than real: James Crawford, *Chance, Order, Change: The Course of International Law* (Leiden: Martinus Nijhoff, 2014), 134–142.

[145] The case for a "general principle" of law would be even more difficult.

means" of ensuring participation? Who is to establish these ways and means? The practice, as we will see, substantiates at least (some) answers to these questions. If a declaration reflects a snapshot moment of consensus, a minimum compromise that all states can live with, the development of customary international law is an 'aggregative approach', a 'conversation across time' that may develop and add substantive flavour to the provisions of a declaration, just as it can '"mould and even modify" the content of otherwise static treaties'.[146]

2.4.5 *The Role of International Organizations in the Formation of Custom*

One more preliminary matter must be dealt with before we can turn to the meat of the study. Because some of the relevant practice (and evidence of *opinio juris*) presented in Chapter 4 can most properly be attributed to specific international organizations, rather than to the member states of those organizations, we need to briefly consider whether and how international organizations can be bound by customary international law, and whether and how they can contribute to its formation.

The first question is more straightforward than the second, although a relevant passage in the ICJ's *WHO-Egypt* opinion – 'obligations incumbent upon international organizations under general rules of international law' – has been much debated. The term 'general rules of international law' is rightly criticized as a 'monument to indeterminacy';[147] it has been used inconsistently by the ICJ at different times to variously mean rules of custom, rules of custom and general principles, or something else entirely.[148] But while some construe the ICJ's statement as excluding the application of rules of custom to international organizations,[149] the more generally accepted view seems to be that international organizations can be subject to customary international law.[150]

146 Crawford, *Chance, Order, Change*, 143.

147 Klabbers, 'Reflections on Accountability', 989.

148 Gennady M. Danilenko, *Law-Making in the International Community* (Leiden: Nijhoff, 1993) 9–10; Prosper Weil, 'Towards Relative Normativity in International Law' (1983) 77 *American Journal of International Law*, 413–442, 436–437.

149 Eyal Benvenisti, 'Upholding Democracy Amid the Challenges of New Technology: What Role for the Law of Global Governance?' (2018) 29(1) *European Journal of International Law*, 9–82, 22–23; José E. Alvarez, 'International Organizations and the Rule of Law' (2016) 14 *New Zealand Journal of Public and International Law*, 3–46, 8–9; Klabbers, 'Reflections on Accountability', 997–998.

150 See, for example, August Reinisch, 'Securing the Accountability of International Organizations' (2001) 7(2) *Global Governance*, 131–149, 136; Michael Wood, 'Do International Organizations Enjoy Immunity under Customary International Law?' (2013) 10

Of course, international organizations will not be affected by all existing rules of custom. Many rules simply do not apply to their activities: rules on state responsibility, self-defence in armed conflict, or territory.[151] Other rules may apply to international organizations as well as to states: custom relating to human rights, for instance. On the other hand, some rules are primarily applicable to international organizations: rules on their responsibility, for instance. The applicability will also differ among international organizations. Thus, it is conceptually possible for international organizations to be bound by a mixture of the same and different obligations than those applicable to states. The ICJ's statement in the *Reparations* advisory opinion supports this notion:[152]

> The subjects of law in any legal system are not necessarily identical in their nature or in the extent of their rights, and their nature depends on the needs of the community.

As the ILC phrased it in its Commentary to the Articles on the Responsibility of International Organizations, international organizations are 'quite different from States and in addition present great diversity among themselves'. Unlike states, they 'do not possess a general competence and have been established in order to exercise specific functions'.[153] In its Commentary to the Draft Conclusions on the Identification of Customary International Law, the ILC further emphasized that international organizations are 'not states' and 'may have their own rights and obligations under international law'.[154]

(2) *International Organizations Law Review*, 287–318; Michael Wood, 'Customary International Law and Human Rights' (European University Institute Working Paper AEL 2016/03); Michael Wood, 'International Organizations and Customary International Law' (2015) 48(3) *Vanderbilt Journal of Transnational Law*, 609–620, 619; Shelton, *Remedies*, 46; Niels Blokker, 'International Organizations and Customary International Law: Is the International Law Commission Taking International Organizations Seriously?' (2017) 14(1) *International Organizations Law Review*, 1–12, 1–10; Daugirdas, 'How and Why', 342–348; August Reinisch, 'Sources of International Organizations' Law: Why Custom and General Principles Are Crucial', in Jean D'Aspremont and Samantha Besson (eds.), *The Oxford Handbook of the Sources of International Law* (Oxford: Oxford University Press, 2017), 1007–1024, 1010.

151 Magdalena Pacholska, 'New Kids on the Block: International Organizations as Customary Rules Creators' (2019) 21(3–4) *International Community Law Review*, 325–343, 338, noting the exception where an international organization operates as a quasi-sovereign functional equivalent of a state.

152 *Reparations*, 178. Also see Jan Klabbers, 'The Transformation of International Organizations Law' (2015) 26(1) *European Journal of International Law*, 9–82, 42.

153 ILC, 'Draft articles on the responsibility of international organizations, with commentaries', para. 7.

154 ILC, 'Draft Conclusions', 88–89.

On the second point, it has long been recognized that international organizations play a role in the formation of custom as fora in which States develop a general practice accepted as law:[155] they can be vehicles through which states act as well as catalysts of state practice.[156]

More recently, it has been acknowledged that the practice of international organizations themselves can contribute to the establishment of custom. Some are of the view that international organizations do not have a role in the creation of custom but can nonetheless be bound by it.[157] However, other commentators, as well as the ILC, are of a different opinion.[158] Conclusion 4 of the 2018 ILC Conclusions provides that, in addition to the practice of states, which is primary:[159]

> 2. In certain cases, the practice of international organizations also contributes to the formation, or expression, of rules of customary international law.

The Commentary to the Conclusions makes clear that it is referring to the practice of international organizations themselves, as opposed to the practice

[155] ILC, 'Draft Conclusions', Conclusion 12; *Barcelona Traction*, Separate Opinion of Judge Ammoun, 303; James D. Fry, 'Formation of Customary International Law through Consensus in International Organizations' (2015) 17(1) *Austrian Review of International and European Law Online*, 49–82; ILC, 'Third report'; Stephen Mathias, 'The Work of the International Law Commission on Identification of Customary International Law: A View from the Perspective of the Office of Legal Affairs' (2016) 15(1) *Chinese Journal of International Law*, 17–31, 24.

[156] Sufyan Droubi, 'Institutionalisation of Emerging Norms of Customary International Law through Resolutions and Operational Activities of the Political and Subsidiary Organs of the United Nations' (2017) 14(2) *International Organizations Law Review*, 254–290.

[157] Lepard, A *New Theory*, 86; Daphna Shraga, 'ILC Articles on Responsibility of International Organizations: The Interplay between the Practice and the Rule (A View from the United Nations)' in Maurizio Ragazzi (ed.), *Responsibility of International Organizations: Essays in Memory of Sir Ian Brownlie* (Leiden: Martinus Nijhoff, 2013), 201, 201–210.

[158] For example, Akehurst, 'Custom as a Source', 11; Gunning, 'Modernizing Customary International Law', 212–213; H. Meijers, 'On International Customary Law in the Netherlands' in Ige F. Dekker and Harry H.G. Post (eds.), *On the Foundations and Sources of International Law* (Utrecht: TMC Asser Press, 2003), 77, 80, 125; Arajärvi, 'From State-Centricism, 23; Danilenko, *Law-Making*, 82–83; Hanna Bokor-Szegö, *The Role of the United Nations in International Legislation* (Amsterdam: North-Holland Publishing Company, 1978), 51; Catherine Brölmann, 'Capturing the Juridical Will of International Organizations' in Sufjan Droubi and Jean D'Aspremont (eds.), International Organizations and Non-State Actors in the Formation of Customary International Law (Manchester: Manchester University Press, 2020), 42–61.

[159] ILC, 'Draft Conclusions', Conclusion 4, commentary para. 2.

of states acting within or through such organizations.[160] By reference to the theory of international organizations explored in Chapter 1, this seems correct.[161] The Commentary states that the practice of international organizations may be particularly relevant 'with rules of customary international law that are addressed specifically to them, such as those on their international responsibility or relating to treaties to which they are parties'.[162]

The Commentary further provides for two cases where such practice is relevant: where member states have transferred exclusive competences to the international organization, such as in the case of the EU, and where member states have conferred on the organization powers functionally equivalent to those exercised by states, such as when organizations are 'concluding treaties, serving as treaty depositaries, in deploying military forces (for example, for peacekeeping), in administering territories, or in taking positions on the scope of the privileges and immunities of the organization and its officials'.[163] These ostensibly exclusive cases are rightly criticized as 'elusive' and 'ill-defined',[164] leaving many unanswered questions, as well as 'overly formalistic' with regard to the role of international organizations in international relations.[165]

A helpful analytical distinction is made by Magdalena Pacholska: between rules applicable only to states, rules applicable to both states and international organizations, and rules applicable only to international organizations.[166] It seems 'self-evident' that international organizations should be able to participate in the formation of the latter two kinds of rules.[167] This notion is supported by the views of states[168] and international organizations[169] and is

[160] Ibid, Commentary to Conclusion 4, para. 3; ILC, 'Third report', 48–49. Also see Wood, 'International Organizations and Customary International Law', 614.

[161] On this point, see Akehurst, 'Custom as a Source', 11.

[162] ILC, 'Draft conclusions', Commentary to Conclusion 4, para. 7.

[163] Ibid., Commentary to Conclusion 4, para. 6.

[164] For example, Blokker, 'Taking International Organizations Seriously', 6, 9; Pacholska, 'New Kids on the Block', 336.

[165] Rossana Deplano, 'Assessing the Role of Resolutions in the ILC Draft Conclusions on Identification of Customary International Law' (2017) 14 *International Organizations Law Review*, 227–253, 228–229.

[166] Pacholska, 'New Kids on the Block', 338.

[167] Ibid., 339. See also Blokker, 'Taking International Organizations Seriously', 10; Brölmann, 'Capturing the Juridical Will', 16–19.

[168] ILC, 'Report of the International Law Commission on the Work of its Sixty-Third Session (2011): Topical Summary of the Discussion Held in the Sixth Committee of the General Assembly during its Sixty-Sixth Session, Prepared by the Secretariat' (2012) UN Doc A/CN.4/650/Add.1, 5–7.

[169] ILC, 'Responsibility of international Organizations, Comments and Observations Received from International Organizations' (2011) UN Doc A/CN.4/637, 7–14.

generally supported by the theory of particular custom.[170] However, to counter the risk that 'IOs might over time be capable of imposing customary rules on States against their will',[171] it is appropriate that the practice of an international organization may only contribute to the creation of custom that binds states if it 'has been generally accepted over time by the organization's member States'.[172]

Regarding the weight to be attributed to the practice of international organizations, the Commentary notes that such practice carries greater weight the more directly it is carried out on behalf of its member states or endorsed by them, and the larger the number of the member states.[173] Thus, for instance, a practice of the UN mandated by a General Assembly resolution would hold great weight. Other factors relevant in weighing the practice include the organization's nature, the nature of the relevant organ, whether the conduct is *ultra vires*, and whether the conduct is 'consonant with that of the member States of the organization'.[174] Otherwise, it is intuitive that similar considerations in assessing the practice and *opinio juris* of states apply to that of international organizations.

A right of Indigenous peoples to participate in international governance would entail obligations for both states and international organizations. Hence, in accordance with Pacholska's suggestion, the practice and *opinio juris* of international organizations themselves, as well as that of states, are relevant for ascertaining whether the right is a rule of custom. The distinction between the practices of international organizations themselves, as opposed to the practice of states acting within international organizations, is not necessarily easy to make.[175] More likely to show evidence of the former are the acts of bodies or officers of international organizations that are not representative of

[170] On particular custom, see Anthony D'Amato, 'The Concept of Special Custom in International Law' (1969) 63 *American Journal of International Law*, 211–223, 212–213; *Asylum*, 276–277; *Case Concerning Rights of Nationals of the United States of America in Morocco* [1952] ICJ Rep 176, 200; *Case Concerning Rights of Passage over Indian Territory*, 39–40; *Nicaragua*, para. 199; *Frontier Dispute (Burkina Faso v. Mali)* (Judgment) [1986] ICJ Rep 554, para. 21; *Dispute Regarding Navigational and Related Rights (Costa Rica v. Nicaragua)* (Judgment) [2009] ICJ Rep 213, paras. 34 and 36; *Fisheries Jurisdiction (United Kingdom v. Iceland)* (Merits) [1974] ICJ Rep 3, 79, and 94, Separate Opinion of Judge de Castro; *North Sea Continental Shelf*, Separate Opinion of President Bustamante y Rivero, 62; *Barcelona Traction*, Separate Opinion of Judge Ammoun, 290–291. Also see ILC, 'Draft Conclusions', Conclusion 16 and commentary thereto.

[171] Pacholska, 'New Kids on the Block', 340.

[172] 2018 States observations on CIL, 18 (New Zealand); discussed ibid., 337, 340–341.

[173] ILC, 'Draft Conclusions', Commentary to Conclusion 4, para. 7.

[174] Ibid.

[175] ILC, 'Third Report', 48–49.

the organization's membership, and the public statements of officers of international organizations. More likely to go towards the latter are decisions of representative bodies of international organizations.

2.4.6 *Summarizing the Framework*

To decide whether practice and *opinio juris* exist or not, as Judge Tanaka pointed out in his dissenting opinion in *North Sea Continental Shelf*, is 'a delicate and difficult matter' not able to be 'mathematically and uniformly decided'.[176] In the following chapters, we will trace the development of a 'conversation across time'[177] – over four decades – taking a traditional approach. We will consider whether the two constituent elements of custom are both, in the end, present: a general practice and acceptance of that practice as law (*opinio juris*).[178] In Chapter 3, we will consider whether prior to 2007, a general practice accepted as law developed such that Articles 18 and 41 of the UNDRIP merely reflected an existing rule. In Chapter 4, we will trace how the Declaration has provided inspiration and impetus for the growth of a general practice accepted as law. It will become clear that the participants of the practice have started to experience 'normative pressure to comply'.[179]

Let us briefly review the methodology for identifying the existence of each element. While a separate inquiry must be carried out in respect of each, the same material may go to evidence both.[180] The type of material that is relevant

[176] *North Sea Continental Shelf*, Dissenting Opinion of Judge Tanaka, 176.

[177] Crawford, *Chance, Order, Change*, 143: 'customary international law is a conversation across time: like good coffee, international law has to be brewed'. And at 142: 'Many ingredients are required to establish customary international law, which interact with, add, modify, accentuate and amplify each other'.

[178] See, for example, *North Sea Continental Shelf*, para. 77; *Jurisdictional Immunities of the State (Germany v. Italy: Greece Intervening)* (Judgment) [2012] ICJ Rep 99, para. 55; *Continental Shelf (Libyan Arab Jamahiriya/Malta)* (Judgment) [1985] ICJ Rep 13, para. 27; *Asylum*, 277; *Case Concerning Right of Passage over Indian Territory* (Merits, Judgment of 12 April 1960) [1960] ICJ Rep 6, 40–43; *WHO Advisory Opinion*, para. 73. Also see ILC Draft Conclusions, Conclusion 2.

[179] This phrase comes from Fernando R Tesón, 'Fake Custom' in Brian D. Lepard (ed.), *Reexamining Customary International Law* (Cambridge: Cambridge University Press, 2017), 86–110, 88 (emphasis removed).

[180] ILC, 'Draft Conclusions', Conclusion 3(2) and commentary paras. 6–8. On what constitutes conduct of the state, see ILC Conclusion 5 and commentary thereto. On forms of practice, see ILC Conclusion 6 and commentary thereto.

will be informed by the circumstances and context.[181] In the following chapters, I draw on evidence of practice in the forms of verbal interventions and written submissions of state representatives to intergovernmental conferences; meetings of international organizations; speeches by state officials; press releases by state officials; decisions of international organizations and their organs; resolutions adopted at intergovernmental conferences; and policy documents adopted by decision-making bodies of international organizations.[182]

It will become apparent that the practice is general, that is, 'sufficiently widespread and representative, as well as consistent'.[183] It is not universal, but as the Commentary to the ILC conclusions explains, universal or uniform practice is not required, although the practice 'should be of such a character as to make it possible to discern a virtually uniform usage'.[184]

The requirement of *opinio juris* entails that the practice must be undertaken with a sense of legal right or obligation, as opposed to mere usage or habit.[185] Broad and representative acceptance is required.[186] Forms of evidence of *opinio juris* that I will discuss include public statements (written and verbal) made on behalf of states, official publications, diplomatic correspondence, treaty provisions, and conduct in connection with resolutions adopted by an international organization or at an intergovernmental conference.[187] As discussed above, I will consider references to the UNDRIP made in the course of explaining or justifying a given instance of practice to constitute evidence of acceptance as law.

The proposed obligation of states, as framed in Chapter 1, is a duty to promote the creation of mechanisms for the participation of affected peoples

181 Ibid, Conclusion 3.1 and commentary paras. 1–5. *North Sea Continental Shelf*, dissenting opinion of Judge Tanaka, 175. For examples of this approach, see *Jurisdictional Immunities*, paras. 55 and 57; *Navigational and Related Rights*, para. 141.

182 ILC, 'Draft Conclusions', Conclusion 6.

183 Ibid, Conclusion 8. *North Sea Continental Shelf*, paras. 74 and 77 (the practice must be 'both extensive and virtually uniform', it must be a 'settled practice').

184 ILC, 'Draft Conclusions', Commentary to Conclusion 8, paras. 2–3 and 7. Also see *Nicaragua*, para. 186 ('The Court does not consider that, for a rule to be established as customary, the corresponding practice must be in absolutely rigorous conformity with the rule. In order to deduce the existence of customary rules, the Court deems it sufficient that the conduct of States should, in general, be consistent with such rules…').

185 ILC, 'Draft Conclusions', Conclusion 9. *North Sea Continental Shelf*, para. 77 ('…they must … be such, or carried out in such a way, as to be evidence of a belief that this practice is rendered obligatory by the existence of a rule of law requiring it').

186 ILC, 'Draft Conclusions', Commentary to Conclusion 9; *WHO Advisory Opinion* para. 67.

187 ILC, 'Draft Conclusions', Conclusion 10.

in international organizations and other international governance bodies. The evidence will include proposals and statements advanced by states in international organizations and other international fora (practice and *opinio juris*), and decisions of bodies of international organizations that are representative of member states with regard to the participation of peoples, as such documents evidence the collective practice and will of states (practice and *opinio juris*).

3

The Proliferation of Indigenous Peoples' Participation, 1982–2007

3.1 INTRODUCTION

On 13 September 2007, the UN Declaration on the Rights of Indigenous Peoples (UNDRIP) was adopted in the General Assembly to much acclaim. This much-anticipated event marked the zenith of a process that had begun more than two decades before with the establishment of the Working Group on Indigenous Populations (WGIP). Created in 1982 under the auspices of the Sub-Commission on the Protection and Promotion of Human Rights,[1] the WGIP introduced to the UN system a practice whereby Indigenous peoples' organizations were allowed to participate in meetings and other activities on what was essentially the same basis as the participation of states. It was the earliest sign, in an intergovernmental setting, of what was over the following decades to prove a sea change in the way that states and international organizations interact with Indigenous peoples in international governance processes. Even in the two and a half decades that passed between the WGIP's establishment and the Declaration's ultimate adoption, it was to inspire, directly or indirectly, similar modalities in numerous other intergovernmental spaces.

3.2 THE PROCESS LEADING TO THE UN DECLARATION ON THE RIGHTS OF INDIGENOUS PEOPLES

The process of the development of the UNDRIP was characterized by what the WGIP's founding Chairperson-Rapporteur, Erica-Irene Daes, termed an 'extraordinarily liberal, transparent and democratic procedure'[2] marked by

[1] The Sub-Commission was itself a subsidiary body of the UN Commission on Human Rights.

[2] Erica-Irene A. Daes, 'The Contribution of the Working Group on Indigenous Populations to the Genesis and Evolution of the UN Declaration on the Rights of Indigenous Peoples' in Claire Charters and Rodolfo Stavenhagen, (eds.), *Making the Declaration Work: The United*

high levels of participation of Indigenous peoples themselves. It was catalysed in large part by the emergence of Indigenous peoples as a political movement in the global arena during the 1960s and 1970s.[3] In turn, the WGIP process was to lead to the emergence and proliferation of mechanisms through which those Indigenous peoples' movements could voice their political demands, at the UN and beyond.

3.2.1 *The Working Group on Indigenous Populations*

The WGIP was established by ECOSOC in 1982 as a subsidiary organ of the Sub-Commission on the Promotion and Protection of Human Rights.[4] Meeting in annual sessions until its dissolution in 2007, it was composed of five independent human rights experts, who were members of the Sub-Commission.[5] The WGIP was mandated to review developments concerning the promotion and protection of Indigenous peoples' rights and to elaborate standards in relation to these rights.[6] From 1985 to 1993, the latter part of this mandate chiefly related to the development of a declaration on the rights of Indigenous peoples, an initiative first begun by the WGIP itself and subsequently authorized by the Sub-Commission.[7]

From the outset, the WGIP established a practice of including Indigenous peoples in its sessions. It decided that in addition to states, and NGOs with consultative status at the ECOSOC, Indigenous peoples' organizations without ECOSOC consultative status would be able to participate as observers.[8]

Nations Declaration on the Rights of Indigenous Peoples (Copenhagen: IWGIA, 2009), 48–77, 74.

3 Sheryl Lightfoot, *Global Indigenous Politics: A Subtle Revolution* (New York: Routledge, 2016).

4 ECOSOC Res. 1982/34 of 7 May 1982. Also see Commission on Human Rights Res. 1982/19 of 10 March 1982.

5 ECOSOC Res. 1982/34, para. 1. For a detailed account of the WGIP's proceedings, see Daes, 'Contribution'.

6 ECOSOC Res. 1982/34, paras. 1–2. The WGIP's mandate was later extended to the preparation of studies on, respectively, the cultural and intellectual property of Indigenous peoples, and treaties between states and Indigenous peoples: ECOSOC decision 1992/256 (20 July 1992); ECOSOC decision 1988/134 (27 May 1988); ECOSOC Res. 1989/77 of 24 May 1989.

7 Sub-Commission on Prevention of Discrimination and Protection of Minorities Res. 1985/22 of 29 August 1985, UN Doc. E/CN.4/Sub.2/1985/22.

8 The barriers faced by Indigenous peoples in accessing ECOSOC observer status will be canvassed in Chapter 4. This decision, which in Stamatopoulou's opinion was taken in response to the informal presence of Indigenous representatives as members of the public at the first and second meetings of the WGIP, was never formalized in writing: Elsa Stamatopoulou, 'Indigenous Peoples and the United Nations: Human Rights as a Developing Dynamic' (1994) 16 *Human Rights Quarterly*, 58–81, 68 note 30. On the rules of

This was a pivotal decision, for it enabled the numerous Indigenous peoples' organizations who did not meet the criteria for consultative status (which were not designed with them in mind), or who did not wish to describe themselves as "nongovernmental" in nature, to participate. Indigenous peoples were placed on the same footing as states in the WGIP's proceedings. Despite the passive connotations of the title "observer," their representatives were not restricted to a passive role. On the contrary, they were permitted to speak, prepare working papers, and make proposals,[9] albeit caveated by the possibility of the WGIP rescinding permission if Indigenous peoples' representatives departed from the applicable procedures.[10]

In practice, Indigenous peoples' representatives took advantage of this status to make formal written and oral presentations, while also informally lobbying WGIP members and state delegates.[11] They convened preparatory meetings before the WGIP's sessions to formulate common positions and initiatives.[12] In addition, several states included Indigenous peoples' representatives on their delegations, including Australia, Norway, and Sweden.[13] Levels of attendance at first were modest:[14] Indigenous representation was limited to delegates from a few higher-income countries, as well as those who happened to be close to Geneva and hence able to travel to the meetings; moreover, a lot of grassroots Indigenous organizations 'totally ignored' the WGIP.[15] However,

participation, see Dorotheé Cambou, 'Enhancing the Participation of Indigenous Peoples at the Intergovernmental Level to Strengthen Self-Determination: Lessons from the Arctic' (2018) 87 *Nordic Journal of International Law*, 26–55, 40; Douglas Sanders, 'The UN Working Group on Indigenous Populations' (1989) 11 *Human Rights Quarterly*, 406–433, 408.

9 Asbjørn Eide, 'The Indigenous Peoples, the Working Group on Indigenous Populations and the Adoption of the UN Declaration on the Rights of Indigenous Peoples' in Claire Charters and Rodolfo Stavenhagen, (eds), *Making the Declaration Work: The United Nations Declaration on the Rights of Indigenous Peoples* (Copenhagen: IWGIA, 2009), 32–47, 34, 36.

10 Augusto Willemsen Diaz, 'How Indigenous Peoples' Rights Reached the UN' in Claire Charters and Rodolfo Stavenhagen, (eds), *Making the Declaration Work: The United Nations Declaration on the Rights of Indigenous Peoples* (Copenhagen: IWGIA, 2009), 16–31, 27.

11 Gudmundur Alfredsson, 'Fourth Session of the Working Group on Indigenous Populations' (1986) 55 *Nordic Journal of International Law*, 22–30, 24.

12 Office of the UN High Commissioner on Human Rights (OHCHR), 'Fact Sheet No. 9 (Rev.1), The Rights of Indigenous Peoples' (1997) 3.

13 Alfredsson, 'Fourth Session of the Working Group', 25. Unfortunately, detail is sparse regarding how these arrangements operated.

14 Andrea Muehlebach, '"Making Place" at the United Nations: Indigenous Cultural Politics at the U.N. Working Group on Indigenous Populations' (2001) 16 *Cultural Anthropology*, 415–448, 420.

15 Rodolfo Stavenhagen, 'The Rights and Participation of Indigenous Peoples: A Challenge for Our Time', in ECOSOC, 'Working Group on Indigenous Populations: Consideration of a Permanent Forum for Indigenous People' (6 July 1995) UN Doc. E/CN.4/Sub.2/AC.4/1995/7/Add.2, para. 3.

over time, the WGIP played host to increasingly large numbers of Indigenous representatives. While in 1988, for instance, 10 Indigenous NGOs and 76 other Indigenous organizations participated,[16] just four years later around a thousand Indigenous participants showed up, representing hundreds of groups from all five UN regions.[17] This represented a huge increase in participant numbers above that which would have been possible had only ECOSOC-accredited organizations been able to participate: As of 1993, only twelve Indigenous peoples' organizations had consultative status with ECOSOC, and of these, only one was from Latin America and none came from the Asia-Pacific region.[18]

As historians have noted, the advocacy of Indigenous peoples themselves was key to creating the conditions for the WGIP and its participatory practices to be brought into being.[19] But the additional role of individual international lawyers should not be overlooked either. Particularly notable is the part one staff member of the Sub-Commission, Augusto Willemsen Diaz, played in promoting this mode of participation.[20] In his own words, Willemsen Diaz proactively 'sought ways of opening [the WGIP] up to the involvement of Indigenous peoples' as he was 'concerned about the restrictive effect' of the requirement for ECOSOC consultative status and 'felt it absurd, and contradictory in the extreme, to create a working group to listen to Indigenous organizations' representatives and then to demand that they have consultative status before they could participate in its sessions', likening it to 'destroying with one hand what you had just finished building with the other'.[21] Indeed, Willemsen Diaz was a key in developing the idea for the WGIP in the first place, presenting the proposal at a symposium at the University of Cambridge in 1974 before proposing it to the UN.[22] The role of Asbjørn Eide, then Chair of the WGIP, is also notable, in taking the decision to admit non-ECOSOC-accredited Indigenous peoples' organizations.[23] Willemsen

16 Sanders, 'The UN Working Group', 410.
17 Willemsen Diaz, 'How Indigenous Peoples' Rights', 27.
18 Commission on Human Rights, 'Future Role of the Working Group: Note by the Chairperson-Rapporteur of the Working Group on Indigenous Populations' (15 July 1993) UN Doc. E/CN.4/Sub.2/AC.4/1993/8, para. 10.
19 Lightfoot, *Global Indigenous Politics*.
20 Willemsen Diaz, 'How Indigenous Peoples' Rights'.
21 Ibid., 26. Willemsen Diaz was the key driver within the UN behind the creation of the WGIP and played a key part in the writing of the Martinez Cobo report as well as the creation of the Voluntary Fund for Indigenous Populations.
22 Ibid., 25.
23 Willemsen Diaz explains the process of how this decision was arrived at, on a proposal of Asbjørn Eide, the then Chair of the WGIP: Ibid., 27.

Diaz writes that it was considered important to 'make sure that those who attended the WGIP were actually the real and legitimate representatives of those peoples and communities and that they were attending to provide information on their problems and contribute to ways of resolving them'.[24] In this latter regard, he notes that '[w]ays of ensuring that the WGIP's sessions were conducted in line with UN standards would be sought and most certainly found ... the WGIP always having the right to bring the behaviour of participants and the practices emerging in the sessions in line with the relevant regulations'. Willemsen Diaz in this way expresses his concerns as to the representativeness of Indigenous attendees, as well as their manner of conduct during meetings. However, it is unclear on the papers whether and to what extent the WGIP exercised oversight regarding the identity of the Indigenous representatives, nor their manner of conduct during meetings. The WGIP's documents do not indicate any criteria that Indigenous participants were required to meet, nor indeed any accreditation process at all. Nor do the records indicate that any restrictions on conduct were used. Willemsen Diaz himself seemed convinced that Indigenous peoples 'would come in good faith' without resorting to 'deviations, excesses or abuses'.[25]

In any case, by the time that the WGIP had been in operation for a few years, states were evidently sufficiently in favour of Indigenous peoples' participation to recognize the need to fund it. In 1985, the General Assembly established the Voluntary Fund for Indigenous Populations (Voluntary Fund), with the purpose of assisting Indigenous representatives to participate in the WGIP's deliberations.[26] The Voluntary Fund, which to this day provides financial assistance for travel and subsistence costs of Indigenous peoples' representatives to various UN processes, funded by voluntary contributions from states and other actors alike, is administered by the Secretary-General on the advice of a five-person board of which one member must be a

24 Rather than, perhaps, to protest or disrupt proceedings: Ibid., 26.

25 Ibid.

26 UNGA Res. 40/131 (13 December 1985). The Fund's mandate has subsequently been expanded to support Indigenous peoples' participation in the PFII, the EMRIP, the Human Rights Council and human rights treaty bodies, and the consultation process on the procedural and institutional steps to enable the participation of Indigenous peoples' representatives and institutions in meetings of relevant UN bodies on issues affecting them during the 70th and 71st sessions of the GA: UNGA Res. 56/140 (19 December 2001); UNGA Res. 63/161 (18 December 2008); UNGA Res. 65/198 (21 December 2010); UNGA Res. 70/232 (23 December 2015). Note that the process of establishing the Fund was in train since the very first session of the WGIP: see Sub-Commission on Prevention of Discrimination and Protection of Minorities Res. 1982/31 (29 September 1982) UN Doc. E/CN.4/Sub.2/RES/1982/31.

representative of an Indigenous peoples' organization.[27] The Fund facilitated relatively small, but not insignificant, numbers of Indigenous representatives to attend the WGIP.[28] The criteria for accessing the fund were that beneficiaries had to be 'representatives of indigenous peoples' organizations and communities', who would not be able to attend the WGIP without the Fund's assistance, and who would be 'able to contribute to a deeper knowledge on the part of the Working Group of the problems affecting indigenous populations and who would secure a broad geographical representation'.[29] According to Willemsen Diaz, who drew up the proposal for the Fund, it was motivated by the need for genuine Indigenous participation in the WGIP: It 'linked to the vital participation of genuine indigenous peoples' and communities' representatives to ensure the authenticity of the presentations' on which the WGIP's actions had to be based.[30] More broadly, the establishment of the Voluntary Fund by the General Assembly also demonstrated member states' collective and implicit acknowledgement, authorization, and support of the practice of enabling participation that had begun on the WGIP's own initiative.

In the WGIP, Indigenous peoples' participation translated into influence over outcomes. While some scholars have dismissed Indigenous peoples' participation at the WGIP as mere 'performance' and 'social drama',[31] the accepted view, as Asbjørn Eide and James Anaya among others have it, is that their views were 'increasingly taken into account'.[32] The first complete draft of the declaration, produced in 1988, 'substantially reflected' proposals submitted by Indigenous peoples' representatives.[33] According to Anaya, the WGIP was an 'important platform for the dissemination of information and exchange

[27] According to a 2010 report, 'in practice, indigenous persons have been regularly appointed as members of the Board': Human Rights Council, 'Practical Implications of a change in the mandate of the Voluntary Fund for Indigenous Populations' (5 July 2010) UN Doc. A/HRC/15/38. At times, the board has been 100% Indigenous: Willemsen Diaz, 'How Indigenous Peoples' Rights', 29.

[28] For instance, the Fund offered financial assistance to twenty-seven people in 1988 and thirty-seven people in 1989: Commission on Human Rights, 'Report of the Working Group on Indigenous Populations on its seventh session' (25 August 1989) UN Doc. E/CN.4/Sub.2/1989/36, para. 25 ("WGIP 7th Session Report").

[29] UNGA Res. 40/131, para. (d).

[30] Willemsen Diaz, 'How Indigenous Peoples' Rights', 29.

[31] Patrick Thornberry, *Indigenous Peoples and Human Rights* (Manchester: Manchester University Press, 2002), 22.

[32] Eide, 'The Indigenous Peoples', 36.

[33] S. James Anaya, *Indigenous Peoples in International Law*, 2nd ed. (Oxford: Oxford University Press, 2004), 63; see Sub-Commission on Prevention of Discrimination and Protection of Minorities, 'Universal Declaration on Indigenous Rights: A Set of Preambular Paragraphs and Principles' (1988) UN Doc. E/CN.4/Sub.2/1988/25. See also Alfredsson, 'Fourth Session of the Working Group', 24.

of views' among Indigenous peoples, states, and NGOs, and the process of drafting the declaration was 'an important means for indigenous peoples to promote their own conceptions about their rights'.[34]

In addition to enabling Indigenous peoples and their organizations to contribute to the development of the UNDRIP and draw attention to domestic situations, the WGIP also provided a platform for Indigenous peoples to advocate for greater participation and representation in other processes. For instance, at the WGIP's fifth meeting, in 1987, Indigenous representatives made statements to the effect that 'indigenous nations, as subjects of international law, should have access to the International Court of Justice and that they should be allowed seats at the General Assembly'.[35] Indigenous representatives also recommended that the ILO's revision process of Convention 107 should have greater Indigenous participation[36] and that multilateral development banks should draft codes of conduct, in consultation with Indigenous representatives, regarding the conditions for loans relating to Indigenous lands, and should accept the principle of active participation by Indigenous peoples in resource development projects.[37] In subsequent years, similar recommendations were made to, among others, the Preparatory Committees of the 1992 Rio Earth Summit,[38] decision-makers regarding the International Year for the World's Indigenous People,[39] and the ILO, the UN Children's Fund, and the UN Educational, Scientific, and Cultural Organization (UNESCO).[40] On several occasions, the WGIP was host to substantial discussions about the idea of a permanent forum within the UN for the consideration of Indigenous peoples' issues.[41]

34 Anaya, *Indigenous Peoples*, 63–64.

35 Commission on Human Rights, 'Report of the Working Group on Indigenous Populations on Its Fifth Session' (24 August 1997) UN Doc. E/CN.4/Sub.2/1987/22, para. 77 ("WGIP 5th Session Report"). As discussed in Chapter 4, this latter demand was to make its way, more than 30 years later, to discussions in the General Assembly.

36 Covered below, section 3.1.

37 WGIP 5th Session Report, 78

38 Commission on Human Rights, 'Report of the Working Group on Indigenous Populations on Its Eighth Session' (27 August 1990) UN Doc. E/CN.4/Sub.2/1990/42, Annex I, para. 12 ("WGIP 8th Session Report").

39 Commission on Human Rights, 'Report of the Working Group on Indigenous Populations on Its Ninth Session' (3 October 1991) UN Doc. E/CN.4/Sub.2/1991/40/Rev.1, Annex I, para. 23.

40 Commission on Human Rights, 'Report of the Working Group on Indigenous Populations on Its 11th Session' UN Doc. E/CN.4/Sub.2/1993/29, paras. 193 and 229 ("WGIP 11th Session Report").

41 See, for example, WGIP 11th Session Report, paras. 190–193; Commission on Human Rights, 'Report of the Working Group on Indigenous Populations on Its Fifteenth Session' (13 August 1997) UN Doc. E/CN.4/Sub.2/1997/14, paras. 109–124 ("WGIP 15th Session Report").

Although the WGIP's and states' practice served as a way for Indigenous peoples to 'make place' for themselves within the UN,[42] strengthen their own identities and sense of solidarity,[43] and participate 'fully and very actively as proponents and direct drafters' in the making of their rights under international law,[44] it cannot be seen as supporting the formation of a rule of custom under the two-element approach. There is no evidence to suggest that the participation of Indigenous peoples was regarded by the Working Group or UN member states as required by law. Rather, according to Willemsen Diaz at least, it seems to have been enabled in response to increased demands by Indigenous peoples, as well due to the recognition that it would be essential in order for the WGIP to 'fulfil its tasks appropriately'.[45] Participants repeatedly stressed the importance of dialogue between representatives of governments and Indigenous peoples in order for the WGIP's standard-setting activities to be effective.[46] These factors continued to carry weight as the draft Declaration advanced further through the UN system.

3.2.2 *The Working Group on the Draft Declaration*

Following a process of revision, in which Indigenous peoples were consulted along with states and other non-state actors,[47] the WGIP completed its final draft Declaration text in 1993.[48] As the WGIP's work on the draft Declaration came to an end, the Commission on Human Rights established a new body with the sole purpose of developing a draft Declaration on the Rights of

42 Muehlebach, 'Making Place', 440.

43 Stamatopoulou, 'Indigenous Peoples and the United Nations', 69.

44 Willemsen Diaz, 'How Indigenous Peoples' Rights', 28.

45 Ibid., 26; Eide, 'The Indigenous Peoples', 34.

46 WGIP 5th Session Report, para. 30.

47 Sub-Commission on Prevention of Discrimination and Protection of Minorities, 'First Revised Text of the Draft Universal Declaration on the Rights of Indigenous Peoples' (1989) UN Doc. E/CN.4/Sub.2/1989/33; Anaya, *Indigenous Peoples*, 84 note 90; Working Group on Indigenous Populations, 'Annotations to the Provisional Agenda' (8 June 1994) UN Doc. E/CN.4/Sub.2/AC.4/1994/1/Add.1, paras. 5–7.

48 WGIP 11th Session Report, Annex I. This was adopted by the Sub-Commission in 1994 and forwarded to the Commission on Human Rights: Sub-Commission on Prevention of Discrimination and Protection of Minorities Res. 1994/45 (26 August 1994), 'Draft United Nations Declaration on the Rights of Indigenous Peoples'; Sub-Commission on Prevention of Discrimination and Protection of Minorities, 'Report on Its 46th Session' (1994) UN Doc. E/CN.4/Sub.2/1994/5. Commission on Human Rights Res. 1995/32 (3 March 1995).

Indigenous Peoples: the Working Group on the Draft Declaration (WGDD).[49]

Emulating the WGIP, the ECOSOC authorized the observer participation of Indigenous peoples' organizations not possessing ECOSOC consultative status for the WGDD's sessions, citing their 'special knowledge and understanding of the current situation of the world's Indigenous people and their human rights needs'.[50] The meetings of the WGDD were declared to be informal – thus avoiding the need for the stringent rules of procedure that would usually apply to such meetings – and Indigenous peoples were entitled to attend WGDD meetings as observers, make oral interventions, and submit written proposals (although the latter were not issued as official documents).[51] In addition, it was agreed that the requisite consensus on the draft text would need to encompass both states and Indigenous peoples.[52] Like the WGIP, then, the WGDD enabled the active participation of Indigenous peoples on the same footing as states, despite the fact that on the face of things the former were labelled "observers," translating into 'significant substantive influence' over the outcome of the draft Declaration.[53]Again echoing the WGIP, in addition to the general WGDD procedures, states such as Denmark and Norway included Indigenous representatives on their delegations.[54]

One difference from the WGIP, however, was that the WGDD required the accreditation of organizations without consultative status. An Indigenous peoples' organization wishing to participate was required to apply to the

[49] Taking into account the WGIP's draft. Commission on Human Rights Res. 1995/32. For detailed accounts of the discussions at the WGDD, see John B. Henriksen, 'The UN Declaration on the Rights of Indigenous Peoples: Some Key Issues and Events in the Process' in Claire Charters and Rodolfo Stavenhagen (eds.), *Making the Declaration Work: The United Nations Declaration on the Rights of Indigenous Peoples* (Copenhagen: IWGIA, 2009), 78–85; Luis Enrique Chávez, 'The Declaration on the Rights of Indigenous Peoples Breaking the *Impasse*: The Middle Ground' in Claire Charters and Rodolfo Stavenhagen (eds.), *Making the Declaration Work: The United Nations Declaration on the Rights of Indigenous Peoples* (Copenhagen: IWGIA, 2009), 96–107.

[50] ECOSOC Res. 1995/32, paras. 4 and 7; Commission on Human Rights Res. 1995/32. The accreditation procedure for such organizations was set out in the Annex to Commission Res. 1995/32, 'Procedures for participation by organizations of indigenous people in the open-ended inter-sessional working group established by the Commission on Human Rights to elaborate a draft declaration on the rights of indigenous peoples' (WGDD Participation Procedures).

[51] WGDD Participation Procedures, paras. 6, 7, and 8.

[52] Henriksen, 'Key Issues and Events', 79.

[53] Ibid., 79. It should be noted that this level of participation was gained in large part by mobilizations from Indigenous peoples' representatives, including a walk out and a hunger strike in the room.

[54] Ibid., 81.

Assistant Secretary-General for Human Rights, in their capacity as Coordinator of the International Decade of the World's Indigenous People, with information on the organization's aims and purposes, its programmes and activities, and its membership.[55] The Coordinator was then required to consult with any state concerned and then forward the application and any information received to the ECOSOC Committee on Non-Governmental Organizations for its decision.[56] Thus, in principle, the state concerned could object to accreditation.[57] In practice, however, states rarely if ever objected,[58] and there is no record of the ECOSOC Committee rejecting an application.[59] Once accredited, an organization was entitled to participate in all future sessions of the WGDD.[60]

The WGDD arrangements for Indigenous peoples' participation have subsequently been widely considered to be "best practice."[61] A World Intellectual Property Organization (WIPO) study considered the WGDD to be 'a good example of an inclusive and participatory UN process that contributed to the legitimacy of its outcome'.[62] It undoubtedly represented the international community's endorsement of the need for Indigenous peoples' participation in the setting of standards on their own rights. However, the level of participation of Indigenous peoples in the process was ultimately limited when the draft Declaration reached the General Assembly.

3.2.3 *Adoption of the Declaration in the General Assembly*

The WGDD process concluded in 2006 with the referral by the Sub-Commission and the subsequent adoption by the Human Rights Council of

55 WGDD Participation Procedures, para. 3.

56 WGDD Participation Procedures, para. 4. The workings of the Council Committee of the Non-Governmental Organizations are governed by ECOSOC Res. 1296 (XLIV) (23 May 1968).

57 Willemsen Diaz, 'How Indigenous Peoples' Rights', 28.

58 Human Rights Council, 'Progress Report on the Study on Indigenous Peoples and the Right to Participate in Decision-Making: Report of the Expert Mechanism on the Rights of Indigenous Peoples' (23 August 2010) UN Doc. A/HRC/15/35, para. 27.

59 For examples of the approval of applications, see ECOSOC, 'Report of the Committee on Non-Governmental Organizations on the First Part of its 1998 Session' (19 June 1998) UN Doc. E/1998/72, Draft Decision III.

60 WGDD Participation Procedures, para. 5.

61 See, for example, Grand Council of the Crees, Letter to Claire Charters (2012), accessible at www.ohchr.org/EN/Issues/IPeoples/Pages/ConsultationonIPparticipationintheUN.aspx.

62 WIPO, 'Draft Study on the Participation of Observers in the Work of the Intergovernmental Committee on Intellectual Property and Genetic Resources, Traditional Knowledge and Folklore' (2012) WIPO Doc. WIPO/GRTKF/IC/20/7, Annex, para. 11.

a draft Declaration.[63] Upon the transferral of the draft Declaration to the General Assembly, Indigenous peoples' representatives who had actively participated in the process for more than 20 years found themselves with a 'greatly diminished voice' by comparison with the process in the WGIP and WGDD.[64] Owing to the strict rules of procedure applicable to the General Assembly and its Third Committee,[65] which states did not feel able to deviate from in this instance, Indigenous peoples could not participate in the discussion. They were cut out of negotiations as a small minority of states that opposed the Human Rights Council's draft pushed to alter provisions relating to the right to self-determination, the definition of Indigenous peoples, and state sovereignty, among other matters, which resulted in the process temporarily stalling for several months.[66] Lobbying from outside the process, perhaps inevitably, did not approach the levels of influence over outcomes that Indigenous peoples had previously exercised from within the process. Indigenous peoples were informed about a final set of changes made by states a week before the UNDRIP's adoption in 2007,[67] but there is no evidence that they were able to exercise any influence over the alterations. The extent of Indigenous peoples' participation in the making of the UNDRIP over the course of 25 years had been substantial, taking place by way of direct negotiations between Indigenous peoples and states, but ultimately came up against hard limits imposed by the centrality of states to the UN. States' willingness to share power with Indigenous peoples stretched only so far; states retained control over the final result.

For this reason, while the novelty and importance of the WGIP's participatory procedures should not be understated – as Daes put it, 'no other UN human rights instrument ha[d] ever been elaborated with so much direct involvement and active participation on the part of its intended

[63] The Council had recently replaced the Commission: Human Rights Council Res. 2006/2 (29 June 2006).

[64] Andrea Carmen, 'International Indian Treaty Council Report from the Battle Field – The Struggle for the Declaration' in Claire Charters and Rodolfo Stavenhagen (eds.), *Making the Declaration Work: The United Nations Declaration on the Rights of Indigenous Peoples* (Copenhagen: IWGIA, 2009), 86–95, 98.

[65] UN, Rules of Procedure of the General Assembly (2021) UN Doc. A/520/Rev.19.

[66] See Joshua Castellino and Cathal Doyle, 'Who Are 'Indigenous Peoples'? An Examination of Concepts Concerning Group Membership in the UNDRIP' in Jessie Hohmann and Marc Weller (eds.), *The UN Declaration on the Rights of Indigenous People: A Commentary* (Oxford: Oxford University Press, 2018), 7–37, 28; Eide, 'The Indigenous Peoples', 38–40.

[67] Carmen, 'Report from the Battle Field', 98. Although these changes were relatively minor, not substantially deviating from the Human Rights Council's draft, with the exception of Article 46.

beneficiaries'[68] – from the perspective of many Indigenous peoples, it represented only a first step. Even though it was the first time that Indigenous peoples had a sustained institutional voice at the UN, the WGIP was 'at the lowest level in the system':[69] Its recommendations had to go through the Sub-Commission, the Commission on Human Rights, the ECOSOC, the Third Committee, and the General Assembly before ultimately being approved. Many Indigenous peoples thus perceived, not unreasonably, that the UN was treating them as 'second-class citizens' as compared with UN member states.[70]

Despite the ultimate limitations of the UNDRIP process, in the course of the late 1980s and early 1990s, the influence of the WGIP's participation practices was already being felt elsewhere in the UN system.

3.3 EARLY RIPPLES, 1988–1993

3.3.1 *ILO Convention No. 169, 1989*

When the WGIP began work towards the elaboration of an instrument on Indigenous peoples' rights in 1985, the ILO was put on notice regarding the need to update its own standards. The ILO's then flagship instrument on Indigenous peoples, the 1957 ILO Convention Concerning the Protection and Integration of Indigenous and Other Tribal and Semi-Tribal Populations in Independent Countries (ILO Convention 107),[71] was premised on the assimilation of Indigenous peoples into dominant political and social orders and was developed without the participation of Indigenous peoples' representatives.[72] While considered by some to be progressive at the time of its adoption, as its objective was to promote improved social and economic conditions for Indigenous populations, by the 1980s its assimilationist approach was subject to increasingly harsh criticism and began to be perceived by states as outdated.[73]

[68] Daes, 'Contribution', 74.

[69] Sanders, 'The UN Working Group', 407.

[70] Julian Burger, 'United Nations Working Group on Indigenous Populations: The United Nations and Indigenous Peoples' in Lydia van de Fliert (ed.), *Indigenous Peoples and International Organizations* (Nottingham: Russel Press, 1994), 90, 92.

[71] Convention concerning the Protection and Integration of Indigenous and Other Tribal and Semi-Tribal Populations in Independent Countries (adopted 26 June 1957 and entered into force 2 June 1959) 328 UNTS 247.

[72] See the discussion in Anaya, *Indigenous Peoples*, 44–45.

[73] Lee Swepston, 'A New Step in the International Law on Indigenous and Tribal Peoples: ILO Convention No. 169 of 1989' (1990) 15 *Oklahoma City University Law Review*, 677–752, 687.

In 1986, the ILO held an expert meeting including Indigenous peoples' representatives, which firmly recommended revision of the Convention.[74] Subsequently, the ILO's Governing Body decided to include the revision of Convention 107 on the agenda of the International Labour Conferences in 1988 and 1989.[75] Since the initiative stemmed from the ILO Secretariat rather than from Indigenous peoples or indeed from the ILO's employers' and workers' constituencies, as Anaya and Rodriguez-Pinero note, there was 'little or no initial involvement from the international Indigenous rights movement and other actors active in the UN discussion'.[76]

This lack of involvement was raised for discussion at the WGIP itself in 1987. Indigenous observers criticized the ILO for not offering Indigenous peoples 'reasonable opportunities for effective consultation, participation and negotiation in the revision process'. In addition, the substance of the draft Convention, in their view, did not sufficiently depart from the old instrument's integrationist and assimilationist approach.[77] While some Indigenous observers seemed more positive about the process, merely encouraging the ILO to allow for Indigenous participation in the drafting process, others suggested that the ILO should defer the consideration of the revision until it had devised new procedures for securing full Indigenous participation.[78] The ILO representative at the WGIP, for his part, acknowledged that the level of participation 'was not as high as the representatives of indigenous and tribal populations would wish', but stressed 'existing possibilities' for Indigenous peoples to participate including official non-governmental observer status or inclusion in government, employer, or worker delegations.[79]

Following the 1987 WGIP meeting, some steps were taken to increase Indigenous peoples' participation in the revision process. The ILO made a then-unprecedented appeal to governments to consult representative

[74] WGIP 5th Session Report, para. 37.

[75] ILO Governing Body, 'Minutes of the 234th Session' (November 1986) ILO Doc. GB.234/PV (Rev.) I/8.

[76] S. James Anaya and Luis Rodríguez-Piñero, 'The Making of the UNDRIP' in Jessie Hohmann and Marc Weller (eds.), *The UN Declaration on the Rights of Indigenous People: A Commentary* (Oxford: Oxford University Press, 2018), 38–62, 144. See also Anaya, *Indigenous Peoples*, 58–61; Luis Rodríguez-Piñero, *Indigenous Peoples, Postcolonialism, and International Law: The ILO Regime (1919–1989)* (Oxford: Oxford University Press, 2005), 291–331.

[77] WGIP 5th Session Report, para. 40.

[78] Ibid., paras. 39–40. The same concerns were raised at the WGIP's 6th Session: Commission on Human Rights, 'Report of the WGIP on its 6th session' (24 August 1988) UN Doc. E/CN.4/Sub.2/1988/24, para. 94.

[79] WGIP 5th Session Report, para. 38.

organizations of Indigenous and tribal people.[80] The responses to this appeal were analysed and summarized in a submission by the International Labour Office to the 1988 International Labour Conference, along with proposed conclusions. After the 1988 Conference, its report was circulated along with a proposed draft to governments, who were again invited to consult with Indigenous peoples. In addition, as Lee Swepston, the then Assistant to the Director of the International Labour Standards Department of the International Labour Office, writes, the ILO made space on many occasions during meetings of the Conference for NGOs representing Indigenous and tribal peoples or speaking on their behalf to address both the plenary and the drafting committee.[81] At the time, this represented a significant procedural innovation for the ILO. The ILO developed the practice of "suspending" a governmental meeting, to enable Indigenous peoples to speak without implying recognition of governmental status.[82] Swepston argues that in this way Indigenous peoples' organizations were able to influence the submission of amendments to the draft texts, as well as through NGO proposals submitted through the workers' group.[83] Swepston's statement is interesting not because it evidences efforts by the ILO to allow Indigenous peoples' representation as much as possible within the bounds of pre-existing rules of procedure but also because it demonstrates a senior ILO official's desire to make it known that the ILO did make efforts to enable Indigenous peoples' participation. In this way, the idea first instantiated in the WGIP that it was important to allow Indigenous peoples to participate in matters concerning them clearly influenced the behaviour of international civil servants in a different organization.

Moreover, some Indigenous peoples participated in the making of ILO Convention 169 through national delegations. For instance, representatives of the Sámi 'were active and played an important role'[84] in the 1988 and 1989 International Labour Conferences, via both the government and worker delegations of Norway, Sweden, and Finland.[85] In addition, the ILO

[80] ILO, Partial revision of the Indigenous and Tribal Populations Convention, 1957 (No. 107), Report VI(1), at 2.

[81] Swepston, 'A New Step', 686.

[82] Russel Lawrence Barsh, 'Indigenous Peoples in the 1990s: From Object to Subject of International Law' (1994) 7 *Harvard Human Rights Journal*, 33–86, 66, note 158.

[83] Swepston, 'A New Step', 686.

[84] Henry Minde, 'Sami Land Rights in Norway: A Test Case for Indigenous Peoples' (2001) 8 *International Journal on Minority and Group Rights*, 107–125, 117.

[85] The latter conference was where ILO Convention 169 was adopted.

Workers Group submitted proposals and voted on the advice of Indigenous representatives, indirectly giving them one-third of the votes in the drafting committee.[86]

Despite these measures, the level of participation of Indigenous peoples in the ILO process, while not nil, was formally much more limited than that in the WGIP. For this reason, following the Convention's adoption at the close of the 1989 International Labour Conference, some Indigenous participants at the WGIP expressed a 'lack of confidence' in the process on the basis of inadequate consultation with Indigenous peoples, although others expressed confidence in the new Convention.[87] What is evident is that the WGIP constituted both a visible example of what Indigenous peoples' participation could (and according to indigenous peoples, should) resemble and a platform by which Indigenous peoples could advocate for more participation in the ILO. It is likely that this had some bearing on the small but not insignificant changes that the ILO and its member states did make to enable a degree of Indigenous peoples' participation in the 1988 and 1989 International Labour Conferences. In the following years, more Indigenous participation was seen in other UN bodies and meetings.

3.3.2 *UN Expert Meetings, 1989–1992*

The UN convened several expert meetings related to Indigenous peoples' issues from 1989 onwards. Following recommendations by the WGIP,[88] a practice was established whereby Indigenous peoples participated on an equal footing with states in these expert meetings.[89] These meetings provided another platform where, in turn, Indigenous peoples could advocate for increased representation and participation in intergovernmental fora, among other demands.

The first such meeting, which considered effects of racism and racial discrimination on the social and economic relations between Indigenous peoples and states, took place in Geneva, Switzerland, in January 1989 as part of the UN's Programme to Combat Racism and Racial Discrimination.[90]

86 Russel Lawrence Barsh, 'An Advocate's Guide to the Convention on Indigenous and Tribal Peoples' (1990) 15 *Oklahoma City University Law Review*, 209–236, 210.

87 WGIP 7th Session Report, para. 31.

88 See, for example, WGIP 8th Session Report, Annex I, para. 15.

89 Commission on Human Rights, 'Future Role of the Working Group', para. 8.

90 The report of the session can be found at Commission on Human Rights, 'Report on the United Nations Seminar on the Effects of Racism and Racial Discrimination on the Social and

According to Russel Barsh, the then Representative of the Mikmaq Grand Council to the UN, aggressive lobbying by the WGIP and Indigenous peoples persuaded the Centre for Human Rights[91] to experiment with including experts nominated by Indigenous organizations as well as by states.[92] Invitations to nominate expert participants were thus extended to fifteen governments and ten Indigenous organizations, on the basis of geographical distribution; when the seminar eventually met, there were nine Indigenous peoples' nominees and ten government nominees.[93] As the then Under-Secretary-General for Human Rights, Jan Martenson, remarked in opening comments, this was the first time that Indigenous peoples' organizations, and in fact any NGO, had nominated experts on an equal basis with governments to take part in a UN seminar.[94] The meeting was welcomed by Indigenous participants in the WGIP as 'the first forum within the context of the United Nations at which government representatives and representatives of indigenous peoples met on an equal footing'.[95]

In addition to the expert participants, several Indigenous peoples' organizations, including both those in consultative status with ECOSOC and those not in possession of such status, sent observers.[96] Further strengthening the level of participation, and representing a further procedural innovation, the participants agreed to elect an Indigenous nominee as the Rapporteur alongside a government nominee as the Chair,[97] as well as to make decisions by consensus among all participants.[98] The procedural inclusion of Indigenous representatives was reflected in the meeting's outputs, which in turn further stressed the need for participation. The recommendations of the meeting reflected Indigenous viewpoints, including the recommendation that Indigenous peoples have the right to self-determination and that their relationships with states 'be based on upon free and informed consent, and co-operation', as well as the incorporation of Indigenous rights in the work of all

Economic Relations Between Indigenous Peoples and States' (1989) UN Doc. E/CN.4/1989/22 ("Geneva Seminar Report").

91 Now the OHCHR.

92 Russel Lawrence Barsh, 'United Nations Seminar on Indigenous Peoples and States' (1989) 83 *American Journal of International Law*, 599–604, 600. As Barsh chronicles, there was a significant political debate over whether Indigenous peoples should be able to nominate experts.

93 Geneva Seminar Report, para. 3; Annex I, 'List of Participants', 15–16.

94 Ibid., Annex II, 'Opening statement by Mr. Jan Martenson', 21.

95 WGIP 7th Session Report, para. 27.

96 Geneva Seminar Report, Annex I, 'List of Participants', 17–18.

97 Geneva Seminar Report, Annex IV, 'Statement by Mrs. Erica-Irene A. Daes', 72.

98 Geneva Seminar Report, para. 40.

international organizations involved with the development process 'with the direct participation of indigenous peoples'.[99]

A second expert meeting, charged with reviewing the experience of countries regarding internal self-government for Indigenous peoples, was convened in Nuuk, Greenland, in September 1991, in connection with the UN's Second Decade to Combat Racism and Racial Discrimination.[100] The first official UN meeting to be held in recognised Indigenous territory, the expert meeting invited sixteen governments and twelve Indigenous organizations, including five that lacked ECOSOC consultative status;[101] ten and eight, respectively, participated.[102] As with the Geneva meeting, Indigenous peoples' organizations both with and without ECOSOC consultative status also attended.[103] The Chair was held by Jonathan Motzfeldt, the former Prime Minister of Greenland and an instrumental figure in the establishment of Greenland Home Rule by which Greenland has full autonomy on most matters; a representative of the Philippines was elected to the role of Rapporteur, continuing the Geneva practice of splitting leadership roles between Indigenous peoples and states.[104] Again, the report of the meeting reflected Indigenous peoples' proposals, affirming Indigenous peoples' right to self-determination and recommending governments periodically review obstacles to Indigenous autonomy and self-government.[105]

The third meeting, on the sustainable self-development of Indigenous peoples, was held in May 1992 as part of preparations for the Rio Conference on Environment and Development, in Santiago, Chile.[106] Like the other seminars, it occurred following the WGIP's recommendation.[107] Invitations to the meeting were extended to fourteen governments and

[99] Ibid., 40(e), 41(a), 41(b), and 41(u).

[100] Commission on Human Rights, 'Report of the Meeting of Experts to Review the Experience of Countries in the Operation of Schemes of Internal Self-government for Indigenous Peoples' (1992) UN Doc. E/CN.4/1992/42 ("Nuuk Report"). See UNGA Res. 42/47 (30 November 1987), Annex, para. 1(b).

[101] Nuuk Report, paras. 2–3.

[102] Nuuk Report, Annex I, 'Attendance', 15.

[103] Ibid., 17.

[104] Nuuk Report, para. 12. However, note the government of Greenland is not equivalent to an Indigenous peoples' organization.

[105] Nuuk Report, para. 54.

[106] Commission on Human Rights, 'Report of the United Nations Technical Conference on Practical Experience in the Realization of Sustainable and Environmentally Sound Self-Development of Indigenous Peoples' (1992) UN Doc. E/CN.4/Sub.2/1992/31 and Add.1 ("Santiago Report").

[107] WGIP 7th Session Report, Annex I, para. 12. Also see Commission on Human Rights Res 1990/62 (7 March 1990); ECOSOC Res. 1990/238 (25 May 1990).

fourteen Indigenous organizations, of which only two had ECOSOC consultative status.[108] All the Indigenous organizations and nine of the governments ultimately sent representatives.[109] In addition, several Chilean Indigenous organizations were permitted to participate as observers, even though they had not specifically been invited by the Secretariat; some fifty-four people from twenty-six Chilean Indigenous peoples' organizations attended.[110] A representative of Chile chaired the meeting, while a representative of the Inuit Circumpolar Council served as Rapporteur.[111]

Ideas raised at the 1992 meeting by Indigenous delegates, independent experts, and government representatives included the setting up of a UN world council of Indigenous elders to advise world political, financial, and religious leaders; the invitation of Indigenous elders to address the UN General Assembly on critical world issues; and the representation of Indigenous peoples in the then-planned Commission on Sustainable Development.[112] The meeting report underscored the potential contributions of Indigenous peoples to economic sustainability and among other things recommended that UN agencies always include Indigenous representation when meeting on issues relevant to Indigenous peoples, that the World Bank and other multilateral financial institutions consult with Indigenous peoples and develop adequate procedures for the participation of Indigenous peoples in the planning, implementation, and evaluation of processes of self-development, and that intergovernmental development organizations, with the active participation of Indigenous peoples, take account of Indigenous knowledge when undertaking environmental rehabilitation work.[113]

A pattern had been set and a precedent established. In the following years, several more expert meetings convened on topics related to Indigenous peoples, in which states and Indigenous peoples participated equally, and chair and rapporteur roles were shared between state and Indigenous delegates.[114] As previously, these meetings provided a further platform for

[108] Santiago Report, paras. 2–3.
[109] Santiago Report, Annex I, para. B.
[110] Santiago Report, para. 5 and Annex I, para. H.
[111] Santiago Report, para. 13.
[112] Ibid., paras. 53 and 57.
[113] Ibid., 19–20.
[114] See, for example, Commission on Human Rights, 'Report of the Expert Seminar on Practical Experience Regarding Indigenous Land Rights and Claims' (25 May 1996) UN Doc. E/CN.4/Sub.2/AC.4/1996/6; Commission on Human Rights, 'Report of the Seminar on the Draft Principles and Guidelines for the Protection of the Heritage of Indigenous People' (19 June 2000) UN Doc. E/CN.4/Sub.2/2000/26; Commission on Human Rights, 'Report on

Indigenous experts to make recommendations regarding Indigenous participation in intergovernmental settings, for instance, in the World Bank, Global Environment Facility, the standard-setting work of the UN,[115] and intergovernmental discussions and negotiations on intellectual property rights.[116] This pattern was to continue in the years following the adoption of the UNDRIP.[117]

3.3.3 *The United Nations Conference on Environment and Development, 1992*

By 1992, Indigenous peoples had been actively and successfully participating at the WGIP for nearly a decade, and their experts had participated in UN expert meetings on the same footing as those of states. The UN Conference on Environment and Development (UNCED), held in Rio in 1992, presented Indigenous peoples with an opportunity for voice in a more visible setting. Indigenous peoples' organizations' attendance at later meetings of the Preparatory Committee led up to the Rio Conference,[118] at which delegates

the Expert Seminar on Indigenous Peoples and the Administration of Justice', November 2003, Madrid (10 June 2004) UN Doc. E/CN.4/Sub.2/AC.4/2004/6; Commission on Human Rights, 'Report on the Second Workshop on Multiculturalism in Africa: Peaceful and Constructive Group Accommodation in Situations Involving Minorities and Indigenous Peoples' (2 April 2001) UN Doc. E/CN.4/Sub.2/AC.5/2001/3; Commission on Human Rights, 'Report on the Third Workshop on Multiculturalism in Africa: Peaceful and Constructive Group Accommodation in Situations Involving Minorities and Indigenous Peoples' (17 June 2002) UN Doc. E/CN.4/Sub.2/AC.4/2002/4; Commission on Human Rights, 'Report of the Seminar on Treaties, Agreements and Other Constructive Arrangements Between States and Indigenous Peoples', Dec 2003, Geneva (1 June 2004) UN Doc. E/CN.4/Sub.2/AC.4/2004/7; Permanent Forum on Indigenous Issues, 'Report of the Workshop on Data Collection and Disaggregation for Indigenous Peoples' (10 February 2004) UN Doc. E/C.19/2004/2; Commission on Human Rights, 'Report on the Expert Seminar on Indigenous Peoples' Permanent Sovereignty over Natural Resources and Their Relationship to Land' (5 May 2006) UN Doc. E/CN.4/Sub.2/AC.4/2006/3.

115 Commission on Human Rights, 'Practical Experience Regarding Indigenous Land Rights and Claims', para. 78.

116 Commission on Human Rights, 'Protection of the Heritage of Indigenous People', para. 51.

117 See, for example, UNPFII, 'Report of the International Expert Group Meeting on Indigenous Languages' (21 January 2008) UN Doc. E/C.19/2008/3; UNPFII, 'Report of the International Expert Group Meeting on Indigenous Peoples and Forests' (11 February 2011) UN Doc. E/C.19/2011/5.

118 Preparatory Committee for the United Nations Conference on Environment and Development, 'Report of the Preparatory Committee for the United Nations Conference on Environment and Development on the Work of its Fourth Session' (12 May 1992) UN Doc. A/CONF.151/PC/128, para. 25; Report of the Preparatory Committee for the United Nations Conference on Environment and Development (21 June 1991) UN Doc. A/46/48, paras. 9 and 56.

considered drafts of the eventual Rio Declaration. Subsequently, participation at the Conference itself was opened up in a way that enabled Indigenous peoples' organizations to participate, alongside myriad other non-state and civil society actors.[119] In 1991, the Preparatory Committee for the Rio Conference invited all 'relevant' organizations to apply directly to the Committee for credentials – normally ECOSOC consultative status would be required – echoing the WGIP's practices.[120] As a result, more than forty Indigenous organizations participated at the Summit, only twelve of which had ECOSOC consultative status.[121] In opening remarks to the conference, UNCED Secretary-General Maurice Strong stressed Indigenous peoples' role as repositories of traditional knowledge and custodians of ecosystems, underscoring the need for the conference to 'hear and heed their voices, learn from their experience and respect their right to live in their own lands in accordance with their traditions, values and cultures'. He stressed that their 'full and informed participation through democratic processes at every level' is 'essential to the achievement of the objectives' of the Conference and that provision for such participation 'must be an essential feature' of the response by intergovernmental institutions to the results of the Conference.[122]

The fruits of Indigenous peoples' participation are evident in Chapter 26 of Agenda 21 on Recognizing and Strengthening the Role of Indigenous People and their Communities,[123] which was based on proposals submitted by Indigenous organizations.[124] Norway and New Zealand, which had Indigenous representatives on their official delegations,[125] agreed to sponsor the Indigenous proposals albeit with several amendments, including replacing wording on a right of Indigenous peoples to veto any development affecting

[119] At the Geneva Preparatory Committee meeting, Chief Oren R. Lyons of the Haudenosaunee addressed the meeting. He said 'Brazil 1992 will also be the 500th anniversary of the landfall of Christopher Columbus in 1492. We now have 500 years of experience and history with which to judge the effects his philosophy had upon our people and our lands. Indigenous people are preparing to meet at the same time in Brazil. … We are in one canoe for better or worse. … We respectfully request a more direct participation in the UNCED conference in Brazil'.

[120] Report of the Preparatory Committee for the United Nations Conference on Environment and Development (1991) UN Doc. A/46/48, Annex 1, dec.2/1, 21.

[121] UN, 'List of Non-governmental Organizations Recommended for Accreditation by the Secretary-General of the Conference: United Nations Conference on Environment and Development' (19 March 1991) UN Doc. A/CONF.151/PC/L.28/Add.9.

[122] UNCED, 'Report of the United Nations Conference on Environment and Development, Volume II: Proceedings of the Conference' (1993) UN Doc. A/CONF.151/26/Rev.1 (Vol. II), 50.

[123] UN Conference on Environment and Development, *Agenda 21* (1992).

[124] Barsh, 'From Object to Subject', 46, note 57.

[125] Ibid.

their territories with references to "partnership" and "collaboration."[126] The chapter has a distinct participatory bent, regarding participation of Indigenous peoples both at the national and at the international level. It states that governments and intergovernmental organizations should, in 'full participation with indigenous people and their communities', aim to fulfil objectives including the establishment of arrangements to strengthen the active participation of Indigenous people and their communities in national law- and policymaking processes, and the establishment of a process to empower Indigenous peoples and their communities.[127] Further, it states that UN organizations as well as other international development and finance organizations should take certain measures to incorporate Indigenous peoples' values, views, and knowledge, 'drawing on the active participation of indigenous people'.[128] One such measure is to organize annual inter-organizational coordination meetings in consultation with governments and Indigenous organizations.[129] Principle 22 of the Rio Declaration on Environment and Development also reflected the result of Indigenous peoples' active efforts. It provided that 'indigenous people and their communities', as well as 'other local communities', 'have a vital role in environmental management and development because of their knowledge and traditional practices'. It went to say that states should enable Indigenous peoples' 'effective participation in the achievement of sustainable development'.[130] This was to be used to bolster Indigenous peoples' arguments to participate in other intergovernmental settings.

At the WGIP's first meeting following the Rio Conference, Under-Secretary-General for Policy Coordination and Sustainable Development Nitin Desai reflected on the involvement of Indigenous peoples leading up to and during the UNCED. He emphasized that it was 'of the greatest importance' to him that the 'dialogue and partnership' with Indigenous people that had begun during the preparation of the Rio Conference be 'maintained and enhanced' in the future.[131] This hope was to bear out in the years to come – and in one instance, very soon.

[126] Ibid.

[127] Agenda 21, para. 26.3.

[128] Agenda 21, para. 26.5.

[129] Agenda 21, para. 26.5(a).

[130] Report of the United Nations Conference on Environment and Development, Annex I: Rio Declaration on Environment and Development (12 August 1992) UN Doc. A/CONF.151/26 (vol. I).

[131] WGIP 11th Session Report, para. 206.

3.3.4 *The International Year for the World's Indigenous People, 1992–1993*

A few months after the Rio Summit, Indigenous peoples' representatives found themselves for the first time addressing states from the podium of the General Assembly. Following Indigenous peoples' repeated calls for an international year to raise global awareness of their situations, in 1990, the General Assembly proclaimed 1993 the International Year of the World's Indigenous People (the Year) with the objective of strengthening international cooperation for solving problems faced by Indigenous peoples in areas such as human rights, the environment, development, education, and health.[132]

Planning for the Year was characterized by contestation as to Indigenous peoples' participation. Canadian Indigenous organizations proposed to the General Assembly that an Indigenous person be appointed as coordinator for the Year and that the Year be planned and evaluated by a formal conference of UN agencies and Indigenous peoples.[133] While neither proposal was adopted,[134] the General Assembly did agree to a technical meeting of agencies and Indigenous peoples' organizations, as well as other NGOs with a special interest in Indigenous matters, in order to devise guidelines for projects carried out under the auspices of the Year and recommend effective means for including Indigenous people in initiating, designing, and implementing projects.[135] However, few Indigenous peoples ultimately attended this meeting because it was convened in Geneva with little advance notice and no funding for travel.[136] The governments that did participate in the meeting recommended a second, more representative meeting.[137] While the second meeting, held in Geneva in August 1992, had much higher levels of participation, the meeting did not result in any decisions, nor a report, partly because the Centre for Human Rights refused to provide full documentation and interpretation services to the meeting, rendering the circulation of proposals and the preparation of a report difficult.[138]

132 UNGA Res. 45/164 (18 December 1990).
133 Barsh, 'From Object to Subject', 63.
134 Antoine Blanca, Under-Secretary-General for Human Rights, was subsequently appointed as Coordinator.
135 UNGA Res. 46/128 (17 December 1991), para. 8(a) at 200.
136 Commission on Human Rights, 'Technical Meeting on the International Year for the World's Indigenous People Convened in Accordance with General Assembly Resolution 48/128' (1992) UN Doc. E/CN.4/1992/AC.4/TM/8, paras. 7 and 25.
137 Commission on Human Rights, 'Technical Meeting on the International Year', 7–9.
138 Barsh, 'From Object to Subject', 64 fn 150.

Despite these difficulties, this second meeting sowed seeds that were to bear fruit nearly a decade later. Here, Indigenous organizations first proposed the establishment of a permanent UN council of Indigenous peoples, which they suggested should be open to the equal participation of representatives of all Indigenous nations and mandated to evaluate progress in achieving Indigenous peoples' rights and aspirations and report annually to the Secretary-General.[139] At the General Assembly shortly afterwards, in November 1992, Canadian Indigenous organizations circulated a proposal that the General Assembly recognize the right of Indigenous peoples to effective participation in UN decisions that affect them directly, and again proposed the creation of a permanent representative advisory council.[140]

Regardless of the challenges faced in the preparation of the Year, a notable event was its opening ceremony on 10 December 1992. There, twenty Indigenous leaders were invited to address a special informal meeting of the General Assembly.[141] This was the first time that Indigenous peoples' representatives had spoken from the podium of the General Assembly. In their remarks, they again called for the creation of a permanent advisory body for Indigenous peoples, and for Indigenous peoples to 'not only have a decisive voice in decisions that affect them directly, but share in all of the decisions that will shape the future of our planet'.[142] Although the ceremony was poorly attended by member states,[143] and despite the contested nature and level of Indigenous peoples' participation in planning for the Year, the symbolic importance of Indigenous peoples' first podium address to the General Assembly should not be underestimated. A mere decade on from the creation of the WGIP, Indigenous peoples had made it from the lowest rungs of the UN system to – if only fleetingly – its highest platform. The Year's influence on the participation of Indigenous peoples at the UN did not end there.

3.3.5 *The World Conference on Human Rights, 1993*

Following the designation of Indigenous peoples as a Major Group at the Rio Conference, and the increasing though still small numbers of Indigenous

[139] Commission on Human Rights, 'Reconvened Technical Meeting on the International Year for the World's Indigenous People Held in Accordance with General Assembly Resolution 46/128: Proposal Submitted by the Mikmaq Grand Council' (1992) UN Doc. E/CN.4/1992/AC.4/TM.2/CRP.1.

[140] Barsh, 'From Object to Subject', 65.

[141] UNGAOR, 47th Session, 82nd Plenary Meeting, UN Doc. A/47/PV.82, 2.

[142] Barsh, 'From Object to Subject', 67.

[143] Ibid., 66.

peoples' organizations qualified for ECOSOC consultative status, such organizations could, and did, participate in UN meetings on the same basis as NGOs. Worth highlighting, however, are occasions where the level of participation for Indigenous peoples exceeded that of NGOs. The UN World Conference on Human Rights, held in Vienna in 1993 (Vienna Conference), was one such case. Governments agreed to set aside one day of the plenary session of the Conference for a commemoration of the International Year of the World's Indigenous People, during which Indigenous representatives, including those not holding ECOSOC consultative status, could address the plenary.[144] More than a hundred Indigenous representatives attended the plenary session for this event.[145]

In the discussions at the Conference, a flashpoint issue was a draft provision of the Vienna Declaration and Programme of Action, which called on governments to 'ensure the full participation of indigenous people in all aspects of society'. During the preparatory meetings and the Conference itself, Indigenous peoples pushed, in particular, for the word 'people' to be made plural and opposed proposals, intended to undercut claims to self-determination, that the exercise of Indigenous peoples rights should only be done 'without detriment to the unity of the State' or only in a manner that contributes 'to the political and social stability of the States in which they live'.[146] The eventual provision urged states to 'ensure the full and free participation of indigenous people in all aspects of society, in particular in matters of concern to them'.[147] The Vienna Declaration also recommended further consideration of the establishment of a permanent forum for Indigenous peoples within the United Nations system, a proposal Indigenous peoples had made in connection with the Year – the first official acknowledgement by any UN body of Indigenous peoples' aspirations for a formal place in the UN system.[148]

As of 1993, then, the practice of including Indigenous peoples' representatives and organizations in intergovernmental processes on matters relating to their rights was well established in a range of UN fora. Indigenous peoples'

[144] The International Year resulted from a proposal of the Sub-Commission on the Promotion and Protection of Human Rights, 'Study of the Problem of Discrimination Against Indigenous Populations; Volume V: Conclusions, Proposals and Recommendations' (1986) UN Doc. E/CN.4/Sub.2/1986/7/Add.4, 46. Also see Sub-Commission Res. 1990/29 (31 August 1990).

[145] Barsh, 'From Object to Subject', 50.

[146] Ibid., 50–51.

[147] Vienna Declaration and Programme of Action (12 July 1993), UN Doc. A/CONF.157/23, paras. 20 and 31.

[148] Vienna Declaration and Programme of Action, para. 32.

participation was enabled over and above that otherwise possible through NGO participation routes, including allowing the attendance of representatives of organizations not accredited with ECOSOC consultative status. While Indigenous representatives used this opportunity to advocate for Indigenous peoples on many fronts, one aspect of this was using these forums as platforms to highlight the need for Indigenous peoples' participation in still other UN and international organization spaces. In this way, the practice of enabling Indigenous peoples to participate spread further and further from its origins in the WGIP.

3.4 THE UN PERMANENT FORUM ON INDIGENOUS ISSUES

A permanent forum on Indigenous issues had first been proposed by Indigenous peoples in 1992 in connection with the Year of the World's Indigenous People. The suggestion was taken up by the Vienna Declaration and Programme of Action, and General Assembly and Commission on Human Rights resolutions followed in 1993 and 1994.[149] Following discussion of the matter by the WGIP at its 12th session in 1994, the Sub-Commission recommended that the Centre for Human Rights organize a workshop with the participation of representatives of governments and of Indigenous organizations, as well as independent experts.[150]

A workshop was held in 1995 to consider the forum's establishment, discussing issues such as its mandate, terms of reference, relationship with the WGIP, and membership. The participants of the workshop included twenty-one representatives of states, twenty-one representatives of Indigenous peoples, and two independent experts.[151] In a background paper for the workshop, Rodolfo Stavenhagen noted that the growing presence of Indigenous peoples in international fora reflected 'not only the justice of [their] demands' but also 'the growing sophistication of their approach' in creating a permanent niche in international organizations.[152] A second

149 UNGA Res. 48/163 (21 December 1993) requested the Commission on Human Rights to give 'priority consideration' to the establishment of a permanent forum for Indigenous people within the UN system. Commission on Human Rights Res. 1994/28 (4 March 1994) requested the WGIP to give the matter consideration at its twelfth session.

150 Sub-Commission Res. 1994/50 (26 August 1994). This was endorsed by Commission Res. 1995/30 (3 March 1995).

151 Commission on Human Rights, 'Consideration of a Permanent Forum for Indigenous People: Report of the Workshop Held in Accordance with Commission Resolution 1995/30' (1995) UN Doc. E/CN.4/Sub.2/AC.4/1995/7.

152 ECOSOC, 'Working Group on Indigenous Populations: Consideration of a Permanent Forum for Indigenous People' (6 July 1995) UN Doc. E/CN.4/Sub.2/AC.4/1995/7/Add.2, 8.

workshop was held in 1997, comprising more than 100 participants. At that workshop, there was consensus that the principle of full participation of Indigenous peoples in the permanent forum would be essential to its success.[153] It was clear that in developing plans for the permanent forum, government and Indigenous representatives were inspired not only by the WGIP but also by other examples discussed elsewhere in this chapter: For instance, in a discussion at the WGIP following the second workshop, a government observer referred to the Fund for the Development of the Indigenous Peoples of Latin America and the Caribbean (FILAC) as a possible model.[154]

The UN Permanent Forum on Indigenous Issues (UNPFII) was finally established in 2000 by consensus resolution as a subsidiary body of the ECOSOC.[155] It was mandated to discuss Indigenous issues relating to economic and social development, culture, the environment, education, health, and human rights, in order to (a) provide advice and recommendations on Indigenous issues to the UN, (b) raise awareness and promote the integration and coordination of activities relating to Indigenous issues within the UN system, and (c) prepare and disseminate information on Indigenous issues.[156] After the passage of the UNDRIP in 2007, it became additionally tasked with promoting 'respect for and full application' of the Declaration's provisions and following up its effectiveness.[157] Made up of sixteen members serving in a personal expert capacity, half of whom are nominated by governments and the other half appointed on the basis of broad consultations with Indigenous organizations including 'local indigenous consultation processes',[158] the UNPFII holds annual two-week sessions[159] and makes recommendations by way of an annual report to the ECOSOC as well as other UN organs, funds, programmes, and agencies.[160]

[153] WGIP 15th Session Report, para. 110.

[154] WGIP 15th Session Report, para. 116.

[155] ECOSOC Res. 2000/22 (28 July 2000). For the procedural background to the establishment of the Forum, see Vienna Declaration and Programme of Action, Part I, section II, para. 32; UNGA Res. 48/163 (21 December 1993); Commission on Human Rights Res. 1994/28 (4 March 1994); ECOSOC, 'Report of the Open-Ended Inter-Sessional Ad Hoc Working Group on a Permanent Forum for Indigenous Peoples in the United Nations System' (1999) UN Doc. E/CN.4/1999/83; Commission on Human Rights Res 2000/87 (28 April 2000).

[156] ECOSOC Res. 2000/22, para. 2.

[157] UNDRIP, Article 42.

[158] ECOSOC Res. 2000/22, para. 1. In practice, these eight members are themselves leaders of Indigenous organizations or peoples: Anaya, *Indigenous Peoples*, 220.

[159] ECOSOC Res. 2000/22, para. 4.

[160] Ibid., para. 5.

Indigenous peoples, through the UNPFII, were hence able to participate in the work of the UN in a double-layered manner: First, through the members of the expert council who are themselves Indigenous, and second, through the participation of Indigenous peoples' organizations as observers. The same procedures applicable to the WGDD also apply to the UNPFII, so that Indigenous peoples' organizations attending the Permanent Forum do not first have to hold consultative status with the ECOSOC.[161] In practice, the UNPFII's meetings are 'always full of indigenous activists from every corner of the globe'.[162]

In the days of the WGIP, Indigenous peoples had pointed out that it was established at a low level in the UN system, with its recommendations needing to pass through several levels of member state-constituted organs. But unlike the WGIP, the UNPFII was established at the highest level within the UN at which a body can be established without constitutional reform;[163] as such, it is a platform through which Indigenous peoples can exercise influence – at least in a recommendatory sense – over other UN organs and bodies. For these reasons, Indigenous peoples' representatives have broadly hailed the UNPFII as a 'historic milestone', being 'the first body within the UN system in which indigenous peoples are represented with the same status as governmental representatives'.[164] The UNPFII is regularly invited to participate in the work of other UN organs and specialized agencies, representing the interests of Indigenous peoples.[165] In this way, it has become the de facto representative of Indigenous peoples at the UN. At the same time, there was from the UNPFII's early days a recognition by many Indigenous organizations that participation through the UNPFII is not 'an end in itself or sufficient', as additional, substantive work must be done in the UN agencies and programmes whose activities affect Indigenous peoples:[166] The UNPFII is only empowered to make non-binding recommendations to other agencies and bodies.

The UNPFII constituted a further forum through which Indigenous peoples could advocate for their inclusion in other UN and international

[161] Ibid., para. 1.

[162] Andrew Erueti, 'The International Labour Organization and the Internationalisation of the Concept of Indigenous Peoples' in Stephen Allen and Alexandra Xanthaki (eds.), *Reflections on the UN Declaration on the Rights of Indigenous Peoples* (London: Hart, 2011), 93–120, 102.

[163] Marjo Lindroth, 'Indigenous-State Relations in the UN: Establishing the Indigenous Forum' (2006) 42 *Polar Record*, 239–428, 246.

[164] Lola García-Alix, *The Permanent Forum on Indigenous Issues* (Copenhagen: IWGIA, 2003), 6.

[165] See, for example, UNESCO, 'Consultation on a UNESCO Policy on Engaging with Indigenous Peoples' (12 July 2017), 26.

[166] García-Alix, *The Permanent Forum*, 6.

organization spaces. At its second meeting alone, the UNPFII called on the UN system and other international organizations to establish 'processes of meaningful participation and partnership with indigenous communities in [sustainable development] processes',[167] recommended that the UN Framework Convention on Climate Change (UNFCCC) establish an 'ad hoc open-ended intersessional working group on indigenous peoples and local communities and climate change' with the guaranteed participation of Indigenous peoples,[168] further recommended that the UN Environment Programme report on the feasibility of developing mechanisms for Indigenous peoples to participate in the monitoring and evaluation process under the Stockholm Convention on Persistent Organic Pollutants,[169] urged the World Health Organization to engage in as global consultation with Indigenous peoples on its participatory research guidelines,[170] recommended that UNESCO incorporate participation, consultation, and dialogue with Indigenous peoples in the drafting of the convention on intangible heritage,[171] and finally recommended that the UN system guarantee Indigenous peoples' 'full and effective participation' in 'appropriate processes and environmental conventions' such as on wetlands, desertification, and climate change.[172] In this way, the UNPFII amplified Indigenous peoples' efforts to secure participation in various other intergovernmental fora.

3.5 ENVIRONMENT AND DEVELOPMENT NEGOTIATIONS, 1994

Meanwhile, in the wake of the UN Conference on Environment and Development, ongoing negotiations were underway in the various treaty bodies that the Conference had established. Of these, Indigenous peoples could and did participate, to differing extents, in UNFCCC and the Convention on Biological Diversity (CBD).

3.5.1 *Convention on Biological Diversity*

The CBD has a tripartite objective: the conservation of biodiversity, its sustainable use, and the fair and equitable sharing of benefits arising from

[167] UNPFII, 'Report on the Second Session' (2003) UN Doc. E/2003/43, 7.
[168] García-Alix, *The Permanent Forum*, 7.
[169] UNPFII, 'Report on the Second Session', 11.
[170] Ibid., 14.
[171] Ibid., 18.
[172] Ibid., 13.

the utilization of genetic resources.[173] It was not long after the treaty's entry into force that Indigenous peoples began to recognize the ways in which it concerned them, and to call for increased participation in its processes.[174] Indigenous peoples' organizations participated as observers from the first session of the Conference of the Parties (COP 1) in 1994,[175] and during COP 3, Indigenous peoples formed the International Indigenous Forum on Biodiversity, a collection of representatives from Indigenous organizations as well as Indigenous scholars and activists, to coordinate their advocacy in CBD meetings.[176] Under the Convention's observer participation policies, Indigenous peoples can participate on the same basis as NGOs and other civil society organizations. They may make formal interventions during sessions and may make textual proposals with the support of at least one state party.[177] In addition, on several occasions, the COP has invited states to include Indigenous peoples' representatives in their official delegations to CBD meetings;[178] a few states, such as Canada, Norway, and Sweden, have done so.[179] By Decision VII/16 in 2004, the COP established a voluntary funding mechanism to facilitate Indigenous peoples' participation,[180] which

173 Convention on Biological Diversity (adopted 5 June 1992 and entered into force 29 December 1993) 1760 UNTS 69 (CBD), Article 1.

174 International Alliance of the Indigenous Peoples of the Tropical Rainforest, 'Submission of the International Alliance to the CBD Secretariat: The Biodiversity Convention – The Concerns of Indigenous Peoples', Reproduced in International Alliance of Indigenous-Tribal Peoples of the Tropical Forest, *Indigenous Peoples, Forest, and Biodiversity* (Copenhagen: IWGIA, 1996), 105–122, 101–106.

175 CBD, 'List of participants' (8 December 1994) UN Doc. UNEP/CBD/COP/1/Inf.11, 116, 121, 123, 130, 132, 133, and 134. The COP is the supreme body of the Convention: CBD, Article 22.

176 International Indigenous Forum on Biodiversity, https://iifb-fiib.org/.

177 CBD, Article 23(5) provides for observer status. See also CBD, Rules of Procedure for Meetings of the Conference of the Parties to the Convention on Biological Diversity, Annex to Decision I/1 and Decision V/20, Rules 7 and 29; CBD, Consolidated *Modus Operandi* of the Subsidiary Body on Scientific, Technical and Technological Advice, decision VIII/10, Annex III, para. 19.

178 CBD, Decision V/16 (2000) UN Doc. UNEP/CBD/COP/DEC/V/6, para. 18; CBD, Decision VII/16 (13 April 2004) UN Doc. UNEP/CBD/COP/DEC/VII/16, para. 29; Decision VIII/5 (15 June 2006) UN Doc. UNEP/CBD/COP/DEC/VIII/5, para. 6(b); Decision X/40 (29 October 2010) UN Doc. UNEP/CBD/COP/DEC/X/40, para. C 3.

179 CBD, 'List of Participants' (30 November 1995) UN Doc. UNEP/CBD/COP/2/Inf.16; CBD, 'List of Participants' (31 March 2006) UN Doc. UNEP/CBD/COP/8/INF/48. See also CBD, 'Mechanisms to Promote the Effective Participation of Indigenous and Local Communities in Matters Related to the Objectives of Article 8(j) and Related Provisions: Note by the Executive Secretary' (28 September 2003) UN Doc. UNEP/CBD/WG8J/3/6, paras. 27–28.

180 Decision VII/16, para. 30. Also see inviting contributions to the fund, CBD, Decision IX/13 (9 October 2008) UN Doc. UNEP/CBD/COP/DEC/IX/13, Decision IX/13 E, para. 4; Decision

appears to receive substantial contributions from states.[181] The COP has also called for capacity building to support, and ensure the efficacy of, Indigenous peoples' participation.[182]

Above and beyond the general level of Indigenous participation permitted in the CBD, in 1998, states parties to the CBD established a working group under which Indigenous peoples have a higher level of participation on a matter affecting them: the Ad Hoc Open-ended Working Group on the Implementation of Article 8(j) and related provisions ("Working Group on Article 8(j)"). Established at COP 4 and first meeting in 2000, the Working Group is tasked with implementing Article 8(j) of the Convention, which concerns traditional knowledge.[183] Its triple mandate is to provide advice on the application and development of legal and other protections for traditional knowledge relevant to the conservation and sustainable use of biodiversity; the implementation of Article 8(j) and related provisions through inter alia the development and implementation of a work programme at national and international levels; and measures and mechanisms to strengthen international cooperation among Indigenous peoples and local communities relevant to the conservation and sustainable use of biodiversity.[184]

Membership of the Working Group was made open to all states parties and observers, including 'in particular' representatives of Indigenous peoples and local communities 'embodying traditional lifestyles relevant to the conservation and sustainable use of biological diversity with participation to the widest possible extent in its deliberations in accordance with the rules of procedure'.[185] The COP heavily encouraged Indigenous peoples to

X/40 C, para. 2; Decision XI/14 (5 December 2012) UN Doc. UNEP/CBD/COP/DEC/XI/14, B, para. 14.

[181] In 2016–2017, it funded the participation of 79 representatives of Indigenous peoples for participation in official meetings under the CBD: 'Report of the CBD to the UNPFII 2017', 9–10, www.un.org/development/desa/indigenouspeoples/wp-content/uploads/sites/19/2018/02/SCBD_UNPFII-QUESTIONNAIRE-SCBD-Response-27-December-2017_vf_JSc-2.pdf.

[182] Decision V/16, para. 12(d); Decision IX/13 E, para. 7; Decision XI/14 B, para. 10; Decision XII/12 (13 October 2014) UN Doc. UNEP/CBD/COP/DEC/XII/12, A, para. 7. Also see reports on capacity-building activities: CBD, 'Participatory Mechanisms for Indigenous and Local Communities in the Work of the Convention: Note by the Executive Secretary' (20 May 2009) UN Doc. UNEP/CBD/WG8J/6/3; CBD, 'Progress Report on Capacity-Building and Development and Participation of Indigenous Peoples and Local Communities in the Work of the Convention' (1 February 2016) UN Doc. UNEP/CBD/SBI/1/INF/1.

[183] Decision IV/9 (1998) UN Doc. UNEP/CBD/COP/DEC/IV/9, para. 1.

[184] Decision IV/9.

[185] Ibid., para. 2.

participate in the Working Group.[186] It called for states parties to include their representatives on their delegations,[187] an invitation taken up by a modest number of countries.[188] In addition, the COP established a voluntary funding mechanism to facilitate the participation of Indigenous and local communities in meetings under the Convention, including though not limited to meetings of the Article 8(j) Working Group.[189]

In practice, nearly 'the fullest possible participation' of Indigenous peoples occurs in the Article 8(j) Working Group, including in contact groups established under it.[190] Over and above the usual rules applicable to CBD meetings, Indigenous peoples' representatives are included as "Friends of the Co-Chairs" and "Friends of the Bureau" – small informal groups often formed during negotiations in order to reach agreement on specific issues – and are appointed as Co-Chairs of contact groups.[191] The Executive Secretary established an Indigenous and local community liaison group to assist in the preparation of documents for the consideration of the Working Group.[192] However, the procedure is still ultimately restricted by the CBD's wider procedural rules in that, for instance, textual proposals by Indigenous peoples' representatives still require the support of at least one state party.[193] In this way, Indigenous peoples participate on almost, but not quite, the same basis as states.

CBD officials view the participation of Indigenous peoples as important for the fulfilment of the objectives of the Convention. At the CBD's second meeting in 2002, the CBD's then Executive Secretary, Hamdallah Zedan, said Indigenous communities' participation was 'critical' as they 'played a vital role in environmental management and development as a result of their knowledge and traditional practices'.[194] In a 2007 statement to the UNPFII,

[186] Ibid., para. 5.

[187] Ibid., para. 3. Also see Decision V/6, para. 18.

[188] CBD, 'Participatory Mechanisms for Indigenous and Local Communities' (27 November 2001), UN Doc. UNEP/CBD/WG8J/2/4, para. 34.

[189] Decision VII/16 G, para. 10.

[190] Elisa Morgera, 'Dawn of a New Day? The Evolving Relationship between the Convention on Biological Diversity and International Human Rights Law' (2018) 53 *Wake Forest Law Review*, 691–712, 692.

[191] CBD, 'Report of the Seventh Meeting of the Ad Hoc Open-Ended Working Group on Article 8(j) and Related Provisions of the Convention on Biological Diversity' (24 November 2011) UN Doc. UNEP/CBD/COP/11/7, paras. 15 and 20.

[192] CBD, 'Participatory Mechanisms for Indigenous and Local Communities' (2001), para. 42.

[193] Morgera, 'Dawn of a New Day', 695.

[194] CBD, 'Report of the Ad Hoc Open-Ended Inter-Sessional Working Group on Article 8(j) and Related Provisions of the Convention on Biological Diversity on the Work of Its Second Meeting' (14 February 2002) UN Doc. UNEP/CBD/COP/6/7, para. 11.

the Executive Secretary of the CBD highlighted that the 'new enhanced phase of the implementation of the Convention ... require[d] the active engagement of indigenous and local communities', which was 'more than ever crucial' to the success of the Convention's implementation.[195] In this regard, he referred to the establishment of the Voluntary Fund and the participation of Indigenous peoples in the negotiations on access and benefit sharing.[196] In a speech to the Indigenous peoples' consultation on access and benefit sharing, he underscored that the participation of Indigenous peoples was 'essential ... to achieve the goals of the Convention'.[197] The Conference of the Parties has also repeatedly stressed the importance of Indigenous peoples' participation in the Article 8(j) Working Group and in other processes under the Convention.[198] States have expressed similar views. For example, at the Working Group's first meeting, the Ambassador of Spain, supporting the participation of Indigenous and local communities in the CBD process, said Indigenous knowledge was 'essential for achieving sustainable development' as Indigenous peoples were 'the best stewards of their ecosystems'.[199] At its fifth meeting, the delegate of Malawi, on behalf of the African Group, said Indigenous and local communities' participation would be 'critical to the success of the meeting'.[200]

The enhanced participatory procedures of the Article 8(j) Working Group were not replicated in other processes under the Convention affecting Indigenous peoples. For instance, the Ad hoc Open-ended Working Group on Protected Areas, established in 2004, does not provide for the participation

[195] CBD, 'Statement by Dr. Ahmed Djoghlaf, Executive Secretary, Convention on Biological Diversity, to the United Nations Permanent Forum on Indigenous Issues at Its Sixth Session' (17 May 2007), 2, www.cbd.int/doc/speech/2007/sp-2007-05-17-unpfii-en.pdf.

[196] Ibid., 2–3.

[197] CBD, 'Statement by Dr. Ahmed Djoghlaf, Executive Secretary of the Convention on Biological Diversity, to the International Indigenous and Local Community Consultation on Access and Benefit-Sharing and the Development of an International Regime' (19 September 2007), 1, www.cbd.int/kb/record/statement/38752?RecordType=statement&Subject=TKIP.

[198] See, for example, Decision V/16, paras. 9 and 11; Decision VI/10 (2002) UN Doc. UNEP/CBD/COP/6/20, Preamble, Recitals Four, Six, and Seven; Decision IX/13 E, para. 2.

[199] CBD, 'Report of the Working Group on the Implementation of Article 8(j) and Related Provisions, Report of the First meeting' (12 April 2000) UN Doc. UNEP/CBD/COP/5/5, para. 6.

[200] CBD, 'Report of the Fifth Meeting of the Ad Hoc Open-Ended Working Group on Article 8(j) and Related Provisions of the Convention on Biological Diversity' (13 November 2007) UN Doc. UNEP/CBD/COP/9/7, para. 23.

of Indigenous peoples except to the default level in Convention processes.[201] Nor did the Ad Hoc Open-ended Working Group on Access and Benefit-sharing (ABS), established in 2000, that through ten years of work ultimately produced the Nagoya Protocol on Access and Benefit Sharing in 2010.[202] Indigenous peoples considered the ABS process critical to protect their traditional knowledge, innovations, and practices associated with genetic resources and ensure the equitable sharing of benefits arising from the use of such resources.[203] While not rising to the standard of the Article 8(j) Working Group, the Working Group on ABS still provided for some degree of Indigenous participation above and beyond regular CBD processes. The COP encouraged the participation of Indigenous peoples in the work of the Working Group on Access and Benefit-sharing,[204] requested the Working Group on Article 8(j) to collaborate with the Working Group on Access and Benefit-sharing in the fulfilment of its mandate,[205] and invited the chair of the group to facilitate the effective participation of Indigenous peoples representatives and to consult them as appropriate.[206] In the process of developing the Nagoya Protocol, there was a consultation in which two members of the

[201] Decision VII/28 (2004) UN Doc. UNEP/CBD/COP/DEC/VII/28 established the Working Group on Protected Areas. In 2008, the UNPFII recommended that it include greater Indigenous peoples' participation: UNPFII, 'Report of the Seventh Session' (2008) UN Doc. E/C.19/2008/13, para. 80.

[202] Decision V/26 (26 May 2000) UN Doc. UNEP/CBD/COP/DEC/V/26. The Working Group was initially tasked with developing guidelines and other approaches to assist parties and stakeholders with the implementation of the access and benefit-sharing provisions of the Convention. By Decision VII/19 D, the Working Group was mandated to negotiate an international instrument on access to genetic resources and benefit sharing. This resulted in the conclusion of the Nagoya Protocol in 2010 (Nagoya Protocol on Access to Genetic Resources and the Fair and Equitable Sharing of Benefits Arising from Their Utilization (concluded 29 October 2010 and entered into force 12 October 2014) UN Doc. UNEP/CBD/COP/DEC/X/1). A 2007 report noted that the lack of adequate resources for Indigenous peoples to engage in effective participation in the access and benefit-sharing process was an obstacle to effective outcomes for Indigenous peoples: UNPFII, 'Report of the International Expert Group Meeting on the International Regime on Access and Benefit-sharing and Indigenous Peoples' Human Rights of the Convention on Biological Diversity' (14 March 2007) UN Doc. E/C.19/2007/8, para. 40.

[203] Acknowledged in CBD, 'Statement by Mr. Ahmed Djoghlaf, Executive Secretary of the Convention on Biological Diversity, on the Occasion of the Opening of the Ninth Session of the United Nations Permanent Forum on Indigenous Issues: "Indigenous Peoples; Development with Culture and Identity"'(19 April 2010), 4–5, www.cbd.int/doc/speech/2010/sp-2010-04-19-UNPFII-en.pdf.

[204] Decision V/16, para. 5.

[205] Decision VIII/5 C, para. 1.

[206] Ibid., para. 7.

UNPFII and twenty representatives of Indigenous peoples' organizations were invited to provide recommendations.[207] The report of the consultation fed into the 5th meeting of the Working Group on Access and Benefit-sharing,[208] although it is unclear to what extent the recommendations were considered or incorporated.[209] Moreover, Indigenous peoples' representatives constituted seven of fifteen observers to the thirty-member Expert Group on Traditional Knowledge Associated with Genetic Resources, established to assist the Working Group with legal and technical advice.[210] But efforts at the Article 8(j) Working Group's fourth meeting, in 2006, to secure Indigenous participation at the meetings of the ABS Working Group on a level comparable to that of the Article 8(j) Working Group did not succeed.[211] This lower level of participation may well have affected the result, as the Protocol has been criticized for not sufficiently respecting the rights of Indigenous peoples.[212]

Other limitations to the CBD's inclusion of Indigenous peoples have been noted. A 2007 international expert group report noted the need for capacity building to allow traditional knowledge holders to become more involved in negotiations,[213] and drew attention to 'an expectation' at some CBD meetings that Indigenous peoples 'will speak with one voice and have one specific position', a situation that the report noted was 'highly unlikely' given that Indigenous peoples are not a homogenous block.[214] The report also noted challenges such as lack of funding and information, as well as limited

[207] Ibid., paras. 3–4.

[208] CBD, 'Statement by Dr. Ahmed Djoghlaf to the International Indigenous and Local Community Consultation on Access and Benefit-Sharing', 3.

[209] See the recommendations in UNPFII, 'Report of the International Expert Group Meeting on Access and Benefit-Sharing', paras. 15–55.

[210] Decision IX/13, para. 11, Annex, paras. 1–3.

[211] See coverage in Soledad Aguilar, Xenya Cherny, Elisa Morgera, Nicole Schabus, and Elsa Tsioumani, 'Summary of the Fourth Meeting of the Working Group on Article 8(j) of the Convention on Biological Diversity' (2006) 9(339) *Earth Negotiations Bulletin*, https://enb.iisd.org/events/4th-meeting-cbd-ad-hoc-open-ended-working-group-article-8j/summary-report-23-27-january-2006.

[212] UN General Assembly, Report of the Special Rapporteur on the Rights of Indigenous Peoples to the General Assembly (2012) UN Doc. A/67/301, para. 58; EMRIP, 'Joint Submission of Grand Council of the Crees, et al.: Nagoya Protocol on Access and Benefit Sharing: Substantive and Procedural Injustices Relating to Indigenous Peoples Human Rights' (2011). However, one outcome has been that Indigenous peoples have two observer seats on the Protocol's Compliance Committee: Decision NP-1/4 (20 October 2014) UN Doc. UNEP/CBD/NP/COP-MOP/DEC/1/4, Annex, para. B.2.

[213] UNPFII, 'Report of the International Expert Group Meeting on Access and Benefit-Sharing', para. 25.

[214] Ibid., para. 23.

translation of documents prepared by Indigenous organizations into UN languages.[215]

3.5.2 *The UN Framework Convention on Climate Change*

Whatever the challenges to Indigenous participation in the CBD, they were at least matched in the UNFCCC during the same time period. Differences in the UNFCCC's rules of procedure limited Indigenous participation in important ways. At UNFCCC COP meetings, each observer constituency is allocated a limited time (usually two minutes) to make formal interventions after the closure of a plenary session, and can provide written input into the negotiations process upon invitation by the Secretariat.[216] Unlike in the CBD, observers cannot intervene during a session, and many state delegates leave the room after the closure of a session and before observer statements.[217] This level of participation is very restricted. Nor, in the period under consideration, was there any subsidiary body that enabled enhanced participation for Indigenous peoples as compared with NGOs.

This was not due to lack of awareness of such possibilities. Beginning in 2003, the UNPFII repeatedly called on the UNFCCC to 'guarantee the full and effective participation of indigenous peoples',[218] establish a working group on Indigenous peoples to study and propose solutions to urgent climate impacts that they face,[219] and develop mechanisms for Indigenous peoples' participation in 'all aspects of the international dialogue on climate change'.[220] However, during the period under examination in this chapter, the UNFCCC's response was very limited. At its 20th session in 2004, the Subsidiary Body for Implementation (SBI), the organ tasked with managing the implementation of the Framework Convention,[221] considered the

[215] Ibid., para. 22.

[216] Constituencies are informal, voluntary groups of organizations representing various categories of stakeholders to the UNFCCC: Joanna Depledge, *The Organization of Environmental Negotiations: Constructing the Climate Change Regime* (London: Earthscan, 2005), 214–216. As of COP 1, three constituencies were recognized: environmental NGOs, business and industry NGOs, and local government and municipal authorities. Indigenous peoples became a recognized constituency in 2001. As of 2021, there are nine constituencies.

[217] Harriet Thew, 'Youth Participation and Agency in the United Nations Framework Convention on Climate Change' (2018) 18 *International Environmental Agreements*, 369–389, 379.

[218] UNPFII, 'Report of the Second Session' (2003) UN Doc. E/C.19/2003/22, para. 61.

[219] UNPFII, 'Report of the Second Session', para. 47; UNPFII, 'Report of the Third Session' (2004) UN Doc. E/C.19/2004/23, para. 78.

[220] UNPFII, 'Report of the Seventh Session', paras. 21 and 30.

[221] UN Framework Convention on Climate Change (concluded 9 May 1992 and entered into force 21 March 1994) 1771 UNTS 107 (UNFCCC), Article 10. All states parties are

UNPFII's recommendations but, stating that the full and effective participation of Indigenous peoples could already be achieved through the existing observer mechanism,[222] merely 'encouraged' Indigenous peoples' organizations to 'make full use of' existing opportunities.[223] While it acknowledged 'the importance of an enhanced participation by indigenous peoples' organizations in the Convention process',[224] the SBI merely invited states parties to 'consider' drawing on Indigenous peoples' organizations' expertise when discussing matters of concern to them,[225] encouraged parties to consider ways of enhancing the participation of Indigenous peoples' organizations in the UNFCCC,[226] and invited the UNFCCC Secretariat and the chairs of relevant UNFCCC bodies to facilitate such participation to the extent possible.[227]

But even without taking procedural barriers into account, by comparison with the CBD, Indigenous peoples' participation under the UNFCCC began later and was not as extensive during the period under consideration in this chapter. Indigenous peoples first participated in the UNFCCC process as members of state government delegations: Canada and to a lesser extent Denmark were active in this regard in the early days of the UNFCCC COPs.[228] No Indigenous representatives appeared as non-state observers until

represented in the SBI, and decisions are taken by consensus. Observer modalities are the same as for the COP.

222 SBI, 'Report of the Subsidiary Body for Implementation on Its Twentieth Session' (2004) UN Doc. FCCC/SBI/2004/10, para. 109.

223 Ibid., para. 106.

224 Ibid., para. 108.

225 Ibid., para. 107.

226 Ibid., para. 107.

227 Ibid., para. 108.

228 Denmark included representatives of the Greenland Home Rule government on its delegation at COPs 3, 6, and 11. Canada first included a representative of the Inuit Circumpolar Conference on its delegation at COP 5, and subsequently at COP 9, COP 10, COP 11, and COP 12. Subsequently, it included representatives of the Grand Chief Council of Yukon First Nations (subsequently known as the Council of Yukon First Nations) (COP 6bis, COP 7, COP 8, COP 9, and COP 11), the Arctic Athabaskan Council (COP 8, COP 9, COP 10, and COP 11), Champagne and Aishihik Nations (COP 9), the Daak-ka Council (COP 9), the Dene Nations (COP 11), the Congress of Aboriginal People (COP 11), the Native Women's Association of Canada (COP 11), the Metis National Council (COP 11 and COP 12), the Blackfoot Confederacy Alberta (COP 12), Inuit Tapiriit Kanatami (COP 11 and COP 12), and the Assembly of First Nations (COP 11 and COP 12). UNFCCC, 'List of Participants' (9 December 1997) UN Doc. FCCC/CP/1997/INF.5; UNFCCC, 'List of Participants' (4 November 1999) UN Doc. FCCC/CP/1999/INF.3; UNFCCC, 'List of Participants' (24 November 2000) UN Doc. FCCC/CP/2000/INF.2; UNFCCC, 'List of Participants' (26 July 2001) UN Doc. FCCC/CP/2001/INF.2; UNFCCC, 'List of Participants' (8 November 2001) UN Doc. FCCC/CP/2001/INF.4; UNFCCC, 'List of Participants' (1 November 2002) UN Doc. FCCC/CP/2002/INF.2; UNFCCC, 'List of Participants' (11

COP 6 in 2000,[229] although subsequently increasing numbers of Indigenous peoples' representatives attended.[230] One reason why Indigenous peoples showed up in the UNFCCC later than in the CBD may be the issue of organizational capacity to track the increasing number of relevant intergovernmental processes. For instance, as Sheila Watt-Cloutier, the then President of the Inuit Circumpolar Conference (ICC) Canada, explains, in the late 1990s, the Inuit were fully engaged in tackling the issue of persistent organic pollutants (POPs). Limited resources made it impossible for the ICC to simultaneously engage in the UNFCCC process, especially since the timing of UNFCCC meetings and negotiations on the POPs treaty often overlapped.[231]

Even where Indigenous peoples are represented on state delegations, the UNFCCC provides one case study of how the extent to which inclusion on state delegations constitutes meaningful participation is subject to delegation structures and practices, individual relationships, and power dynamics. This is illustrated by Watt-Cloutier's experience representing the Inuit Circumpolar Conference on the Canadian delegation to COP 9 and COP 10. She writes that her request to the Canadian head of delegation at COP 9 to be allowed to make an intervention in the plenary was denied; nor was the head of delegation willing to make statements on behalf of the peoples of the Arctic. Watt-Cloutier eventually connected with delegates from the Samoan government delegation who were willing to highlight the Arctic in one of their interventions.[232] While individual experiences will have varied, certain structural elements are likely to be common across government delegations.

3.5.3 *The World Intellectual Property Organization's Intergovernmental Committee*

The World Intellectual Property Organization (WIPO) differs from the UNFCCC and CBD in several obvious respects. It is an international

December 2003) UN Doc. FCCC/CP/2003/INF.1; UNFCCC, 'List of Participants' (17 December 2004) UN Doc. FCCC/CP/2004/INF.3; UNFCCC, 'List of Participants' (9 December 2005) UN Doc. FCCC/CP/2005/INF.2 (Parts 1 and 2); UNFCCC, 'List of Participants' (16 November 2006) UN Doc. FCCC/CP/2006/INF.1.

229 UNFCCC, 'List of Participants' (2000). Sheila Watt-Cloutier, *The Right to Be Cold* (Minneapolis: University of Minnesota Press, 2018), 197.

230 UNFCCC, 'List of Participants' (26 July 2001); UNFCCC, 'List of Participants' (8 November 2001); UNFCCC, 'List of Participants' (2002); UNFCCC, 'List of Participants' (2003); UNFCCC, 'List of Participants' (2005); UNFCCC, 'List of Participants' (2006).

231 See below, Section 7.3. Watt-Cloutier, *The Right to Be Cold*, 197.

232 Watt-Cloutier, *The Right to Be Cold*, 228–229.

organization, not a treaty. It deals with intellectual property, not environmental issues. Unlike the Rio Conventions, nobody but member states, observer states, and IGOs may participate in the general activities of the organization.[233] But there are also important similarities. Like the CBD and to a different extent the UNFCCC, WIPO's standard-setting activities have a bearing on Indigenous peoples' traditional knowledge. In addition, like the CBD, WIPO has instituted *sui generis* rules of procedure to enable Indigenous peoples' participation in a specific sub-organ that concerns traditional knowledge: the Intergovernmental Committee on Intellectual Property and Genetic Resources, Traditional Knowledge and Folklore (IGC).

From the earliest stages of WIPO's consideration of traditional knowledge, there was a recognition within the organization that it should reach out 'to identify and explore the intellectual property needs and expectations of new beneficiaries, including the holders of indigenous knowledge and innovations'.[234] This recognition was helped along by the work that Indigenous peoples had done during the 1990s, including the Mataatua Declaration on Cultural and Intellectual Property Rights of Indigenous Peoples adopted at the First International Conference on Cultural and Intellectual Property Rights of Indigenous Peoples in 1993,[235] as well as a study on intellectual and cultural property of Indigenous peoples carried out under the auspices of the WGIP.[236]

At the IGC's first meeting in 2001, a fast-track accreditation procedure for ad hoc observers was established to allow Indigenous communities without WIPO permanent observer status to participate in the IGC's meetings.[237]

[233] WIPO, General Rules of Procedure, No. 399 (FE) Rev. 3, 1998. (Adopted 28 September 1970; amended 27 November 1973, 5 October 1976, and 2 October 1979), Rules 7 and 8.

[234] WIPO Budget Committee, 'Draft Program and Budget 1998–1999' (1998) WIPO Doc. WO/BC/18/2—A/32/2 107. See IGC, 'Participation of Local and Indigenous Communities in the Work of the Committee' (2002) WIPO Doc. WIPO/GRTKF/IC/4/12, paras. 3–8.

[235] First International Conference on the Cultural and Intellectual Property Rights of Indigenous Peoples, *The Mataatua Declaration on Cultural and Intellectual Property Rights of Indigenous Peoples* (June 1993).

[236] Commission on Human Rights, 'Study on the Protection of the Cultural and Intellectual Property of Indigenous Peoples' (28 July 1993) UN Doc. E/CN.4/Sub.2/1993/28.

[237] IGC, 'Rules of Procedure' (2001) WIPO Doc. WIPO/GRTKF/IC/1/2, paras. 6 and 8; IGC, 'Report on the First Session' (2001) WIPO Doc. WIPO/GRTKF/IC/1/13, paras. 17–18. Although it should be noted that the "fast track" procedure has been criticized for still taking up to a year for Indigenous peoples' organizations to be approved: Veronica Gordon, 'Appropriation without Representation? The Limited Role of Indigenous Groups in WIPO's Intergovernmental Committee on Intellectual Property and Genetic Resources, Traditional Knowledge, and Folklore' (2014) 16 *Vanderbilt Journal of Entertainment and Technology Law*, 629–667, 654.

Under these rules, Indigenous peoples' organizations may apply to the IGC for *ad hoc* observer status. Once such status has been obtained, Indigenous peoples' organizations, along with all other participants, are allowed to speak at the beginning of the IGC sessions and are also permitted some speaking time during the sessions.[238] From the beginning of the IGC's work, many Indigenous organizations were accredited and attended as ad hoc observers.[239] By 2007, the number of accredited observers had risen to nearly 200.[240] In practice, the Chair of the IGC has allowed Indigenous peoples' representatives to intervene on any agenda item and to make drafting proposals on negotiating texts and other working documents for consideration by member states. Such proposals are incorporated in the text if supported by at least one member state, and are reflected in the reports of the sessions.[241] On occasion, Indigenous peoples' representatives have served as rapporteurs for contact drafting groups, an influential role.[242] In addition, several states have from time to time included representatives of Indigenous organizations on their delegations,[243] a practice encouraged by the WIPO General Assembly.[244] These arrangements give Indigenous peoples the ability to make meaningful inputs into the IGC's standard-setting process.

WIPO provides some practical support for the participation of Indigenous peoples, although this is limited in important ways. The Secretariat facilitates preparatory consultative arrangements for Indigenous representatives through an Indigenous Consultative Forum before each IGC meeting and provides a dedicated room for Indigenous peoples and local communities' representatives to hold consultations throughout the meetings, as well as an office.[245]

[238] IGC, 'Report on the Seventh Session' (2005) WIPO Doc. WIPO/GRTKF/IC/7/15, para. 63.

[239] See, for example, IGC, 'Report on the First Session', para. 18, Annex I.

[240] WIPO, 'WIPO General Assembly, Thirty-Fourth (18th Ordinary) Session, Report' (12 November 2007) WIPO Doc. WO/GA/34/16, para. 254.

[241] IGC, 'Draft Study on the Participation of Observers in the Work of the Intergovernmental Committee on Intellectual Property and Genetic Resources, Traditional Knowledge and Folklore' (13 January 2012) WIPO Doc. WIPO/GRTKF/IC/20/7, Annex, para. 24.

[242] IGC, 'Intersessional Working Group (IWG) 2, March 2011' (2011) WIPO Doc. WIPO/GRTKF/IWG/2/3.

[243] For instance, Brazil, Denmark, the United States, Mexico, and New Zealand: IGC, 'Report on the Fifth Session' (2003) WIPO Doc. WIPO/GRTKF/IC/5/15, Annex; IGC, 'Report on the Seventh Session', Annex.

[244] WIPO, 'Assemblies of the Member States of WIPO, Thirty-Seventh Series of Meetings, General Report' (2002) WIPO Doc. A/37/14, para. 290(ii). The IGC itself considered in 2005 that states 'should make every effort' to include such representatives in their delegations: IGC, 'Report on the Fifth Session', para. 206.

[245] IGC, 'Practical Guide for Observers', 4, www.wipo.int/export/sites/www/tk/en/igc/pdf/observers_practical_guide.pdf.

In addition, pursuant to a proposal by the European Community and its member states in 2001,[246] since 2005, WIPO has nominally funded, with member states' contributions, the participation of accredited Indigenous peoples and local communities' organizations through the WIPO Voluntary Fund.[247] However, although the Voluntary Fund was initially well funded,[248] in the following years, it frequently became depleted and in reality financed the attendance of only a few representatives;[249] in addition, states have opposed the funding of Indigenous peoples' participation from WIPO's core budget.[250]

We must distinguish the above form of participation in the substantive negotiations themselves, from another form of so-called "participation" that does not add to Indigenous peoples' substantive influence but rather functions as a tokenistic exercise. Since 2005, pursuant to a proposal made by New Zealand,[251] the sessions of the IGC have been opened by panels of representatives of Indigenous and traditional communities presenting on their concerns and experiences.[252] According to the WIPO Secretariat, these panels are 'a rich source of information on the experiences, concerns and aspirations of indigenous and local communities concerning the protection, promotion and preservation of traditional knowledge, traditional cultural expressions and genetic resources'.[253] Summaries of their proceedings are recorded in

[246] WIPO/GRTKF/IC/4/12, para. 11. See the discussion in WIPO, 'WIPO General Assembly, Thirtieth (16th Ordinary) Session, Report' (1 October 2003) WIPO Doc. WO/GA/30/8, 12–19, where the proposal was also supported by Colombia and Venezuela. Express support was later expressed by Mexico (WIPO, 'WIPO General Assembly, Thirty-First (15th Extraordinary) Session, Report' (5 October 2004) WIPO Doc. WO/GA/31/15, para. 91), Switzerland for Group B and Morocco for the African Group, Turkey, Peru, Kyrgyzstan, Trinidad and Tobago, New Zealand, Nigeria, Malaysia, Ethiopia, and Antigua and Barbuda (WIPO, 'WIPO General Assembly, Thirty-Second (17th Ordinary) Session, Report' (5 October 2005) WIPO Doc. WO/GA/32/13, paras. 170, 172, 187, 191, 192, 195–199, and 201).

[247] WIPO, 'Establishment of the WIPO Voluntary Fund for Accredited Indigenous and Local Communities' (2005) WIPO Doc. WO/GA/32/6, Annex.

[248] See, for example, IGO, 'Report of the Eleventh Session', paras. 54–55.

[249] See, for example, IGC, 'Report of the Thirty-Sixth Session' (2018) WIPO Doc. WIPO/GRTKF/IC/36/11, para. 31; 'Report on the Thirty-Fifth Session' (2018) WIPO Doc. WIPO/GRTKF/IC/35/10, para. 36. See also Gordon, 'Appropriation without Representation', 655.

[250] IGC, 'Report on the Twenty-Eight Session' (2014) WIPO Doc. WIPO/GRTKF/IC/28, para. 34.

[251] IGC, 'New Zealand Proposal – Practical Participation of Indigenous and Local Communities' (2005) WIPO Doc. WIPO/GRTKF/IC/7/14.

[252] IGC, 'Report on the Seventh Session', para. 63(iv).

[253] WIPO, 'Presentations on Indigenous and Local Community Experiences', www.wipo.int/tk/en/igc/panels.html.

WIPO's reports of the IGC meetings,[254] and presentations made by panel participants are made available on the IGC website.[255] Although one might argue that the panels heighten the visibility of Indigenous peoples and increase awareness of their concerns and experiences, in practice state representatives often leave the room during the presentations,[256] and there is no formal mechanism by which the panel discussions can feed into the process. There is no evidence that any increased awareness, even if the panels do result in raising the level of awareness of the few state representatives who attend, influences outcomes. The panels have thus been criticized as increasing 'apparent participation while not improving their influence' and sidelining Indigenous peoples' views.[257]

There was a level of recognition by both states and the IGC itself that, normatively speaking, Indigenous peoples ought to be able to participate in the IGC, due to both their affectedness by the IGC's activities and the importance of their participation for the IGC's mandate to be fulfilled, including for legitimizing the IGC process.[258] The IGC decided in 2005 that 'there was a unanimous view that the participation of local and indigenous communities was of great importance' for its work.[259] According to New Zealand's 2004 proposal, 'the subject matter' of the IGC meant that 'indigenous and local communities have a very high stake in the outcomes of its deliberations'.[260] Similarly, the delegation of Portugal on behalf of Group B,[261] at IGC 4, declared that since Indigenous and local communities were directly affected by the IGC's work, it was important that the IGC should

[254] IGC, 'Draft Study on the Participation of Observers in the Work of the Intergovernmental Committee on Intellectual Property and Genetic Resources, Traditional Knowledge and Folklore', Annex, para. 37.

[255] WIPO, 'Intergovernmental Committee IGC' https://wipo.int/tk/en/igc/.

[256] Gordon, 'Appropriation without Representation', 655.

[257] Ibid.

[258] For instance, Spain, Norway, Venezuela (for the Group of Latin American and Caribbean Countries), Peru, Belgium, Thailand, Côte d'Ivoire, Switzerland, Mexico, Portugal (for Group B countries), Barbados, Algeria (for the African Group), Denmark (for the European Community and its member states), Romania (for the Central European and Baltic States), Zambia, Canada, New Zealand, Brazil, South Africa, and the Russian Federation: IGC, 'Report on the First Session', paras. 33 and 147; IGC, 'Report on the Second Session' (14 December 2001) WIPO Doc. WIPO/GRTKF/IC/2/16, paras. 18, 69, 72, 75, 122, 124, 128, 150, and 187; IGC, 'Report on the Third Session' (21 June 2022) WIPO Doc. WIPO/GRTKF/IC/3/17, paras. 25 and 28; IGC, 'Report on the Fourth Session' (17 December 2002) WIPO Doc. WIPO/GRTKF/IC/4/15, paras. 21–42.

[259] IGC, 'Report on the Fifth Session', para. 206.

[260] IGC, 'New Zealand Proposal', Annex, para. 1.

[261] Group B, broadly speaking, is made up of industrialized countries.

continue its work to facilitate their involvement.[262] Other states expressing similar sentiments included Brazil,[263] Mexico,[264] and Namibia.[265]

More instrumentally, Switzerland opined that the 'active and direct participation' of Indigenous communities was 'a crucial prerequisite for the success of its efforts'.[266] Morocco for the African Group, at the WIPO General Assembly meeting in 2005, said the participation of Indigenous communities in the IGC's work would 'consolidate the progress made' in the committee, as well as make the IGC's work 'more visible and adding to its value'.[267] The following year, Kenya said Indigenous peoples' participation would be 'fundamental in orientating the ongoing deliberations', while South Africa believed that Indigenous peoples' 'voice and experience' had been a 'vital contribution' to the IGC's work.[268] Similar sentiments have subsequently been expressed by states including Group B,[269] Central European and Baltic States,[270] the Group of Latin American and Caribbean States,[271] the European Union,[272] the Regional Group of Central Asian, Caucasus and Eastern European Countries,[273] Australia,[274]

262 IGC, 'Report on the Fourth Session', para. 21.

263 Highlighting the fact that Indigenous communities had 'much at stake' in the IGF: IGC, 'Report on the Fourteenth Session' (1 October 2009) WIPO/GRTKF/IC/14/12, para. 183.

264 IGC, 'Report on the Sixteenth Session' (10 December 2010) WIPO/GRTKF/IC/16/8, para. 40.

265 IGC, 'Report on the Twentieth Session' (13 July 2012) WIPO/GRTKF/IC/20/10, para. 723.

266 IGC, 'Report on the Fourth Session', para. 26; also see IGC, 'Report on the Twenty-Seventh Session' (2 July 2014) WIPO/GRTKF/IC/27/10, para. 20.

267 WIPO, 'WIPO General Assembly, Thirty-Second Session', para. 172. Also see subsequent statements by the African Group, including IGC, 'Report on the Thirty-Eighth Session', para. 14; IGC, 'Report on the Nineteenth Session' (23 February 2012) WIPO/GRTKF/IC/19/12, para. 479; IGC, 'Report on the Twenty-Seventh Session', para. 24; and IGC, 'Report on the Twenty-Eighth Session', para. 57.

268 WIPO, 'WIPO General Assembly, Thirty-Third (16th Extraordinary) Session, Report' (3 October 2006) WIPO Doc. WO/GA/33/10, paras. 152–153.

269 Describing Indigenous peoples as having a 'valuable and essential role' for the work of the IGC: IGC, 'Report on the Thirty-Fifth Session', para. 20. Also see subsequent statements, for example, IGC, 'Draft Report on the Fortieth Session' (30 September 2019) WIPO Doc. WIPO/GRTKF/IC/40/20 PROV.2, para. 21.

270 IGC, 'Report on the Thirty-Sixth Session', para. 20.

271 IGC, 'Report on the Thirty-Eighth Session' (2019) WIPO Doc WIPO/GRTKF/IC/38/16, para. 15. See also IGC, 'Report on the Fifteenth Session' (14 May 2010) WIPO Doc. WIPO/GRTKF/IC/15/7, para. 33.

272 IGC, 'Report on the Fourteenth Session', para. 18 (Indigenous communities 'integral to finding a solution for the protection of GR, TK and TCEs').

273 IGC, 'Report on the Fifteenth Session', para. 35.

274 IGC, 'Draft Report on the Twenty-Fifth Session' (18 October 2013) WIPO Doc. WIPO/GRTKF/IC/25/8 PROV.2, para. 17; IGC, 'Report on the Twenty-Seventh Session', para. 22 (stating that Indigenous participation was important to maintain the IGC's 'credibility, transparency and relevance'); IGC, 'Report on the Twenty-Eighth Session', para. 30; IGC,

Brazil,[275] Canada,[276] Chile,[277] Colombia,[278] New Zealand,[279] Pakistan,[280] and Peru.[281] Further support for Indigenous peoples' participation in the IGC – without naming reasons, but nonetheless demonstrating wide support – was expressed by South Africa,[282] the Asia and the Pacific Group,[283] the Like-Minded Countries,[284] the United States,[285] Egypt,[286] Israel,[287] Guatemala,[288] Venezuela,[289] Thailand,[290] and the Republic of Korea.[291]

The level of practice under the CBD's Article 8(j) Working Group and the WIPO IGC was certainly more than under the UNFCCC during the period under consideration, which in turn was more than nothing. However, it was lower than what had been concurrently occurring in the WGIP and WGDD. It did not place Indigenous peoples on the same footing as states.[292] While

'Report on the Thirty-Third Session' (12 June 2017) WIPO Doc. WIPO/GRTKF/IC/33/7, para. 32.

275 IGC, 'Report on the Sixteenth Session', para. 33.

276 IGC, 'Report on the Nineteenth Session', para. 555.

277 IGC, 'Report on the Twenty-Eighth Session', para. 32.

278 IGC, 'Report on the Twentieth Session', para. 758.

279 IGC, 'Draft Report on the Twenty-Fifth Session', para. 16; IGC, 'Report on the Twenty-Seventh Session', para. 23.

280 WIPO Secretariat, 'Note on Existing Mechanisms for Participation of Observers in the Work of the WIPO Intergovernmental Committee on Intellectual Property and Genetic Resources, Traditional Knowledge and Folklore' (10 October 2011), Annex, Comments of the Intellectual Property Organisation of Pakistan, 1 (encouraging 'strengthening the capacity' of observers to contribute to the process, citing their 'valuable inputs').

281 IGC, 'Report on the Twenty-Eighth Session', para. 33 (noting the legitimizing function of Indigenous participation).

282 IGC, 'Report on the Thirty-Seventh Session' (2019) WIPO Doc. WIPO/GRTKF/IC/37/17, para. 36; IGC, 'Report on the Twentieth Session', para. 750; IGC, 'Report on the Twenty-Seventh Session', para. 27.

283 IGC, 'Report on the Thirty-Ninth Session' (2019) WIPO Doc. WIPO/GRRTKF/IC/39/18, para. 187.

284 Ibid.

285 Ibid., para. 196.

286 IGC, 'Report on the Fifteenth Session', para. 53.

287 IGC, 'Report on the Sixteenth Session', para. 54.

288 IGC, 'Report on the Eighteenth Session' (29 July 2011) WIPO/GRTKF/IC/18/11, para. 386.

289 IGC, 'Report on the Twentieth Session', para. 791.

290 IGC, 'Report on the Twenty-Seventh Session', para. 28.

291 Ibid., para. 32.

292 In relation to the WIPO IGC, this point has been made by, for example, Gordon, 'Appropriation without Representation'; Lawson, Bikundo, and Tranter, 'The Perils of Parliamentarism'; Maui Solomon, 'An Indigenous Perspective on the WIPO IGC' in Daniel F. Robinson, Ahmed Abdel-Latif, and Pedro Roffe (eds.), *Protecting Traditional Knowledge: The WIPO Intergovernmental Committee on Intellectual Property and Genetic Resources, Traditional Knowledge and Folklore* (Oxford: Routledge, 2017), 219–229; Boehme et al., 'Cultural Diversity and the Politics of Recognition in International Organizations'.

Indigenous peoples can make textual proposals and amendments in both forums, these require the support of at least one state in order to be reflected in the text.[293] Proposals made by states, on the other hand, encounter no such gatekeeping. A common element, from the WGIP to the WIPO IGC, is that Indigenous peoples cannot vote on final outcomes: just as Indigenous peoples lost influence over the final version of the UNDRIP when it entered the General Assembly, they will not be able to vote on the adoption of any eventual instrument emerging from the IGC in the WIPO General Assembly.[294]

3.6 DEVELOPMENT INSTITUTIONS

Meanwhile, steps towards increased participation of Indigenous peoples were being made in international development and finance organizations. This section considers three examples: the World Bank, the UN Development Programme (UNDP), and the International Fund for Agricultural Development (IFAD). In all cases, the influence of ILO Convention 169, with its emphasis on Indigenous peoples' participation and free, prior, and informed consent, is clear. These policies and practices represented advances compared with previous policies and paved the way for further advances over time.

3.6.1 *The World Bank*

The effect of the WGIP's example, as well as the substantive provisions of ILO Convention 169, became apparent at the World Bank in 1991. The Bank had first addressed the situation of Indigenous peoples in a 1982 policy document entitled "Tribal People in Bank-Financed Projects." The document outlined procedures for protecting the rights of "tribal people," recognizing that they were 'more likely to be negatively impacted than helped' by development projects.[295] The 1982 policy did not extend as far as to provide for the participation of such peoples in the lending and development process, however. Indeed, it was elaborated without any participation by Indigenous peoples. Moreover, like ILO Convention 107, it took an assimilationist approach premised on the integration of Indigenous peoples

[293] Gordon, 'Appropriation without Representation', 632.

[294] Lawson, Bikundo, and Tranter, 'The Perils of Parliamentarism', 307, 309.

[295] World Bank, Operational Manual Statement, 'Tribal People in Bank-Financed Projects', OMS 2.34 (1982), para. 5.

into Western society.[296] A 1987 review recommended revising the policy, suggesting that the World Bank should promote the direct participation of Indigenous peoples in the planning of development projects, as without such participation there were 'several dangers that development projects will not only fail to satisfy the manifest needs of indigenous peoples, but may also be initiated and developed at their expense'.[297] That same year, in a meeting with the then President of the Bank, three Indigenous leaders from Colombia, Peru, and Bolivia recommended that tripartite agreements be adopted between the World Bank, the borrowing country, and affected Indigenous peoples in all cases where loan operations affected their communities and territories.[298] This was followed up in 1990 when Indigenous organizations recommended a policy of requiring the informed consent of affected Indigenous peoples for development projects in Indigenous areas to take place, participation of organizations representing the affected Indigenous peoples throughout the full project cycle, and the establishment of tripartite commissions to oversee project implementation.[299]

3.6.1.1 Operational Directive 4.20, 1991

Beginning in 1991, with the Bank's adoption of Operational Directive 4.20 on Indigenous peoples,[300] the Bank began to develop a more participatory approach, although it did not go as far as Indigenous peoples' proposals. The policy provided that, with a view to ensuring that Indigenous peoples would not be 'subject to adverse effects during the development process' and would receive 'culturally compatible social and economic benefits',[301] 'the strategy for addressing the issues pertaining to indigenous peoples must be based on the *informed participation* of the indigenous peoples themselves'.[302] Operational Directive 4.20 further provided that mechanisms should be

[296] Shelton H. Davis, 'The World Bank and Operational Directive 2.0' in Lydia van de Fliert (ed.), *Indigenous Peoples and International Organizations* (Nottingham: Russell Press, 1994), 75, 76.

[297] World Bank, Office of Environmental and Scientific Affairs, 'A Five-Year Implementation Review of OMS 2.34 (1982–1986)' (June 1987).

[298] Tom Griffiths, 'Indigenous Peoples and the World Bank: Experiences with Participation' (Forest Peoples Programme, July 2005), 3.

[299] Referenced in Griffiths, 'Indigenous Peoples and the World Bank', 3.

[300] World Bank, Operational Directive 4.20, Indigenous Peoples (World Bank 1991).

[301] Ibid., para. 6.

[302] Ibid., para. 8 (emphasis in original).

established for Indigenous peoples' participation 'throughout project planning, implementation and evaluation', noting the existence of Indigenous peoples' organizations 'that provide effective channels for communicating local preferences' and that 'traditional leaders' should be brought into the planning process. It stated that due concern should be given to ensuring 'genuine representation', while noting that no 'foolproof methods' exist for guaranteeing full participation at the local level.[303] It called for borrowing countries to prepare Indigenous Peoples Development Plans in all projects affecting Indigenous peoples, with the participation of the affected people(s).[304] In practice, this was mainly carried out through consultations.[305]

The reader may question the relevance of this example, which is different from the others canvassed so far in this chapter. It does not concern Indigenous peoples' participation in the making of an international instrument or standard regarding their rights, or in an international conference on matters concerning them, but rather relates to participation in planning and decision-making regarding lending for development projects. Moreover, it could be viewed as merely being an instance of Indigenous peoples' participation in national policymaking processes: the Directive mandates that the national borrower establish mechanisms for Indigenous peoples' participation. However, one can also view this as an instance of Indigenous peoples' participation in decision-making processes at the international level, i.e. those of the World Bank. Although under the Directive the Indigenous peoples concerned did not engage directly with the Bank, by mandating receiving countries to carry out participatory processes, the Bank created a dynamic whereby Indigenous participation was required for the disbursement of funds by the Bank. In other words, Indigenous participation was critical to the Bank's decision regarding whether or not to fund a given project.

At the UN Expert Seminar in 1992,[306] a representative of the World Bank elaborated on the motivations behind the Operational Directive. He stated that the Directive started from the premise that Indigenous peoples were

303 Ibid., para. 15(d).

304 Ibid., paras. 13, 14, and 15.

305 World Bank Country Evaluation and Regional Relations Operations Evaluation Department, *Implementation of Operational Directive 4.20 on Indigenous Peoples: An Evaluation of Results* (10 April 2003) Report No. 23754, paras. 3.7–3.8.

306 See above, Section 3.2.

'more likely to be harmed by development projects' as they were especially vulnerable due to 'discrimination, marginalization, inadequate legal frameworks and above all, lack of safe access to natural resources upon which they depended'. He stressed that development decisions 'should be left to indigenous peoples themselves', which meant that they 'should participate in the formulation, design and implementation of the programmes that affected them'.[307]

The implementation of the Directive was imperfect. According to an internal review conducted in 2003, while there was a 'marked increase' in Indigenous peoples' participation in the design and implementation of projects where the directive was applied, their participation in decision-making and financial management was low, in part due to national regulations controlling the use of public funds. Moreover, in a third of projects where Indigenous people were affected, the Operational Directive was not applied. In addition, World Bank projects typically lacked adequate indicators for Indigenous participation, and some lacked monitoring systems altogether, meaning that for many projects it was impossible to verify if Indigenous peoples had participated, let alone assess the quality of participation.[308] Civil society organizations documented the continuing prominence of top-down World Bank interventions, including cases where consultations were organized only with the objective to stem Indigenous communities' criticism of proposed projects, as well as the use of "participation" as a government tool for social control and co-option.[309] Recognition of this led to a revised policy.

3.6.1.2 World Bank Operational Policy 4.10, 2005

Operational Policy 4.10 replaced Operational Directive 4.20 in 2005,[310] following several years of development including consultations with Indigenous peoples' organizations.[311]

307 Santiago Report, para. 58.

308 World Bank Operations Evaluation Department, *Implementation of Operational Directive 4.20 on Indigenous Peoples: An Independent Desk Review* (10 January 2003) Report No. 25332, para. 3.21 and table 3.4.

309 Griffiths, 'Indigenous Peoples and the World Bank'.

310 World Bank, Operational Manual: OP 4.10 – Indigenous Peoples (World Bank 2005), and Bank Procedure 4.10 on Indigenous Peoples (20 May 2005).

311 World Bank, 'Summary of Consultations with External Stakeholders regarding the World Bank Draft Indigenous Peoples Policy, Draft OP/BP 4.10' (18 April 2002). However, note that the consultation process was condemned by Indigenous peoples for being rushed, lacking time for open discussion, poor moderation, and translation facilities, and not sufficiently timely

The Policy requires a borrowing country to engage in a process of 'free, prior and informed consultation' on all projects potentially affecting Indigenous peoples.[312] The borrowing country is required to establish an appropriate framework that provides opportunities for consultation at each stage of project preparation and implementation, use consultation methods appropriate to the local conditions and values of the relevant communities, and provide them with all relevant information about the project.[313] It is then required to ascertain whether there is 'broad support' from the affected Indigenous communities and to prepare a detailed report on the process of consultation and measures that may be required to address adverse effects on Indigenous peoples and to provide them with project benefits.[314] The borrowing country then prepares, in consultation with the affected communities, an Indigenous Peoples Plan that sets out the measures by which it will ensure that affected Indigenous peoples receive culturally appropriate social and economic benefits.[315] Under the Policy, the Bank will finance a project only when free, prior, and informed *consultation* results in 'broad community support to the project by the affected indigenous peoples'.[316] The Bank is then required to review the process and outcome of the consultation to satisfy itself that the affected Indigenous communities 'have provided their broad support to the project'.[317] This, notably, stops short of recognizing the right to free, prior, and informed *consent* in all cases.[318] The Policy clarifies that the provisions on consultation cannot be interpreted in the sense of according a veto right to individuals or groups.[319] In this way, as Stefanie Errico points out, ultimately 'the only option that indigenous peoples have is to work to improve the conditions of the project involving their land and resources without having the power to stop it'.[320] Operational Policy 4.10, then, while

prior provision of relevant documentation: Griffiths, 'Indigenous Peoples and the World Bank', 4–6.

[312] World Bank, 'OP 4.10', para. 10.

[313] Ibid., para. 10.

[314] Ibid., para. 11.

[315] Ibid., para. 12.

[316] Ibid., para. 1.

[317] Ibid., para. 11.

[318] On the failure to recognize FPIC, see Stefania Errico, 'The World Bank and Indigenous Peoples: The Operational Policy on Indigenous Peoples (O.P. 4.10) between Indigenous Peoples' Rights to Traditional Lands and to Free, Prior, and Informed Consent' (2006) 13 *International Journal on Minority and Group Rights*, 367–390.

[319] World Bank, 'OP 4.10', para. 1.

[320] Errico, 'The World Bank and Indigenous Peoples', 372.

representing an advance over the previous policy, still falls short of the standard of free, prior, and informed consent as contained in ILO Convention 169.[321]

3.6.1.3 The Grants Facility for Indigenous Peoples/Indigenous Peoples Assistance Facility

In September 2003, the World Bank announced it would fund a Grants Facility for Indigenous Peoples to support development projects planned and implemented by and for Indigenous peoples. It disbursed grants of between US$10,000 and 30,000. The Facility was governed by a board consisting in majority of Indigenous peoples' leaders, as well as representatives from governments, donors, civil society organizations, the UNPFII, and the World Bank.[322]

The Facility operated for three years under the auspices of the World Bank – during which time the Bank noted that the governance structure 'had worked well, that there was significant interest in the Facility, that the quantity and quality of the proposals had been high, and that the approach of working directly with communities for the self-identification of activities had been successful'.[323] Then it was transferred to IFAD[324] in September 2006.[325] At IFAD, the facility was renamed the Indigenous Peoples Assistance Facility (IPAF).

Under IFAD, IPAF has given small grants of US$20–50,000 to Indigenous and tribal peoples to enable them to design and implement grassroots development projects based on their own priorities.[326] The board of the IPAF,

[321] Fergus MacKay, 'The Draft World Bank Operational Policy 4.10 on Indigenous Peoples: Progress or More of the Same?' (2005) 22 *Arizona Journal of International & Comparative Law*, 65–98, 68; Errico, 'The World Bank and Indigenous Peoples', 380ff.

[322] World Bank, 'About the Grants Facility for Indigenous Peoples' (World Bank, 2004) http://web.worldbank.org/archive/website00524/WEB/OTHER/GLOBAL-3.HTM.

[323] IFAD, 'IFAD's Engagement with Indigenous Peoples' (2 August 2006), IFAD Doc EB 2006/88/R.34, para. 32.

[324] IFAD, a specialized agency of the UN, was established in 1977 to finance agricultural development projects, primarily for food production in developing countries: Agreement Establishing the International Fund for Agricultural Development (opened for signature 20 December 1976 and entered into force 30 November 1977) 1059 UNTS 191.

[325] IFAD, 'Letter Agreement between IFAD and the International Bank for Reconstruction and Development for the Transfer of the Grants Facility for Indigenous Peoples' (2 August 2006) IFAD Doc EB 2006/88/R.40.

[326] IFAD, 'Indigenous Peoples Assistance Facility' (IFAD, n.d.) www.ifad.org/en/ipaf.

which makes decisions about which proposals to finance, since its inception has consisted in majority of Indigenous peoples' leaders: four representatives of Indigenous peoples' organizations from different regions, as well as one representative each of the UNPFII and IFAD.[327] At the regional level, the IPAF is co-managed by Indigenous peoples' organizations.[328] The IFAD has described the IPAF as a 'listening and learning instrument' on the needs, solutions, and innovations of Indigenous peoples.[329] Thus, Indigenous peoples have delegated power over some decisions of the IFAD that directly affect them.[330]

3.6.2 *The UN Development Programme and the Policy of Engagement with Indigenous Peoples, 2001*

Following, and going beyond, the World Bank's example, in 2001 UNDP adopted a policy on engagement with Indigenous peoples, developed as a result of consultation with Indigenous peoples' organizations.[331] The policy recognized that UNDP needed to develop its own capacity to enable Indigenous peoples' full participation in the design and implementation of UNDP projects and programmes.[332] The policy went on to state that UNDP 'promotes and supports' the right to free, prior, and informed consent regarding development projects and programmes affecting Indigenous peoples, '[c]onsistent with United Nations conventions such as ILO Convention 169'.[333] It highlighted that consultation should include representatives from Indigenous peoples' organizations, and the need for the use of culturally appropriate consultation methods and respect for Indigenous peoples' concepts of time.[334] It encouraged UNDP country offices to develop their own strategies for engaging with Indigenous peoples, including building

[327] IFAD, *IFAD Policy on Engagement with Indigenous Peoples* (IFAD, 2009), 16 and 29–30.
[328] For the most recent IPAF cycle, these were Foro Internacional de Mujeres Indígenas, Samburu Women Trust, and Tebtebba Foundation: IFAD, 'Good Practices in IFAD's Engagement with Indigenous Peoples' (IFAD 2021) 4, www.ifad.org/documents/38714170/44358796/IPs_engagement_Good_Practices.pdf/deaa1849-6518-e223-8274-d672f1081499?t=1651742225818.
[329] IFAD, 'Policy on Engagement', 29.
[330] Not all decisions, as the Executive Board still makes decisions on proposals of larger amounts, many of which affect Indigenous peoples.
[331] UNDP, *UNDP and Indigenous Peoples: A Policy of Engagement* (UNDP 2001), para. 4.
[332] Ibid., paras. 22–23.
[333] Ibid., para. 28.
[334] Ibid., paras. 60–61.

the capacity of Indigenous peoples' organizations to participate in the design of development activities affecting them.[335]

This policy is partly motivated by the need to fulfil UNDP's mandate. The 2001 policy points to the importance of Indigenous peoples' participation for the organization's objectives.[336] It highlights that ensuring participation is 'critical in preventing and resolving conflict, enhancing democratic governance, reducing poverty and sustainably managing the environment'.[337] Similarly, remarks delivered to the UNPFII by the Associate Administrator of the UNDP highlighted that improving Indigenous peoples' participation was 'crucial' for generating inclusive development.[338] There is also evidence that as early as 2001, UNDP perceived its participation policies as required by international law: the 2001 Policy states that it is 'informed and underpinned by the international human rights framework', as well as by 'the international conventions, declarations and programmes of action that recognize indigenous peoples' rights'.[339] This is the earliest such recognition by any of the international organizations studied in this chapter.

3.7 REGIONAL PROCESSES

3.7.1 *The Arctic*

At the same time, as developments regarding Indigenous peoples' participation were occurring in UN expert meetings, the Rio Conference and other UN conferences, the UNFCCC, CBD, WIPO, and international development institutions, Indigenous peoples' participation in regional governance processes was also evolving. The Arctic is a case in point. Since the early 1990s, a trend of Arctic Indigenous peoples' participation has been established in realms such as the Arctic Council, the Barents regional cooperation, the negotiations towards the Stockholm Convention on Persistent Organic Pollutants, and Sámi participation in the negotiations towards the Nordic Saami Convention. In the Arctic, perhaps to a greater extent than anywhere

[335] Ibid., para. 47.
[336] Ibid., para. 5.
[337] Ibid., para. 3.
[338] UNDP, 'Rebecca Grynspan: Remarks at UN Permanent Forum on Indigenous Issues' (16 May 2011) (speech delivered to UNPFII) www.undp.org/content/undp/en/home/presscenter/speeches/2011/05/16/rebeca-grynspan-remarks-at-un-permanent-forum-on-indigenous-issues-.html.
[339] UNDP, *UNDP and Indigenous Peoples*, para. 7.

else, states have shared the power with Indigenous peoples in regional governance processes.

3.7.1.1 The Arctic Council

THE ARCTIC ENVIRONMENTAL PROTECTION STRATEGY The prehistory of the Arctic Council dates back to at least June 1991 with the adoption of the Arctic Environmental Protection Strategy (AEPS) by Norway, Sweden, Finland, Canada, Denmark, the then Soviet Union, and the United States.[340] Three Indigenous peoples' organizations – the Inuit Circumpolar Council, the Saami Council, and the Russian Association of Indigenous Peoples of the North (RAIPON) – among other "observers," had assisted in preparing the text of the AEPS.[341] The AEPS related to cooperation on scientific research regarding pollution, the assessment of potential environmental impacts of development activities, and implementation of measures to control pollutants and reduce their adverse impacts on the Arctic environment, among other matters.[342]

Under the Declaration on the Protection of the Arctic Environment, by which the participating states adopted the AEPS, participating states agreed 'to continue to promote cooperation with the Arctic Indigenous peoples and to invite their organizations to future meetings as observers'.[343] Chapter 10 of the AEPS stated that the three Indigenous peoples' organizations that had contributed to the preparation of the text would be invited to meetings of the AEPS states, as observers.[344] The motivation for this stemmed from states' recognition of 'the special relationship of the indigenous peoples and local populations to the Arctic and their unique contribution to the protection of the Arctic Environment'.[345] This status in the AEPS was a strong foundation on which Arctic Indigenous peoples were to build.

The second ministerial meeting of the AEPS states, in 1993, presented a first opportunity to consolidate Indigenous peoples' participation. In 1993, Indigenous peoples' active participation at the Rio Earth Summit was presumably fresh in the minds of Arctic Indigenous participants; indeed, the

340 Arctic Environmental Protection Strategy (14 June 1991) ("AEPS").
341 AEPS, 1.
342 Ibid., 2.
343 Declaration on the Protection of the Arctic Environment, AEPS at 3, 3.
344 AEPS, 42.
345 Declaration on the Protection of the Arctic Environment, preamble, fifth recital.

Nuuk Declaration adopted by states at that 1993 meeting affirmed in its preamble Principle 22 of the Rio Declaration.[346] By the Nuuk Declaration, states pronounced that they would 'promote [Indigenous peoples'] effective participation in the achievement of sustainable development in the Arctic'.[347] In the report on the session, ministers agreed to 'explore various sources of support for indigenous organizations accredited to the AEPS, to enable them to determine how best they should participate in the AEPS', and also agreed to 'continue to promote cooperation with the Arctic indigenous peoples'.[348]

The Nuuk Declaration shows how Arctic states' motivations for enabling Indigenous peoples' participation were both instrumental and affectedness orientated: they regarded Indigenous peoples' traditional knowledge as greatly important for the AEPS to succeed, but also acknowledged that Indigenous peoples were affected by environmental issues. The preamble of the declaration recognizes that Indigenous peoples are particularly at risk from environmental degradation in the Arctic.[349] In the operative part of the declaration, states recognized 'the special role of the indigenous peoples in environmental management and development in the Arctic, and of the significance of their knowledge and traditional practices'.[350] The report of the session stated that 'it is of great importance for the success' of the AEPS that their ecological and environmental knowledge is 'effectively incorporated into the process'.[351]

Building on this momentum, as well as that from the Rio Conference, Indigenous leaders persuaded the Senior Arctic Affairs Officials (SAAOs) – the designated points of contact in each state for Arctic issues – to allow Indigenous peoples to attend and intervene in meetings of the SAAOs.[352] This development, in turn, led to the three Indigenous peoples' groups being

[346] Nuuk Declaration on Environment and Development in the Arctic (16 September 1993), preamble, ninth recital.

[347] Ibid., para. 7.

[348] Marine Mammal Commission, *The Marine Mammal Commission Compendium of Selected Treaties, International Agreements, and Other Relevant Documents on Marine Resources, Wildlife, and the Environment*, First Update (Washington, D.C.: The Marine Mammal Commission, 1994), 279–287, 'The Nuuk Declaration on Environment and Development in the Arctic, Nuuk, 1993, Report', https://iea.uoregon.edu/MarineMammals/engine/Documents/1-0279-0287.htm ('The Nuuk Declaration Report').

[349] Nuuk Declaration on Environment and Development in the Arctic, third recital.

[350] Ibid., para. 7.

[351] Marine Mammal Commission, 'The Nuuk Declaration Report'.

[352] Timo Koivurova, 'The Status and Role of Indigenous Peoples in Arctic International Governance' (2011) 3 *Yearbook of Polar Law*, 169–192, 178.

deemed Permanent Participants to the AEPS, at the third AEPS ministerial in 1996.[353] Alongside this, in 1994 the Indigenous Peoples' Secretariat, tasked with facilitating the Indigenous organizations' participation in the work of the AEPS, enhancing their capacity, and facilitating dialogue among them, was established by the Danish government.[354] The Inuvik Declaration of the third AEPS ministerial meeting recognized and affirmed 'the right of all Arctic indigenous peoples to be represented in the AEPS', acknowledged the contributions of the Permanent Participants, and encouraged them and other Indigenous peoples' organizations 'to participate actively in the work of the AEPS'.[355] This is the first known instance of states using the language of human rights to support Indigenous peoples' participation in regional governance.

By this time, negotiations towards the establishment of the Arctic Council were already underway. Recounting this period, Koivurova notes that even though three Indigenous organizations were already Permanent Participants at the AEPS, 'it was by no means clear that they would be able to retain their position'.[356] The United States, especially, 'found it difficult to accept indigenous peoples gaining an influential status as permanent participants in the founding document of a new high-level inter-governmental forum', a position that only changed in the final stages of the negotiations.[357]

THE ARCTIC COUNCIL In 1996, negotiations bore fruit in the establishment of the Arctic Council. Building on the AEPS, the Arctic Council is a 'high level forum' established to, among other objectives,[358]

> provide a means for promoting cooperation, coordination and interaction among the Arctic States, *with the involvement of the Arctic indigenous communities and other Arctic inhabitants on common Arctic issues*, in particular issues of sustainable development and environmental protection in the Arctic.

The involvement of Arctic Indigenous peoples was thereby built into the Arctic Council from the very beginning. The Ottawa Declaration on the

353 Inuvik Declaration (21 March 1996), paras. 6 and 8.
354 Ibid., para. 7.
355 Ibid., para. 8.
356 Koivurova, 'The Status and Role', 179.
357 Ibid; David Scrivener, 'Arctic Environmental Cooperation in Transition' (1999) 35 *Polar Record*, 51–58, 54.
358 Declaration on the Establishment of the Arctic Council (1996) 35 ILM 1387 ("Ottawa Declaration"), Article 1(a) (emphasis added).

Establishment of the Arctic Council recognized in its preamble 'the special relationship and unique contributions to the Arctic of indigenous people and their communities' and noted states' desire to 'ensure full consultation with and the full involvement of indigenous people and their communities and other inhabitants of the Arctic' in activities to address Arctic issues requiring circumpolar cooperation.[359]

Similarly to the AEPS, in addition to its eight member states, the Arctic Council created a Permanent Participant status for Arctic organizations of Indigenous peoples, intended to 'provide for active participation and full consultation with the Arctic indigenous representatives within the Arctic Council'.[360] Article 2 of the Ottawa Declaration granted such status to the Inuit Circumpolar Conference, the Saami Council, and RAIPON – the same three organizations that had held that status in relation to the AEPS – while leaving the door to Permanent Participant status open to other Arctic organizations of Indigenous peoples with majority Arctic Indigenous constituency, representing either a single Indigenous people resident in more than one Arctic state or more than one Arctic Indigenous people resident in a single Arctic state, with the caveat that the number of Permanent Participants should be less than that of member states.[361] Since its establishment, the Arctic Council has welcomed the Aleut International Association, the Gwich'in Council International, and the Arctic Athabascan Council as additional Permanent Participants.[362] Indigenous peoples' participation is clearly distinct from that of NGOs and other entities: an observer status, which entails fewer rights than Permanent Participant status, is open to NGOs as well as non-Arctic states, IGOs, and inter-parliamentary organizations.[363]

The Council structured its work through (i) biennial ministerial meetings, (ii) working groups to carry out the technical and research work of identifying and analysing challenges to the Arctic environment, and (iii) meetings of the Senior Arctic Officials occurring at least twice a year and serving as a liaison between the ministerial and the working groups.[364] Under the Council's

359 Ottawa Declaration, preamble, recitals 1 and 6.

360 Ottawa Declaration, Article 2. The United States attempted to block the status of Indigenous peoples as permanent participants until late in the negotiations on the Declaration: Timo Koivurova and Leena Heinämäki, 'The Participation of Indigenous Peoples in International Norm-Making in the Arctic' (2006) 42 *Polar Record*, 101–109, 105.

361 Also see Arctic Council, *Arctic Council Rules of Procedure* (revised version, 2013) ("Rules of Procedure"), Rule 34.

362 Koivurova and Heinämäki, 'The Participation of Indigenous Peoples', 107.

363 Ottawa Declaration, Article 3.

364 See Svein Vigeland Rottem, 'A Note on the Arctic Council Agreements' (2015) 46 *Ocean Development and International Law*, 50–59, 51.

Rules of Procedure, Permanent Participants have been permitted to participate in all meetings and activities of the Council and to be represented by 'a head of delegation and such other representatives as each Arctic State and Permanent Participant deems necessary'.[365] The principle of active participation and full consultation with the Permanent Participants has applied to 'all meetings and activities' of the Council,[366] and while decision-making has been by consensus of the member states,[367] Permanent Participants could propose agenda items for ministerial meetings[368] and make proposals for cooperative activities.[369]

Indigenous peoples thus have had 'almost equal participatory rights as the state members'.[370] Despite the stipulation that only states hold formal decision-making power, the fact that the Permanent Participants must be fully consulted on decisions has functioned as 'close to a *de facto* power of veto should they all reject a particular proposal'.[371] Moreover, the 'fluid manner in which many decisions are made in the council's working groups and task forces' has meant that 'it is seldom clear when a formal decision is being taken'.[372] Significant, too, is the element of institutional memory: many of the heads of delegation of the Permanent Participants 'have been involved in the council much longer than their government counterparts', enabling them to be 'highly effective – and influential' participants.[373] Further, Indigenous peoples' organizations have in fact been highly influential. They played an active role in the negotiation of two legally binding instruments negotiated under the Council's auspices – the Arctic Search and Rescue Agreement of 2011 and the Agreement on Cooperation on Marine Oil Pollution Preparedness and Response in the Arctic of 2013[374] – and in both cases

365 Rules of Procedure, Rule 4.

366 Ibid., Rule 5.

367 Ottawa Declaration Article 7; Rules of Procedure, Rule 7.

368 Rules of Procedure, Rule 19.

369 Ibid., Rule 26.

370 Margherita Paola Poto, 'Participatory Engagement and the Empowerment of the Arctic Indigenous Peoples' (2017) 19 *Environmental Law Review*, 30–47, 40.

371 Koivurova and Heinämäki, 'The Participation of Indigenous Peoples', 104.

372 Brian R. Israel, 'International Law and Governance in a Changing Arctic' (2014) 108 *American Journal of International Law*, 348–359, 357.

373 Israel, 'Changing Arctic', 357.

374 Agreement on Cooperation on Aeronautical and Maritime Search and Rescue in the Arctic (signed 12 May 2011 and entered into force 19 January 2013) 50 ILM 1119; Agreement on Cooperation on Marine Oil Pollution Preparedness and Response in the Arctic (signed 15 May 2013 and entered into force 25 March 2016), https://oaarchive.arctic-council.org/handle/11374/529.

managed to have their rights reflected in the text of the agreements.[375] In addition, two proposals submitted by the Saami Council were chosen by ministers at the Iqaluit ministerial meeting in 1998 for completion and implementation under the guidance of SAAOs.[376] Another example is the policy discussions and scientific research efforts towards the Arctic Climate Impact Assessment (ACIA), which was launched in 2000.[377] As Sheila Watt-Cloutier writes, the ACIA research efforts drew upon both science and Inuit traditional knowledge, and many researchers worked directly with Inuit hunters and elders, as a result of Permanent Participants' suggestions.[378] In the policy discussions, the Permanent Participants managed, after some struggle, to have their recommendations reflected in the ACIA policy recommendations report.[379]

3.7.1.2 Barents Regional Cooperation

While undoubtedly the most well-known, the Arctic Council is far from the only instance of Indigenous participation in Arctic regional governance. The Barents regional cooperation is another such case. Initiated by the Kirkenes Declaration of 1993 between Sweden, Finland, Norway, Denmark, Iceland, Russia, and the EU, the Barents cooperation consists principally of two organs, the Barents Euro-Arctic Council (BEAC) and the Barents Regional Council (BRC).[380] The BEAC convenes once a year at ministerial level, serving as a forum for cooperation in multiple fields, including economy, trade, science and technology, tourism, and the environment, among others.[381] The BRC consists of delegates of the regional governments of the sub-national counties or provinces that make up the region.[382] Structurally, the Barents cooperation

375 Poto, 'Participatory Engagement and Empowerment', 46; Margherita Paola Poto, 'Participatory Rights of Indigenous Peoples: The Virtuous Example of the Arctic Region' (2016) 28 *Environmental Law & Management*, 81–89, 88.

376 Evan T. Bloom, 'Current Developments: Establishment of the Arctic Council' (1999) 93 *American Journal of International Law*, 712–722.

377 Arctic Council, Barrow Declaration (13 October 2000), accessible at https://oaarchive.arctic-council.org/handle/11374/87.

378 Watt-Cloutier, *The Right to Be Cold*, 200–201.

379 Ibid., 201–215.

380 Declaration on Cooperation in the Barents Euro-Arctic Region, Conference of Foreign Ministers in Kirkenes, 11 January 1993 (Kirkenes Declaration).

381 Kirkenes Declaration, Annex: Terms of Reference for the Council of the Barents Euro-Arctic Region, paras. 1, 3, and 5.

382 The Protocol Agreement from the Statutory Meeting of the Regional Council of the Barents Region (the Euro-Arctic Region) adopted by the Regional Council of the Barents Region, Kirkenes, 11 January 1993. The participating regions currently include Nordland Fylke,

is supported by the International Barents Secretariat,[383] and the two councils have established thematic working groups, including on culture, education and research, energy, health and social issues, tourism, rescue cooperation, and economic cooperation.[384] Most of the cooperation takes place through the activities of these working groups.[385] In addition, the BEAC is supported by a Committee of Senior Officials (CSO), which acts as its executive organ.

From the beginning, the documents attest to a clear imperative felt by member states to involve Indigenous peoples in the cooperation process. The Kirkenes Declaration expressly noted that the BRC will include 'representation of the indigenous peoples of the Region'[386] and in addition 'reaffirmed' the participating states' 'commitment to the rights of the indigenous peoples in the North' in keeping with Chapter 26 of Agenda 21.[387] In addition, it contained their 'commitment to strengthen the indigenous communities of the Region, and to ensure that the cooperation now being initiated will take the interests of indigenous peoples into consideration'. It 'took note of' a proposal to establish a Working Group for Indigenous Issues with representatives from Indigenous peoples and government authorities from Finland, Norway, Russia, and Sweden and agreed various tasks that the Working Group might undertake.[388] At the second session of the BEAC, the following year, these sentiments were repeated and the Council expressed the hope that the proposed Working Group would 'contribute to ensure broad consideration of indigenous issues in all aspects of the Barents Cooperation and to facilitate active indigenous participation in the work of the Regional Council', as well as agreeing that it would have a 'special advisory role' in relation to the BRC.[389]

Troms Fylke, and Finnmark Fylke (Norway); Västerbotten Län and Norrbotten Län (Sweden); Kainuu, Oulu, and Lapland (Finland); Murmansk Oblast, the Republic of Karelia, Arkhangelsk Oblast, Nenets Autonomous Okrug, and the Republic of Komi (Russia): Barents Euro-Arctic Cooperation, 'The Barents Regional Council' (n.d.) www.barentscooperation.org/en/Barents-Regional-Council.

383 Established under the Agreement on the Establishment of an International Barents Secretariat for the Cooperation in the Barents Euro-Arctic Region, 15 November 2007.

384 Barents Euro-Arctic Cooperation, 'About Us' (n.d.) www.barentscooperation.org/en/About.

385 Sébastien Duyck, 'Participation of Non-state Actors in Arctic Environmental Governance' (2012) 40 *Nordia Geographical Publications*, 99–110, 108.

386 Kirkenes Declaration, 2.

387 Ibid., 4.

388 Ibid., 4. These sentiments were repeated at the BEAC's second session: Joint Statement, Barents Euro-Arctic Council, Second session, 14th–15th September 1994, Tromso, Norway, accessible at www.barentsinfo.fi/beac/docs/499_doc_Tromsocommunique_1994_e.pdf.

389 Joint Statement, Barents Euro-Arctic Council, Second session, 3.

The Working Group for Indigenous Peoples was subsequently established in 1995.[390] According to its most recent terms of reference, its purpose is 'to serve as a forum for indigenous co-operation in the Barents Euro-Arctic Region' and to ensure their involvement 'in the decision-making processes and their participation in the co-operation'.[391] It exists on a permanent basis, playing an advisory role to both Councils.[392] The Working Group consists of six members: one Sámi representative from each of Finland, Norway, Russia, and Sweden; one representative of the Nenets; and one representative of the Veps.[393] The Sámi members from the Nordic countries are appointed by the Saami Parliamentary Council,[394] while the Nenets, Veps, and Russian Sámi members are nominated by the relevant Indigenous organizations.[395] In addition to its six full members, the Working Group has four observers from relevant Indigenous peoples' organizations: one each from the Saami Council, the Association of World Reindeer Herders, RAIPON, and Ga'ldu – Resource Centre for Rights of Indigenous Peoples.[396] It meets twice a year, with decisions taken unanimously by its full members.[397] The Working Group is supported by a secretariat consisting of the advisor on Indigenous peoples at the Norwegian Barents Secretariat, and the head of the Barents Indigenous Peoples Office.[398] Its costs are covered by the Norwegian Barents Secretariat, the Ministries of Foreign Affairs of Finland, Norway, Sweden, and Russia, and other sources via the Norwegian Barents Secretariat.[399]

The Working Group provides a platform for Indigenous participation in the rest of the Barents system. The Chair of the Working Group is a member of

390 Barents Euro-Arctic Cooperation, 'Working Group of Indigenous Peoples' (n.d.) www.barentscooperation.org/en/Working-Groups/Working-Group-of-Indigenous-Peoples.

391 Terms of Reference for the Working Group of Indigenous Peoples in the Barents Euro-Arctic Region (15 December 2010) ("Terms of Reference"), para. 1.

392 Terms of Reference, para. 2. See also Barents Regional Council, 'Barents Regional Committee, Terms of Reference' (14 November 2012), Article 16.

393 Terms of Reference, para. 4a.

394 Ibid., para. 5a.

395 Ibid., para. 5b. These are the Guolnegk Soamet Sobbar for the Sami in Russia, Yasavey for the Nenets, and the Veps Culture Society for the Veps.

396 Terms of Reference, para. 4d.

397 Ibid., paras. 8 and 11.

398 Ibid., para. 4c. The Barents Indigenous Peoples Office, established in 2003, is financed by the Norwegian Saami Parliament and located in Murmansk, Russia. It provides services and information for partners and participants within the Indigenous peoples' cooperation in the Barents Euro-Arctic Region: 'Working Group of Indigenous Peoples in the Barents Euro-Arctic Region, Action Plan for Indigenous Peoples in the Barents Euro-Arctic Region, 2013–2016' (2012), 4.

399 Terms of Reference, para. 15.

the CSO and the BRC.[400] Additionally, the Working Group can submit proposals to both Councils, as well as participate in all sessions of other working groups. In addition, the Working Group has regular meetings and dialogue with the CSO, a practice that the BEAC has welcomed and instructed the CSO to continue.[401] The annual reports of the Working Group reveal an extensive programme of participation in meetings and activities of the BEAC, the BRC, and its various subsidiary bodies.[402] In 2015, the BEAC member states agreed to ensure permanent funding for the Working Group.[403]

In addition to its participatory activities, the Working Group is mandated to determine and implement an Action Plan for Indigenous Peoples, on a four-yearly cycle. The Action Plan is meant to lay out priorities, propose practical solutions, and recommend decisions to be made.[404] Typically, the action plans encompass activities for cooperation among Indigenous peoples, for instance, on language education, health, culture, and reindeer husbandry.[405] Furthermore, the Working Group hosts a Barents Indigenous Peoples Congress on a biennial basis.[406]

When examining how the Councils and their member states justified the participation of the Sámi, Nenets, and Vepsians in their resolutions, communiques, and statements, it is apparent that, on the one hand, the commitment of the BEAC and BRC to Indigenous peoples' participation in the Barents cooperation appeared to stem from a recognition of their 'special relationship and unique contributions to the region'.[407] Indigenous peoples, the BEAC noted in 1996, have a 'specific role in promoting sustainable development and preserving traditional ways of life'.[408] At other times, the reasoning became

[400] Ibid., paras. 12 and 13.

[401] BEAC, 'Ninth Session of the Barents Euro-Arctic Council (BEAC), Joint Communique' (Umea 2–3 October 2003), para. 4.

[402] See, for example, Working Group of Indigenous Peoples in the Barents Euro-Arctic Region, 'Annual Report 2008' (2008), www.barentsinfo.fi/beac/docs/BEAC_Working_Groups_Annual_Reports_2008.pdf, 22–25; Working Group of Indigenous Peoples in the Barents Euro-Arctic Region, 'Annual Report 2019', www.barentsinfo.fi/beac/docs/WGIP_Annual_Report_2019.pdf.

[403] Resolution from the Third Barents Indigenous Peoples' Congress (14 April 2015), at 3.

[404] Terms of Reference, para. 3. See, for example, Working Group of Indigenous Peoples in the Barents Euro-Arctic Region, Action Plan for Indigenous Peoples in the Barents Euro-Arctic Region, 2013–2016 (2012) ("2013–2016 Action Plan").

[405] See, for example, 2013–2016 Action Plan.

[406] Terms of Reference, para. 6. In practice, this has occurred in 2010, 2012, 2015, and 2019.

[407] Barents Euro-Arctic Council, 'Third Session, October 9–10, 1995, Rovaniemi, Joint Statement' (1995), para. 8.

[408] BEAC, 'Joint Statement of the Fourth Session of the Council of the Barents Euro-Arctic Region, 5–6 November 1996, Petrozavodsk' (1996), para. 3.13.

more explicitly instrumental, and Indigenous peoples' participation is seen as supporting the ultimate goals of cooperation in the region. The Fifth Parliamentary Barents Conference, in this vein, underlined that enhanced participation by Indigenous peoples 'would greatly contribute' to the Barents regional cooperation.[409] According to a speech given by the Finnish Foreign Minister Erkki Tuomioja, at the BEAC's 13th session, Indigenous peoples are 'natural partners' in the regional cooperation since they 'enrich the economic activities' while concurrently 'assuring the environmental protection', and hence their full participation in the activities of the BEAC is 'of utmost importance'.[410] Indigenous peoples' traditional knowledge is seen as particularly valuable. Norwegian Foreign Minister Jonas Gahr Støre positioned the traditional knowledge of the Indigenous peoples of the region as 'invaluable', stressing that they must play 'an active role in the modern development' of the Barents region.[411] Other times, there was no stated reason, just a repeated refrain that the participation of Indigenous peoples in decision-making and policymaking is 'important' or 'crucial'.[412] Conversely, there was also the idea that Indigenous peoples' participation would help to 'further improve' their 'economic, social, environmental and cultural situation'.[413] The BRC has stated that Indigenous peoples' active participation is important 'to secure indigenous peoples' rights, foundation for trade, society, culture and language'.[414] Other times, the justification is heard that Indigenous peoples 'should be involved in decision-making in cases where their interests are

409 Resolution of the Fifth Parliamentary Barents Conference, Lulea, 20 May 2011, 1. See also Conference Resolution, Sixth Barents Parliamentary Conference, 23–24 April in Harstad, Norway, para. 6.

410 Barents Euro-Arctic Council, 'Thirteenth Session, 12 October 2011, Speeches and Statements' (2011), 5.

411 Ibid., 25. See also 'Declaration on the Twentieth Anniversary of the Barents Euro-Arctic Cooperation, Kirkenes, Norway, 3–4 June 2013' (2013), 6. Also see the Statement of Minister Timo Soini to the XV Session of the BEAC, 15 October 2015, 2: www.barentsinfo.fi/beac/docs/Soini-BEAC-kokouspuhe-2015.pdf.

412 See, for example, Barents Euro-Arctic Council, Seventh Meeting of Environment Ministers, Declaration, 19 October 2005, para. 35; Barents Euro-Arctic Council, 12th Session of the Barents Euro-Arctic Council, Joint Communique, Murmansk, 15 October 2009, para. 11; Barents Euro-Arctic Council, XIII Session of the Barents Euro-Arctic Council, Joint Communique, Kiruna, 12 October 2011, para. 25; Barents Euro-Arctic Council, 13th Session, 12 October 2011, Speeches and Statements, Speech of Foreign Minister Jonas Gahr Støre, Norway, 8.

413 Resolution of the Fifth Parliamentary Barents Conference, 2.

414 'Joint Statement of the Barents Regional Council on the XIV Session of the Barents Euro-Arctic Council, 29 October 2013, Tromso, Norway' (2013), 2. Also see Barents Euro-Arctic Council, 'Third Session, Joint Statement', para. 8.

affected'.[415] As Dorotheé Cambou puts it, the Working Group enables Indigenous organizations to have direct access to, and maintain a constructive dialogue with, state authorities and thus 'constitutes an important platform for indigenous organisations to strengthen their political stance at the inter-regional level and also to enhance their cooperation with the state, regional and local authorities in the Barents region'.[416]

3.7.1.3 Stockholm Convention on Persistent Organic Pollutants

In addition to the Arctic Council and the Barents regional cooperation, notable too are the ways in which, during the period under consideration, Arctic Indigenous peoples, specifically the ICC, engaged in the process towards the adoption of the Stockholm Convention on Persistent Organic Pollutants,[417] through the Canadian government delegation. The motivation on the ICC's side stemmed from recognition that pollution from POPs, which are heavy metals and synthetic chemicals used in pesticides, herbicides, industrial chemicals, and pharmaceuticals,[418] was disproportionately affecting Indigenous peoples in the Arctic.[419] Transported over long ranges through atmospheric and oceanic currents from warmer to colder parts of the planet and absorbed into the food chain, POPs accumulate in fatty tissues of animals and do not disperse, increasing in concentration at higher levels of the food chain.[420] This had led to very high concentrations of POPs in top predator species. Inuit and other Arctic Indigenous peoples, who rely on seal, whale, walrus, and other marine mammals as a major component of their diet and a central aspect of their culture, were thereby disproportionately exposed to high

415 'Second Barents Parliamentary Conference, Conclusions of the Chair, CSO Information document' (22 August 2005) Doc.BEAC.CSO.2005.25, 2.

416 Cambou, 'Enhancing the Participation'.

417 Stockholm Convention on Persistent Organic Pollutants (adopted 22 May 2001 and entered into force 17 May 2004) 2256 UNTS 119.

418 Perhaps the most well-known is the pesticide dichlorodiphenyltrichloroethane (DDT). Other POPs include aldrin, chlordane, dieldrin, endrin, heptachlor, hexachlorobenzene, mirex, toxaphene, polychlorinated biphenyls (PCBs), dioxins, and furans.

419 Bruce E. Johansen, 'The Inuit's Struggle with Dioxins and Other Organic Pollutants' (2002) 26 *American Indian Quarterly*, 479–490; Harriet V. Kuhnlein, Laurie Hing Man Chan, Grace Egeland, and Olivier Receveur, 'Canadian Arctic Indigenous Peoples, Traditional Food Systems, and POPs' in David Leonard Downie and Terry Fenge (eds.), *Northern Lights against POPs: Combatting Toxic Threats in the Arctic* (Montreal: McGill-Queen's University Press, 2003), 22–40.

420 Eric Dewailly and Christopher Furgal, 'POPs, the Environment, and Public Health' in David Leonard Downie and Terry Fenge (eds.), *Northern Lights against POPs: Combatting Toxic Threats in the Arctic* (Montreal: McGill-Queen's University Press, 2003), 3–21, 4.

levels of persistent organic pollutants. Human exposure to POPs causes numerous ill effects on health, including various cancers and reproductive, endocrine, and neurological disorders.[421] The Stockholm Convention sets out a range of control measures to eliminate the production and use of specified persistent organic pollutants, eliminate trade in specified persistent organic pollutants, minimize emissions of those that cannot be eliminated, and avoid the production and use of new persistent organic pollutants.[422] It contains a process and criteria by which new persistent organic pollutants may be identified, evaluated, and added to the control regime.[423]

While several Indigenous peoples' organizations took part as observers in sessions of the intergovernmental negotiating committee[424] – which by itself is not unusual for environmental negotiations of this kind – of more interest is that a representative of Canadian Indigenous peoples was also included on the Canadian delegation.[425] According to a first-person account from Sheila Watt-Cloutier, the then President of the Canadian branch of the ICC, who spearheaded the ICC's work on POPs, the various Indigenous organizations formed a 'fruitful' working relationship with the Canadian delegation and managed to contribute substantively to the process.[426] By this route, combined with their active participation as observers,[427] Arctic Indigenous peoples

[421] See, for example, Esther Vizcaino, Joan O. Grimalt, Ana Fernández-Somoano, and Adonina Tardon, 'Transport of Persistent Organic Pollutants across the Human Placenta' (2014) 65 *Environment International*, 107–115; Terri Damstra, 'Potential Effects of Certain Persistent Organic Pollutants and Endocrine Disrupting Chemicals on the Health of Children' (2002) 40 *Clinical Toxicology*, 457–465; David O. Carpenter, 'Polychlorinated Biphenyls (PCBs): Routes of Exposure and Effects on Human Health' (2006) 21(1) *Reviews on Environmental Health*, 1–23; Anne Vested, Aleksander Giwercman, Jens Peter Bonde, and Gunnar Toft, 'Persistent Organic Pollutants and Male Reproductive Health' (2014) 16(1) *Asian Journal of Andrology*, 71–80.

[422] See, for example, Articles 3, 5, and 6.

[423] See, for example, Article 8.

[424] Including the Inuit Circumpolar Conference, the International Indian Treaty Council, the Council of Yukon First Nations, the Teslin Tlingit Council, and the Denendeh National Office: see UNEP, 'List of participants' (10 August 1998) UN Doc. UNEP/POPS/INC.1/INF/15.

[425] 'List of Participants' (11 September 1999) UN Doc. UNEP/POPS/INC.3/INF/17; 'Provisional List of Delegations' (24 March 2000) UN Doc. UNEP/POPS/INC.4/INF/11/Rev.1; 'Provisional List of Participants' (9 December 2000) UN Doc. UNEP/POPS/INC.5/INF/11/Rev.1; 'List of Participants' (26 June 2001) UN Doc. UNEP/POPS/CONF/INF/4/Rev.1. A list of participants is not available for the first meeting of the intergovernmental negotiating committee in 1997, but first-hand accounts report that Canada included an Indigenous peoples' representative on its delegation there too: Watt-Cloutier, *The Right to Be Cold*, 140.

[426] Watt-Cloutier, *The Right to Be Cold*, 156–157.

[427] The 'extraordinary' level of participation by representatives of Indigenous communities is remarked on in Peter L. Lallas, 'The Stockholm Convention on Persistent Organic Pollutants'

wielded a high level of moral influence in the negotiations and 'played a significant role in shaping' the outcome.[428]

Looking beyond the negotiation of the Convention and into the implementation phase, of interest is that while the meetings of the Conference of the Parties allow the participation of observers in the subsidiary body that reviews proposals submitted by parties regarding adding new chemicals to the control regime, the rules do not specifically contemplate Indigenous peoples' participation.[429]

3.7.1.4 Nordic Saami Convention

The reverberations of the UNDRIP process, as well as the influence of the Arctic Council, were also seen in the process of drafting the Nordic Saami Convention, in which Nordic states and Nordic Sámi were equally represented.[430] The origins of the Convention date back concurrently with the early days of the WGIP. As Nigel Bankes and Timo Koivurova document, the Saami Council proposed in the mid-1980s that Sweden, Norway, Finland, and Russia along with the Saami develop a Convention to address the situation of the Saami as an Indigenous people divided by international

(2001) 95 *American Journal of International Law*, 692–708, 707. The level of activity of Indigenous peoples' organizations is evident in reports from the conferences: see, for example, Richard Campbell, Jonathan Krueger, Leila Mead, and Tiffany Prather, 'POPS INC-1 Highlights Monday, 29 June 1998' (29 June 1998) 15(6) *Earth Negotiations Bulletin*, https://enb.iisd.org/events/1st-session-inc-international-legally-binding-instrument-implementing-international-action-1.

428 Henrik Selin and Noelle Eckley Selin, 'Indigenous Peoples in International Environmental Cooperation: Arctic Management of Hazardous Substances' (2008) 17 *Review of European Community & International Environmental Law*, 72–83, 82. Also see Terry Fenge, 'POPs and Inuit: Influencing the Global Agenda' in David Leonard Downie and Terry Fenge (eds.), *Northern Lights against POPs: Combatting Toxic Threats in the Arctic* (Montreal: McGill-Queen's University Press, 2003) , 192–213, 201–204; John Anthony Buccini, 'The Long and Winding Road to Stockholm: The View from the Chair' in David Leonard Downie and Terry Fenge (eds.), *Northern Lights against POPs: Combatting Toxic Threats in the Arctic* (Montreal: McGill-Queen's University Press, 2003), 224–255, 239; Watt-Cloutier, *The Right to Be Cold*, 153–179.

429 Art 19(8) Convention; Rule 7(1), UNEP, Conference of the Parties of the Stockholm Convention on Persistent Organic Pollutants, 'Report of the Conference of the Parties of the Stockholm Convention on Persistent Organic Pollutants on the work of its first meeting' (6 May 2005) UN Doc. UNEP/POPS/COP.1/31, 14, Decision SC-1/1, 'Rules of procedure'. Also see Basel, Rotterdam and Stockholm Conventions, 'Guidelines for the participation of representatives of observers at meetings of the conferences of the Parties to the Basel, Rotterdam and Stockholm conventions (BRS) and their subsidiary bodies' (July 2016).

430 The text of the Convention in English can be found at www.sametinget.se/105173 (unofficial translation).

boundaries.[431] In 1995, the Nordic Council took up this idea and appointed a committee to review the issue. This committee, in turn, recommended that the governments establish a Working Group on the matter. In 2002, the governments of Sweden, Norway, and Finland established an Expert Group, consisting of six members: three appointed by the three states, and three appointed by the three Saami Parliaments. The Expert Group produced a draft Convention in 2005.[432] To look beyond the temporal scope of this chapter for a moment, while it was expected that negotiations between the three Nordic states and the Saami of those states would commence in 2007, the process was delayed and ultimately resumed in 2011;[433] negotiations concluded in 2017, but the Saami Parliaments subsequently tabled proposals for some additional amendments to the draft Convention, which as of 2020 are still being considered by the three Nordic governments.[434]

Not only did the Saami Parliaments have a very strong role in negotiating the Convention, but they also have a high profile in all aspects of its operation, despite the fact that the Saami Parliaments are not, strictly speaking, contracting parties to the Convention. They must approve the Convention before it can be ratified,[435] and can reject any amendment to the Convention.[436] In addition, they are equally represented with states in bodies established to implement the Convention. Under Article 44 of the Convention, a Cooperation Council composed of the state ministers for Saami affairs and the presidents of the Saami Parliaments is to convene regularly to promote the objectives of the Convention and consider relevant Saami matters of common interest. Furthermore, Article 45 establishes a Nordic Saami Convention Committee to monitor the implementation of the Convention, made up of six members with one appointed by each state and each Saami Parliament. The Committee is empowered to submit reports and proposals aimed at

[431] Nigel Bankes and Timo Koivurova, 'Introduction' in Nigel Bankes and Timo Koivurova (eds.), *The Proposed Nordic Saami Convention: National and International Dimensions of Indigenous Property Rights* (Oxford: Hart, 2013) 1–18, 2.

[432] See discussion in Timo Koivurova, 'The Draft Nordic Saami Convention: Nations Working Together' (2008) 10 *International Community Law Review*, 279–293.

[433] Timo Koivurova, 'Can Saami Transnational Indigenous Peoples Exercise Their Self-determination in a World of Sovereign States?' in Nigel Bankes and Timo Koivurova (eds.), *The Proposed Nordic Saami Convention: National and International Dimensions of Indigenous Property Rights* (Oxford: Hart, 2013), 105–124, 122.

[434] International Work Group for Indigenous Affairs, *The Indigenous World 2020* (Copenhagen: IWGIA, 2020), 532.

[435] Articles 48 and 49.

[436] Article 51, read with Article 48.

strengthening the objective of the Convention to the governments and the Saami Parliaments, and additionally may deliver opinions in response to questions from individuals and groups. This all constitutes perhaps the highest level of involvement a non-state body can have without being a state, stretching the limits of state-centrality in the international community.

Article 19 of the Convention states that Saami Parliaments shall represent the Saami in intergovernmental matters and that furthermore the three states shall promote Saami representation in international institutions and Saami participation in international meetings. The eventual Convention will thus provide for a high level of Arctic Indigenous participation in global governance. But whether the Convention is ultimately passed or not, the process by which Indigenous peoples and states were equally involved in negotiating it is testament to the very high extent to which the norm of Indigenous peoples' equal representation in international law-making has permeated the Arctic region.

3.7.2 *Latin America and the Caribbean*

The second regional case study is that of Latin America and the Caribbean. While less extensive than in the Arctic region, the work of international organizations to enable Indigenous peoples' participation still deserves note. Beginning in the early 1990s, the Fund for the Development of the Indigenous Peoples of Latin America and the Caribbean (FILAC) and a decade later the Andean Community have enabled the participation of the Indigenous peoples of the region. In the case of FILAC, this amounts to power sharing with Indigenous peoples.

3.7.2.1 The Fund for the Development of the Indigenous Peoples of Latin America and the Caribbean

The FILAC[437] is an international organization established in 1992 under an agreement signed at the Second Ibero-American Summit.[438] With the objective of supporting Indigenous peoples' self-development,[439] it provides funding

[437] In Spanish: El Fondo para del Desarrollo de los Pueblos Indígenas de América Latina y el Caribe. See generally www.filac.org.

[438] Agreement establishing the Fund for the Development of the Indigenous Peoples of Latin America and the Caribbean (signed 24 July 1992 and entered into force 4 August 1993) 1728 UNTS 380 ("FILAC Agreement").

[439] Ibid., Article 1.1.

for projects and programmes organized by Indigenous peoples in the region.[440] In a speech to the Rio Conference, the President of Bolivia explained the rationale for the establishment of the Fund: because the governments of the region 'consider[ed] indigenous people to be the natural focal points and protagonists of a genuine policy of sustainable development'.[441]

Indigenous peoples are represented at the highest levels of FILAC. The supreme organ of FILAC is its General Assembly, made up of representatives of each of the twenty-two member states and eighteen representatives of Indigenous peoples, one from each of its Latin American and Caribbean member states.[442] Indigenous peoples' representatives are elected by Indigenous peoples themselves, in processes beginning at the local level and culminating in national assemblies of Indigenous peoples.[443] Decisions are taken by a majority both of member states and Indigenous delegates.[444] Indigenous peoples are also permitted to attend as observers or guests and may speak during the meetings,[445] an opportunity which they have taken up with 'considerable enthusiasm'.[446] FILAC's Council, which carries out governance activities, is composed of six member state representatives and six Indigenous peoples' representatives.[447] FILAC is thus a setting where Indigenous peoples and states share power.

440 Ibid., Article 1.2.

441 Statement by H.E. Mr Jaime Paz Zamora, President of the Republic of Bolivia, in UN, 'Report of the United Nations Conference on Environment and Development' (1993) UN Doc. A/CONF.151/26/Rev.1 (Vol. 111) 169.

442 FILAC Agreement, Article 3.2.

443 FILAC, Operational Directive No. 11, 'Establecimiento de la representación de los pueblos indígenas ante la Asamblea General del Fondo Indígena', in FILAC, *Normatividad Institucional* (n.d.) www.filac.org/wp/wp-content/uploads/2017/10/Jerarquia-Normativa.pdf.

444 FILAC, *XIII Asemblea General – Sesión Extraordinaria: Minuta de Resoluciones* (FILAC, 2016), Resolution XIII AG/FILAC/003.

445 FILAC, *Acta de la Primera Asamblea General Ordinaria del Fondo para el Desarrollo de los Pueblos Indigenas de America Latina y el Caribe, Santa Cruz de la Sierra, Bolivia, 22 a 25 de mayo de 1995* (FILAC, 1995), para. 11. Also see 'Reglamento de la Asamblea General' (13 September 2006), Article 22, in FILAC, *Normatividad Institucional* (n.d.) www.filac.org/wp/wp-content/uploads/2017/10/Jerarquia-Normativa.pdf.

446 ECOSOC, 'Working Group on Indigenous Populations: Consideration of a Permanent Forum for Indigenous People' (6 July 1995) UN Doc E/CN.4/Sub.2/AC.4/1995/7/Add.2, para. 13.

447 FILAC Agreement, Article 3.3; 'Reglamento del Consejo Directivo y de la Secretaría Técnica' (24 June 2004), Article 3, in FILAC, *Normatividad Institucional* (n.d.) www.filac.org/wp/wp-content/uploads/2017/10/Jerarquia-Normativa.pdf.

3.7.2.2 The Andean Community Working Group on the Rights of Indigenous Peoples

The Andean Community (Comunidad Andina) is a sub-regional economic integration organization, initially created in 1969 as the Andean Pact pursuant to the Cartagena Agreement between Bolivia, Colombia, Ecuador, Peru, and Chile.[448] The Community is made up of its member states in addition to the Andean Integration System, which is comprised of several bodies and institutions largely emulating those of the European Community, including a Commission, the Andean Presidential Council, the Council of Foreign Ministers, General Secretariat, Court of Justice, the Andean Parliament, and several specialized organs.[449] The Andean Presidential Council is the Community's highest body, made up of the heads of state of the member countries, and issues guidelines that are carried out by the other bodies.[450] The Commission, consisting of a member and an alternate from each of the member states, is the principal policymaking and operational body, tasked with carrying out and evaluating sub-regional integration policy.[451] The Council of Foreign Ministers, composed of Ministers of Foreign Affairs of the member states, formulates and evaluates general sub-regional integration policy, as well as member states' foreign policy on matters of sub-regional interest.[452] The General Secretariat is the administrative executive body,[453] while the Andean Parliament is the deliberative body, composed partly of individuals directly elected by the people of the member states and partly by individuals appointed by the national parliaments of the member states.[454]

448 Agreement on Andean Subregional Integration (Cartagena Agreement) (signed 26 May 1969 and entered into force 16 October 1969) (1969) 8 ILM 910. Chile withdrew from the Agreement in 1973. Venezuela became a member in 1973 but withdrew in 2006. The Cartagena Agreement has subsequently been modified by the Protocol of Amendment Establishing the Andean Community and the Andean Integration System (signed 10 March 1996 and entered into force 3 June 1997) (Protocol of Trujillo) – by which the Andean Pact was renamed the Andean Community, the Protocol of Sucre (signed 25 June 1997 and entered into force 14 April 2003), and the Additional Protocol to the Cartagena Agreement (signed 10 June 2000, not yet in force). On the background, history, and development of the Andean Community, see Richard V. Adkisson, 'The Andean Group: Institutional Evolution, Intraregional Trade, and Economic Development' (2003) 37(2) *Journal of Economic Issues*, 371–379.

449 Cartagena Agreement, Articles 5 and 6.

450 Ibid., Articles 11–14.

451 Ibid., Articles 21–28.

452 Ibid., Articles 15–20.

453 Ibid., Articles 29–39.

454 Ibid., Article 42.

Within this elaborate apparatus, a specific niche was created for Indigenous peoples of the region to feed into the organization. In 2001, the Declaration of Machu Picchu on Democracy, the Rights of Indigenous Peoples, and the Fight Against Poverty ordered the establishment of a working group on the rights of Indigenous peoples within the Community's institutional framework, 'with the participation of indigenous organizations, human rights organizations, civil society and representatives of each one of the member states, with the purpose of fully integrating indigenous peoples into the economic, social and political life of our countries, while respecting and promoting their cultural diversity'.[455]

A year later, the Council of Foreign Ministers established the Working Group on the Rights of Indigenous Peoples,[456] in order to promote the active participation of Indigenous peoples in matters related to sub-regional integration.[457] The Working Group's functions included the issuance of opinions to the Commission, Council of Foreign Ministers, or General Secretariat on matters related to the participation of Indigenous peoples in the process of sub-regional integration; the recommendation of measures to promote Indigenous peoples' rights; and the recommendation of joint positions in international forums dealing with issues related to Indigenous peoples.[458]

The Working Group was mandated to comprise thirty-five members – seven for each country, plus seven advisory members. For each country, there would be three Indigenous delegates elected by representative organizations of the country's Indigenous peoples 'in accordance with their respective internal democratic and participatory procedures', as well as three government delegates and a delegate from the national office of the ombudsperson.[459] The advisory members would include an independent expert for each member country, a representative of the Coordinator of Indigenous Organizations of the Amazon Basin (COICA), and a representative of the FILAC.[460] This unwieldy structure was later simplified by introducing a Steering Committee – made up of one member from each country, which would carry out the majority of the functions.[461]

455 Declaration of Machu Picchu on Democracy, the Rights of Indigenous Peoples and the Fight against Poverty (2001), para. 9.

456 Decision 524 (9 July 2002) Official Gazette of the Cartagena Agreement, No. 814, Article 1.

457 Ibid., Article 1.

458 Ibid., Article 3.

459 Ibid., Article 4(a).

460 Ibid., Article 4(b).

461 Draft Internal Regulation on the Working Group on the Rights of Indigenous Peoples (17 May 2003) Doc No. SG/dt 215, Articles 6–10.

However, following this initial momentum, the Working Group never commenced its functions. The reasons are somewhat mysterious. An internal paper from 2006 noted that 'various circumstances' had so far prevented the holding of the first working meeting of the group, 'since to date it has not been possible to complete the designation and accreditation of all its members before the General Secretariat'.[462] It is unclear why the members of the Working Group had not been chosen and accredited. This may have been due to, for instance, delays in the internal selection processes of Indigenous peoples' organizations, or a failure by national governments to designate their delegates. The Declaration of Tarija by the 17th Andean Presidential Council in 2007 suggests that at least the failure was not down to a lack of political will by the collected member states: it 'affirmed the conviction' that the participation of Indigenous peoples' in the Andean Community 'allows the consolidation of democracy and the generation of conditions for sustainable development' and recommended the earliest implementation of the Working Group.[463] While the Andean Community Working Group was ultimately non-viable, it points to the spread of the idea that Indigenous peoples should be able to participate in regional governance processes.

3.7.3 *The European Council*

As a coda to this chapter, we will briefly explore how the European Union treated Indigenous peoples during the period under consideration. Beginning in the 1990s, organs of the European Union took some notice of Indigenous peoples in respect of its development cooperation activities. In 1994, the European Parliament called for criteria to be drawn up on the financing of European Community projects in the light of the rights of Indigenous peoples, and for these peoples to be directly involved in projects concerning them.[464] In 1998, in response to an invitation from the Council of Ministers of Development Co-operation, the European Commission presented a working document on support for Indigenous peoples in the European Community's development cooperation.[465] Indigenous peoples were

[462] Draft Internal Regulation on the Working Group on the Rights of Indigenous Peoples (Second Version) (8 March 2006) Doc No. SG/dt 215/Rev.1, 1.

[463] Declaration of Tarija, XVII Andean Presidential Council (27 September 2007), para. 12.

[464] European Parliament, 'Resolution on Action Required Internationally to Provide Effective Protection for Indigenous Peoples' (9 February 1994) Doc PV 58(II).

[465] Commission of the European Communities, 'Commission Working Document on Support for Indigenous Peoples in the Development Co-operation of the Community and the Member States' (11 May 1998) SEC(1998) 773 final.

consulted in the development of the working document.[466] It began by noting that while the vast majority of Indigenous peoples experience marginalization, 'many of them inhabit areas which are considered crucial for the conservation of biodiversity and maintain social and cultural practices which permit a sustainable use of these resources',[467] and expounded on Indigenous peoples' relationship with land, as well as their vulnerability to development and environmental change, in some detail.[468] Referencing the Vienna Declaration and Programme of Action, the ILO Convention 169, as well as the 1994 Draft Declaration on the Rights of Indigenous Peoples, the working document said participation must be 'an integrated part of any attempt to address these peoples', but noted the difficulty posed by 'different and overlapping institutions' that makes it 'difficult to identify unquestioned authority'.[469] Nonetheless, it stressed the need for policies on Indigenous participation in the design and implementation of development projects, and 'free and informed consent' where any project would affect their land and livelihood.[470] Free and full participation was 'regarded as fundamental', including elements such as 'prior consultation with indigenous peoples, their consent to envisaged activities, their control over activities affecting their lives and land, and the identification of their own priorities for development'.[471] The document stressed culturally appropriate means of communication, working consistently with Indigenous notions of time and decision-making, taking into account women's interests and needs, and allowances for long-term, small-scale involvement.[472]

On the basis of the Commission's working document, the European Council prepared a resolution on Indigenous peoples and development cooperation. In this resolution, the European Council took note of international instruments on Indigenous peoples[473] and noted that Indigenous cultures 'constitute a heritage of diverse knowledge and ideas, which is a

[466] European Commission, 'Report from the Commission to the Council – Review of Progress of Working with Indigenous Peoples' COM(2002) 291 final, 13.
[467] Ibid., 2.
[468] Ibid., 6–7, 12.
[469] Ibid., 11.
[470] Ibid., 13.
[471] Ibid., 13.
[472] Ibid., 13.
[473] Council Resolution 'Indigenous Peoples within the Framework of the Development Cooperation of the Community and the Member States' (30 November 1998) C/98/421, para. 1.

potential resource to the entire planet',[474] and that many Indigenous peoples 'inhabit areas crucial for the conservation of biodiversity, and maintain social and cultural practices by way of which Indigenous peoples have a special role in maintaining and enhancing biological diversity and in providing unique sustainable development models'.[475] It acknowledged the importance that Indigenous peoples attach to their "self-development" – which the resolution defines as 'the shaping of their own social, economic and cultural development and their own cultural identities', including participating 'fully and freely' in the development process.[476] The resolution recognized that participation of Indigenous peoples was 'essential for the objectives of poverty elimination, [and] sustainable development of natural resources'.[477] It invited the Commission to develop a comprehensive policy on engaging Indigenous peoples in development cooperation.[478]

Building on this, in 2002 the European Council set out principles to be applied in EU strategies and financing instruments, including the full and effective participation of Indigenous peoples at all stages of the project cycle, and the importance of building the capacities of Indigenous peoples' organizations.[479] Further, it suggested that the Commission and member states should create specific practical procedures for its aid practitioners and that the proposed measures should be 'discussed with indigenous peoples and other partners'.[480]

A 2002 report of the European Commission detailed efforts undertaken by the Commission to consult widely with Indigenous peoples to identify their priorities for development, the results of which were to feed into project design and implementation as well as the EU's wider development cooperation strategy.[481] Further, it highlights 'practical mechanisms' set up by the Commission to ensure the consultation of Indigenous peoples in policies and activities that affect them, such as contact points to liaise with Indigenous peoples, an informal network of Indigenous peoples' organizations with whom the Commission consulted, and wide consultations with

[474] Ibid., para. 2.
[475] Ibid., para. 4.
[476] Ibid., para. 2.
[477] Ibid., para. 5.
[478] Ibid., para. 9.
[479] 2002 Council Conclusions on Indigenous peoples, General Affairs and External Relations, 2463rd Council meeting, document 13466/02 (18 November 2002), para. 8.
[480] Ibid., para. 10.
[481] European Commission, 'Review of Progress of Working with Indigenous Peoples', 13.

Indigenous peoples to identify their own priorities for the development process.[482]

3.8 A PICTURE COMING INTO FOCUS

From its beginnings at the margins of the UN system in 1982, by the time of the adoption of the UN Declaration on the Rights of Indigenous Peoples in 2007, the practice among states and international organizations of including Indigenous peoples in international governance processes had spread widely, motivated by a raft of concerns, including a broad recognition of Indigenous peoples' affectedness by contemporary global issues as well as the usefulness of their traditional knowledge to environmental protection and development and hence the fulfilment of the missions of various international organizations and treaties. The WGIP, the WGDD, and the UNPFII, among others, all served as platforms and role models for increased Indigenous peoples' participation in more and more settings. Alongside this, states such as Australia, Brazil, Canada, Denmark, Finland, Mexico, New Zealand, Norway, Sweden, and the United States began to include Indigenous peoples' representatives on their delegations, albeit with varying levels of regularity.

From these promising, albeit ultimately restricted, beginnings, the practice of including Indigenous peoples in international governance was to spread even further and, crucially, begin to be accompanied by a belief that doing so was required by law.

[482] Ibid., 12–13.

4

Emerging Legal Status? Participation of Indigenous Peoples, 2007–2022

Although in one sense the adoption of the UN Declaration on the Rights of Indigenous Peoples (UNDRIP) in September 2007 marked the end of a long process of negotiation, contestation, and struggle, in another sense it heralded a beginning. The codification of Indigenous peoples' rights into the UNDRIP's provisions breathed new momentum into ongoing struggles for their recognition, respect, and protection. In respect of participation, specifically, Articles 18 (right to participate in decision-making), 19 (obligation to consult and cooperate in good faith), and 41 (ways and means of ensuring participation shall be established) were to prove especially influential.

Of course, the post-2007 period did not decisively break from the past. For one thing, participatory forms developed in the period leading up to the Declaration's adoption – not least the WGIP – continued to inspire and serve as a model for Indigenous peoples' demands elsewhere, as in the pre-UNDRIP period. For another, the general trend of proliferation of participatory policies and mechanisms identified in Chapter 3 only intensified. Organizations that had not previously sought to include Indigenous peoples in a systematic way adopted mechanisms and policies to do so; organizations that had previously instituted such mechanisms or policies sought to enhance them. The UNPFII and Indigenous peoples' organizations continued to play a key driving role in these transformations. The UNDRIP provided an institutional stepping stone that Indigenous advocates could use to further advocate for their participation at the United Nations, especially at the General Assembly.

4.1 BUILDING ON THE UNDRIP AT THE UNITED NATIONS, 2007–2022

4.1.1 *The Expert Mechanism on the Rights of Indigenous Peoples: A Champion of the Right to Participate*

On 14 December 2007, a few months after the UNDRIP's adoption, the Human Rights Council established a new subsidiary body. The Expert Mechanism on the Rights of Indigenous Peoples (EMRIP) was mandated to provide the Council with thematic expertise and research-based advice on the rights of Indigenous peoples.[1] The EMRIP was initially made up of five independent experts and later expanded to seven – one from each of the seven Indigenous sociocultural regions – who serve three-year terms.[2] While the Council's usual process for the selection of experts applies to the EMRIP,[3] so that members may be self-nominated or proposed by NGOs, governments, national human rights institutions, and others—unlike the UNPFII, where half the members are nominated by Indigenous peoples and half by member states—the Council is strongly recommended to give 'due regard' to 'experts of indigenous origin' as well as 'recognized competence and experience in the rights of indigenous peoples'.[4] In practice, many current and former EMRIP members are Indigenous people, and at times the Mechanism has been fully comprised of Indigenous members.[5] Despite this, some Indigenous peoples have felt a lack of control over the member selection process, as the nomination structures are inconsistent across regions.[6]

The EMRIP followed a similar approach to that of the WGIP and WGDD in respect of accreditation and participation of Indigenous peoples' organizations. Meetings, occurring annually in a five-day session, were opened to

1 Human Rights Council Res. 6/36 (14 December 2007), para. 1. The mandate was reviewed and updated in 2016, discussed below.

2 Ibid., paras. 3 and 6; Human Rights Council Res. 33/25 (5 October 2016), paras. 4 and 7. The seven Indigenous sociocultural regions are Africa; Asia; Central and South America, and the Caribbean; the Arctic; Central and Eastern Europe, the Russian Federation, Central Asia, and Transcaucasia; North America; and the Pacific.

3 Human Rights Council Res. 6/36, para. 3; Human Rights Council Res, 33/25, para. 4; Human Rights Council Res. 5/1 (18 June 2007), Annex, paras. 39–53.

4 Human Rights Council Res. 6/36, para. 4; Human Rights Council Res. 33/25, para. 6.

5 Office of the High Commissioner on Human Rights (OHCHR), 'Current Experts in the Expert Mechanism on the Rights of Indigenous Peoples' (n.d.) www.ohchr.org/EN/Issues/IPeoples/EMRIP/Pages/Membership.aspx.

6 Henrike Narr, 'Nothing about Us without Us: Access for Indigenous Peoples to the United Nations and Perceptions of Legitimacy' (PhD thesis, University of Tübingen, 2019), 122–123.

Indigenous peoples' organizations 'whose aims and purposes are in conformity with the spirit, purposes and principles of the Charter of the United Nations', based on ECOSOC accreditation arrangements 'and practices observed by the Commission on Human Rights', through an 'open and transparent accreditation procedure' in accordance with the Human Rights Council's rules of procedure.[7] In practice, the Office of the High Commissioner for Human Rights requests all non-state bodies that wish to participate to seek EMRIP accreditation, irrespective of any entitlement to accreditation under ECOSOC procedures.[8] First-person accounts from Indigenous representatives attending EMRIP sessions illustrate how Indigenous observers frequently make oral interventions,[9] and Indigenous peoples' organizations frequently make written submissions, for instance, towards studies prepared by the Expert Mechanism.[10] Indigenous representatives may apply to the Voluntary Fund for assistance with attendance costs; in 2010, the General Assembly expanded the mandate of the Voluntary Fund to assist representatives of Indigenous peoples' organizations to participate in sessions of the Human Rights Council, the EMRIP, the UNPFII, as well as human rights treaty bodies.[11] In many ways, the EMRIP has inherited, and continues, the legacy of the WGIP, alongside the UNPFII and the Special Rapporteur on the rights of Indigenous peoples. When the EMRIP's mandate was reviewed eight years after its creation, written submissions were invited from Indigenous peoples as well as from states,[12] and the reviewed mandate allowed the EMRIP to assist

7 Human Rights Council Res. 6/36, para. 9; Human Rights Council Res. 33/25, para. 13.

8 Human Rights Council, 'Ways and means of promoting participation at the United Nations of indigenous peoples' representatives on issues affecting them' (2012) UN Doc. A/HRC/21/24, para. 19.

9 Tammy Solonec, 'UN Mechanisms for Indigenous Peoples: A Personal Account of Participation in 2010' (2010) 7 *Indigenous Law Bulletin*, 8–12.

10 See, for example, the submissions contributed towards the Mechanism's report on cultural heritage: Office of the High Commissioner on Human Rights, 'Promotion and Protection of the Rights of Indigenous Peoples with Respect to Their Cultural Heritage: Report' (19 August 2015) www.ohchr.org/EN/Issues/IPeoples/EMRIP/Pages/Studyonculturalheritage.aspx.

11 UNGA Res. 65/198 (21 December 2010), para. 3.

12 Subsequent to Human Rights Council Res. 30/11 (11 October 2015), para. 1; OHCHR, 'About the Mandate of the Expert Mechanism on the Rights of Indigenous Peoples' (n.d.) www.ohchr.org/EN/Issues/IPeoples/EMRIP/Pages/Reviewofthemandate.aspx. In the course of that consultation, several states expressed strong support for the full participation of Indigenous peoples in the EMRIP, including Argentina, Canada, and Chile: OHCHR, 'Summary of Responses to the Questionnaire on the Review of the Mandate of the Expert Mechanism on the Rights of Indigenous Peoples' (April 2016), www.ohchr.org/EN/Issues/IPeoples/EMRIP/Pages/Reviewofthemandate.aspx; Human Rights Council, 'Expert Workshop to Review the Mandate of the Expert Mechanism on the Rights of Indigenous Peoples: Report' (10 May 2016) UN Doc. A/HRC/32/26, para. 51.

Indigenous peoples on request with advice regarding the development of domestic legislation and policies related to Indigenous peoples' rights, among other changes.[13]

The EMRIP views these participatory practices as required by law. Indeed, from its beginnings, it has been a strong proponent of the right of Indigenous peoples to participate in global governance. In a 2010 progress report on the right to participation in decision-making, it stated that the right to self-determination as a 'normative framework' underlies a legal right to participation. In its view, an 'appropriate goal' was 'the full and direct participation of indigenous peoples in all international processes on matters that particularly concern them'.[14] Its final report built on these concepts, calling for the establishment of 'a permanent mechanism or system for consultations with indigenous peoples' governance bodies … to ensure effective participation at all levels of the United Nations'.[15] In 2013, the then EMRIP Chair, Wilton Littlechild, in a presentation to the Human Rights Council regarding the upcoming World Conference on Indigenous Peoples, stressed the right of Indigenous peoples to participate in decision-making.[16] In its 2021 report on self-determination, it stated that participation of Indigenous peoples at the UN and other international policy forums and decision-making bodies was 'an example of the exercise of external self-determination', recommending that states support Indigenous peoples' effective involvement in such forums, ensure their protection from reprisals, and establish a process to consider ways to enhance the participation of Indigenous peoples in the work of the Human Rights Council.[17]

Over the years, the Expert Mechanism has often functioned as a platform where Indigenous peoples can assert claims to be heard in other UN spaces, similarly to the WGIP before it and the UNPFII alongside it. In relation to the COVID-19 pandemic in 2020, it called on relevant UN agencies to 'ensure

13 Human Rights Council Res. 33/25.

14 Human Rights Council, 'Progress Report on the Study on Indigenous Peoples and the Right to Participate in Decision-Making: Report of the Expert Mechanism on the Rights of Indigenous Peoples' (23 August 2010) UN Doc. A/HRC/15/35, paras. 30 and 95–96.

15 Human Rights Council, 'Final Report of the Study on Indigenous Peoples and the Right to Participate in Decision-Making: Report of the Expert Mechanism on the Rights of Indigenous Peoples' (17 August 2011) UN Doc. A/HRC/18/42, para. 36.

16 Human Rights Council, 'Half-Day Panel Discussion on the World Conference on Indigenous Peoples: Human Rights as a Cross-Cutting Theme in the World Conference on Indigenous Peoples' (17 September 2013), 10.

17 EMRIP, 'Efforts to Implement the United Nations Declaration on the Rights of Indigenous Peoples: Indigenous Peoples and the Right to Self-Determination' (2021) UN Doc. A/HRC/48/75, paras. 17, 31, 61, and 74.

that indigenous peoples become [their] partners' and seek free, prior, and informed consent (FPIC) for measures that may affect Indigenous peoples.[18] Later that year, it proposed that the Human Rights Council call on the World Health Organization (WHO) to work in collaboration with Indigenous peoples' representatives and institutions to recognize and respect Indigenous peoples' rights.[19] It further proposed that the Council encourage states to continue to promote the participation of Indigenous peoples 'within global mechanisms that may benefit from indigenous contributions in particular mechanisms dealing with issues that threaten indigenous peoples lives such as climate change, migration and COVID-19',[20] presumably referring to institutions like the UNFCCC and the WHO.

One result of the EMRIP's early work on participation was, in 2011, a resolution of the Human Rights Council that called on the Secretary-General to prepare a report on the ways and means of promoting participation at the United Nations of Indigenous peoples' representatives on issues affecting them.[21] This report was to prove influential in later discussions on the status of Indigenous peoples at the UN.

4.1.2 *The 2012 "Ways and Means" Report*

In the 2012 report on ways and means of promoting Indigenous peoples' participation at the United Nations,[22] the Secretary-General began by outlining ways in which Indigenous peoples' representative organizations and institutions differ 'qualitatively and functionally' from NGOs:[23] Indigenous peoples' organizations often represent Indigenous individuals, collectives, families, and extended families;[24] membership can be hereditary and/or based on Indigenous legal and cultural norms;[25] they have often been recognized, whether constitutionally, legally, or politically, by the state concerned;[26] and their purposes may include the public governance of their peoples and/or

[18] EMRIP, 'COVID-19: Yet Another Challenge for Indigenous Peoples' (6 April 2020), www.un.org/development/desa/indigenouspeoples/wp-content/uploads/sites/19/2020/04/EMPRIP-English.pdf.
[19] EMRIP, 'Proposals for the Human Rights Council' (July 2020) www.ohchr.org/sites/default/files/ProposalsHRCChairsProposal.pdf, para. 7.
[20] Ibid., para. 11.
[21] Human Rights Council Res. 18/8 (13 October 2011), para. 12.
[22] Human Rights Council, 'Ways and Means of Promoting Participation'.
[23] Ibid., para. 7.
[24] Ibid., para. 7.
[25] Ibid., para. 7.
[26] Ibid., para. 8.

territories – that is, they are not "non-governmental" in nature.[27] Accordingly, the report noted, an Indigenous peoples' organization might not choose to seek accreditation as an NGO under the ECOSOC rules even if technically eligible.

The report then outlined the difficulty that many Indigenous peoples' organizations face in meeting the criteria for consultative status at the ECOSOC,[28] even if they choose to seek accreditation. Often, for example, they will not be registered or even recognized by the relevant state, have an executive officer, headquarters, or the requisite documentation, nor be broadly representative of major segments of society in a large number of countries in different regions of the world.[29]

As a result, the Secretary-General explained, Indigenous peoples can find themselves unable to participate in UN meetings of direct relevance to them.[30] The report went on to outline four preliminary issues to be considered by states in partnership with Indigenous peoples before deciding on solutions:[31] what should the criteria be for eligibility for accreditation?[32] Who should decide who is eligible? What should be the nature and membership of such an accrediting body?[33] What sort of information should a would-be Indigenous peoples' representative be required to submit?[34] Finally, what measures, such as technical and administrative support and training, are required to ensure that participation is meaningful and effective?[35]

At the time, the Secretary-General's report was noted with appreciation by the Human Rights Council, which invited the General Assembly to include the issue in its agenda based on the possible steps elaborated in the report.[36] The General Assembly subsequently took note of the report.[37] As we will see, it has been instrumental in subsequent developments, and resolution of the four issues it raised has not proved uncomplicated.

27 Ibid., para. 9.
28 ECOSOC Res. 1996/31 (25 July 1996), principles 9, 10, and 22.
29 Human Rights Council, 'Ways and Means of Promoting Participation', para. 10.
30 Ibid., para. 11.
31 Ibid., paras. 57–58.
32 Ibid., paras. 61–62.
33 Ibid., para. 63.
34 Ibid., para. 64.
35 Ibid., para. 65.
36 Human Rights Council Res. 21/24 (11 October 2012), para. 10.
37 UNGA Res. 67/153 (20 December 2012), para. 3. See also UNGA Res. 68/149 (18 December 2013), para. 8.

4.1.3 *The World Conference on Indigenous Peoples*

Meanwhile, efforts were underway to organize a high-level plenary meeting of the General Assembly, known as the World Conference on Indigenous Peoples (WCIP). In a resolution initially co-sponsored by Bolivia, Ecuador, Guatemala, Mexico, and Nicaragua[38] – later joined by several other states[39] – the General Assembly decided in December 2010 to hold the WCIP in order to 'share perspectives and best practices' on the realization of Indigenous peoples' rights, 'including to pursue the objectives of the [UNDRIP]'.[40] The Assembly launched a preparatory process, inviting its President to conduct open-ended consultations on the modalities for the meeting, including the participation of Indigenous peoples, with member states and Indigenous peoples' representatives within the framework of the UNPFII, as well as with the EMRIP and the Special Rapporteur on the rights of Indigenous peoples.[41]

Indigenous peoples engaged comprehensively in the preparatory process,[42] which was co-led by state and Indigenous representatives. In April 2012, the General Assembly President appointed John Henriksen of the Sámi Parliament of Norway and the Ambassador of Mexico, Luis Alfonso de Alba, as co-facilitators for the consultations on the modalities and arrangements for the World Conference process.[43] In January 2012, Indigenous peoples established an Indigenous Global Coordinating Group through which to organize themselves to engage in the process, composed of members from the seven Indigenous-identified sociocultural world regions, as well as the Indigenous youth and Indigenous women's caucuses.[44] The Coordinating Group met

38 See the draft resolution at General Assembly, Third Committee, 'Indigenous Issues: Draft Resolution' (18 October 2010) UN Doc. A/C.3/65/L.22.

39 Argentina, Australia, Benin, Cuba, Denmark, Dominican Republic, El Salvador, Finland, Honduras, Norway, Panama, Peru, Uruguay, and Venezuela: Third Committee, 'Indigenous Issues: Revised Draft Resolution' (12 November 2010) UN Doc. A/C.3/65/L.22/Rev.1.

40 UNGA Res. 65/198 (21 December 2010), para. 8.

41 Ibid., para. 8.

42 General Assembly, 'Outcome Document of the High-Level Plenary Meeting of the General Assembly Known as the World Conference on Indigenous Peoples' (15 September 2014) UN Doc. A/69/L.1 ("WCIP Outcome Document"), para. 2.

43 President of the General Assembly, 'Letter Dated 5 April 2012 to All Permanent Missions and Permanent Observer Missions to the United Nations Appointing Co-chairs to Lead the Informal Consultations for the High Level Meeting on Indigenous Issues', http://cendoc.docip.org/collect/cendocdo/index/assoc/HASH9ea4/2914b6ff.dir/Informalmeeting_Indigissues_letten1.pdf.

44 The UNPFII welcomed the establishment of the Indigenous Global Coordinating Group in UNPFII, 'Report on the Eleventh Session' (2012) UN Doc. E/C.19/2012/13, para. 70. Also see President of the General Assembly, 'Letter dated 5 April 2012'. See also UNPFII, 'Political

regularly and organized regional preparatory meetings in late 2012 and early 2013 in Kenya, Guatemala, the United States, Greenland, Thailand, Australia, and Russia, as well as meetings of the Global Indigenous Women's Caucus and the Global Indigenous Youth Caucus.[45] Indigenous peoples' bodies at the UN also dedicated themselves to the WCIP preparations. The UNPFII, during its 10th and 11th sessions in 2011 and 2012, respectively, devoted time to discussing the WCIP's modalities in dialogues with the President of the General Assembly and issued recommendations on the organization of the WCIP and its preparatory process, particularly regarding the equal, direct, and meaningful participation of Indigenous peoples.[46] The EMRIP affirmed these recommendations and called on the Human Rights Council to support the full and effective participation of

Position Document and Plan of Action of the World's Indigenous Women Adopted in the World Conference of Indigenous Women' (2014) UN Doc. E/C.19/2014/CRP.1, 4.

45 See 'African Declaration on the World Conference on Indigenous Peoples 2014' (21 November 2012) http://cendoc.docip.org/collect/cendocdo/index/assoc/HASH0176/0f3c47ed.dir/WCIP_Afridecl_en.pdf; Foro Indígena de Abya Yala, 'Declaration of the Indigenous Forum of Abya Yala' (13 April 2013) http://cendoc.docip.org/collect/cendocdo/index/assoc/HASH017a/6014b4a5.dir/WCIP_AbyaYaladecl_en.pdf; North American Indigenous Peoples' Caucus, 'Decisions and Recommendations of the North American Indigenous Peoples' Caucus Regarding the UN High-Level Plenary Meeting to Be Called a World Conference on Indigenous Peoples' (3 March 2013) http://cendoc.docip.org/collect/cendocdo/index/assoc/HASH01f5/624f3354.dir/WCIP_NAIPC_Declaration_ENG.pdf; Representatives of Inuit and Sami peoples, 'Arctic Declaration on the World Conference on Indigenous Peoples 2014: The Arctic Preparatory Meeting in Nuuk, Greenland' (24 October 2012) http://cendoc.docip.org/collect/cendocdo/index/assoc/HASH1e2e/4e5c63dc.dir/WCIP_Nuuk_ENG.pdf; 'WCIP – Asia Declaration' (9 November 2012) http://cendoc.docip.org/collect/cendocdo/index/assoc/HASH0176/8f7023dd.dir/WCIP_asiedecl_en.pdf; 'The Pacific Declaration of the Preparatory Meeting for Pacific Indigenous Peoples on the World Conference on Indigenous Peoples 2014' (21 March 2013) http://cendoc.docip.org/collect/cendocdo/index/assoc/HASH01f3/69157d75.dir/WCIP_Pacifidecl_en.pdf; Indigenous Peoples of the North, Siberia and the Far East, 'Salekhard Declaration' (29 March 2013) http://cendoc.docip.org/collect/cendocdo/index/assoc/HASHf411/953b9d0d.dir/WCIP_RussiaDecl_en.pdf; Global Indigenous Women's Caucus, 'Recommendations for Outcome of UNGA High Level Plenary Also to Be Called the World Conference on Indigenous Peoples' (30 March 2013) http://cendoc.docip.org/collect/cendocdo/index/assoc/HASH01f5/8707c3a9.dir/WCIP_Women_Declaration_ENG.pdf; Global Indigenous Youth Caucus, 'Global Indigenous Youth Caucus Declaration on the World Conference on Indigenous Peoples 2014' (2013) http://cendoc.docip.org/collect/cendocdo/index/assoc/HASH0106/75023a4a.dir/WCIP_Youth_Declaration_ENGa.pdf.

46 See, for example, UNPFII, 'Report on the Eleventh Session' (2012) UN Doc. E/C.19/2012/13, paras. 74, 75, 79, 81, 82, 83, 84, 85, 86, and 87–89. UNPFII, 'Report on the Tenth Session' (2011) UN Doc. E/C.19/2011/14, paras. 122, 123, 127, 128, 129, and 130. These recommendations were reiterated and extended in UNPFII, 'Report on the Twelfth Session' (2013) UN Doc. E/C.19/2013/25, paras. 78–90.

Indigenous peoples in the Conference.[47] In turn, the Human Rights Council encouraged states to continue to promote and support Indigenous peoples' participation in the WCIP preparatory process.[48]

4.1.3.1 The September 2012 Resolution on Participatory Modalities for the Conference

Based on those consultations, the General Assembly at its next session in September 2012 passed a resolution setting the date and organizational arrangements for the WCIP, including the modalities for participation. These largely mirrored the UNPFII's recommendations. Recalling the UNDRIP, the resolution encouraged Indigenous peoples' full and effective participation in the Conference, as well as their continued active engagement in its preparation.[49] It encouraged member states to consider including Indigenous peoples' representatives in their delegations to the WCIP.[50] More concretely, it decided that the WCIP would consist of three roundtable discussions and one panel discussion, enclosed by opening and closing sessions.[51] In the opening session, speaking slots would be held by the Chair of the UNPFII, and three Indigenous peoples' representatives nominated by Indigenous peoples, alongside the General Assembly President, the Secretary-General, the UN High Commissioner on Human Rights, and several heads of state.[52]

The three roundtables and the panel would each be co-chaired by one Indigenous peoples' representative and one member state delegate.[53] During the roundtable and panel discussions, Indigenous peoples would participate on the same footing as member states, as well as other observers, civil society organizations, and national human rights institutions.[54] The accreditation of Indigenous peoples' organizations would be arranged 'in accordance with the established practice for the accreditation of representatives of organizations and institutions of indigenous peoples' under the WGDD and EMRIP,

[47] EMRIP, 'Report of the Expert Mechanism on the Rights of Indigenous Peoples on Its Fifth Session' (17 August 2012) UN Doc. A/HRC/21/52, 5. EMRIP, 'Report of the Expert Mechanism on the Rights of Indigenous Peoples on Its Sixth Session' (31 July 2013) UN Doc. A/HRC/24/49, para. 6.

[48] Human Rights Council Res. 21/24, para. 9.

[49] UNGA Res. 66/296 (17 September 2012), preamble, recitals 1, 4, and 8.

[50] Ibid., para. 4.

[51] Ibid., para. 3(a).

[52] Ibid., para. 3(b).

[53] Ibid., para. 3(c).

[54] Ibid., para. 3(g).

whereby organizations 'whose aims and purposes are in conformity with the spirit, purposes and principles of the Charter of the United Nations' were invited to apply to the Secretariat for accreditation 'through an open and transparent procedure'.[55] The Assembly expanded the mandate of the Voluntary Fund to assist Indigenous peoples' representatives to participate in the WCIP, including the preparatory process.[56]

In the same resolution, the Assembly requested the President of the General Assembly to prepare a draft text for the Conference's outcome document – intended to contribute to the realization of Indigenous peoples' rights, pursue the UNDRIP's objectives, and promote the achievement of internationally agreed development goals – on the basis of consultations with Indigenous peoples and member states, and by taking into account the views emerging from the preparatory process, and to convene 'inclusive and open informal consultations' to enable sufficient consideration by member states and agreement by the General Assembly before formally endorsing the outcome document at the WCIP.[57]

4.1.3.2 The Alta Conference

As the preparatory process continued, in June 2013 a Global Indigenous Preparatory Conference convened in Alta, Norway, hosted by the Sámi Parliament of Norway. Seven regional Indigenous preparatory processes had already convened in the build-up to the Alta Conference. At the Alta Conference, more than 600 Indigenous peoples' representatives and observers, according to media reports,[58] gathered to exchange views and proposals and develop collective recommendations for the WCIP outcome. The result was the Alta Outcome Document, which proposed four thematic focus areas for the Conference as well as recommendations under each theme.[59]

55 Ibid., para. 3(h).
56 Ibid., para. 13.
57 Ibid., paras. 9 and 10.
58 Nunatsiaq News, 'Indigenous Peoples Meet in Arctic Norway to Prepare 2014 UN Conference' (*Nunatsiaq News*, 10 June 2013, https://nunatsiaq.com/stories/article/65674indigenous_peoples_meet_in_arctic_norway_to_prepare_un_conference/).
59 Alta Outcome Document, in UN General Assembly, 'Letter Dated 10 September from the Permanent Representatives of the Plurinational State of Bolivia, Denmark, Finland, Guatemala, Mexico, New Zealand, Nicaragua, Norway and Peru to the United Nations Addressed to the Secretary General' (13 September 2013) UN Doc. A/67/994, Annex. The UNPFII considered that the themes proposed should be considered as a firm basis for the identification of themes for the round-table and panel discussions: 'Report on the Twelfth Session', para. 78.

While it covered the gamut of Indigenous peoples' rights, several of the Alta Outcome Document's recommendations were especially relevant to participation, not just in the WCIP but also in the UN more widely. In this regard, it seemed to be influenced by the Secretary-General's 'Ways and Means' report of the year prior – as well as a continuation of Indigenous peoples' decades-long push for full membership of the international community. First, the Alta Conference recommended that the General Assembly appoint an Under-Secretary-General for Indigenous Peoples in order to strengthen the UN's capacity and efforts towards ensuring the inclusion and reflection of Indigenous peoples' rights, 'including the right to full and effective participation in decision-making', in all UN activities.[60] Second, it recommended that all UN agencies, funds, and programmes engaging in activities that impact Indigenous peoples form advisory councils or forums composed of Indigenous peoples' representatives 'to engage in dialogue and provide advice on policymaking and country- and regional-level operations'.[61] Third, it called for, pursuant to the right of self-determination, 'permanent observer status' within the UN system to enable Indigenous peoples' direct participation through their own governments and parliaments.[62] Finally, the Alta Outcome Document recommended that 'in keeping with [the] right of self-determination and free prior and informed consent', Indigenous peoples 'participate fully and effectively in the negotiations of all relevant international agreements that may affect them, including multilateral and bilateral trade and investment agreements and organizations, including in the review of existing agreements'.[63] The Alta Outcome Document was endorsed by the UNPFII, and by members of the EMRIP,[64] and the Indigenous Global Coordinating Group suggested that it should be the foundation of the outcome document of the WCIP.[65]

60 Alta Outcome Document, 6. This proposal has not been taken up.
61 Alta Outcome Document, 7.
62 Alta Outcome Document, 7.
63 Alta Outcome Document, 9.
64 UNPFII, 'Report on the Twelfth Session', para. 78. EMRIP, 'Report on Its Sixth Session', 4, paras. 6(b) and 31–34.
65 See, for example, John Henriksen for the Indigenous Global Coordinating Group, 'Second Round of Consultations Organized by the President of the General Assembly, Opening Intervention' (16 July 2014) http://cendoc.docip.org/collect/cendocdo/index/assoc/HASH2d41/e4092f25.dir/WCIP_2nd160714_GCGOpening_en.pdf.

4.1.3.3 Further Preparations in 2014 towards the WCIP Outcome

Throughout the preparations for the WCIP, many states had expressed support for Indigenous peoples' participation, including in terms suggesting acceptance as law. At a meeting of the Third Committee in December 2012, several state delegations had stressed the importance of Indigenous peoples' representatives' participation in the WCIP: Australia, Suriname, and Denmark for the Nordic countries, and Mexico.[66] In particular, Denmark for the Nordic countries said that the participation of Indigenous peoples in decisions affecting their rights was fundamental to the UNDRIP, but that there were barriers hindering the participation of such representatives in UN bodies – suggesting that Denmark and the Nordic countries considered the participation of Indigenous peoples' representatives in UN bodies to be not only required under but also fundamental to the UNDRIP.[67] Mexico also said that the participation of Indigenous peoples' representatives in the WCIP was 'in line with' UNDRIP.[68]

In September 2013, the Human Rights Council held a panel discussion on the WCIP and human rights. Several states used the meeting as a chance to express support for Indigenous peoples' participation in the WCIP. Finland supported Indigenous peoples' full and effective 'participation and consultation' in the preparation for the WCIP as well as during the Conference itself, 'stressing the vision of Indigenous peoples' self-determination and their free, prior and informed consent'.[69] The European Union said Indigenous peoples' participation in the WCIP was 'essential' for its success, while Estonia stressed the importance of Indigenous peoples' participation in decision-making at the UN more broadly.[70]

Following on from the Alta Conference, at least four rounds of informal consultations and interactive hearings towards the WCIP outcome document were convened between June and August 2014.[71] The President of the

66 UNGAOR, 67th Session, 3rd Committee, 18th Meeting, UN Doc. A/C.3/67/SR.18, paras. 44, 56, 69, 74, and 88.
67 Ibid., para. 74.
68 Ibid., para. 88.
69 Human Rights Council, 'Half-Day Panel Discussion on the World Conference on Indigenous Peoples', p. 15.
70 Ibid., p. 18.
71 President of the General Assembly, 'Letter Dated 30 May 2014 to Representatives of Indigenous Peoples' (30 May 2014), http://cendoc.docip.org/collect/cendocdo/index/assoc/HASH4a77/6cf01eaa.dir/PGALetter_toIP_wcip_300514.pdf; General Assembly, 'World Conference on Indigenous Peoples – Documents' (n.d.) www.un.org/en/ga/69/meetings/indigenous/documents.shtml.

General Assembly conducted the consultations, assisted by two advisors from Costa Rica and Slovenia, respectively, and two from Indigenous peoples, Myrna Cunningham and Les Malezer.[72] Indigenous representatives engaged extensively in the consultation process. A zero draft of the outcome text was released in July 2014 (and discussed at the EMRIP's thirteenth session),[73] followed by four further iterations of draft text.[74] Echoing the Alta Outcome Document, permanent observer status was a key demand that Indigenous peoples' representatives raised throughout these sessions.[75]

During the consultations, several states expressed explicit support for Indigenous peoples' full and meaningful participation at the WCIP, as well as more generally. At the informal consultation on 3 June, Norway's representative expressed the 'fundamental importance' of Indigenous peoples' involvement in the WCIP preparatory process and negotiations towards the outcome document, referencing ILO Convention 169.[76] At the same meeting, the United States' representative supported the full and meaningful participation of Indigenous peoples in the WCIP and full consultation in respect of its outcome. The United States said it had 'consistently reiterated its support for meaningful indigenous participation in the UN' and agreed with Indigenous peoples that 'existing arrangements for indigenous peoples' participation in the UN are not satisfactory', particularly with respect to the US federally recognized tribes that are 'governments with inherent powers of self-governance'. The United States' representative said 'a promising route', following the 2012 Ways and Means report, 'may be to seek broadened and enhanced indigenous peoples' participation in UN meetings ... addressing development matters' and welcomed continued dialogue with Indigenous peoples on this

[72] President of the General Assembly, 'Letter Dated 30 May 2014 to Representatives of Indigenous Peoples'.

[73] General Assembly, 'The World Conference on Indigenous Peoples: Consultations' (n.d.) www.un.org/en/ga/69/meetings/indigenous/consultations.shtml; EMRIP, 'Report of the Expert Mechanism on the Rights of Indigenous Peoples on Its Seventh Session' (8 August 2014) UN Doc. A/HRC/27/64, paras. 34–51.

[74] General Assembly, 'World Conference on Indigenous Peoples – Documents'.

[75] See, for example, General Assembly, 'Informal Interactive Hearing in preparation for the World Conference on Indigenous Peoples, 17–18 June, United Nations Headquarters, New York, Summary Report',www.un.org/en/ga/69/meetings/indigenous/consultations.shtml, 2.

[76] Norway, 'GA: Informal on the Outcome of the High-Level Meeting Indigenous Peoples, Statement Held by Iselin Hebbert Larsen on Behalf of Norway' (3 June 2014) http://cendoc.docip.org/collect/cendocdo/index/assoc/HASH0174/1f5036d0.dir/WCIP_infcons03042014_iselinnorway.pdf.

issue.[77] At the second informal consultation, Guatemala advocated promoting the participation of Indigenous peoples' organizations at the national, regional, and international levels.[78]

Indigenous peoples' participation in the negotiations towards the outcome document was not unqualified. Although the first stages of the drafting and consultation were carried out with member states and Indigenous peoples, the final stage in the General Assembly was carried out among member states only, echoing the process of adopting the UNDRIP.[79] Among Indigenous peoples and observers, this approach remained controversial.[80]

4.1.3.4 The World Conference and Its Outcomes

After the long preparatory period, the WCIP opened on 22 September 2014. In opening remarks to the plenary, Indigenous peoples' participation in the WCIP as well as in the UN more generally received sustained attention. The President of the General Assembly, Sam Kutesa, welcomed Indigenous peoples' active participation in the Conference's preparation, as well as the cooperation between member states and Indigenous peoples in the preparation of the outcome document.[81] Secretary-General Ban Ki-moon stressed that Indigenous peoples are 'concerned about issues that top the global agenda', including climate change – being 'deeply connected to Mother Earth', human rights, and global development. He said the success of the WCIP is 'integral to progress for all humankind'.[82] The President of Finland, for the Group of Western European and Other States, said the participation of Indigenous Peoples' representatives in the WCIP and its preparatory process

77 United States, 'U.S. Statement at Informal Consultation on the World Conference on Indigenous Peoples, June 3 2014' (3 June 2014) http://cendoc.docip.org/collect/cendocdo/index/assoc/HASH05e5/4e03feba.dir/WCIP_infconso3042014_terryus.pdf.

78 Guatemala, 'Intervención de la Delegación de Guatemala, Connie Taracena – Ministra Consejera, Dialogo interactivo organizado por el Presidente de la Asamblea General sobre la Conferencia Mundial sobre los Pueblos Indigena' (17 June 2014) http://cendoc.docip.org/collect/cendocdo/index/assoc/HASH012d/279f0c00.dir/IIH_WCIP170614_connieguatemala1.pdf.

79 EMRIP, 'Report on Its Seventh Session', para. 47.

80 Natural Justice, 'WCIP Concludes in New York with Adoption of Outcome Document' (Natural Justice, 2 October 2014, https://naturaljustice.org/wcip-concludes-in-new-york-with-adoption-of-outcome-document/); IWGIA, *The Indigenous World – 2014* (Copenhagen: IWGIA, 2014), p. 14.

81 General Assembly, 'Press Release: UN Member States Reaffirm Commitment to the Rights of Indigenous Peoples at First World Conference on Indigenous Peoples' (United Nations, 22 September 2014) www.un.org/en/ga/69/meetings/indigenous/pdf/Press-Release_final.pdf.

82 UNGAOR, 69th Session, 4th Plenary Meeting, UN Doc. A/69/PV.4, pp. 2–3.

'reinforces our joint commitment to the [UNDRIP]' and marks an important step in fulfilling the recommendation of the Alta Conference that Indigenous peoples should have the right to participate in matters concerning them in the UN. In justifying the importance of Indigenous peoples' participation at the UN, he said '[o]nly true dialogue with all relevant stakeholders will yield solid results beneficial for all'.[83] The President of Estonia said 'it is unfortunate that the participation of indigenous peoples in UN fora is constantly questioned', calling it 'incomprehensible, if not to say bizarre and shameful that some states attempt to hinder the participation of indigenous peoples' and expressing the hope that Indigenous peoples would soon have 'a strong voice in the international community'. In his statement, the President of Estonia invoked his own identity as 'a member of an indigenous people', noting that Estonians had lived on their present territory for several thousand years and had experienced 'both sides, as an oppressed indigenous people and now as a member of the United Nations'.[84] Both the President of Estonia and the President of Finland expressed concern about reported Russian attempts to prevent Koola Sami from attending the meeting.[85] The President of Mexico spoke in favour of Indigenous peoples participating in the UN under a separate status from that of NGOs.[86] The Republic of the Congo, speaking for the Group of African States, expressed its 'deep appreciation' for Indigenous peoples' 'valuable contributions' to the preparatory process, highlighting the establishment of the International Forum on Indigenous Peoples of Central Africa as an integral part of the operational bodies of the Economic Community of Central African States, and a platform for integration and cooperation in the Congo Basin on Indigenous issues.[87]

In the outcome document of the WCIP, member states, reaffirming their support for the UNDRIP and their 'solemn commitment to respect, promote

[83] The President of the Republic of Finland, 'Statement by President of the Republic of Finland Sauli Niinistö at the World Conference on Indigenous Peoples (WCIP) United Nations, New York 22 September 2014' (22 September 2014) http://cendoc.docip.org/collect/cendocdo/index/assoc/HASH018a/44a49367.dir/WCIP14PMniistoFinland004.pdf.

[84] Estonia, 'President Ilves at the United Nations World Conference on Indigenous Peoples, 22 September 2014' (22 September 2014) http://cendoc.docip.org/collect/cendocdo/index/assoc/HASHbcba/63c4d6c5.dir/WCIP14PMilvesEstonia006.pdf.

[85] The President of the Republic of Finland, 'Statement by President of the Republic of Finland'; Estonia, 'President Ilves'.

[86] Mexico, 'Palabras del Presidente de Los Estados Unidos Mexicanos, Licenciado Enrique Peña Nieto, durante La Sesión Plenaria de La Conferencia Mundial de Los Pueblos Indígenas' (22 September 2014) http://cendoc.docip.org/collect/cendocdo/index/assoc/HASH01d0/c7a5b270.dir/WCIP14PMenriqueMexico007.pdf.

[87] UNGAOR, 69th Session, 5th Plenary Meeting, UN Doc. A/69/PV.5, pp. 6–7.

and advance and in no way diminish the rights of indigenous peoples and to uphold the principles of the Declaration',[88] committed to considering, at the 70th session of the General Assembly, 'ways to enable the participation of indigenous peoples' representatives and institutions in meetings of relevant United Nations bodies on issues affecting them'.[89] To inform this meeting, they requested the Secretary-General to submit, taking into account Indigenous peoples' views, specific proposals to enable such participation, building on his 2012 report.[90] Ban Ki-moon welcomed this mandate as 'critical for indigenous communities – and for our world', stressing that the UN 'will do everything possible to support indigenous peoples' and counts on 'their engagement in our global drive for a more sustainable future'.[91] Countries also expressed support for these provisions in their statements. The United States called for the UN to 'establish procedures that recognize tribal leaders and tribal governments for who they are – persons and governments who are distinct from NGO representatives and who represent their own constituencies'.[92] The Peruvian delegate said Peru intended for UNFCCC COP 20, to be held in December 2014 in Lima, to mark a 'positive turning point' in Indigenous peoples' participation in discussion and decision-making regarding climate change, 'in explicit recognition of the central role they play in any definitive solution to this immense challenge'.[93]

The President of the General Assembly described the outcome document as 'unique because of the inclusive way in which indigenous peoples and Member States turned their shared goals into a reality', and the inclusive approach 'made this Conference a success'.[94] Representatives of Indigenous peoples' organizations also spoke out strongly in favour of the participation-related provisions in the Outcome Document, as well as participation at the

88 WCIP Outcome Document, paras. 3–4.

89 Ibid., para. 33.

90 Ibid., para. 40.

91 UNGAOR, 69th Session, 4th Plenary Meeting, UN Doc. A/69/PV.4, p. 3.

92 United States, 'WCIP Roundtable 1: "UN System Action for the Implementation of the Rights of Indigenous Peoples," United States Statement by Ambassador Keith Harper' (22 September 2014) http://cendoc.docip.org/collect/cendocdo/index/assoc/HASH013e/1a524365.dir/WCIP14R1keithUSA023.pdf, 1.

93 However, this hope was not to materialize. Peru, 'Intervención del señor Gabriel Quijandría, Viceministro de Desarrollo Estratégico de los Recursos Naturales en la Mesa Redonda Tierras, Territorios y Recursos de los Pueblos Indígenas' (23 September 2014) http://cendoc.docip.org/collect/cendocdo/index/assoc/HASH0183/31ca808c.dir/WCIP14R3gabrielPeru005.pdf, 2.

94 Closing statement made by the President of the UNGA: UNGA, Sixty-ninth session, 5th plenary meeting, UN Doc. A/69/PV.5, 8.

UN on issues affecting them,[95] and used the WCIP as a platform to advocate for Indigenous peoples' full and effective participation in processes such as the process towards the 2030 Agenda and the Sustainable Development Goals.[96]

It was on the basis of this mandate that work proceeded at the UN on the status of Indigenous peoples.

4.1.4 *Towards an Enhanced Status of Indigenous Peoples at the United Nations, 2015–2021*

Following the WCIP, the task of implementation took centre stage. In March 2015, some seven months after the WCIP, several Indigenous peoples' organizations hosted a follow-up meeting in Geneva to hold informal discussions among Indigenous peoples on the way forward.[97] The meeting strongly recommended, '[c]onsistent with the right of self-determination', 'broad, full and effective participation in all bodies of the United Nations in terms of where Indigenous Peoples' representative institutions themselves determine that issues under discussion in those bodies and processes would affect their rights'.[98] It emphasized the UNDRIP as the 'minimum' standard for Indigenous peoples' participation, particularly Articles 3 (right to self-determination) and 18 (right to participate in decision-making), noting the then current rules on Indigenous peoples' participation were insufficient to ensure full and effective participation. It recalled the Alta Outcome Document's demand for permanent observer status, as well as paragraph 33 of the WCIP Outcome Document, reiterating the intention to find ways and means for Indigenous Peoples' representative institutions to participate fully and effectively under a new status.[99] The meeting proposed that a new category, permanent observer status, should be created for Indigenous peoples' representatives; a new committee should be created by the General Assembly in order to carry out the accreditation process for such status; "participation"

[95] See, for example, President of the Sami Parliament of Norway, 'Remarks by Aili Keskitalo, President of the Sami Parliament of Norway, 22 Sep. 2014, World Conference on Indigenous Peoples' (22 September 2014) http://cendoc.docip.org/collect/cendocdo/index/assoc/HASHabe4/9acd9dab.dir/WCIP14PMailiSaami009.pdf, 2.

[96] Asia Indigenous Peoples' Caucus and Asia Indigenous Peoples Pact, 'Statement of the Asia Indigenous Peoples Caucus and the Asia Indigenous Peoples Pact' (22 September 2014) http://cendoc.docip.org/collect/cendocdo/index/assoc/HASH01be/440d5885.dir/WCIP14R1AIPP007.pdf, 2.

[97] EMRIP, 'Report of the Open-Ended Meeting of Indigenous Peoples on the Follow-Up to the World Conference of Indigenous Peoples' (10 July 2015) UN Doc. A/HRC/EMRIP/2015/CRP.2, 3.

[98] Ibid., 5.

[99] Ibid., 5.

should include the ability to attend meetings and conferences, make written and oral statements, and participate in drafting resolutions in the same manner as member states, as well as to propose agenda items; participation should be permitted in all bodies and agencies relevant to Indigenous interests, as determined by Indigenous peoples' representative institutions; and Indigenous peoples' representatives should be able to fully participate in the process of accreditation, including determining criteria for accreditation and implementing an accreditation process.[100]

Indigenous peoples' demands were thus clear from an early stage in the process. But the multilateral process would take time. In December 2015, the General Assembly passed resolution 70/232. This requested the President of the Assembly to conduct consultations, on possible measures necessary to enable the participation of Indigenous peoples' representatives and institutions in meetings of relevant UN bodies on issues affecting them, with member states, Indigenous peoples' representatives and institutions, and existing UN mechanisms. The Assembly also requested the President to prepare a compilation of the views presented during the consultations, including good practices within the UN regarding the participation of Indigenous peoples, to form the basis of a draft text to be adopted by the General Assembly at its following session.[101] The President of the General Assembly appointed four advisors to conduct the consultations: two state representatives – Finland and Ghana – and two Indigenous peoples' delegates, Claire Charters and James Anaya.[102]

4.1.4.1 Informal Consultations and Intergovernmental Negotiations towards a General Assembly Resolution in 2017

The four advisors carried out consultations with member states and Indigenous peoples between March and June 2016, via an electronic consultation and three consultation meetings on successive draft compilations of

[100] Ibid., 5–6.

[101] UNGA Res. 70/232 (23 December 2015), para. 19.

[102] 70th President of the General Assembly, 'Letter Appointing the Four Advisers Who Will Assist Him in Conducting Consultations on the Participation of Indigenous Peoples at the United Nations' (18 February 2016), www.un.org/development/desa/indigenouspeoples/participation-of-indigenous-peoples-at-the-united-nations.html. General Assembly, 'Compilation of Views on Possible Measures Necessary to Enable the Participation of Indigenous Peoples' Representatives and Institutions in Relevant United Nations Meetings on Issues Affecting Them, and of Good Practices within the United Nations Regarding Indigenous Peoples' Participation' (25 July 2016) UN Doc. A/70/990, 1. HRC, 'Report of the Expert Mechanism on the Rights of Indigenous Peoples on Its Ninth Session, Geneva, 11–15 July 2016' (8 August 2016) UN Doc. A/HRC/33/56, paras. 36–37.

views.[103] The electronic consultation invited views on, inter alia, procedures and modalities that would make the participation of Indigenous peoples' representatives meaningful and effective; eligibility criteria for accreditation as Indigenous peoples' representatives; nature and membership of a body to determine such eligibility; and details of the process, including information required to be submitted to obtain accreditation.[104] The final compilation of views, which included proposed elements for a draft General Assembly resolution, was presented in July of 2016.[105] The four advisors were then re-appointed and conducted further consultations with member states and Indigenous peoples between December 2016 and February 2017 on successive drafts of the elements paper.[106]

A draft text was published in April 2017,[107] and, after further consultations with states and Indigenous peoples during UNPFII 16, four rounds of intergovernmental negotiations took place in May and June punctuated by three further iterations of draft text.[108] Indigenous peoples were not included in

[103] President of the General Assembly, 'Letter Enclosing the Communication from the Advisers on the Way Forward on the Consultations on the Participation of Indigenous Peoples at the United Nations' (9 March 2016), www.un.org/development/desa/indigenouspeoples/participation-of-indigenous-peoples-at-the-united-nations.html.

[104] President of the General Assembly, 'Letter Enclosing the Communication from the Advisers'.

[105] General Assembly, 'Compilation of Views on Possible Measures'. For the draft elements, see Annex II.

[106] 'Letter by the President of the General Assembly Re-appointing the Four Advisors and Convening a Meeting on the Issue of Participation of Indigenous Peoples at the United Nations' (28 September 2016) www.un.org/esa/socdev/unpfii/documents/2016/Docs-updates/PGA-Letter-Invitation-IP-Consultation-October-2016.pdf. Advisors to the President of the General Assembly, 'Elements for Discussion during the 71st Session of the General Assembly' (December 2016) www.un.org/esa/socdev/unpfii/documents/2016/Docs-updates/PGA_Elements_for_further_discussion_22_Dec_final.pdf ("Revised Draft Elements"); Advisors to the President of the General Assembly, 'Elements for Discussion during the 71st Session of the General Assembly' (February 2017) www.un.org/esa/socdev/unpfii/documents/2017/PGA_Consultations/Clean_Elements_paper_February_2017.pdf ("Second Revised Draft Elements").

[107] General Assembly, 'Draft Resolution by the General Assembly on Enabling the Participation of Indigenous Peoples' Representatives and Institutions in Meetings of Relevant United Nations Bodies on Issues Affecting Them' (21 April 2017) www.un.org/development/desa/indigenouspeoples/wp-content/uploads/sites/19/2016/02/CLEAN-FINAL-ZERO-DRAFT-21-APRIL-2017-RESOLUTION-ON-IP-PARTICIPATION.pdf ("Zero Draft").

[108] General Assembly, 'Draft Resolution by the General Assembly on Enabling the Participation of Indigenous Peoples' Representative Institutions in Meetings of Relevant United Nations Bodies on Issues Affecting Them (REV 1)' (19 May 2017) www.un.org/pga/71/wp-content/uploads/sites/40/2015/08/Participation-of-indigenous-peoples.pdf ("First Revised Draft"); General Assembly, 'Draft Resolution by the General Assembly on Enabling the Participation of Indigenous Peoples' Representative Institutions in Meetings of Relevant United Nations Bodies on Issues Affecting Them (REV 2)' (6 June 2017) www.un.org/pga/71/wp-content/

these negotiations. By the end of the fourth round of negotiations, it was clear that an impasse had been reached.[109] As a result, the advisors circulated a shorter, procedural draft resolution, which deferred action on the issue but laid the groundwork for it to be addressed again in future.[110] That resolution was eventually adopted.[111] It requested the Secretary-General to produce a further report on 'achievements, analysis and concrete recommendations' on 'possible further measures necessary to enable participation' by the 74th session of the General Assembly,[112] and asked its President to hold 'informal interactive sessions' during the 72nd, 73rd, and 74th sessions of the Assembly and to prepare summaries of these.[113] The General Assembly decided to continue its consideration of the matter at its 75th session in 2020.[114]

The principal issues of contention were the venues for participation by Indigenous peoples' representative institutions (IPRIs), the application process, and the selection criteria to determine which organizations are representative of one or more Indigenous people. In what follows, I explore how these issues evolved throughout the course of consultations and negotiations, before turning to examine how the process has unfolded since 2017.

VENUES A key disagreement centred on the issue of which UN bodies Indigenous peoples should be able to participate in. In informal consultations,

uploads/sites/40/2015/08/Indigenous-peoples-6-June-2017.pdf ("Second Revised Draft"); General Assembly, 'Draft Resolution by the General Assembly on Enabling the Participation of Indigenous Peoples' Representative Institutions in Meetings of Relevant United Nations Bodies on Issues Affecting Them (REV 2, Technical Update)' (16 June 2017) www.un.org/pga/71/wp-content/uploads/sites/40/2015/08/Indigenous-peoples-16-June-2017.pdf ("Updated Second Revised Draft").

109 Dr Claire Charters gave an update to the 10th session of the EMRIP, in July 2017: UN Web TV, 'Item 7: Indigenous Peoples' Participation – 5th Meeting, 10th Session Expert Mechanism on Rights of Indigenous Peoples' https://media.un.org/en/asset/k1d/k1d8z1yoa6 ("Claire Charters' Update").

110 General Assembly, 'Draft Resolution on Enhancing the Participation of Indigenous Peoples' Representatives and Institutions in Meetings of Relevant United Nations Bodies on Issues Affecting Them' (10 August 2017) www.un.org/pga/71/wp-content/uploads/sites/40/2015/08/Indigenous-peoples.pdf.

111 General Assembly, 'Draft Resolution submitted by the President of the General Assembly: Enhancing the Participation of Indigenous Peoples' Representatives and Institutions in Meetings of Relevant United Nations Bodies on Issues Affecting Them' (15 August 2017) UN Doc. A/71/L.82; UNGA Res. 71/231 (8 September 2017).

112 UNGA Res. 71/231, para. 5. At para. 6, it requested the Secretary-General, in doing so, to seek input from Indigenous peoples from all regions of the world.

113 Ibid., para. 8. At para. 9, the General Assembly expanded the mandate of the Voluntary Fund in order to assist Indigenous peoples to participate in these hearings.

114 Ibid., para. 7.

some states, like the EU, Canada, Australia, New Zealand, Norway, Sweden, and Denmark and Greenland, were in favour of access to the General Assembly and its committees.[115] Others, such as the United States, favoured participation only in the ECOSOC, the Human Rights Council, and their subsidiary bodies.[116] Still others thought that Indigenous peoples should have the right to participate in all UN bodies that Indigenous peoples themselves judge to affect their interests.[117] Russia initially did not expressly favour any increase in participation, preferring that more information about already existing opportunities be provided,[118] but later supported Indigenous peoples' enhanced participation in UN bodies and venues where non-state actors such as NGOs already participated, including in the Human Rights Council and its subsidiary bodies.[119]

Paragraphs in the draft texts regarding ECOSOC, the Human Rights Council, and other UN bodies did not seem to attract much opposition. Invitations to the ECOSOC to ensure that IPRIs can attend and participate 'in all its meetings on issues affecting them' including in its functional commissions, and to the Human Rights Council 'to make the necessary arrangements for [IPRIs] to attend and participate at its meetings', remained consistent throughout the drafts.[120] Furthermore, all iterations of the draft text included a paragraph urging 'all bodies and organisations throughout the United Nations System, including Charter and functional bodies, and United Nations funds, programmes and specialized agencies, to enable the participation of Indigenous Peoples' representative institutions on issues affecting them'.[121] The texts also reaffirmed that IPRIs may be invited to attend 'conferences, summits and other meetings convened by the General

[115] Claire Charters' Update (the EU favoured enhanced participation in all General Assembly meetings, as well as meetings of its Second and Third Committees).

[116] General Assembly, 'Compilation of Views on Possible Measures', para. 18. General Assembly, 'Compilation of Submissions to IP Advisers Email Address' (20 May 2016) www.un.org/esa/socdev/unpfii/documents/2016/Docs-updates/Compilation_of_submission_to_GAConsultation_08_07_2016-rev3.pdf, pp. 83–84.

[117] General Assembly, 'Compilation of Views on Possible Measures', para. 23.

[118] General Assembly, 'Compilation of Submissions', p. 100.

[119] Human Rights Council, 'Intersessional Round Table on Ways to Enhance the Participation of Indigenous Peoples' Representatives and Institutions in Meetings of the Human Rights Council on Issues Affecting Them' (11 January 2022) UN Doc. A/HRC/49/69, para. 44.

[120] Zero Draft, OP6 and OP7; First Revised Draft, OP3 Alternatives 1, 2, and 3; Second Revised Draft, OP4(b) and (c); Updated Second Revised Draft, OP4(b) and (c).

[121] Updated Second Revised Draft, OP4. Also see Second Revised Draft, OP4; First Revised Draft, OP6; Zero Draft, OP11. Changes to this paragraph throughout the iterations were minimal. At the Second Revised Draft stage, the caveat 'as appropriate to the intergovernmental character of the United Nations' was added.

Assembly on issues affecting them',[122] although a commitment to ensure that in the modalities for future conferences convened by the General Assembly IPRIs are granted 'at a minimum, similar rights to attend and participate in those conferences as established in the modalities herein' was included in the first two drafts but was not present in later drafts.[123]

The prospect of IPRIs' participation in the General Assembly, on the other hand, attracted the most opposition. The zero draft included options for inviting IPRIs to attend and participate in 'all meetings of the General Assembly and its Main Committees on issues affecting them', or 'all meetings of the General Assembly as well as the General Assembly's Second Committee and Third Committees on issues affecting them' as well as additional meetings in the General Assembly's Main and other committees and its subsidiary bodies at the invitation of the President of the General Assembly.[124] Some states objected to both of these options, including for reasons of "practicality." This resulted in the inclusion, in the first revised draft, of an option involving no invitation to participate in the General Assembly or its committees.[125] The second revised draft proposed a compromise: IPRIs would be invited to participate in the General Assembly and its committees 'on issues affecting them', but the President of the General Assembly in consultation with member states and IPRIs would determine which meetings, or parts thereof, address issues affecting Indigenous peoples, although at minimum this would include the parts of meetings of the General Assembly and its committees under agenda items referring specifically to "Indigenous" or "Indigenous Peoples."[126]

However, a number of states continued to express 'considerable resistance' to including the General Assembly as a participation venue.[127] A further compromise text, drafted in a final attempt to break the impasse, would have excluded any participation in the General Assembly, inviting only the ECOSOC to enable IPRIs' participation, in combination with other provisions discussed below. However, states could not agree even to this level of compromise.[128]

122 Zero Draft, OP9; First Revised Draft, OP4; Second Revised Draft, OP5; Updated Second Revised Draft, OP5.
123 Zero Draft, OP10; First Revised Draft, OP5.
124 Zero Draft, OP6 Alternatives 1 and 2.
125 First Revised Draft, OP3 Alternative 3.
126 Second Revised Draft, OP4(a); Updated Second Revised Draft, OP4(a).
127 Claire Charters' Update.
128 Claire Charters' Update.

MODALITIES OF PARTICIPATION At the intergovernmental negotiation stage, states seemed united on appropriate participatory modalities – or at least, provisions were quickly reached that did not conflict with any states' red lines. The drafts envisaged that IPRIs would be allowed to make oral statements and to submit written statements, in one of the official languages of the UN.[129] The drafts consistently positioned IPRIs' participation at a lower level than that of states. While early drafts envisaged that Indigenous peoples could be offered the right of reply 'where appropriate, and when invited by the chairperson of the meeting',[130] this was excluded in later drafts.[131] The drafts were, however, unanimous that IPRIs would not have the right to vote, to raise points of order, to submit, move amendments to, or co-sponsor resolutions, or to 'take decisions or exercise other prerogatives of Member States',[132] although different views had been expressed at the consultation stage.[133] Moreover, the draft resolution did not envisage unlimited speaking slots for IPRIs, stating that these 'shall be arranged in a balanced way' taking into account equitable representation, efficiency, and fairness between all participants – unlike for states.[134] Likewise, IPRIs were to be allocated 'appropriate seating arrangements' that would 'not be overly burdensome' for the UN but would take equitable regional representation into account.[135] The drafts sidestepped the issue of whether IPRIs would take priority over NGOs in terms of speaking order or seating arrangements.[136]

A provision inviting the ECOSOC and HRC to apply these provisions 'mutatis mutandis' was later altered to provide that these provisions would 'serve as guidance for other relevant United Nations meetings'.[137]

[129] Zero Draft, OP12(a); First Revised Draft, OP7(a); Second Revised Draft, OP6(a); Updated Second Revised Draft, OP6(a).

[130] Zero Draft, OP12(b); First Revised Draft, OP7(b).

[131] Second Revised Draft, OP6(c); Updated Second Revised Draft, OP6(c).

[132] Zero Draft, OP12(d); First Revised Draft, OP7(d); Second Revised Draft, OP6(c); Updated Second Revised Draft, OP6(c). Some states, such as Mexico, held the position that accredited IPRIs should have voting rights, but this appears not to have been a red line: Claire Charters' Update.

[133] General Assembly, 'Compilation of Views on Possible Measures', paras. 25–27.

[134] Zero Draft, OP12(c); First Revised Draft, OP7(c); Second Revised Draft, OP6(b); Updated Second Revised Draft, OP6(b).

[135] Zero Draft, OP12(e); First Revised Draft, OP7(e); Second Revised Draft, OP6(d); Updated Second Revised Draft, OP6(d).

[136] Disagreements on this issue had been expressed at consultation stage: General Assembly, 'Compilation of Views on Possible Measures', para. 29.

[137] Zero Draft, OP4; First Revised Draft, OP37; Second Revised Draft, OP6; Updated Second Revised Draft, OP6.

APPLICATION MECHANISM At the consultation stage, views diverged on whether a new body should be established to accredit IPRIs. Most favoured the establishment of a new body, although views diverged on whether it should consist of representatives of both Indigenous peoples and states, those of only states, or if it should consist of independent experts.[138] Some thought the PFII should be mandated to oversee accreditation,[139] while others thought accreditation should be carried out by a "non-objection" procedure, and still others thought the final decision should rest with the General Assembly.[140]

At the negotiation stage, the draft resolution was clear that a new committee would be established to review and decide on IPRIs' applications for participation at the UN.[141] Many Indigenous peoples' organizations had opposed any state involvement in accrediting IPRIs, but early drafts of the resolution all included state involvement, with the most equal option providing that the accrediting committee would consist of experts on the rights of Indigenous peoples, with half the members appointed in consultation with member states and half appointed in consultation with Indigenous peoples.[142]

In later drafts, however, control of the accreditation process shifted towards states. Because of 'considerable resistance from a number of states' to a committee that included Indigenous delegates,[143] the membership of the committee would have excluded any Indigenous peoples' representatives or experts. Rather, it would consist solely of representatives of member states.[144] The committee would be assisted by an Expert Advisory Group, composed of seven experts selected by the President of the General Assembly on the basis of proposals by and consultation with Indigenous peoples.[145] The relevant member states were to be notified and invited to provide information when an IPRI applied to the committee.[146] The application process would have consisted of two stages. At the first stage, the Expert Advisory Group would

[138] General Assembly, 'Compilation of Views on Possible Measures', paras. 31 and 33.
[139] Ibid., 32.
[140] Ibid., 33.
[141] Zero Draft, OP13; First Revised Draft, OP7; Second Revised Draft, OP7; Updated Second Revised Draft, OP7.
[142] Zero Draft, OP14; First Revised Draft, OP9.
[143] Claire Charters' Update.
[144] Second Revised Draft, OP8; Updated Second Revised Draft, OP8.
[145] Second Revised Draft, OP9; Updated Second Revised Draft, OP9.
[146] Zero Draft, OP18; Second Revised Draft, OP14; Updated Second Revised Draft, OP11.

make a recommendation; at the second stage, the committee of state representatives would take a decision by majority vote, 'taking into account' the Expert Advisory Group's recommendation.[147] In addition, the member state concerned could request a General Assembly vote to reverse a decision of the committee.[148]

Even this large degree of control over Indigenous peoples' accreditation proved impossible for some states to accept. The third revised draft resolution, upon which states were unable to agree, would have streamlined the application process such that applicant IPRIs that were not queried by a relevant state would acquire a separate participatory status in the ECOSOC, but if a relevant state chose to object, the application process might be discontinued unless a resolution between the concerned state and the Indigenous applicant could be found or the ECOSOC voted to grant the application.[149] Under a further proposed compromise, a state would be able to object to an IPRI's application, but state recognition would not be a mandatory criteria. However, some states were not able to accept an objection procedure, while others were not able to agree without one.[150] There was ultimately no agreement on this issue.

SELECTION CRITERIA The final tricky issue was the selection criteria that IPRIs would have to meet. Throughout the process, successive draft texts consistently proposed that IPRIs selected for participation should be 'genuinely representative of one or more people or community that qualify as indigenous'.[151] Under this approach, IPRIs seeking accreditation would have to 'show persuasive evidence that they are the legitimate representative of one or more Indigenous people or community', with relevant evidence including 'written documentation and, where appropriate, oral testimony', although evidence 'must not be so difficult to establish as to limit the ability of an

[147] Second Revised Draft, OP10; Updated Second Revised Draft, OP10. This was reflected in the Zero Draft, OP19 Alternative 2; First Revised Draft, OP9 Alternative 2.

[148] Second Revised Draft, OP18; Updated Second Revised Draft, OP18. Earlier options regarding an appeal procedure, by which either the IPRI or member state concerned could appeal and appeals would be considered by the same committee that made the original decision, were removed: Zero Draft, OP24–OP27; First Revised Draft, OP18–OP21.

[149] Claire Charters' Update.

[150] Claire Charters' Update.

[151] Updated Second Revised Draft, OP24; Second Revised Draft, OP24; First Revised Draft, OP28 ('one or more community, nation or people'); Zero Draft, OP34 ('one or more people'). Also see General Assembly, 'Compilation of Views on Possible Measures', para. 37.

Indigenous Peoples' representative institution to be selected'. Relevant evidence would include 'authority under Indigenous law and customs and/or national legislation'; 'election as the representative body'; 'permanent physical presence of the institution and its personnel within the territory of the people they represent'; and existence as an institution for at least two years.[152] All drafts were clear that once IPRIs were accredited by the committee, they would 'have full authority to select their own delegates'.[153]

An initial point of contention was whether IPRIs should be limited to Indigenous governance institutions. Some held the view that it should be so limited, including governing councils, parliaments, and traditional authorities. Others pointed out that not all IPRIs can be accurately described as governing, in some cases because of the impact of colonization and/or dispossession.[154] The second revised draft resolution attempted to resolve this issue by providing that IPRIs were 'those governance and other bodies of indigenous traditional or elected authorities that are constituted or adopted by Indigenous peoples themselves in the exercise of their inherent right of self-determination'.[155] In the updated second revised draft, this language was changed to 'those governance *or* other bodies of indigenous traditional or *other, including elected*, authority that are constituted or adopted by Indigenous Peoples *to represent themselves*'.[156] As such, there seems to have been broad agreement that IPRIs were not necessarily 'governance' bodies, but would have to have some form of 'authority' – although some states clearly objected to the second revised draft's explicit linkage with self-determination. Across all drafts, IPRIs were clearly differentiated from NGOs 'that are created or led by Indigenous individuals apart from indigenous governance or authority structures, or that are established primarily to address sectoral concerns or particular issues of relevance to indigenous peoples'.[157]

The more difficult issue was the factors the committee would take into account in determining whether an IPRI was representative of one or more *Indigenous peoples*. Initially there had been some debate about whether a

[152] Zero Draft, OP37(b) and (c); First Revised Draft, OP31(b) and (d); Second Revised Draft, OP27(b); Updated Second Revised Draft, OP27(b).
[153] Zero Draft, OP39; First Revised Draft, OP32; Second Revised Draft, OP28; Updated Second Revised Draft, OP28.
[154] General Assembly, 'Compilation of Views on Possible Measures', para. 43.
[155] Second Revised Draft, OP2.
[156] Updated Second Revised Draft, OP2 (emphasis added).
[157] Second Revised Draft, OP2; Updated Second Revised Draft, OP2.

definition of Indigenous peoples would be required,[158] but the draft resolution contained a list of relevant factors to be flexibly considered.[159] It recognized that the situation of Indigenous peoples 'varies from region to region and from country to country and that the significance of national and regional particularities and various historical and cultural backgrounds should be taken into consideration'.[160] Some factors proved largely uncontroversial, appearing throughout the drafts, such as self-identification; a unique relationship with lands, territories, and resources; cultural distinctiveness including Indigenous languages; entry into treaties, agreements, or other constructive arrangements; occupation of ancestral lands, territories, and resources over a long period of time, often reflected in prior occupancy; traditional authority under Indigenous law; the exercise of collective rights; the practice of self-government; recognition as Indigenous by other Indigenous peoples; and a history of dispossession and/or colonization.[161] While there was disagreement about which of these factors should be considered primary, and which secondary, their mention in the text did not cross any states' red lines.[162]

By contrast, proposed criteria relating to state recognition and approval proved most difficult. The first two iterations of the draft resolution listed state recognition, and 'recognition under domestic laws and policies', as relevant factors among the undifferentiated list.[163] But in the later drafts, state recognition was proposed as a primary factor: 'the existence and terms of domestic laws or policies of the State concerned that are specifically aimed at addressing Indigenous peoples (whether or not referred to explicitly as "Indigenous"), apart from others residing within the State's territory, because of historical

[158] General Assembly, 'Compilation of Views on Possible Measures', para. 38. For instance, France and China favoured elaborating a definition of Indigenous peoples: General Assembly, 'Compilation of Submissions', pp. 104 and 112.

[159] Zero Draft, OP36; First Revised Draft, OP26; Second Revised Draft, OP26; Updated Second Revised Draft, OP26.

[160] Zero Draft, OP35; First Revised Draft, OP29; Second Revised Draft, OP25; Updated Second Revised Draft, OP25.

[161] Zero Draft, OP37(a); First Revised Draft, OP31(a); Second Revised Draft, OP27(a); Updated Second Revised Draft, OP27(a). Compare the Cobo definition.

[162] While the Zero Draft simply laid out a list of relevant factors without distinguishing among them, the First Revised Draft had a list of factors followed by a list of 'other factors that can be applied', and the Updated Second Revised Draft distinguished between 'primary factors' and 'other factors that can be applied'.

[163] Zero Draft, OP37(a); First Revised Draft, OP31(a) ('recognition by the state concerned of Indigenous people with a status distinct from other non-Indigenous people in the state').

factors and/or conditions of vulnerability'.[164] The 'reasoned views of the State concerned' were also to be a primary factor. This in itself was a carefully worded compromise. Some states took the view that state recognition should be a necessary condition, while others (as well as Indigenous peoples) could not accept such a provision.[165] Consensus could not be found, even on a further proposed compromise under which, while state recognition would not be a mandatory criterion, a state could object to an IPRI's application.[166]

In this light, it is unsurprising that Indigenous peoples were deeply concerned about the potential for the draft resolution to undermine existing standards and norms on the rights of Indigenous peoples, including the Declaration.[167] If the final compromise text had been adopted, an Indigenous people's application for status at the General Assembly would have been decided on by a committee of states, with recognition and views of the state concerned as primary factors in the committee's decision. Further, the state concerned would have been able to object to the Indigenous people's application. In addition, an Indigenous applicant would have had to show potentially burdensome evidence of representativeness. Overall, if the draft resolution in its ultimate compromise form had been adopted, this would have represented a step back for self-determination. It remains to see how these issues can be resolved.

In the course of the consultations and negotiations, several states expressed the view that the participation of IPRIs at the General Assembly and in other UN bodies was required by law. For instance, Australia, in the course of a statement on behalf of Canada, Australia, and New Zealand expressing support for Indigenous peoples' participation in the General Assembly and its committees, said that '[i]n line with the [WCIP Outcome Document] and with the aims of the Declaration and the rights of indigenous peoples, we believe that indigenous peoples have the right to participate and be heard in decisions that affect them at the United Nations'.[168] Similarly, Denmark on behalf of Norway, Sweden, and Greenland said that enabling IPRIs' participation in meetings would reflect the exercise of 'their right to participate in meetings of all relevant UN bodies on issues affecting them … as set out in UNDRIP'.[169] In a separate submission, Denmark and Greenland said that

164 Second Revised Draft, OP27(a) (using the term 'benefiting' instead of 'addressing'); Updated Second Revised Draft, OP27(a).

165 Claire Charters' Update.

166 Claire Charters' Update.

167 See comments by Indigenous peoples' representatives, in Claire Charters' Update.

168 Claire Charters' Update.

169 Claire Charters' Update.

establishment of a separate accreditation category would be consistent with Articles 18 and 41 of the UNDRIP.[170] Other states, such as Mexico and Peru, expressed support for Indigenous peoples' participation without reference to law.[171]

4.1.4.2 The Process Subsequent to 2017

The 2017 resolution envisaged that the process would continue via three 'informal interactive hearings' with Indigenous peoples on the margins of the UNPFII's sessions, convened by the President of the General Assembly, as well as a further report to be prepared by the Secretary-General. The issue would then be taken up again at the General Assembly's 75th session in 2020, with a view to reaching agreement. But external events intervened. Two of the informal hearings were held as planned, in 2018 and 2019, respectively,[172] but then the COVID-19 pandemic forced the third hearing to be postponed twice, to 2022.[173] The continuation of the General Assembly's consideration of possible further measures necessary to enhance the participation of Indigenous peoples' representatives and institutions was similarly postponed until its 77th session.[174] In addition, Indigenous peoples organized two international dialogue meetings to discuss their enhanced participation, in 2016 and 2020, the second of which resulted in the creation of an Indigenous coordinating body to facilitate the cooperation of Indigenous peoples in the enhanced participation process.[175]

170 General Assembly, 'Compilation of Submissions to IP Advisers Email Address', 55–56.

171 See, for example, statements of Mexico and Peru, in Claire Charters' Update.

172 General Assembly, 'First Informal Interactive Hearing with Indigenous Peoples, President's Summary' (31 May 2018) www.un.org/development/desa/indigenouspeoples/wp-content/uploads/sites/19/2019/06/Informal-interactive-hearing-Letter-to-Indigenous-Peoples-31-May.pdf; General Assembly, 'Second Informal Interactive Hearing with Indigenous Peoples on Indigenous Peoples enhanced participation in the United Nations, President's Summary' (20 May 2019) www.un.org/pga/73/wp-content/uploads/sites/53/2019/05/Summary-of-the-Informal-interactive-hearing-with-indigenous-peoples.pdf. See also UNGA Res. 72/155 (19 December 2017); UNGA Res. 73/156 (17 December 2018), para. 32.

173 UNGA decision 74/565 of 12 August 2020, in General Assembly, 'Resolutions and Decisions Adopted by the General Assembly during Its Seventy-Fourth Session, Volume III' GAOR 74 Supp. 49 (2020) UN Doc. A/74/49 (Vol. III); UNGA decision 75/561 of 16 April 2021, in General Assembly, 'Resolutions and Decisions Adopted by the General Assembly during Its Seventy-Fifth Session, Volume III' GAOR 75 Supp. 49 (2021) UN Doc. A/75/49 (vol. III).

174 UNGA Res. 76/459 (16 December 2021), para. 43.

175 General Assembly, 'Enhancing the Participation of Indigenous Peoples' Representatives and Institutions in Meetings of Relevant United Nations Bodies on Issues Affecting Them: Report of the Secretary-General' (27 July 2020) UN Doc. A/75/255, para. 40.

In the first and second hearings, disagreement persisted on many of the same issues that had characterized disagreement during the 2017 negotiations. On venues of participation, some states continued to favour IPRIs' participation in all General Assembly meetings, as well as the ECOSOC and Human Rights Council, while others preferred merely enhancing existing mechanisms like the UNPFII and EMRIP.[176] On selection criteria, some states preferred self-identification as the primary criterion, while states disagreed on whether state recognition and/or non-objection should be required.[177] On selection mechanism, states disagreed on whether the selection body should be composed of Indigenous peoples' representatives.[178]

In 2020, the Secretary-General released a report that summarized the discussions to date.[179] It recommended that the General Assembly organize further informal consultations with Indigenous peoples and states organize national and regional consultations.[180] Further, the report identified a lack of common understanding of "Indigenous peoples' representatives" and "Indigenous peoples' representative institutions," proposing an in-depth study of existing representative institutions and their practices.[181] The process is still ongoing, and it remains to be seen how the outstanding issues can be resolved in a way that is satisfactory to states as well as to Indigenous peoples.

4.1.5 *Towards Enhanced Participation at the Human Rights Council*

Following the passage of General Assembly resolution 70/232, alongside the ongoing discussions in the General Assembly, a parallel push took place for Indigenous peoples' participation in the Human Rights Council, especially in respect of its activities that expressly relate to Indigenous peoples. In particular, the Council holds an annual half-day discussion on the rights of Indigenous peoples, as well as dialogues with the EMRIP and the Special Rapporteur on the rights of Indigenous peoples. The EMRIP, at its ninth and tenth meetings in 2016 and 2017, respectively, proposed to the Human Rights Council that,

[176] General Assembly, 'First Informal Interactive Hearing', para. 22.
[177] General Assembly, 'First Informal Interactive Hearing', para. 24; General Assembly, 'Second Informal Interactive Hearing', 4.
[178] General Assembly, 'Second Informal Interactive Hearing', 5.
[179] General Assembly, 'Enhancing the Participation of Indigenous Peoples' Representatives'.
[180] Ibid., paras. 60–61.
[181] Ibid., para. 62. The General Assembly subsequently took note of the report: UNGA Res. 75/475 (16 December 2020), para. 35; UNGA Res. 76/459, para. 41.

'without prejudice' to the ongoing process in the General Assembly, the Council make further efforts to enhance the participation of Indigenous peoples' representatives and institutions in its work, including all meetings relevant to Indigenous peoples' rights.[182]

At its 39th meeting in 2018, the Human Rights Council resolved to hold a half-day inter-sessional interactive dialogue on ways to enhance the participation of Indigenous peoples' representatives and institutions in meetings of the Human Rights Council on issues affecting them, at the 12th session of the EMRIP in 2019.[183] In the preamble to that resolution, the Council appreciated 'the current efforts towards the promotion, protection and fulfilment of the rights of indigenous peoples', recalling the General Assembly's commitment in the WCIP Outcome Document to consider ways to enhance Indigenous peoples' participation at the UN on issues affecting them – implying that the Council considered such participation to be a right of Indigenous peoples.[184]

The inter-sessional interactive dialogue took place on 15 July 2019. In opening remarks, the President of the General Assembly, María Fernanda Espinosa Garcés, stated that '[t]he full and effective participation of indigenous peoples in processes that affect their rights is enshrined in the UN Declaration of the Rights of Indigenous Peoples' and that 'it is vital that the UN sets an example in this regard'.[185] She called for 'broad, flexible mechanisms and processes that can accommodate the various forms of indigenous peoples' organizations'.[186] Representatives from the OHCHR and EMRIP underscored the UNDRIP Article 41 requirement to establish ways and means of ensuring participation of Indigenous peoples on issues affecting them.[187] In addition to the rights-based justification, UN representatives highlighted instrumental justifications for the participation of Indigenous peoples: Garcés said it 'would make a substantive contribution to the UN's work, and

[182] EMRIP, 'Report of the Expert Mechanism on the Rights of Indigenous Peoples on Its Ninth Session, Geneva, 11–15 July 2016' (8 August 2016) UN Doc. A/HRC/33/56, para. 9; EMRIP, 'Annual Report of the Expert Mechanism on the Rights of Indigenous Peoples' (8 August 2017) UN Doc. A/HRC/36/57, para. 11. The EMRIP has since echoed these proposals repeatedly: see, for example, EMRIP, 'Proposals for the Human Rights Council', para. 1.

[183] Human Rights Council Res. 39/13 (28 September 2018), para. 11.

[184] Ibid., preamble, recital 5.

[185] All speeches from the inter-sessional interactive dialogue, referred to in the following notes, are available at https://hrcmeetings.ohchr.org/HRCSessions/RegularSessions/41Session/Pages/Statements.aspx?SessionId=30&MeetingDate=15/07/2019%2000:00:00.

[186] Ibid.

[187] See, for example, speech by Paulo David, Chief of Indigenous Peoples and Minorities Section, OHCHR; speech by Erika Yamada, EMRIP.

expand the ways in which we see the world',[188] while the EMRIP representative stated that when Indigenous peoples participate 'positive outcomes are achieved' and such participation is 'crucial to informing our understanding of indigenous peoples' human rights issues and proposing realistic measures to address them in context'.[189]

Indigenous speakers used the opportunity presented by the dialogue to continue to advocate for enhanced participation not just at the Human Rights Council but at the General Assembly and all bodies and organizations throughout the UN system.[190] They said that requiring IPRIs register as NGOs in order to participate was 'unfair' and 'unjust', stressing that they are not NGOs.[191]

Many states spoke in support of enhancing Indigenous participation in the Human Rights Council,[192] though not all supported the idea.[193] States discussed possible modalities, including speaking rights, the right to provide written information, and the right to propose candidates for special procedures mandates such as the Special Rapporteur on the rights of Indigenous peoples.[194] Discussions on accreditation processes mirrored those in the General Assembly process.[195]

Several states expressed the view that Indigenous peoples' participation at the UN is required by law. For Bolivia, Indigenous peoples' representatives' 'full and effective participation … in the United Nations system and its organs on matters that concern them or affect their rights is a fundamental priority' under the UNDRIP, the ILO Convention 169, and the WCIP Outcome Document.[196] Indigenous peoples' participation was fundamentally important for the implementation of Indigenous peoples' individual and collective rights.[197] Canada, for Canada, Australia, and New Zealand, stressed the importance for the Human Rights Council 'to take concrete steps to reflect in [its] own mechanisms the [UNDRIP] and include Indigenous peoples' representatives and institutions'.[198]

188 Ibid.
189 Speech by Erika Yamada.
190 See, for example, speech by Asia Indigenous Peoples Pact representative.
191 See, for example, speech by Kenneth Deer, Haudenosaunee External Relations Committee.
192 See, for example, Bolivia, Canada, Australia, New Zealand, the EU, Mexico, Peru, Sweden, Norway, Iceland, Finland, and Denmark.
193 Brazil spoke against, expressing the wish to avoid the proliferation of negotiations in different fora.
194 Intervention by a representative of the EU; intervention by a representative of Sweden, for Iceland, Norway, Finland, Denmark together with Greenland, and Sweden.
195 See, for example, speech by a representative of Peru; speech by a representative of the EU.
196 Speech by a representative of Bolivia.
197 Ibid.
198 Speech by a representative of Canada.

Other states, without expressing *opinio juris*, supported the participation of Indigenous peoples in the Human Rights Council for the reason that it would strengthen the achievement of its mandate or benefit "everyone" including via internationally agreed objectives. Canada, for Canada, Australia, and New Zealand, said Indigenous peoples' participation would strengthen the Human Rights Council's ability to promote and protect human rights and to address situations of human rights violations.[199] The EU, similarly, said Indigenous peoples' participation would contribute effectively to strengthening the Human Rights Council's and its principles and objectives.[200] Sweden, for Iceland, Norway, Finland, Denmark 'together with Greenland' and Sweden, said enhancing Indigenous peoples' participation 'will benefit all'.[201] Peru positioned Indigenous peoples' participation as necessary to achieving the substantive rights of Indigenous peoples contained in the UNDRIP.[202] For Mexico, Indigenous peoples' participation was necessary to achieving the Sustainable Development Goals and implementing the 2030 Agenda.[203]

All these discussions in the Human Rights Council have taken place without the full participation of Indigenous peoples. Under the Council's rules, Indigenous peoples' participation is restricted to those Indigenous organizations that have ECOSOC consultative status.[204]

In July 2021, the Human Rights Council held a further inter-sessional roundtable, on possible steps to be taken to enhance the participation of Indigenous peoples' representatives and institutions in Human Rights Council meetings on issues affecting them. Co-chaired by an Indigenous representative and the President of the Human Rights Council,[205] the roundtable heard statements from Indigenous peoples' representatives from the

[199] Speech by a representative of Canada.

[200] Speech by a representative of the EU.

[201] Speech by a representative of Sweden.

[202] Speech by a representative of Peru.

[203] Speech by a representative of Mexico.

[204] As highlighted by the Sami Parliament of Finland, in a submission to the EMRIP of 2 December 2020. The Sami Parliament of Finland also pointed to the difficulty of participating in virtual meetings: EMRIP, '13th Session/Regional Meetings of the Expert Mechanism on the Rights of Indigenous Peoples' (2020) (OHCHR, www.ohchr.org/EN/Issues/IPeoples/EMRIP/Pages/Session13.aspx). Several states pointed to this in the 2021 roundtable, including Canada, Denmark, and New Zealand: Human Rights Council, 'Intersessional Round Table on Ways to Enhance the Participation', paras. 14, 21, and 36.

[205] Human Rights Council Res. 42/19 (26 September 2019), paras. 12 and 13. Also see paras. 10 and 11. Preamble recital 4 implies that the Council considers Indigenous peoples' participation to be required as a right of Indigenous peoples. The roundtable was initially scheduled for 2020, but was postponed until July 2021 due to the COVID-19 pandemic: Human Rights Council Res. 45/12 (6 October 2020), para. 15.

seven sociocultural regions. They called for an intergovernmental negotiation process under the Human Rights Council mandated to develop draft modalities for the participation of Indigenous peoples in the work of the Council, to culminate in a Human Rights Council resolution to enable the participation of IPRIs in meetings of the Council on issues affecting them.[206] As steps towards this outcome, their suggestions included that the Human Rights Council should convene workshops open to the equal participation of States and Indigenous peoples and call for written submissions to identify the best possible ways of enhancing the participation of Indigenous peoples in the Council[207] and that the President of the Council should appoint co-facilitators to conduct consultations with states and Indigenous peoples' representatives on the procedure and modalities.[208] Similarly, Megan Davis, Chair of the EMRIP, proposed that the Council should hold an expert workshop with the equal participation of states, Indigenous peoples, and relevant institutions and organizations, with the objective of proposing recommendations for possible ways to ensure the enhanced participation of Indigenous peoples in the Council.[209]

States were generally supportive of Indigenous peoples' participation in the Human Rights Council.[210] States identified substantive questions that would need to be resolved. Denmark, for example, identified the definition and accreditation of Indigenous peoples, who would decide who had the right to speak, what practical modalities would apply, in which specific meetings Indigenous peoples would participate, and how much time would be allotted to them.[211] On a different note, Russia questioned who would determine the representativeness of IPRIs, situations where one people had more than one representative body, what would happen if a state did not recognize the existence of Indigenous peoples on its territory, how to deal with 'cross-border realities', and pointed to a lack of common understanding of IPRIs.[212] There was some initial discussion of substantive matters, with, for instance, Canada stressing the need for a mechanism or procedure for Indigenous peoples' accreditation based on self-determination and self-identification,[213] while the Philippines supported the establishment of a category 'that reflected

[206] Human Rights Council, 'Intersessional Round Table on Ways to Enhance the Participation', paras. 19 and 20.

[207] Ibid., paras. 25, 43, and 56.

[208] Ibid., paras. 47–48.

[209] Ibid., para. 52.

[210] Ibid., para. 57.

[211] Ibid., para. 23.

[212] Ibid., paras. 45 and 46.

[213] Ibid., para. 17.

authentic indigenous political structures, and took into account indigenous customary laws and practices'.[214] States discussed selection criteria, including whether state recognition and objection procedures would be relevant, and suggested establishing a body composed of states and Indigenous representatives to accredit IPRIs.[215]

Several states referred to the UNDRIP in justifying Indigenous participation. The representative of Canada, recalling UNDRIP provisions including the right to self-determination and the right to take part in decision-making, urged the Human Rights Council and the wider UN system to take concrete steps to reflect the UNDRIP in its mechanisms by including the participation of Indigenous peoples' representatives.[216] The delegate of Ecuador underscored the importance of strengthening the UNDRIP's implementation, pointing out that Indigenous peoples' participation in processes concerning them was enshrined in the Declaration and that this provided the Human Rights Council with an opportunity.[217] Denmark called for progress on Indigenous peoples' participation at the Human Rights Council, expressing support for Indigenous peoples to enjoy their UNDRIP Article 18 rights.[218] New Zealand 'firmly believed that all indigenous peoples should be able to participate and be heard in decisions that affected them at all levels, both domestically and internationally, as safeguarded in the UNDRIP', specifically referring to the rights to self-determination and to participate in decisions affecting them, while stressing New Zealand's commitment to upholding those rights and exploring ways to enhance the participation of Indigenous peoples at the UN, including in the Human Rights Council.[219]

Apart from referring to the UNDRIP, Canada pointed to the lack of recognition of the rights of Indigenous peoples in many countries as a reason for why their participation in the Council was critically important, as well as saying that the UN had to be relevant to all people.[220] For Ecuador, the voices of Indigenous peoples had been 'central' to the work of the Human Rights Council.[221] The Russian Federation simply acknowledged 'the importance of the participation of indigenous peoples within the UN system'.[222]

[214] Ibid., para. 40. See also paras. 60–62.
[215] Ibid., para. 62.
[216] Ibid., para. 15.
[217] Ibid., para. 27.
[218] Ibid., para. 22.
[219] Ibid., para. 35.
[220] Ibid., para. 16.
[221] Ibid., para. 29.
[222] Ibid., para. 44.

Among the recommendations emerging from the roundtable were that the Human Rights Council should 'take leadership over the process of enhancing the full and effective participation of indigenous peoples' representatives and institutions' in the UN 'and thereby serve as an example' for all UN agencies;[223] an expert workshop should be held on the measures necessary to enhance Indigenous peoples' participation in the Council, including on the procedural and institutional steps and selection criteria, with the engagement of all stakeholders including Indigenous peoples not accredited by the ECOSOC, and with co-facilitators appointed on the basis of nominations from states and Indigenous peoples;[224] that a new status, not based on ECOSOC accreditation requirements, should be developed to allow Indigenous peoples to participate in Human Rights Council meetings;[225] and that in any future discussions in the Human Rights Council on the enhanced participation of Indigenous peoples, IPOs and IPRIs should be allowed to participate without ECOSOC accreditation.[226]

Subsequently, the Human Rights Council resolved to convene a four-day expert workshop in 2022 on possible ways to enhance the participation of Indigenous peoples in the work of the Human Rights Council, open to the participation of both states and Indigenous peoples, and to invite written submissions.[227] It invited the board of the Voluntary Fund to assist Indigenous peoples' representatives to participate in the workshop.[228] As of this writing, the workshop has not yet taken place.

4.1.6 *What Now for Indigenous Peoples at the UN?*

Active discussions on Indigenous peoples' participation are ongoing at both the General Assembly and in the Human Rights Council. As of this writing, it is not yet clear whether and how these discussions will be resolved. As has been seen, a substantial number of states are committed to advancing Indigenous peoples' participation at the UN. Indigenous organizations have been advancing their case for membership of the UN for nearly 50 years. It seems unlikely that the issue will fall off the intergovernmental agenda. However, for some states difficult questions still remain. Some states still seek

223 Ibid., para. 71.
224 Ibid., paras. 72–74.
225 Ibid., para. 75.
226 Ibid., para. 78.
227 Human Rights Council Res. 48/11 (8 October 2021), paras. 15–16.
228 Ibid., para. 17.

a level of control over Indigenous participation that is inconsistent with Indigenous peoples' aspirations. It is not clear that any of the issues that ultimately sank the process in 2017 have yet been resolved. What is nevertheless demonstrated is the number of states that consider Indigenous peoples' enhanced participation in the UN, including in the General Assembly and the Human Rights Council, to be a requirement of the UNDRIP.

4.2 EVOLUTIONS IN INDIGENOUS PEOPLES' PARTICIPATION IN ENVIRONMENT AND DEVELOPMENT STANDARD-SETTING

Concurrently with the process unfolding at the heart of the UN, from 2007 onwards Indigenous peoples made strides in enhancing their participation at UN specialized agencies, in treaty bodies, and outside the UN system. In particular, several new policies and mechanisms were created for Indigenous peoples' participation: in the UN Framework Convention on Climate Change (UNFCCC), the UN Food and Agriculture Organization (FAO), the Intergovernmental Science-Policy Platform on Ecosystem Services (IPBES), the UN Educational, Scientific and Cultural Organization (UNESCO), and the International Union for the Conservation of Nature (IUCN). In Chapter 3 we saw how, from the 1990s onwards, UN processes on environment and development increasingly made space for Indigenous peoples' participation, beginning with the Rio Conference and extending into the Convention on Biological Diversity, and the WIPO Intergovernmental Committee on traditional knowledge. Here we see how these mechanisms provided inspiration for similar ones in other fora. And, as in Chapter 3, we see how the ongoing processes taking place at the heart of the UN system continued to provide inspiration and momentum, and a platform by which Indigenous peoples could advocate for participation in other fora.

4.2.1 *The UNFCCC Local Communities and Indigenous Peoples Platform*

Indigenous peoples had sought more voice in the UNFCCC since its early days. As early as 2003, the UNPFII had recommended that the UNFCCC develop an 'ad hoc open-ended inter-sessional working group on Indigenous peoples and local communities and climate change', with Indigenous peoples' guaranteed participation.[229] A decade later, this call still resonated. At COP 20 in 2014, the International Indigenous People's Forum on Climate Change

[229] Lola García-Alix, *The Permanent Forum on Indigenous Issues* (Copenhagen: IWGIA, 2003), p. 7. See further Chapter 3.

(IIPFCC), the coalition of Indigenous peoples' organizations working in UNFCCC processes, called for the COP to set up an Indigenous peoples' experts and knowledge holders advisory body, elected by Indigenous governments and organizations, to act as a technical advisory body to the 'design, implementation, monitoring and evaluation of all UNFCCC subsidiary bodies, activities, mechanisms and programmes'.[230] The IIPFCC repeated this demand at COP 21.[231] In addition, individual Indigenous organizations put forward similar proposals. For example, the Saami Council proposed that formal structures similar to those within the Convention on Biological Diversity be established to ensure Indigenous peoples' full and effective participation within the UNFCCC's work, specifically engaging the IIPFCC 'in an advisory role' within the UNFCCC decision-making bodies and processes.[232]

These advocacy efforts were to bear fruit at COP 21 in 2015. In the decision accompanying the Paris Agreement, the COP '[r]ecognize[d] the need to strengthen knowledge, technologies, practices and efforts of local communities and Indigenous Peoples related to addressing and responding to climate change', and to this end established 'a platform for the exchange of experiences and sharing of best practices on mitigation and adaptation in a holistic and integrated manner'.[233] This was not entirely consonant with the ambition of the IIPFCC's demands, but rather reflected a compromise position, albeit a more ambitious one than earlier drafts of the decision had envisaged, under which the platform would have taken the form of an annual high-level event taking place for four years.[234] This platform came to be known as the Local Communities and Indigenous Peoples Platform ("LCIPP" or "the Platform").

As the COP did not further specify the Platform's mandate or form, the task of operationalizing the LCIPP fell to successive sessions of the Subsidiary Body for Scientific and Technological Advice ("SBSTA").[235]

230 IIPFCC, 'Executive Summary of Indigenous Peoples' Proposals to the UNFCCC COP 20 and COP21' (30 November 2014), 3, www.iipfcc.org/resources.

231 IIPFCC, 'Our Proposals to Governments' (27 November 2015), 3, www.iipfcc.org/resources.

232 Saami Council, 'Saami Council Position Paper' (11 October 2015), 2, www.iipfcc.org/resources.

233 UNFCCC, '2019 Report to the UNPFII' (8 January 2019) 3, www.un.org/development/desa/indigenouspeoples/wp-content/uploads/sites/19/2019/01/Questionnaire-to-Agencies-Nov-2018_UNFCCC-input-v-8-Jan.pdf.

234 UNFCCC, 'Draft Paris Outcome' (9 December 2015) https://unfccc.int/sites/default/files/resource/docs/2015/cop21/eng/da01.pdf, para. 129(d); UNFCCC, 'Draft Paris Outcome (10 December 2015) https://unfccc.int/sites/default/files/resource/docs/2015/cop21/eng/da02.pdf, para. 129(d).

235 The SBSTA is the organ established by states parties under the UNFCCC to provide advice on scientific and technological matters: UNFCCC, Article 9. Like the SBI, decisions in the SBSTA are taken by consensus among all states parties. Observer modalities are the same as for the COP.

4.2.1.1 The Operationalization of the Platform

Indigenous peoples were involved on substantially the same footing as states at nearly every step of the way when deciding how the Platform would work. Following informal consultations at COP 22 in 2016, in which some states included Indigenous peoples' representatives on their delegations,[236] an open multi-stakeholder dialogue was convened during by the SBSTA in May 2017, co-moderated by a representative of Indigenous peoples' organizations and a state party. In the dialogue, the LCIPP's structure, functions, and possible ways and modalities of fulfilling those functions were discussed by states parties, Indigenous peoples' representatives, and others.[237] Written submissions were sought, in advance of the session, from states, Indigenous peoples' organizations, IGOs, and other observers.[238]

A variety of visions for the Platform were put forward. At COP 22, the IIPFCC held the position that, in addition to providing a 'full program on Indigenous Peoples under the COP that will enhance the participation of Indigenous Peoples in the implementation of the Paris Agreement', the Platform would provide avenues for Indigenous peoples' knowledge, practices, and perspectives to inform decisions and actions on mitigation and adaptation at the national and international level, for knowledge sharing among Indigenous peoples and states and for capacity building to strengthen Indigenous peoples' efforts to respond to climate change.[239] Although states' submissions varied, in broad terms states also proposed that the Platform should provide the opportunity for knowledge sharing, capacity building, and for Indigenous peoples to inform and influence parties' climate policies

[236] Canada, first submission, Local Communities and Indigenous Peoples Platform (April 2017) 1. All submissions can be found at UNFCCC, 'Submission Portal', www4.unfccc.int/sites/submissionsstaging/Pages/Home.aspx.

[237] COP 22 requested that the Chair of the SBSTA convene the dialogue and prepare a report on the dialogue for consideration at SBSTA 47: SBI, 'Report of the Subsidiary Body for Implementation on Its Forty-Fifth Session' (2017) UN Doc. FCCC/CP/2016/20, paras. 167(b), (c), and (d). The dialogue is noted in the report of SBSTA 46: UNFCCC, 'Report of the Subsidiary Body for Scientific and Technological Advice on Its Forty-Sixth Session' (30 June 2017) UN Doc. FCCC/SBSTA/2017/4, para. 8.

[238] All submissions can be found at UNFCCC, 'Submission Portal', www4.unfccc.int/sites/submissionsstaging/Pages/Home.aspx. Also see SBSTA, 'Local Communities and Indigenous Peoples Platform: Proposals on Operationalization Based on the Open Multi-stakeholder Dialogue and Submissions: Report by the Secretariat' (2017) UN Doc. FCCC/SBSTA/2017/6.

[239] IIPFCC, 'IIPFCC Proposals for the Indigenous Peoples Knowledge-Sharing Platform' (10 November 2016), 2–3, http://cendoc.docip.org/collect/cendocdo/index/assoc/HASH9abd/808d79dd.dir/IIPFCC%20propIndPeoplesknowledgeplatform_EN.pdf.

and actions.[240] But while some states thought the Platform should mainly consist of a web platform,[241] others disagreed, proposing annual events, workshops, and other technical work.[242] Australia, the EU, Canada, and Ecuador, in particular, strongly supported Indigenous peoples' participation in the work of the Platform.[243]

As a result of this process, in 2017, COP 23 decided that the LCIPP would have a threefold purpose:[244]

> to strengthen the knowledge, technologies, practices and efforts of local communities and indigenous peoples related to addressing and responding to climate change, to facilitate the exchange of experience and the sharing of best practices and lessons learned related to mitigation and adaptation in a holistic and integrated manner, and to enhance the engagement of local communities and indigenous peoples in the UNFCCC process.

Pursuant to these purposes, the COP decided that the Platform would have three functions: knowledge sharing, capacity building, and facilitating climate

[240] EU, 'Submission by the Republic of Malta and the European Commission on Behalf of the European Union and Its Member States' (21 March 2017), 2; Canada, 'Canada's Second Submission on the Local Communities and Indigenous Peoples Platform (the Platform)' (30 October 2017), 2–3; Brazil, 'Views of Brazil on the on Local Communities and Indigenous Peoples Platform Referred to in Paragraph 135 of 1/CP.21' (7 May 2017), para. 6; Ecuador, 'Ecuador's Submission on Local Communities and Indigenous Peoples Platform, Referred to in Paragraph 135 of Decision 1/CP.21' (17 April 2017), 2; New Zealand, 'Submission to the COP on the Local Communities' and Indigenous Peoples Platform' (30 April 2017), para. 11.

[241] Brazil, 'Views of Brazil on the on Local Communities and Indigenous Peoples Platform Referred to in Paragraph 135 of 1/CP.21' (7 May 2017), para. 9.

[242] Australia, 'Australia's Submission on the Local Communities and Indigenous Peoples Platform' (3 May 2017), 2; Canada, 'Local Communities and Indigenous Peoples Platform' (21 April 2017), 2; Canada, 'Canada's Second Submission on the Local Communities and Indigenous Peoples Platform (the Platform)' (30 October 2017), 4.

[243] Canada, 'Local Communities and Indigenous Peoples Platform' (21 April 2017), 1–2; EU, 'Submission by the Republic of Malta and the European Commission on Behalf of the European Union and Its Member States' (21 March 2017), 3; Australia, 'Australia's Submission on the Local Communities and Indigenous Peoples Platform' (3 May 2017), 3; Canada, 'Canada's Second Submission on the Local Communities and Indigenous Peoples Platform (the Platform)' (30 October 2017), 3–4; Ecuador, 'Ecuador's Submission on Local Communities and Indigenous Peoples Platform, Referred to in Paragraph 135 of Decision 1/CP.21' (17 April 2017), 1.

[244] UNFCCC, 'Report of the Conference of the Parties on Its Twenty-Third Session, Held in Bonn from 6 to 18 November 2017, Addendum: Decisions Adopted by the Conference of the Parties' (8 February 2018) UN Doc. FCCC/CP/2017/11/Add.1, Decision 2/CP.23, 'Local Communities and Indigenous Peoples Platform', para. 5.

policy and climate action.[245] On the first function, the COP decided that the Platform[246]

> should promote the exchange of experience and best practices with a view to applying, strengthening, protecting and preserving traditional knowledge, knowledge of indigenous peoples and local knowledge systems, as well as technologies, practices and efforts of local communities and indigenous peoples related to addressing and responding to climate change, taking into account the free, prior and informed consent of the holders of such knowledge, innovations and practices.

Regarding the second function, the LCIPP should[247]

> build the capacity of indigenous peoples and local communities to enable their engagement in the UNFCCC process and the capacity of Parties and other relevant stakeholders to engage with the platform and with local communities and indigenous peoples, including in the context of the implementation of the Paris Agreement and other climate change related processes.

In terms of the third, the Platform should[248]

> facilitate the integration of diverse knowledge systems, practices and innovations in designing and implementing international and national actions, programmes and policies in a manner that respects and promotes the rights and interests of local communities and indigenous peoples. The platform should also facilitate the undertaking of stronger and more ambitious climate action by indigenous peoples and local communities that could contribute to the achievement of the nationally determined contributions of the Parties concerned.

This mandate does not explicitly provide any role for the Platform in terms of giving advice or feeding into other policy- or decision-making processes under the UNFCCC, contrary to proposals made by Indigenous peoples' organizations during the consultations on the Platform's operationalization.[249] Rather, the mandate focuses on exchanging experiences and best practices, building

[245] Ibid., para. 6.
[246] Ibid., para. 6(a).
[247] Ibid., para. 6(b).
[248] Ibid., para. 6(c).
[249] For example, the Assembly of First Nations proposed that Indigenous peoples be granted Permanent Participant status at the UNFCCC, as in the Arctic Council: Assembly of First Nations, 'Submission of the Assembly of First Nations (AFN) on the Purpose, Content and Structure for the Indigenous Peoples' Traditional Knowledge Platform', 5.

the capacity of Indigenous peoples to engage in the UNFCCC, and promoting climate action by Indigenous peoples themselves so as to contribute to states' achievement of their national climate goals.

On participation, the decision provided that the operationalization of, and processes under, the Platform should take into account the full and effective participation of Indigenous peoples, the equal status of Indigenous peoples and states parties, 'including in leadership roles', the self-selection of Indigenous peoples' representatives in accordance with their own procedures – reflecting provisions in the draft resolutions under the General Assembly to that effect – and the need for adequate funding from the UNFCCC Secretariat and states parties.[250]

In December 2018, COP 24 established a Facilitative Working Group for the LCIPP, with the objective of 'further operationalizing the Platform and facilitating the implementation of its functions'.[251] The Facilitative Working Group was composed of fourteen individuals, equally divided: seven representatives of states parties and seven representatives of Indigenous peoples' organizations, appointed by Indigenous peoples through their focal points.[252] Co-Chair and Vice Co-Chair positions were, similarly, equally split between states and Indigenous peoples.[253] Meeting twice a year and taking decisions by consensus, the Working Group's sessions were made open to states parties and observers including Indigenous peoples' organizations that have qualified as observers to the UNFCCC, but not to Indigenous peoples' organizations and representatives that do not qualify, or have not qualified, for admission as observers.[254] This does limit the organizations that can participate, since the procedure for admission as observers is not trivial.[255]

At COP 25, the Working Group adopted the LCIPP's first three-year workplan.[256] Its activities included thematic training workshops to build the capacity of parties and other stakeholders to engage with Indigenous peoples,

[250] Decision 2/CP.23, para. 8.

[251] UNFCCC, 'Local Communities and Indigenous Peoples Platform: Draft Conclusions Proposed by the Chair' (7 December 2018) UN Doc. FCCC/SBSTA/2018/L.18, Decision 2/CP.24, paras. 1–2. See also Decision 2/CP.23, para. 5.

[252] Decision 2/CP.24, paras. 3 and 6. The number seven was chosen to enable representation of the seven sociocultural regions of the world's Indigenous peoples.

[253] Ibid., para. 9.

[254] Ibid., paras. 15, 17, and 29.

[255] UNFCCC, 'How to Obtain Observer Status' (n.d.) https://unfccc.int/process-and-meetings/parties-non-party-stakeholders/non-party-stakeholders/overview/how-to-obtain-observer-status.

[256] SBSTA, 'Local Communities and Indigenous Peoples Platform: Draft Conclusions Proposed by the Chair' (5 December 2019) UN Doc. FCCC/SBSTA/2019/L.13, para. 3; UNFCCC,

the development of draft recommendations on the engagement and input of Indigenous peoples across the UNFCCC process, and the mapping of existing policies and practices for Indigenous peoples' participation in climate change-related bodies and processes. These activities were carried out during 2020 and 2021.[257] At COP 26, the Working Group's mandate was extended, and a second three-year workplan was approved.[258] The workplan includes activities such as convening dialogues to advance Indigenous peoples' participation in designing and implementing climate policies and actions, inviting various UNFCCC constituted bodies to collaborate on engaging Indigenous peoples in their work, and organizing annual meetings to enhance the inclusion of Indigenous peoples' knowledge in addressing and responding to climate change.[259]

The LCIPP, then, in one sense embodies unprecedented space for Indigenous peoples within UNFCCC processes. In itself, it represents a partnership wherein power is distributed between states and Indigenous peoples. However, it has very a limited mandate, and outside the LCIPP, Indigenous peoples have the same level of participation in the UNFCCC as other observer constituencies. Its second workplan shows that while it is beginning to engage with other UNFCCC constituted bodies, this is a slow process.

4.2.1.2 States' Motivations Include Requirement of Law

In states' submissions during the establishment of the LCIPP,[260] there was a broad recognition that the voices of Indigenous peoples ought to be heard for reasons of intrinsic importance. For instance, Australia stated that because Indigenous peoples 'are directly affected by climate change', the country was a 'strong advocate' for their full and effective participation and is 'supportive and encouraging' of the LCIPP as 'an avenue' by which Indigenous peoples can

'The 1st Meeting of the Facilitative Working Group of the Local Communities and Indigenous Peoples Platform' (18 September 2019) UN Doc. FCCC/SBSTA/2019/4, Annex I.

257 UNFCCC, 'Report of the Facilitative Working Group of the Local Communities and Indigenous Peoples Platform' (20 August 2021) UN Doc. FCCC/SBSTA/2021/1.

258 Decision 16/CP.26, 'Local Communities and Indigenous Peoples Platform', in UNFCCC, 'Part Two: Action Taken by the Conference of the Parties at Its Twenty-Sixth Session' (8 March 2022) UN Doc. FCCC/CP/2021/12/Add.2, 11, paras. 5–6.

259 UNFCCC, 'Report of the Facilitative Working Group 2021', Annex IV.

260 All submissions can be found at UNFCCC, 'Submission Portal', www4.unfccc.int/sites/submissionsstaging/Pages/Home.aspx.

contribute to implementing the Paris Agreement.[261] Similarly, Canada stressed the need to operationalize the Platform so as to respect and recognize 'the importance [of] indigenous peoples to be self-represented, have a stronger voice, and enhance their participation'.[262] In a similar vein, New Zealand supported providing Indigenous peoples with 'a clear voice' in decision-making in the UNFCCC and 'an active role in helping to shape climate action'.[263] Ecuador strongly underlined 'the importance of an active, permanent role and involvement of' Indigenous peoples in 'all relevant UNFCCC negotiations and decisions', going so far as to say that they should be heard first, before states.[264]

But states also tended to cite the instrumental value of Indigenous peoples' participation in the achievement of international objectives on climate action. In this vein, the preamble of decision 2/CP.23 emphasizes the role of Indigenous peoples in achieving the targets and goals set out in the UNFCCC, the Paris Agreement, and the 2030 Agenda.[265] Decision 16/CP.26 in its preamble recognizes the role of Indigenous peoples and local communities in relation to the stewardship of and living in harmony with nature, and the LCIPP's role in bringing together Parties and Indigenous peoples and local communities to work towards achieving the objectives of the Convention and the Paris Agreement.[266] Australia stated that Indigenous knowledge systems and practices are 'important resources for adaptation to climate change', constituting 'unique' and 'highly valuable' knowledge that can 'help inform climate-related decision-making at the UNFCCC'.[267] Brazil emphasized the potential role of the LCIPP in strengthening and facilitating the promotion and integration of traditional knowledge into mitigation and adaptation action.[268] Similarly Canada, when stressing its commitment to 'enhancing the voices of Indigenous Peoples in the work of the UNFCCC', underscored that states parties can 'benefit greatly' from their participation in

[261] Australia, 'Australia's Submission on the Local Communities and Indigenous Peoples Platform' (3 May 2017), 2.

[262] Canada, first submission, 'Local Communities and Indigenous Peoples Platform' (April 2017), 2.

[263] New Zealand, 'Submission to the COP on the Local Communities' and Indigenous Peoples Platform' (April 2017), paras. 3, 11, and 12.

[264] Ecuador, 'Ecuador's Submission on Local Communities and Indigenous Peoples Platform' (2017), 1.

[265] Decision 2/CP.23, preamble, third recital.

[266] Ibid., fifth and sixth recitals.

[267] Australia, 'Australia's submission', 2.

[268] Brazil, 'Views of Brazil on the on Local Communities and Indigenous Peoples Platform' (2017), 1.

addressing climate change.[269] The EU noted that the LCIPP would 'help to create … more effective, coherent and inclusive climate policies'.[270]

In addition to instrumental justifications, some states, as well as the COP itself, have stated that the participation of Indigenous peoples in the LCIPP is required by the UNDRIP. The preamble of decision 2/CP.23 recalls the UNDRIP,[271] as does that of decision 2/CP.24, which also emphasizes that the purpose and functions of the LCIPP and the Facilitative Working Group will be 'carried out consistent with international law'.[272] In its report to the UNPFII, the UNFCCC highlighted that the Platform 'serves as an inclusive and participatory space … in a manner that abides by the principles based on the UNDRIP'.[273] States have also highlighted the UNDRIP in their submissions. Australia stated that the Platform should 'take into account the broader developments' related to Indigenous peoples' representation and participation, including the UNDRIP, the EMRIP, and the UNPFII, and states that it 'could support the collective rights enshrined in the UNDRIP' including self-determination and FPIC.[274] Supporting the consultation of Indigenous peoples in the process of operationalizing the LCIPP, Australia also noted that giving them a 'strong role in organisation and participation' would be '[c]onsistent with the aims of the UNDRIP'.[275] Similarly, Canada referenced Article 41 of the UNDRIP (participation in matters affecting them at the UN), as well as the rights to self-determination and participation in decision-making affecting them as 'context' that 'reaffirm[ed] the importance of the Platform as a tool for enhancing and supporting the full and effective participation of Indigenous Peoples and local communities in the work of the UNFCCC'.[276] The EU and New Zealand also recalled the UNDRIP in their submissions.[277] The OHCHR, stressing the disproportionate negative impacts of climate change and mitigation and adaptation actions on Indigenous peoples, as well as their

269 Canada, first submission, 'Local Communities and Indigenous Peoples Platform', 1.

270 EU, 'Submission by the Republic of Malta and the European Commission on Behalf of the European Union and Its Member States' (21 March 2017), 2.

271 Decision 2/CP.23, preamble, first recital.

272 Decision 2/CP.24, preamble, fourth recital.

273 UNFCCC, '2019 report to the UNPFII', 3.

274 Australia, 'Australia's Submission', 1. However, Australia does not accept that the UNDRIP represents binding international law, so it is unlikely that this statement can be viewed as an instance of *opinio juris*.

275 Ibid., 3.

276 Canada, 'Canada's Second Submission on the Local Communities and Indigenous Peoples Platform' (October 2017), 2.

277 EU, 'Submission by the Republic of Malta', 1; New Zealand, 'Submission to the COP on the Local Communities' and Indigenous Peoples Platform' (April 2017), para. 10.

role in supporting adaptation efforts, cited Common Article 1 of the Human Rights Covenants and the UNDRIP in support of the increased participation of Indigenous peoples in the UNFCCC by way of the LCIPP.[278]

The LCIPP, then, is a good example of a mechanism for Indigenous participation – on equal terms with states – in international governance that states are beginning to accept as required by law. But ultimately the stakes of participation are limited by the LCIPP's positioning in the work of the UNFCCC as a whole.

4.2.2 *The International Union for the Conservation of Nature (IUCN)*

Let us now turn to a very different case. The International Union for the Conservation of Nature (IUCN) is not an intergovernmental organization strictly speaking. Rather, it is composed of both government and civil society organizations. Its objective is to 'influence, encourage and assist societies throughout the world to conserve the integrity and diversity of nature and to ensure that any use of natural resources is equitable and ecologically sustainable'.[279] Every four years, the IUCN hosts a meeting of the World Conservation Congress, its highest organ. The Congress consists of delegates of its members and defines the IUCN's policies, makes recommendations to governments and organizations, and considers the programme for the next four-year period.[280] In addition to the World Conservation Congress, the IUCN has a Council that provides oversight and sets strategic direction for the IUCN;[281] National and Regional Committees;[282] a Secretariat;[283] and Commissions, networks of expert volunteers tasked with developing IUCN's institutional knowledge and experience.[284]

Indigenous peoples had been involved in the IUCN's work on an ad hoc basis as early as 1983. According to Dalee Sambo Dorough, as of writing the International Chairperson of the Inuit Circumpolar Council (ICC), in that year the ICC was actively involved in the redrafting of the IUCN's World

[278] OHCHR, 'Response to the UNFCCC Secretariat Request for Submissions on: Possible Elements of a Local Communities and Indigenous Peoples' Traditional Knowledge Platform' (16 May 2017), 1–2.

[279] IUCN Statutes (adopted 5 October 1948 and last amended 27 September 2016), in IUCN, *Statutes, including Rules of Procedure of the World Conservation Congress, and Regulations* (Switzerland: IUCN, 2022), Article 2.

[280] IUCN Statutes, Articles 18–20.

[281] IUCN Statutes, Articles 37–46.

[282] IUCN Statutes, Articles 66–72.

[283] IUCN Statutes, Articles 78-.

[284] IUCN Statutes, Articles 73–77.

Conservation Strategy.[285] Indigenous peoples' involvement ramped up from the early 2000s. At the 2004 World Parks Congress, over 120 Indigenous peoples' representatives were present and spoke at the opening plenary, on panels and in workshops. This was facilitated by the creation, in 2003, of an Indigenous Peoples Ad Hoc Working Group for the World Parks Congress, which lobbied to secure speaking slots, sought funding for Indigenous participation, coordinated regional meetings, and organized a preparatory conference immediately before the Congress.[286] At the 2008 World Conservation Congress, Indigenous peoples' organizations were again in attendance.[287] At the 2014 World Parks Congress one workstream, on the theme of respecting Indigenous and traditional knowledge and culture, was led by Indigenous organizations.[288] Meanwhile, the IUCN Council had included Indigenous leaders in its membership since at least the early 2000s.[289]

In 2016, however, a step-change in Indigenous peoples' participation in the IUCN occurred. At the World Conservation Congress that year, the IUCN Members Assembly resolved to amend the IUCN statutes by creating a new membership category for Indigenous peoples' organizations, which it defined as 'institutions and associations established by indigenous peoples for the advancement of indigenous communities'.[290] IUCN documents explain how this was done to 'better accommodate indigenous peoples' representative institutions', 'giv[e] them a clearer identity as a distinct constituency and amplify[y] their voice in the internal policy making of IUCN and the general life of the institution', as well as to set 'an example of the ways in which international organizations can better integrate indigenous peoples in their institutional architecture and at decision-making levels'.[291]

[285] Dalee S. Dorough, 'The Rights, Interests and Role of the Arctic Council Permanent Participants' in Robert C. Beckman, Tore Henriksen, Kristine Dalaker Kraabel, Erik J. Molenaar, and J. Ashley Roach (eds.), *Governance of Arctic Shipping: Balancing Rights and Interests of Arctic States and User States* (Leiden: Brill Nijhoff, 2017), 68–106, 73.

[286] J. Peter Brosius, 'Indigenous Peoples and Protected Areas at the World Parks Congress' (2004) 18 *Conservation Biology*, 609–612, 609.

[287] Nels Paulson, Ann Laudati, Amity Doolittle, Meredith Welsh-Devine, and Pablo Pena, 'Indigenous Peoples' Participation in Global Conservation: Looking beyond Headdresses and Face Paint' (2012) 21 *Environmental Values*, 255–276.

[288] IUCN, 'Advancing Indigenous Peoples' Rights in IUCN's Conservation Programme: Information for the Expert Group Meeting on Conservation and the Rights of Indigenous Peoples Nairobi, Kenya – January 23–25, 2019' (IUCN, 2019) www.un.org/development/desa/indigenouspeoples/wp-content/uploads/sites/19/2019/01/IUCN_EGM-Jan-2019.pdf, 2.

[289] Ibid., 2.

[290] WCC-2016-Res-004, 'Including Indigenous Peoples' Organisations in the Structure of the Union'; IUCN Statutes, Articles 4 and 5(e).

[291] IUCN, 'Advancing Indigenous Peoples' Rights', 2.

The criteria for an Indigenous peoples' organization to be admitted are that (a) it shares and supports the IUCN's objectives, (b) it has, as one of its central purposes, the achievement of the IUCN's objectives and a substantial record of activity in the conservation of nature and natural resources, and (c) its objectives and track record substantially embody the conservation of the integrity and diversity of nature, the aim to ensure that any use of natural resources is equitable and ecologically sustainable, or a dedication to influencing, encouraging, and assisting societies to meet the objectives of the IUCN.[292] In addition, the organization must be a not-for-profit entity conforming to the law of the state in which it is based, have existed for at least three years, be autonomous in administration and governance, and have Indigenous peoples as its primary constituency.[293]

To be admitted, an Indigenous peoples' organization applies to the Director General of the IUCN – the organization's chief executive – including information about how it meets the criteria, documentation of its activities in conservation of nature and natural resources over at least a three-year period, and a written statement of endorsement of the IUCN's objectives.[294] The Director General then notifies existing members (including states as well as non-state members) of the application.[295] Members can object to admission on the grounds that the applicant does not meet the criteria.[296] The applicant is given an opportunity to respond to any objection.[297] Applications are decided by the IUCN Council, on a two-thirds majority of votes to admit the applicant.[298] An admission may be reversed upon an appeal by ten members within six months of the decision, then a two-thirds majority vote of member states as well as a combined two-thirds majority vote of non-governmental and Indigenous peoples' organizations at the World Conservation Congress.[299]

Indigenous peoples' organizations' members of the IUCN have nearly the same procedural rights as NGOs and states. They can participate in the

[292] IUCN Statutes, Article 7.

[293] IUCN Regulations (last amended 11 February 2020), in IUCN, *Statutes, including Rules of Procedure of the World Conservation Congress, and Regulations* (Switzerland: IUCN, 2022), Regulation 5bis.

[294] Ibid., Regulations 7, 8, and 9.

[295] Ibid., Regulation 14.

[296] Ibid., Regulations 15–16.

[297] Ibid., Regulation 17.

[298] IUCN Statutes, Articles 8 and 9; IUCN Regulations, Regulation 18.

[299] IUCN Statutes, Article 10; IUCN Regulations, Regulation 19.

World Conservation Congress, as well as the IUCN's national and regional committees, nominate candidates for IUCN offices, submit motions, and vote on decisions taken in the World Conservation Congress.[300] Most decisions of the World Conservation Congress require a simple majority of votes cast by states, and of votes cast by NGOs and Indigenous peoples' organizations combined.[301] The difference between state and other IUCN members is in the number of votes: while each state member has three votes, NGOs and Indigenous peoples' organizations each have one vote.[302]

As of 2022, twenty-five Indigenous peoples' organizations are members of the IUCN.[303] A follow-up resolution at the 2020 World Conservation Congress calls on the IUCN's Director General and Council to 'promote the full and effective participation of Indigenous peoples' organizations, in the ongoing work of the Union, and to strengthen those organizations through regional focal points', and urges them to consider the development of mechanisms for the full and effective participation of Indigenous peoples' organizations and the regional focal points, including in the formulation, implementation, and monitoring of policies, projects, and guidelines for the management of protected natural areas and Indigenous territories. It also called on the Commissions to advance the representation of Indigenous peoples in their steering committees and work programmes.[304] An additional resolution modified the IUCN statutes to establish an elected Indigenous Councillor as part of the IUCN Council,[305] following the 2018 appointment of the first Indigenous peoples' organizations' member of the Council.[306]

We can observe how although IUCN is one of the only organizations in which Indigenous peoples have their own category of membership separate from NGOs but substantially on par with that of states, they still lack the same voting rights as states, and the informal nature of the organization means that its formal powers are limited.

[300] IUCN Statutes, Article 12(a) and (b).
[301] IUCN Statutes, Articles 30–31.
[302] IUCN Statutes, Articles 34–35.
[303] IUCN, 'IUCN Members' (n.d.) www.iucn.org/about/members/iucn-members.
[304] IUCN, 'Strengthened Institutional Inclusion Concerning Indigenous Peoples' (2020) WCC-2020-Res-002, paras. 2, 3, and 5.
[305] IUCN, 'Establishment of an Elected Indigenous Councillor Position' (2020) WCC-2020-Dec-140.
[306] Referred to in WCC-2020-Res-002, preamble, recital 5.

4.2.3 *The Intergovernmental Science-Policy Platform on Biodiversity and Ecosystem Services (IPBES)*

Turning now to another organization at the science-policy interface, the Intergovernmental Science-Policy Platform on Biodiversity and Ecosystem Services (IPBES) was established in 2012 to perform regular assessments of knowledge on biodiversity and ecosystem services.[307] Its secretariat is hosted by the UN Environment Programme (UNEP),[308] and its assessments feed into other international governance processes, most notably the CBD and UNFCCC. In its first decade of operation, it completed eight assessments, including the 2019 IPBES Global Assessment on Biodiversity and Ecosystem Services.[309]

At the fifth IPBES plenary meeting in 2017, following a suggestion from Indigenous peoples' organizations,[310] IPBES member states agreed to establish a participatory mechanism to facilitate the effective engagement of Indigenous peoples and local communities and their organizations or networks in IPBES assessments and other areas of the organization's work.[311] The participatory mechanism aims to 'facilitate the effective and meaningful engagement of Indigenous and local knowledge holders, Indigenous and local knowledge experts and their organizations or networks in order to strengthen their ability to contribute to and benefit from IPBES at all scales'.[312] Under the participatory mechanism, Indigenous peoples are included in collaboratively defining problems and goals for an assessment, incorporating into the assessment a wide array of evidence and data from multiple sources of Indigenous knowledge, appropriately engaging Indigenous peoples in reviewing drafts, and sharing knowledge and insights gained through an

307 Resolution on the Intergovernmental Science-Policy Platform on Biodiversity and Ecosystem Services (second session of the plenary meeting to determine the modalities and institutional arrangements for IPBES, 21 April 2012). See also UNGA Res. 65/162 (20 December 2010).

308 IPBES, 'IPBES Administrative and Institutional Arrangements' (2013) Decision IPBES/1/4.

309 IPBES, *Global Assessment Report on Biodiversity and Ecosystem Services of the Intergovernmental Science-Policy Platform on Biodiversity and Ecosystem Services* (Bonn: IPBES Secretariat, 2019).

310 International Indigenous Forum on Biodiversity and Ecosystem Services (IIFBES), 'Report of the Task Force on Indigenous and Local Knowledge' (12 January 2015), www.asianindigenouswomen.org/index.php/component/k2/item/118-statement-by-the-international-indigenous-forum-on-biodiversity-and-ecosystem-services-iifbes.

311 IPBES, 'Report of the Plenary of the Intergovernmental Science-Policy Platform on Biodiversity and Ecosystem Services on the Work of Its Fifth Session' (11 April 2017) UN Doc. IPBES/5/15.

312 Ibid., Annex II, para. 26.

assessment with Indigenous peoples afterwards.[313] In particular, elements of the mechanism include the representation of Indigenous experts in the expert groups that scope and perform the assessments; web-based consultations to ensure broad participation by Indigenous peoples, and the reflection of their perspectives and of Indigenous knowledge, throughout all phases of an assessment; dialogue workshops to bring together a representative selection of experts on Indigenous knowledge and representatives of Indigenous peoples; the synthesis of Indigenous knowledge gathered through these procedures; local dialogue workshops; and building the capacity of Indigenous peoples to engage in and benefit from IPBES.[314] For each assessment, an Indigenous and local knowledge liaison group is established to develop the key questions and topics pertaining to Indigenous peoples to be covered in the assessment, synthesizing all relevant knowledge, and ensuring that the assessment adequately reflects the perspectives resulting from different knowledge systems.[315]

In addition to the participatory mechanism, at the seventh session of the IPBES plenary in 2019, member states established a Task Force on Indigenous and Local Knowledge. Under the Task Force's terms of reference, its mandate is to oversee and take part in the implementation of IPBES' work with Indigenous and local knowledge systems.[316] The Task Force meets annually and comprises up to fourteen members, including up to four members of the IPBES Bureau and its Multidisciplinary Expert Panel, representatives of Indigenous peoples and local communities, representatives of scientific organizations including experts on Indigenous and local knowledge, and recognized individual experts on Indigenous and local knowledge.[317] Representatives of Indigenous organizations may also be invited to participate in the Task Force as resource persons, at the co-chairs' invitation.[318]

These participatory mechanisms are justified by reference to Indigenous knowledge as well as affectedness. According to IPBES, Indigenous peoples 'possess detailed knowledge on biodiversity and ecosystem trends', formed through their 'direct dependence on their local ecosystems, and observations and interpretations of change generated and passed down over many

[313] Ibid., paras. 12–17.
[314] Ibid., para. 17.
[315] Ibid., para. 23.
[316] IPBES, 'Report of the Plenary of the Intergovernmental Science-Policy Platform on Biodiversity and Ecosystem Services on the Work of Its Seventh Session' (22 May 2019) UN Doc. IPBES/7/10, Annex II, para. 14.
[317] Ibid., para. 15. As of 2022, the task force has six Indigenous members.
[318] Ibid., para. 17.

generations, and yet adapted and enriched over time'.[319] But in addition, they 'suffer directly from the pressures of expanding agriculture frontiers and commodity production' and are 'often better placed than scientists to provide detailed information on local biodiversity and environmental change'.[320] Hence, Indigenous peoples' participation is crucial for developing its assessments 'in ways that recognize the role of Indigenous and local knowledge in biodiversity conservation' and for enabling its work to be of use to Indigenous peoples themselves.[321]

4.2.4 *The UN Educational, Scientific and Cultural Organization (UNESCO)*

4.2.4.1 The UNESCO Policy on Engaging with Indigenous Peoples, 2018

In 2018, UNESCO adopted a policy on engaging with Indigenous peoples,[322] which was developed through a process that included meetings and workshops between Indigenous peoples and UNESCO staff, as well as submissions.[323] In their submissions, several states called for improving Indigenous peoples' participation. For instance, Canada's submission expressly supported the possibility of UNESCO establishing formal partnerships with Indigenous peoples' organizations.[324] Chile proposed a 'dialogue and participation mechanism' between Indigenous peoples, states, and UNESCO to 'allow the collection of information on policy implementation'.[325] Colombia supported Indigenous peoples' 'full and effective participation and inclusion leading to empowerment' at all levels 'including the decision-making and strategic levels' and at all stages 'including planning, programming, implementation, monitoring and evaluation'; this should include 'continued and direct dialogue and interaction with indigenous

[319] IPBES, 'Indigenous and Local Knowledge in IPBES' (n.d.) https://ipbes.net/indigenous-local-knowledge.
[320] Ibid.
[321] IPBES, 'Participation of IPLC in IPBES' (n.d.) https://ipbes.net/participation-iplc-ipbes/.
[322] UNESCO, 'UNESCO Policy on Engaging with Indigenous Peoples' (2018) UNESCO Doc. No. 201 EX/6 ("UNESCO Policy"); UNESCO, 'Decisions Adopted by the Executive Board at Its 202nd Session' (2017) UNESCO Doc. No. 202 EX/DECISIONS, 16. See also UNESCO, 2014–2021 *Medium-Term Strategy* (2014) UNESCO Doc. 37 C/4, pp. 17 and 21.
[323] UNESCO Policy, p. 4.
[324] UNESCO, 'Consultation on a UNESCO Policy on Engaging with Indigenous Peoples, Comments' (12 July 2017), 7, www.unesco.org/new/fileadmin/MULTIMEDIA/HQ/SC/pdf/170712-UNESCO-IPP-MSConsultation-Compilation-comments.pdf.
[325] Ibid., 8.

peoples through their freely chosen representatives'.[326] In making this submission, Colombia referred explicitly to Article 41 of the UNDRIP. Denmark suggested UNESCO consider establishing an advisory body of Indigenous peoples' representatives, highlighting that this would 'ensure that the voice of indigenous peoples is heard, and taken into account by UNESCO on a systematic basis'.[327]

In the end result, the 2018 Policy sets out provisions of the UNDRIP of specific relevance to UNESCO's work, before stating that UNESCO, '[i]n line with all relevant articles of the UNDRIP … commits to respect, protect and promote' Indigenous peoples' rights to 'full and effective participation in matters affecting their lives and cultures' and to 'take part in the development of policies concerning their cultures, cultural expressions and heritage, including through effective participation in relevant consultative bodies and coordination mechanisms'.[328] In addition, the Policy provides that UNESCO will '[i]mprove participation of indigenous peoples' organizations through promoting official partnerships between their organizations and UNESCO'[329] and 'promote dialogue and participatory mechanisms between indigenous people[s], Member States and UNESCO that allows the collection of information on the implementation of activities relevant for indigenous peoples and within the framework of the policy'.[330]

It is not yet clear how this policy will be implemented. There are a few isolated examples of the participation of Indigenous peoples in UNESCO's activities to date: in a workshop on Indigenous knowledge and climate change in October 2017;[331] in the preparatory process for the 8th World Water Forum in March 2018;[332] in a high-level policy forum and international conference on language and education in 2019;[333] in sessions of the Open Science Forum for Latin America and the Caribbean in 2018;[334] in consultations towards the UN Decade of Ocean Science for Sustainable

[326] Ibid., 10.
[327] Ibid., 13.
[328] Ibid., paras. 77(b) and (d).
[329] Ibid., para. 102(a).
[330] Ibid., para. 105.
[331] UNESCO, '2017 Report to the UNPFII' (2018), 14, www.un.org/development/desa/indigenouspeoples/wp-content/uploads/sites/19/2018/02/UNESCO_03012018Questionnaire-to-Agencies-Nov-2017.pdf.
[332] Ibid.
[333] UNESCO, '2018 Report to the UNPFII' (2019), 13, www.un.org/development/desa/indigenouspeoples/wp-content/uploads/sites/19/2019/01/PFII-Questionnaire-to-Agencies-UNESCO.pdf.
[334] Ibid, 8.

Development;[335] and in consultations towards the adoption of the Recommendation on Open Science in 2021.[336] Additionally, in 2021 the International Decade of Indigenous Languages 2022–2032 was launched, coordinated by a Global Task Force consisting of a Steering Committee and an Advisory Group.[337] The Steering Committee is formed of six member state representatives, seven Indigenous peoples' representatives, one representative each of the UNPFII, EMRIP, and Special Rapporteur on the rights of Indigenous peoples, and representatives from UNESCO, UNDESA, and OHCHR. The Advisory Group is formed of twelve member state representatives, fourteen representatives of Indigenous peoples, as well as representatives of the UNPFII, EMRIP, Special Rapporteurs, and the Inter-Agency Support Group.[338] These instances represent a promising beginning, but are far from the more systematic participation that is envisaged in the Policy.

4.2.4.2 Justifications

UNESCO has justified its 2018 Policy primarily by reference to its mandate. The Policy states that Indigenous peoples' concerns are 'also the heart of the concerns of UNESCO's mandate', as they are living manifestations of cultural diversity, the stewards of rare languages, and 'essential partners in building knowledge societies and achieving the 2030 Agenda'.[339]

Mandate-related motivations aside, other statements point to UNESCO's awareness of the value of Indigenous knowledge, and the impacts of environmental change on Indigenous peoples. In 2012, Bokova noted that Indigenous peoples have valuable knowledge of sustainability and face challenges due to discrimination and marginalization, stating that 'sustainable development must be inclusive' and '[a]ll voices must not only be heard but

335 UNESCO, 'Indigenous Peoples and UNESCO 2020: Outcomes of Questionnaire for the UN Permanent Forum on Indigenous Issues' (2020), 31, www.un.org/development/desa/indigenouspeoples/wp-content/uploads/sites/19/2021/04/UNESCO_Consolidated-SWAP-Report-UNPFII-20-final-clean.pdf.

336 UNESCO, 'Indigenous Peoples and UNESCO 2021: Outcomes of the Questionnaire for 22nd Session of the UN Permanent Forum on Indigenous Issues' (31 December 2021), 12, www.un.org/development/desa/indigenouspeoples/wp-content/uploads/sites/19/2022/03/UNESCO-Consolidated-Report-UNPFII-22_final.pdf.

337 UNESCO, 'UNESCO Launches the Global Task Force for Making a Decade of Action for Indigenous Languages' (22 March 2021) https://en.unesco.org/news/unesco-launches-global-task-force-making-decade-action-indigenous-languages.

338 UNESCO, 'Open Call for Nominations Addressed to the Indigenous Peoples and Indigenous Peoples' Organizations' (14 October 2020) https://iyil.ph/documents/61/Open_Call_For_Nomination_Indigenous_Peoples_Document.pdf.

339 UNESCO Policy, 1.

listened to'.[340] That same year, the Chief of UNESCO's Small Islands and Indigenous Knowledge Section and the organization's focal point for Indigenous peoples stated that 'the active participation of Indigenous peoples within the framework of UNESCO is extremely important'.[341] In 2015, Bokova, in an address to an international conference on Indigenous peoples and climate change, said UNESCO was 'the house of all peoples' and stressed the importance of ensuring 'the voices of indigenous peoples are heard' in combating climate change due to the impacts of climate change on Indigenous peoples.[342]

But the Policy also justifies itself by reference to UNDRIP. The Policy states that it is a means by which 'UNESCO reaffirms its commitment to implement the [UNDRIP]'.[343] Referring to Articles 18 and 41, it recognized that the governing bodies of UNESCO's conventions, such as the World Heritage Committee, 'can play an important role in developing relevant standards, guidance and operational mechanisms to ensure full and effective participation and inclusion of indigenous peoples in the processes of these instruments'.[344] As mentioned above, it discusses the right to participation – which it links to self-determination and FPIC – in stating that UNESCO should include Indigenous peoples in the development of policies concerning them. In a statement to the UNPFII, UNESCO noted that the Policy 'explicitly adheres to article 41 of the UNDRIP'.[345]

Successive statements made by UNESCO's senior officials bolster the notion that the Policy was adopted with the acceptance that it was required by the UNDRIP. In a message on the occasion of the International day of the World's Indigenous People in 2008, then Director-General of UNESCO, Koïchiro Matsuura, emphasized the importance of implementing the – then newly adopted – UNDRIP via 'concrete policies that will enable indigenous peoples to participate fully and equally in the national and international life' and expressed hope that the Declaration 'will serve as a platform for genuine

340 UNESCO, 'Message from Ms Irina Bokova, Director-General of UNESCO on the Occasion of the International Day of the World's Indigenous People' (9 August 2012) UNESCO Doc. DG/ME/ID/2012/015, 1.

341 IWGIA, *International Expert Workshop on the World Heritage Convention and Indigenous Peoples* (Copenhagen: IWGIA, 2012), 20.

342 UNESCO, 'Address by Irina Bokova, Director-General of UNESCO on the Occasion of the Closing of the Conference "Resilience in a Time of Uncertainty: Indigenous Peoples and Climate Change"' (27 November 2015) UNESCO Doc. DG/2015/235, 1 and 4.

343 UNESCO Policy, 1.

344 Ibid.

345 UNESCO, 'Indigenous Peoples and UNESCO 2020', 37.

dialogue between indigenous and non-indigenous partners'.[346] The next year, Matsuura, after invoking the UNDRIP, called on the international community 'to engage in genuine dialogue with indigenous peoples', and, noting that Indigenous voices had 'remained largely on the sidelines' of international debates on climate change despite Indigenous communities facing the first and worst impacts, drew attention to a UNESCO-launched internet forum providing 'a space for local and indigenous voices to contribute to decision-making' in the lead-up to the 2009 UN Climate Change Conference in Copenhagen.[347] In 2018, Director-General Audrey Azoulay 'reaffirm[ed]' UNESCO's 'full commitment' to the UNDRIP.[348] In 2019, Azoulay underscored that UNESCO was 'committed to … enabling [Indigenous peoples] to participate fully and equally at national and international levels', highlighting their knowledge 'crucial' for achieving the Sustainable Development Goals and drawing attention to several UNESCO programmes relevant to Indigenous peoples.[349]

4.2.4.3 Indigenous Peoples and the UNESCO World Heritage Committee

A particular area of UNESCO's work with the potential to impact on Indigenous peoples is the protection of world heritage. Despite the potentially serious impacts of decisions to place a site on the World Heritage List ("the List"), affected Indigenous peoples have historically been overlooked by the World Heritage Committee ("WHC"), which consists of twenty-one representatives of states parties to the World Heritage Convention and holds annual sessions to decide on whether nominated sites are to be inscribed on the List, examine reports on the state of conservation of listed properties, and make other decisions on the implementation of the Convention.[350]

346 UNESCO, 'Message from Mr Koïchiro Matsuura, Director-General of UNESCO on the Occasion of the International Day of the World's Indigenous People' (9 August 2008) UNESCO Doc. DG/ME/ID/2008/011 REV, 1 and 3.

347 UNESCO, 'Message from Mr Koïchiro Matsuura, Director-General of UNESCO on the Occasion of the International Day of the World's Indigenous People' (9 August 2009) UNESCO Doc. DG/ME/ID/2009/12, 2–3.

348 UNESCO, 'Message from Ms Audrey Azoulay, Director-General of UNESCO, on the Occasion of International Day of the World's Indigenous Peoples – Migration and Movement' (9 August 2018) UNESCO Doc. DG/ME/ID/2018/26, 2.

349 UNESCO, 'Message from Ms Audrey Azoulay, Director-General of UNESCO on the Occasion of the International Day of the World's Indigenous Peoples' (9 August 2019) UNESCO Doc. DG/ME/ID/2019/26, 1.

350 Convention concerning the Protection of the World Cultural and Natural Heritage (adopted 16 November 1972; entry into force 17 December 1975), 1037 UNTS 151, Articles 8, 9, 11, and 13.

Since at least 2005, the General Assembly,[351] UNPFII,[352] EMRIP,[353] the Special Rapporteur on the Rights of Indigenous Peoples,[354] the ACHPR,[355] and IUCN[356] have all expressed concern about the lack of participation of Indigenous peoples in the nomination, inscription, and management of World Heritage Sites. A joint statement from Indigenous peoples' organizations to the UNPFII in 2011 emphasized that[357]

> [t]here are numerous examples of Indigenous sites on the World Heritage List that have been inscribed without the free, prior and informed consent of the Indigenous peoples concerned. In many cases Indigenous peoples were not even consulted when their territories were designated as World Heritage sites, although this designation can have far-reaching consequences for their lives and human rights, their ability to carry out their subsistence activities, and their ability to freely pursue their economic, social and cultural development in accordance with their right of self-determination.

The joint statement named three nominations, then under consideration by the Committee, that had been prepared without the meaningful involvement or consultation of affected Indigenous peoples; all three were subsequently inscribed on the List despite Indigenous peoples' concerns.[358]

[351] General Assembly, 'Programme of Action for the Second International Decade of the World's Indigenous People' (2005) UN Doc. A/60/270, para. 16.

[352] UNPFII, 'Report on the Tenth Session' (2011) E/C.19/2011/14, p. 14, and 'Report of the Second Session' (2003) UN Doc. E/C.19/2003/22, 18.

[353] EMRIP, 'Report on Its Fifth Session', 7; EMRIP, 'Final Report of the Study on Indigenous Peoples and the Right to Participate in Decision-Making', Annex, para. 38; EMRIP, 'Advice No 2 (2011): Indigenous Peoples and the Right to Participate in Decision-Making' (2011) UN Doc. A/HRC/18/42, 11; EMRIP, 'Advice No 8 (2015): Promotion and Protection of the Rights of Indigenous Peoples with Respect to Their Cultural Heritage' (2015) UN Doc. A/HRC/30/53, Annex, 10, 20, and 23.

[354] Human Rights Council, 'Report of the Special Rapporteur on the Rights of Indigenous Peoples' (2012) UN Doc. A/HRC/21/47.

[355] African Commission on Human and Peoples' Rights, 'Resolution on the Protection of Indigenous Peoples' Rights in the Context of the World Heritage Convention and the Designation of Lake Bogoria as a World Heritage Site' (5 November 2011) ACHPR Res. 197 (L)2011, paras. 2–3.

[356] IUCN, 'Resolution on the Intergovernmental Science-Policy Platform', para. 2.

[357] Endorois Welfare Council et al., 'Joint Statement on Continuous Violations of the Principle of Free, Prior and Informed Consent in the Context of UNESCO's World Heritage Convention' (Statement to the PFII, New York, 17 May 2011) https://aippnet.org/joint-statement-on-continuous-violations-of-the-principle-of-free-prior-and-informed-consent-in-the-context-of-unescos-world-heritage-convention/.

[358] Stefan Disko, Helen Tugendhat, and Lola García-Alix, 'World Heritage Sites and Indigenous Peoples' Rights: An Introduction' in Stefan Disko and Helen Tugendhat (eds.), *World Heritage Sites and Indigenous Peoples' Rights* (Copenhagen: IWGIA, 2014), 3–38, 25.

Pressure from Indigenous advocates led to changes. In 2015, the Committee changed the Operational Guidelines of the Convention to include Indigenous peoples in a list of potential 'partners in the protection and conservation of World Heritage' and encourage states to obtain their FPIC when nominating sites for the List.[359] However, FPIC was a recommended practice rather than obligatory, and Indigenous peoples were referred to as "stakeholders" rather than rights-holders.[360]

The Guidelines were further updated in 2019.[361] The 2019 Guidelines encouraged states parties to ensure the 'full, effective and gender-balanced participation' of 'a wide variety of stakeholders and rights-holders', including Indigenous peoples, to prepare their tentative lists of sites for nomination.[362] Further, in cases of sites affecting the lands, territories, or resources of Indigenous peoples, states parties were now required to 'consult and cooperate in good faith with the indigenous peoples concerned through their own representative institutions in order to obtain' FPIC before the sites could be included on the tentative list of properties for nomination.[363] At the nomination stage, the guidelines provide that states parties '"shall" demonstrate, as appropriate, that the free, prior and informed consent of indigenous peoples has been obtained, through, inter alia making the nominations publicly available in appropriate languages and public consultations and hearings'.[364] Thus the consent of affected Indigenous peoples is now required before the WHC makes a decision to inscribe a property on the List.

In addition to the rules on FPIC, Indigenous peoples have long sought a direct participatory mechanism to the Committee. Successive attempts have proved unsuccessful. At its 24th and 25th sessions in 2000–2001, the WHC considered a proposal, submitted by a forum of Indigenous peoples, for the establishment of a World Heritage Indigenous Peoples Council of Experts ("WHIPCOE") as a consultative body to the Committee.[365]

359 World Heritage Committee (WHC), 'Operational Guidelines for the Implementation of the World Heritage Convention' (2015) UNESCO Doc. WHC.15/01, paras. 40 and 123.

360 UNPFII, 'Statement of O. Lorde on Behalf of the UNPFII at the World Heritage Committee', 39th Session (29 June 2015); see also Ana Filipa Vrdoljak, 'Indigenous Peoples, World Heritage, and Human Rights' (2018) 25 *International Journal of Cultural Property*, 245–281, 269.

361 UNESCO, 'Decisions Adopted during the 43rd Session of the World Heritage Committee' (2019) UNESCO Doc. WHC/19/43.COM/18, Decision 43 COM 11A, Annex.

362 Ibid., paras. I.C.12 and II.C.64.

363 Ibid., para. II.C.64.

364 Ibid., para. III.A.123.

365 WHC, 'Report of the Twenty-Fifth Session' (2002) UNESCO Doc. WHC-2001/CONF.205/WEB.3.

The forum had proposed that, given the 'lack of involvement of Indigenous peoples in the development and implementation of laws, policies and plans ... which apply to their ancestral lands',[366] a WHIPCOE should sit alongside, and 'add value [to] rather than displace',[367] the Committee's existing advisory bodies.[368] It would provide 'expert Indigenous advice on the holistic knowledge, traditions and cultural values of Indigenous Peoples relative to the implementation of the World Heritage Convention', including on 'the appropriate identification, evaluation and management of "mixed" properties and "cultural" properties with indigenous associations and the identification, management and possible renomination of properties listed for their "natural" World Heritage values that may also hold indigenous values'.[369] The proposal stated that it was designed as a 'means of giving Indigenous people greater responsibility for their own affairs and an effective voice in decisions on matters which affect them'.[370]

Although the proposal was initially 'warmly received' by the WHC and the World Heritage Centre conducted a feasibility study on the proposal including developing draft terms of reference with the assistance of the Indigenous representatives who had made the proposal,[371] the Committee ultimately did not approve the request, owing to 'a number of legal concerns and issues relating to the funding, legal status, role and relationships (with the States Parties, Advisory Bodies, World Heritage Committee and World Heritage Centre)', as well as the fact that '[s]ome members of the Committee questioned the definition of indigenous peoples and the relevance of such a distinction in different regions of the world'.[372]

366 World Heritage Committee, 'Supporting Paper to the Submission of the Indigenous Peoples Forum Presented to the 24th Session of the World Heritage Committee' (28 November 2000) UNESCO Doc. WHC-2001/CONF.205/WEB.3, Annex 1, 2.

367 Ibid., 3.

368 The IUCN, the International Council on Monuments and Sites (ICOMOS), and the International Centre for the Study of the Preservation and Restoration of Cultural Property (ICCROM): Article 8.3, World Heritage Convention.

369 WHC, 'Report on the Proposed World Heritage Indigenous Peoples Council of Experts (WHIPCOE)' (2001) UNESCO Doc. WHC-01/CONF.208.24.

370 WHC, 'Supporting Paper to the Submission of the Indigenous Peoples Forum', 12.

371 WHC, 'Progress Report on World Heritage Indigenous Peoples Council of Experts (WHIPCOE)' (2001) UNESCO Doc. WHC-2001/CONF.208/13, 1.

372 WHC, 'Report of the Twenty-Fifth Session', 57. For more detail, see Lynn Meskell, 'UNESCO and the Fate of the World Heritage Indigenous Peoples Council of Experts (WHIPCOE)' (2013) 20 *International Journal of Cultural Property*, 155–174.

In 2017, Indigenous peoples' organizations set up the International Indigenous Peoples' Forum on World Heritage (IIPFWH) as a 'standing global body aiming to engage with the WHC during its meetings, in order to represent the voices of indigenous peoples with regard to the World Heritage Convention'.[373] The WHC 'noted the establishment' of the IIPFWH 'as an important reflection platform on the involvement of Indigenous Peoples in the identification, conservation and management of World Heritage properties',[374] but so far this development has not resulted in any changes in Indigenous peoples' participation in the Committee, which 'continues to be marginal'.[375] This is despite the fact that UNESCO presented the launch of the IIPFWH to the UNPFII, in 2019, as a 'major step in engaging indigenous peoples'.[376] Given that UNESCO also said in its statement to the UNPFII that the World Heritage Centre is 'continuously liaising with the forum regarding the next steps',[377] it may be that this is a quickly changing area and that enhanced participation of Indigenous peoples in the work of the Committee will soon ensue. But as of the WHC's 44th session in 2021, the IIPFWH continued to push for increased participation in the WHC, lamenting that its interventions are heard only after decisions on nominations are already adopted.[378] For now, the prospect of an Indigenous advisory body to the UNESCO WHC remains 'perpetually deferred'.[379]

4.2.5 *The UN Food and Agriculture Organization's Committee on Food Security*

Beginning in 2009, Indigenous peoples have been included in the FAO Committee on Food Security.[380] Reporting to the ECOSOC as well as the FAO Conference, the Committee on Food Security develops policy recom-

373 See International Indigenous Peoples' Forum on World Heritage (IIPFWH), 'International Indigenous Peoples' Forum on World Heritage' (n.d.), www.iipfwh.org. This is not an official advisory body to the WHC.

374 WHC, 'State of Conservation of the Properties Inscribed on the World Heritage List' (2017) Decision 41 COM 7.

375 IWGIA, *The Indigenous World – 2019* (Copenhagen: IWGIA, 2019), 664.

376 UNESCO, '2018 Report to the UNPFII (2019)', 13.

377 Ibid.

378 IIPFWH, 'Statement of the International Indigenous Peoples' Forum on World Heritage, Item 7B – State of Conservation of Properties Inscribed on the World Heritage List' (July 2021), https://iipfwh.org/publications/.

379 Vrdoljak, 'Indigenous Peoples, World Heritage', 271.

380 FAO Constitution, Article IV.9; General Rules of the Organization, Rule XXXIII; both in *Basic Texts of the Food and Agriculture Organization of the United Nations* (FAO 2017).

mendations and guidance on food security and nutrition. Unlike the FAO's other committees, in which states are the primary (and only) actors, 2009 reforms saw the Committee opened to a broader range of participants, including civil society organizations and NGOs 'with strong relevance to issues of food security and nutrition' particularly organizations representing, among others affected by food insecurity, Indigenous peoples.[381] As participants, Indigenous peoples may intervene in plenary and breakout discussions of the Committee to contribute to preparing meeting documents and agendas, submit and present documents, and make formal proposals.[382] They have a higher level of participation than that of an observer, a status that the new rules preserve for other interested organizations.[383] In its reports to the UNPFII, the FAO has highlighted its support for the participation of Indigenous peoples in the Committee, including by ensuring the participation of the UNPFII Chair and representatives of Indigenous youth.[384]

The UNPFII evidently considers this level of participation insufficient: in successive recommendations to the FAO, it has suggested that it establish a dedicated mechanism for partnership with Indigenous peoples, such as a working group,[385] and has requested FAO to enhance the participation of Indigenous peoples in the work of its other committees, in particular the Committees on Agriculture, Forestry, Fisheries, World Food Security, and Genetic Resources for Food and Agriculture.[386]

4.2.6 *Moves towards Acceptance as Law in the WIPO IGC and the CBD?*

Indigenous peoples have gained procedural footholds, then, in the UNFCCC, IUCN, IPBES, UNESCO, and FAO. In all but the IUCN and

[381] FAO, 'Report of the Thirty-Fifth Session of the Committee on World Food Security' (2009) FAO Doc. C 2009/21-Rev.1, Appendix H, para. 11. See also Rules of Procedure of the Committee on World Food Security, in *Basic Texts of the Food and Agriculture Organization of the United Nations* (FAO 2017), Rule I.

[382] FAO, 'Report of the Thirty-Fifth Session', para. 12.

[383] Ibid., paras. 13–15.

[384] FAO, '2017 Report to the UNPFII' (2018), www.un.org/development/desa/indigenouspeoples/wp-content/uploads/sites/19/2018/02/FAO-Questionnaire-to-Agencies-UNFPII-2017.pdf, 6–8.

[385] UNPFII, 'Report on the Fourteenth Session' (2015) UN Doc. E/2015/43-E/C.19/2015/10, para. 27, and 'Report on the Tenth Session', para. 6.

[386] UNPFII, 'Report on the Seventeenth Session' (2018) UN Doc. E/2018/43*-E/C.19/2018/11*, para. 112; UNPFII, 'Report on the Eighteenth Session' (2019) UN Doc. E/2019/43-E/C.19/2019/10, para. 91.

IPBES, these have been justified by states and international officials by reference to the UNDRIP. In other mechanisms for Indigenous peoples' participation that were established pre-2007, discussed in Chapter 3, we can observe a move post-2007 towards justifying the mechanisms on the basis of the UNDRIP.

In decision IX/8 of 2008, the COP noted the UNDRIP and recognized the need for Indigenous peoples' participation in the work on protected areas.[387] In a statement on the adoption of the UNDRIP, the CBD Executive Secretary said that states parties were 'committed to the participation of indigenous peoples in issues affecting them', consistent with Articles 40 and 41 of the UNDRIP.[388]

In the WIPO, a 'Practical Guide for Observers' in the IGC published on the WIPO Secretariat website states:[389]

> Indigenous peoples and local communities in particular need to be able to participate, express their views and have their voices heard in the IGC decision-making process, in accordance with the 2007 UN Declaration on the Rights of Indigenous Peoples, as the outcome of the IGC negotiations will affect their rights.

This statement suggests that WIPO views the participation of Indigenous peoples in the IGC as required by the UNDRIP. Several states have also expressed this view in the IGC from 2009 onwards, including Mexico,[390] Bolivia,[391] and Canada.[392]

387 Decision IX/8 (9 October 2008) UN Doc. UNEP/CBD/COP/DEC/IX/8.

388 CBD, 'Press Release: The Executive Secretary of the Convention on Biological Diversity Welcomes the Adoption of the Declaration on the Rights of Indigenous Peoples' (30 June 2006) www.cbd.int/doc/press/2006/pr-2006-07-06-drip-en.pdf.

389 WIPO IGC, 'Practical Guide for Observers' (n.d.), www.wipo.int/export/sites/www/tk/en/igc/pdf/observers_practical_guide.pdf, 1.

390 IGC, 'Report on the Thirteenth Session' (30 April 2009) UN Doc. WIPO/GRTKF/IC/13/11, para. 21 ('it was important to continue listening to … indigenous organizations … bearing in mind the [UNDRIP]').

391 IGC, 'Report on the Fourteenth Session' (1 October 2009) UN Doc. WIPO/GRTKF/IC/14/12, para. 32 ('although indigenous participation in the discussions of the Committee was sought, participation of those directly involved had not been sufficient for their concerns to be taken into account, as established in the latest progress made in the multilateral legal system such as the [UNDRIP]').

392 IGC, 'Report on the Thirty-Ninth Session' (2019) UN Doc. WIPO/GRRTKF/IC/39/18, para. 29 (the IGC's work 'closely aligns with the implementation of UNDRIP', and any international framework developed in the IGC 'has to be informed by the views of and involve the active participation of representatives of IPLCs from around the world, as the holders of such knowledge and cultural expressions').

4.3 EVOLUTIONS IN INDIGENOUS PEOPLES' PARTICIPATION IN INTERNATIONAL DEVELOPMENT AND FINANCIAL ORGANIZATIONS

As was seen in Chapter 3, from the early 1990s, the World Bank and the UN Development Programme pioneered policies for Indigenous peoples' participation in development decision-making and project implementation. In the years following the adoption of the UNDRIP, more and more development organizations adopted policies on Indigenous peoples, very often with the involvement and consultation of Indigenous peoples' organizations. While these policies tended to cover the full range of Indigenous peoples' rights as reflected in the UNDRIP, they contained a particular focus on participation in international policymaking and decision-making including, where appropriate, FPIC. Through these policies, international organizations typically require FPIC – or at minimum consultations to obtain FPIC – of Indigenous peoples before making a decision to invest in, or carry out, development projects with the potential to affect them. In addition, they sometimes also provide for Indigenous peoples' membership on decision-making bodies, or on advisory boards. These aspects are addressed here in turn.

A crucial factor in the development of these policies was the 2008 release by the UN Development Group of Guidelines on Indigenous Peoples' Issues (UNDG Guidelines).[393] Coming soon after the adoption of the UNDRIP, these guidelines clearly influenced what were to follow.

4.3.1 *The UN Development Group Guidelines on Indigenous Peoples' Issues, 2008*

The UNDG Guidelines provided an overview of the situation of Indigenous peoples, existing international norms and standards on Indigenous peoples' rights, and programmatic implications for United Nations Country Teams (UNCTs) for addressing and mainstreaming Indigenous peoples' issues.[394] They named Indigenous peoples' participation as an 'overarching principle' for UNCTs.[395] It cited ILO Convention 169 and the UNDRIP, specifically Article 41, as providing 'a framework for strengthened engagement on

[393] UN Development Group, *Guidelines on Indigenous Peoples' Issues* (UN 2008) https://unsdg.un.org/sites/default/files/UNDG_guidelines_EN.pdf.

[394] Ibid., p. 5.

[395] Ibid., p. 4.

indigenous peoples' issues at the country level'.[396] The Guidelines said the right to self-determination may be addressed through respect for the principle of FPIC, 'full and effective participation of indigenous peoples at every stage of any action that may affect them direct or indirectly', and 'consultation with the indigenous peoples concerned prior to any action that may affect them, direct or indirectly'.[397] The guidelines called for 'effective participation of indigenous peoples and their representatives, including indigenous women, throughout programming cycles and strategic planning processes'.[398] On participation, it said participation 'implies going further than mere consultation and should lead to concrete ownership of projects by indigenous peoples' and that although mechanisms for participation can vary, Indigenous peoples 'should participate in regular participatory mechanisms put in place by UNCTs'.[399] It outlined elements of FPIC[400] and mapped ways to involve Indigenous peoples during the UNCT planning process.[401]

This guidance was broadly framed. However, in the years to follow, various international development organizations translated it into more concrete policies.

4.3.2 *Free, Prior, and Informed Consent (FPIC) Policies*

4.3.2.1 The International Fund for Agricultural Development (IFAD) Policy on Engagement with Indigenous Peoples, 2009

The first such policy was produced by the International Fund for Agricultural Development (IFAD), in 2009.[402] The IFAD Policy on Engagement with Indigenous Peoples of 2009[403] was developed by a group of IFAD staff in

396 Ibid., 6–7.

397 Ibid., 15.

398 Ibid., 26.

399 Ibid., 27.

400 Ibid., 30.

401 Ibid., 31–35.

402 The IFAD's main decision-making body is the Governing Council, consisting of representatives of the IFAD's 177 member states, while decisions on whether to approve projects and programmes are made by an Executive Board composed of eighteen member state representatives: Agreement Establishing the International Fund for Agricultural Development (opened for signature 20 December 1976 and entered into force 30 November 1977) 1059 UNTS 191, Articles 6.1(a), 6.2, 6.5, 6.6, and 7.2(c)–(d), and Schedule II. IFAD also has a President and staff responsible for conducting its business: Article 6.8.

403 IFAD, *Engagement with Indigenous Peoples: Policy* (IFAD, 2009). Also see IFAD, 'Executive Board: Minutes of the Ninety-seventh Session' (2009) IFAD Doc. Document EB 2009/97/R.3/Rev.1.

consultation with Indigenous peoples' representatives and the UNPFII and subsequently approved by its Executive Board.[404] It sets out principles of engagement for IFAD to follow in its work with Indigenous peoples, whether in the formulation of country strategies, in policy dialogue, or throughout the project cycle.[405] Aiming 'to enhance IFAD's development effectiveness in its engagement with indigenous peoples' communities in rural areas, and especially to empower them to overcome poverty by building on their identity and culture',[406] the policy lists FPIC as one of the nine fundamental principles.[407]

On FPIC, the Policy states that IFAD, when working with member states on projects targeting or affecting Indigenous peoples, shall support 'the participation of indigenous peoples' communities in determining priorities and strategies for their own development'.[408] '[C]onsultation to obtain' FPIC is a criterion for project approval.[409] IFAD's detailed policies on how consultations are to be carried out broadly mirror accepted principles.[410] Consultations should be carried out through Indigenous peoples' freely chosen representatives and institutions, without coercion, intimidation, or manipulation, with sufficient time and information, and with the expected outcome of consent.[411] Consent, not just consultation, is clearly required when a project would result in physical displacement or impacts on access to land or other resources.[412]

Prior to project approval, the Policy also provides for the participation of Indigenous peoples. Before specific projects are carried out, IFAD works with a country receiving funds to create a "country strategic opportunities programme" that defines priority objectives and presents concepts for projects, providing a framework for IFAD's work in the country.[413] IFAD's policy provides that for countries where Indigenous peoples are relevant to issues of rural poverty, IFAD 'will' invite Indigenous peoples' representatives to be part

404 Ibid, 6; Acknowledgements.

405 IFAD, *Engagement with Indigenous Peoples*, 15.

406 Ibid., 6.

407 Ibid., 4.

408 Ibid., 13.

409 Ibid., 13.

410 See IFAD, 'Social, Environmental and Climate Assessment Procedures' (IFAD, 2017) ("SECAP"), 230; IFAD, 'How to Do Seeking Free, Prior and Informed Consent in IFAD Investment Projects' (IFAD, 2015). See also IFAD, 'Policy on Improving Access to Land and Tenure Security' (IFAD, 2008); IFAD, 'Policy on Environment and Natural Resource Management' (IFAD, 2011).

411 IFAD, 'How to Do Seeking', 2 and 5–8.

412 IFAD, 'SECAP', 9.

413 IFAD, 'Operational Procedures and Guidelines for Country Strategies' (IFAD, n.d.), 2.

of the team that prepares the country strategic programme.[414] In addition, IFAD will invite representatives to participate in the country project management team or in the preparation of the project.[415] According to the Policy, arrangements for implementing a project 'should facilitate a direct role by indigenous peoples in managing resources', including capacity-building measures where needed to enable affected Indigenous peoples' organizations to 'assume effective control over the resources to be invested in their communities'.[416] An IFAD internal review found that the Policy has largely been adhered to in practice.[417]

One reason for IFAD's adoption of practices regarding the participation of Indigenous peoples in activities of the Fund that affect them, as evidenced by its publicly available documents and statements, is to better fulfil its own mandate and bolster its own legitimacy. But there is also evidence to suggest that it regards this as required by the UNDRIP. Regarding the former, the Policy on Engagement with Indigenous Peoples begins with the acknowledgement that 'reaching indigenous peoples with agricultural development' – recognized by the Fund as an important part of fulfilling its mandate – 'requires tailored approaches that respect their values and build upon their strengths'.[418] It goes on to express the aim of enhancing IFAD's development effectiveness in its engagement with Indigenous peoples' communities in rural areas.[419] The Policy further states that a participatory approach can 'better address complexity and diversity' and make programmes more 'responsive to local problems and to the goals and visions of indigenous peoples'.[420] The Strategic Framework 2016–2024 further supports this view, stating that because of its responsiveness to the needs and priorities of Indigenous peoples, 'IFAD's interventions, and their targeting will be improved'.[421] In a speech to

[414] IFAD, *Engagement with Indigenous Peoples*, 15. For an example of COSOPs adopted using this approach, see IFAD, 'India: Country Strategic Opportunities Programme 2018–2024' (21 August 2018) IFAD Doc. EB 2018/124/R.19.

[415] IFAD, *Engagement with Indigenous Peoples*, 15.

[416] Ibid., 16.

[417] See, for example, IFAD, 'IFAD's Progress in Its Engagement with Indigenous Peoples in the Biennium 2017–2018' (IFAD, 2018), particularly 6, 8, and 9.

[418] Ibid., 4.

[419] Ibid., 6.

[420] Ibid., 11.

[421] IFAD, *Strategic Framework 2016–2024* (IFAD, 2015), 19. For further examples, see IFAD, 'The Traditional Knowledge Advantage: Indigenous Peoples' Knowledge in Climate Change Adaptation and Mitigation Strategies' (IFAD, 2016), 7 ('IFAD has made significant progress in enhancing its development effectiveness with regard to indigenous peoples. It established instruments to support indigenous peoples' self-driven development and their full and effective participation at all levels'); IFAD, 'IFAD's Statement by Mattia Prayer Galletti Lead Technical

the 2014 World Conference on Indigenous Peoples, the President of the Fund stated that working with Indigenous peoples as equal partners through inclusive processes was necessary to fulfilling development objectives.[422]

However, there are also reasons to believe that IFAD's practices are partly motivated by the belief that they are required by the UNDRIP. The Policy on Engagement with Indigenous Peoples states that it was developed in response to 'rapidly evolving national and international normative frameworks on the rights of indigenous peoples', including the adoption of policies on Indigenous peoples by other international financial institutions,[423] and cites the international legal framework on Indigenous peoples' rights including ILO 169 and the UNDRIP, which it says 'promotes [Indigenous peoples'] full and effective participation in all matters that concern them'.[424] A 2021 IFAD publication stressed that FPIC was recognized in the UNDRIP.[425] In addition, in 2017 the President of IFAD stated in a speech that IFAD had 'become a role model for how institutions can build relationships with indigenous peoples based on inclusive and horizontal partnerships, in line with UNDRIP's article on self-determined development'.[426] In a speech to the UNPFII in 2019, a representative of IFAD stated that 'giving Indigenous Peoples the driving seat' was 'in line with the principles of UNDRIP'.[427] At the World Conference on Indigenous Peoples in 2014, the President emphasized Article 18 of the UNDRIP.[428] On other occasions, the President has stated that the Fund wants 'to support [Indigenous peoples'] efforts to make yourselves heard in the defence of [their] rights, which are established by international conventions and declarations'[429] and that the Forum was

Specialist at UNPFII' (26 April 2019), www.ifad.org/en/web/latest/speech/asset/41123449; IFAD, 'Welcoming Remarks by Gilbert Houngbo, President of IFAD at the Fourth Indigenous Peoples' Forum' (12 February 2019) www.ifad.org/en/web/latest/speech/asset/41016256 ('We believe that ownership is essential to development.... Dialogue has vastly improved our understanding').

422 IFAD, 'Statement by IFAD President to Roundtable at the World Conference on Indigenous Peoples (22 September 2014)', www.ifad.org/en/web/latest/speech/asset/39030687.

423 IFAD, *Engagement with Indigenous Peoples*, 6.

424 Ibid., 7.

425 IFAD, 'Good Practices in IFAD's Engagement with Indigenous Peoples' (IFAD, 2021), 3, www.ifad.org/documents/38714170/44358796/IPs_engagement_Good_Practices.pdf/deaa1849-6518-e223-8274-d672f1081499?t=1651742225818.

426 IFAD, 'Proceedings of the Third Global Meeting of the Indigenous Peoples Forum at IFAD' (IFAD, 2017), 7.

427 IFAD, 'IFAD's Statement by Mattia Prayer Galleti'.

428 IFAD, 'Statement by IFAD President to World Conference on Indigenous Peoples'.

429 IFAD, 'Welcoming Remarks by Gilbert Houngbo'.

established 'within the framework of' the UNDRIP.[430] The repetitive reference to the UNDRIP in the course of outlining IFAD's procedures for Indigenous peoples' participation strongly suggests that IFAD views such processes as in line with UNDRIP. IFAD officials have repeatedly emphasized the Fund's commitment to ensuring that Indigenous peoples' voices are heard on the global stage, stressing that its Engagement Policy represents '[t]he right thing to do'.[431]

4.3.2.2 The UN Food and Agriculture Organization (FAO) Policy on Indigenous and Tribal Peoples, 2010

The year after the IFAD policy was adopted, a similar policy was established by the UN Food and Agriculture Organization (FAO). The 2010 FAO Policy on Indigenous and Tribal Peoples addresses Indigenous peoples' participation in policymaking and standard-setting activities affecting them, recognizing that Indigenous peoples are specifically affected by the FAO's work as they face unique challenges in relation to nutrition and food security due to the ongoing effects of colonialism.[432] Itself prepared through consultations with Indigenous peoples' representatives and the UNPFII, among others,[433] the Policy recognizes Indigenous peoples' right to full and effective participation 'at every stage of any action that may affect them directly or indirectly'[434] and further states:[435]

> FAO will facilitate the direct and effective participation of indigenous peoples in current and future FAO programmes and activities that affect indigenous peoples. It will support enabling environments to foster inclusion of indigenous peoples in the design, execution and evaluation of policies and programmes that concern and/or affect them.

The Policy envisages that this will be implemented, firstly, by way of 'policy dialogue' between the FAO and Indigenous peoples 'in order to communicate effectively what can be done for and with them as stipulated by FAO's

430 IFAD, 'Closing Remarks by IFAD President at the Indigenous People's International Conference on Sustainable Development and Self-Determination' (19 June 2012) www.ifad.org/en/web/latest/speech/asset/39034628.

431 See, for example, IFAD, 'Proceedings of the Second Global Meeting of the Indigenous Peoples Forum at IFAD' (IFAD, 2015), 10; IFAD, 'Governing Council Report, Fortieth Session' (2017) IFAD Doc. GC 40, 73 and 82.

432 FAO, *FAO Policy on Indigenous and Tribal Peoples* (FAO, 2010), 1–2.

433 Ibid., 1.

434 Ibid., 5.

435 Ibid., 12.

mandate and operational boundaries'.[436] Noting the need for a representative body of Indigenous peoples with which to engage, it notes that Indigenous peoples' representatives at the Civil Society Forum at the World Food Summit in 2010 discussed forming a committee, stating that if such a body were established, FAO would 'consider it a counterpart through which partnership and dialogue can move forward'.[437] No such committee has subsequently been established, however. The "policy dialogue" element of the Policy does not appear to have been carried out. Moreover, it may be observed that this provision of the Policy focuses on one-way communication *from* the FAO *to* Indigenous peoples; the Policy speaks of 'clarifying' to Indigenous peoples 'what can be realistically expected'.[438] Similar emphasis is not placed on the potential role policy dialogue could play in conveying Indigenous peoples' concerns and views to the FAO.

Other parts of the Policy have been implemented. The Policy elsewhere envisages the participation of Indigenous peoples through multi-stakeholder consultations with member states, research institutions, UN agencies, private sector organizations, and civil society organizations,[439] as well as in FAO committees, conferences, and regional conferences through FAO's internal civil society liaison or via its internal private sector cooperation group.[440] With respect to the participation of Indigenous peoples in multi-stakeholder consultations, for instance, FAO mentions in its reporting to the UNPFII that it supported the participation of Indigenous peoples in a regional and global consultation on farmers' rights, the outcomes of which were presented at the 7th meeting of the Governing Body of the International Treaty on Plant Genetic Resources for Food and Agriculture.[441] In addition, according to the FAO, Indigenous peoples have participated in FAO committees through the civil society mechanism.[442]

Like IFAD's policy, FAO's policy also covers Indigenous peoples' participation and FPIC in field programmes and projects affecting them. The 2010 Policy emphasizes that FAO is required to 'facilitate the direct and effective participation' of Indigenous peoples in programmes and activities affecting

[436] Ibid., 16.
[437] Ibid., 16–17.
[438] Ibid., 16.
[439] Ibid., 17.
[440] Ibid., 17.
[441] FAO, '2017 Report to the UNPFII', 12.
[442] FAO, 'FAO Activities 2018' (2018), www.un.org/development/desa/indigenouspeoples/wp-content/uploads/sites/19/2018/12/2018-FAO-UNPFII-Questionnaire.pdf, 6.

them and support enabling environments to foster their inclusion.[443] Further, the FAO is required to[444]

> establish measures to collaborate with indigenous peoples and discourage ventures that will have an adverse impact on their communities. When there is a direct impact or relation to indigenous peoples' issues, it will follow the provisions of the [UNDRIP] that relate to free, prior and informed consent.

Elaborating on FPIC, the Policy provides that the FAO will seek FPIC when its projects directly affect Indigenous peoples.[445] It clarifies that FPIC must be obtained before adopting and implementing projects affecting them, that there must be no act of coercion, intimidation, or manipulation, and that Indigenous peoples should be included as 'competent and legitimate stakeholders' in projects affecting them.[446]

Building on this, the FAO Environmental and Social Management Guidelines of 2015 clarify the FAO's requirement that before implementing projects and programmes that may affect Indigenous peoples' rights, lands, natural resources, territories, livelihoods, knowledge, social fabric, traditions, governance systems, or culture or heritage, FPIC is required 'in all cases'.[447] Environmental and Social Standard 9 provides that in the process of obtaining FPIC, complete information must be disclosed to the Indigenous peoples in a timely manner, with sufficient time for them to carry out internal deliberations, in accordance with their traditions and customs, in their local language, and in an environment and in ways to which the Indigenous peoples can relate.[448] Where FPIC is given, the Standard requires that a plan be prepared in full consultation with the affected peoples to avoid, minimize, mitigate, or compensate for any adverse impacts.[449]

The FAO's own discourse reveals a threefold motivation behind the 2010 Policy. The first is the imperative to achieve its own mandate. In the introduction to the 2010 Policy, the FAO states that '[t]he fight against hunger

443 FAO, *Policy on Indigenous*, 12.
444 Ibid., 13.
445 Ibid., 14.
446 Ibid., 5.
447 FAO, *Environmental and Social Management Guidelines* (FAO, 2015), Environmental and Social Standard 9 ("ESS 9"), paras. 6 and 9. Further on FPIC, see FAO, 'Free Prior and Informed Consent: An Indigenous Peoples' Right and a Good Practice for Local Communities: Manual for Project Practitioners' (FAO, 2016); FAO, 'Respecting Free, Prior and Informed Consent: Practical Guidance for Governments, Companies, NGOs, Indigenous Peoples and Local Communities in Relation to Land Acquisition' (FAO, 2014).
448 FAO, ESS 9, para. 7.
449 Ibid, paras. 8 and 10.

cannot be won without [Indigenous peoples]', who may 'bring novel solutions' to the table.[450] Thus it considers Indigenous peoples 'an undeniable stakeholder in a development agenda shaped by such a mandate'.[451] The engagement of Indigenous peoples is framed as a means by which the organization can better achieve its ends.[452] Second, the FAO evidently recognizes the importance of Indigenous peoples being heard on matters affecting them. The document outlining the reforms to the Committee on Food Security highlights the importance of ensuring that the 'voices of all relevant stakeholders are heard in the policy debate on food and agriculture'.[453] The FAO Strategy for Partnerships with Civil Society Organizations states that 'the increasing participation of indigenous peoples and other ethnic minorities in public policy debates and fora is an important step towards strengthening their rights and improving their situation'.[454] Thirdly, the 2010 Policy also cites Article 41 of the UNDRIP, suggesting that FAO sees the policy as required by law.[455]

4.3.2.3 The Global Environment Facility (GEF) Principles and Guidelines for Engagement with Indigenous Peoples, 2012

The Global Environment Facility (GEF) is an international organization that serves as the financial mechanism to five multilateral environmental agreements including the UNFCCC and CBD, providing new and additional grant and concessional funding to assist developing countries in meeting the objectives of the conventions it serves.[456] In 2012, the GEF adopted Principles and Guidelines for Engagement with Indigenous Peoples.

[450] FAO, *Policy on Indigenous*, 1–2.

[451] Ibid., 2.

[452] Also see ibid., 7–8.

[453] FAO, Committee on World Food Security, 'Reform of the Committee on World Food Security' (2009) FAO Doc. CFS:2009/2 Rev.2, paras. 2 and 7.

[454] FAO, 'Report of the Council of FAO, Hundred and Forty-Sixth Session' (2013) FAO Doc. CL 146/REP, Appendix F, FAO Strategy for Partnerships with Civil Society Organizations, para. 18.

[455] FAO, *Policy on Indigenous*, 2.

[456] Global Environment Facility (GEF), *Instrument for the Establishment of the Restructured Global Environment Facility* (GEF, 2015), Articles I.2 and I.6. The relevant conventions are the UNFCCC, the CBD, the Stockholm Convention on Persistent Organic Pollutants, the UN Convention to Combat Desertification in those Countries Experiencing Serious Drought and/or Desertification, particularly in Africa (signed 14 October 1994 and entered into force 26 December 1996) 1954 UNTS 3, and the Minamata Convention on Mercury (signed 10 October 2013 and entered into force 16 August 2017), 3202 UNTS.

Unlike the IFAD and FAO, the GEF's 2012 Principles and Guidelines require FPIC before deciding to finance a project only for countries that have acceded to ILO Convention No. 169 or that are required to seek FPIC under another domestic or international legal obligation.[457] For other countries, the 2012 Principles and Guidelines merely 'recogni[se] the recommendation from Indigenous Peoples that FPIC be applied to GEF-financed activities on, or significantly impacting, their traditional and user rights on their land, territories and resources, consistent with the [UNDRIP]'.[458] In cases where the country is not required to seek FPIC, the GEF merely requires consultations resulting in 'broad community support' for the project, rather than consent.[459]

The policy further provides that the GEF will ensure the full and effective participation of Indigenous peoples in GEF activities that may impact them or infringe upon their rights, meaning that Indigenous peoples should be identified in a timely manner and participate in impact assessments and in the identification, development, implementation, monitoring, and evaluation of relevant projects.[460]

While it falls below the UNDRIP's standard of participation, the 2012 Principles and Guidelines suggest that this practice was nonetheless adopted in the belief that it would allow the GEF to meet the UNDRIP's requirements, as well as to better fulfil its mandate. Regarding the latter, the GEF acknowledges 'the important role' of Indigenous peoples in the GEF's activities, 'both as valuable contributors in the project development stages, and as potential partners and stakeholders in the identification, development, implementation, monitoring, and evaluation stages'.[461] It acknowledges the importance of Indigenous peoples' efforts in 'fulfilling [the GEF's] mandate to protect the global environment',[462] and states that it 'acknowledges' the UNDRIP and 'supports' the realization of its provisions.[463] In a separate document, the GEF similarly states that it supports, through its operations and policies, the realization of the UNDRIP.[464]

457 GEF, 'GEF Policy on Agency Minimum Standards on Environmental and Social Safeguards' (2011) GEF Doc. GEF/C.41/Rev.1, 18; GEF, 'Principles and Guidelines for Engagement with Indigenous Peoples' (2012) GEF Doc. GEF/C.42/Inf.03/Rev.1, paras. 36(e) and 37.

458 GEF, 'Principles and Guidelines', para. 38.

459 GEF, 'Policy on Minimum Standards', 18.

460 GEF, 'Principles and Guidelines', para. 36(a).

461 GEF, 'Principles and Guidelines', para. 14.

462 Ibid., para. 34(i).

463 Ibid., para. 34(vii).

464 GEF, *User Guide: Indigenous Peoples and GEF Project Financing* (GEF, 2016), 3. Also see GEF, 'Partnering with Indigenous Peoples to Conserve the Global Environment' (8 August 2014) www.thegef.org/news/partnering-indigenous-peoples-conserve-global-environment.

4.3.2.4 The UN Environment Programme, 2012–2015

In the race among international organizations to adopt policy guidance on Indigenous peoples, the UN Environment Programme (UNEP) was not far behind. Two policy documents were critical in orienting UNEP's subsequent work in respect of Indigenous peoples.

UNEP AND INDIGENOUS PEOPLES: A PARTNERSHIP IN CARING FOR THE ENVIRONMENT, 2012 In 2012, UNEP adopted policy guidance on Indigenous peoples,[465] which aimed among other things to ensure that UNEP 'appropriately considers Indigenous Peoples in its activities'[466] and to 'promote the synergies and linkages between Indigenous Peoples and the global, regional and national environment policy development, policy decision-making and implementation'.[467] It expressly considered Indigenous peoples as an 'important partner', since they 'inhabit large areas of the Earth's surface' and each Indigenous group 'has developed over the millennia a unique relationship with its traditional land, territory, and related natural resources as well as with the ecosystems they inhabit'.[468] Further, it stated that Indigenous peoples' economic practices 'can be considered as "green" and have been proven to be sustainable and equitable, and also to assist the environment in its rehabilitation and resilience'.[469] The document further cited the need to empower Indigenous peoples in their efforts to live in a sustainable way with nature and to support their continued existence.[470] On the other hand, the document recognized the impacts of climate change on Indigenous peoples.[471] Therefore, UNEP recognized 'the importance of Indigenous Peoples' participation at all levels of policy and programme development and implementation stages in order to achieve sustainable development in a holistic and integrated manner', and also 'respects the valuable inputs that these holders of traditional knowledge and heritage ... can contribute to environmental assessments and sustainable ecosystem

[465] UN Environment Programme, 'UNEP and Indigenous Peoples: A Partnership in Caring for the Environment, Policy Guidance' (UNEP, November 2012) https://wedocs.unep.org/bitstream/handle/20.500.11822/11202/UNEP_Indigenous_Peoples_Policy_Guidance_endorsed_by_SMT_26_11_12.pdf?sequence=1&isAllowed=y.
[466] Ibid., 1.
[467] Ibid., 4.
[468] Ibid., 5.
[469] Ibid., 5.
[470] Ibid., 5.
[471] Ibid., 14.

management'.[472] In addition to these instrumental motivations, the policy guidance also explicitly stated that participation is in line with the UNDRIP.[473] The document goes on to quote Article 41 of the UNDRIP.[474]

The objectives of the policy guidance included strengthened institutional interaction between UNEP and Indigenous peoples 'to tap into Indigenous Peoples' knowledge, expertise and experiences, for the benefit of the environmental decision-making processes', and increased Indigenous peoples' participation in policy development and decision-making and implementation 'that could contribute to improved international and national environmental governance'.[475]

The guidance stated that UNEP would 'encourage and enhance' Indigenous peoples' accreditation to facilitate meaningful participation in the UNEP Governing Council, the Global Ministerial Environmental Forum, and the Global Major Groups and Stakeholders Forum.[476] At the programmatic level, UNEP would 'utilize relevant mechanisms to regularly engage and consult' with Indigenous peoples when developing and implementing programmes of work.[477] It included suggested actions that UNEP staff and partners should take during project design, development, implementation, and monitoring and evaluation, such as stakeholder involvement, regular stakeholder meetings, and Indigenous involvement in project implementation.[478]

At the early design phase of projects, the project manager would determine whether Indigenous peoples are present in, or have a collective attachment to, the project area. If so, the project manager would bring this to the attention of UNEP's Indigenous Peoples Focal Point, 'with a view to involving relevant expertise and encouraging the application of the principle of free, prior and informed consent'.[479] However, the policy was light on detail as to what the FPIC principle concretely required, only stipulating that it required that 'third parties enter into an equal and respectful relationship with them based on the principle of informed consent' and 'processes that allow and support meaningful choices by Indigenous Peoples about their development path'.[480]

[472] Ibid., 5.
[473] Ibid., 1.
[474] Ibid., 5, 8.
[475] Ibid., 6.
[476] Ibid., 11.
[477] Ibid., 12.
[478] Ibid., 13.
[479] Ibid., 12.
[480] Ibid., 12.

ENVIRONMENTAL, SOCIAL AND ECONOMIC SUSTAINABILITY FRAMEWORK, 2015 Building on the 2012 policy, the 2015 Environmental, Social and Economic Sustainability Framework of the UNEP included a standard that applies whenever Indigenous peoples are or may be present in an area affected by a project supported by UNEP.[481] It provides that when Indigenous peoples may be affected, UNEP and its implementing and/or executing partners will prepare a plan in conjunction with Indigenous peoples, assessing potential socioeconomic impacts and risks, and will apply the principle of FPIC with full consideration given to options preferred by the affected peoples.[482] Further, it provides that when it is impossible to avoid restricting Indigenous peoples' access to legally designated parks and protected areas, UNEP will ensure that the affected Indigenous peoples 'fully and effectively participate' in the design, implementation, monitoring, and evaluation of area management plans.[483]

The purpose of the standard is to ensure that UNEP projects respect Indigenous peoples' rights and take into account their views and needs to avoid any harm and promote opportunities to improve their livelihoods.[484]

4.3.2.5 The UN-REDD Programme Operational Guidance and Guidelines, 2013

The UN Programme on Reducing Emissions from Deforestation and Forest Degradation (UN-REDD Programme) is a joint initiative of FAO, UNDP, and UNEP that supports developing countries on nationally led REDD+ processes.[485] Its 2009 Operational Guidance on Engagement of Indigenous Peoples & Other Forest Dependent Communities, developed in consultation with Indigenous peoples,[486] provides that FPIC 'must be adhered to', as must

481 UNEP, *UNEP Environmental, Social and Economic Sustainability Framework* (UNEP, 2015), Safeguard Standard 5: Indigenous Peoples, 20.

482 Ibid., para. 5.3. On FPIC, see further UNEP, 'UNEP and Indigenous Peoples: A Partnership in Caring for the Environment: Policy Guidance' (UNEP, 2012), 9.

483 UNEP, 'Safeguard Standard 5', para. 5.5.

484 UNEP, 'Safeguard Standard 5', 20.

485 UN Collaborative Programme on Reducing Emissions from Deforestation and Forest Degradation in Developing Countries (UN-REDD Programme), *Framework Document* (UN-REDD Programme, 2008). REDD+ refers to reducing emissions from deforestation and forest degradation and the role of conservation, sustainable management of forests, and enhancement of forest carbon stocks in developing countries.

486 UN-REDD Programme, 'UN-REDD Programme Operational Guidance: Engagement of Indigenous Peoples & Other Forest Dependent Communities' (UN-REDD Programme, 2009), 1.

the full and effective participation of Indigenous peoples in policymaking and decision-making in UN-REDD Programme activities.[487] The Operational Guidance suggests that all this is required under the UNDRIP.[488]

Further, the UN-REDD Programme's 2013 Guidelines on Free, Prior and Informed Consent set out specific requirements for FPIC that correspond to the accepted principles of FPIC in terms of the manner in which consultations are to be carried out, and in terms of an acknowledgement that while consent will not always be required, it will be under certain circumstances.[489] The Guidelines state that FPIC is a 'legal norm under international law' while also acknowledging that it is 'essential to the success of REDD+'.[490] This is evidence of a dual motivation: the fulfilment of the Programme's objectives, as well as a belief that the participation of affected peoples in terms of FPIC is required by law.

4.3.2.6 The UN Development Programme's Social and Environmental Standard on Indigenous Peoples, 2014

Building on its policies highlighted in Chapter 3, and based on recommendations of the UNPFII, the UNDP undertook to revise its policies on engagement with Indigenous peoples. This culminated in 2014, with the approval of the Social and Environmental Standard on Indigenous Peoples. The Standard aims to ensure that projects that may impact Indigenous peoples are designed 'in a spirit of partnership with them, with their full and effective participation' and with the objective of securing their FPIC where their rights, lands, resources, territories, or traditional livelihoods may be affected.[491] It requires that mechanisms be identified and implemented to guarantee their meaningful, effective, and informed participation on all matters throughout the project cycle,[492] and these mechanisms are articulated in a stakeholder engagement plan that is incorporated in project documentation.[493] Further, it requires that 'culturally appropriate consultation' is carried out with the objective of

487 Ibid., paras. 2–3.
488 Ibid., para. 1.
489 UN-REDD Programme, 'Guidelines on Free, Prior and Informed Consent' (UN-REDD Programme, 2013), 18–20 and 24–29. The provisions are substantially similar to those of the World Bank, so are omitted to avoid repetition.
490 Ibid., 8 and 9.
491 UNDP, *Social and Environmental Standards* (UNDP, 2014), Standard 6: Indigenous Peoples, 36.
492 Ibid., 38.
493 UNDP, *Guidance Note: UNDP Social and Environmental Standards, Standard 6: Indigenous Peoples* (UNDP, 2017), 9.

achieving agreement and that FPIC is obtained on any matters affecting them before any project activities are carried out.[494] Consultation and FPIC processes must be culturally appropriate and conducted in good faith, exercised through Indigenous peoples' own governance structures and chosen representatives and in accordance with their own laws and customs for decision-making.[495] It emphasizes that FPIC is required before any relocation of Indigenous peoples may occur.[496] In addition, it requires the development of a plan in accordance with Indigenous peoples' effective and meaningful participation, to avoid, minimize, and mitigate any adverse effects of a project.[497]

Guidance to the Standard notes that it is guided by 'international human rights standards' such as the ICCPR, ICESCR, ILO Convention 169, and the UN Declaration on the Rights of Indigenous Peoples.[498]

4.3.2.7 The World Bank Environmental and Social Standards, 2016

Following on from its earlier policies, the World Bank's 2016 Environmental and Social Framework ("ESF") contains an Environmental and Social Standard ("ESS") on Indigenous Peoples and Sub-Saharan African Historically Underserved Traditional Local Communities.[499] Applicable whenever Indigenous peoples 'are present in, or have collective attachment to a proposed project area',[500] the ESS aims to ensure that Indigenous peoples 'are fully consulted about, and have opportunities to actively participate in, project design and the determination of project implementation arrangements'.[501]

494 Ibid., 38–39. The elements of FPIC are further elaborated in UNDP, *Guidance Note*, 6–7.
495 UNDP, *Guidance note*, 9.
496 UNDP, *Standard* 6, 38.
497 Ibid., 39.
498 UNDP, *Guidance Note*, 3.
499 World Bank, *The World Bank Environmental and Social Framework* (World Bank, 2017), Environmental and Social Standard 7. The category of 'Sub-Saharan African Historically Underserved Traditional Local Communities' reflects the rejection by many African nations of the term "Indigenous peoples" with respect to their countries: Corinne Lewis and Carl Söderbergh, 'The World Bank's New Environmental and Social Framework: Some Progress but Many Gaps Regarding the Rights of Indigenous Peoples' (2019) 23 *International Journal of Human Rights*, 63–86, 69. Here I will continue referring to "Indigenous peoples" for simplicity. On issues with the "historically underserved" terminology, see Lewis and Söderbergh, 69–70.
500 World Bank, *Environmental and Social Framework*, Standard 7, para. 7.
501 Ibid., para. 11.

CONSULTATION TOWARDS THE ESF The ESF was developed in a process involving extensive consultation with governments, international organizations, experts, civil society groups, and Indigenous peoples.[502] The consultation proceeded in three phases. First, the Bank prepared a paper on its approach to the new safeguards and opened it up to public consultation,[503] part of which consisted of sixteen dedicated dialogues with Indigenous peoples.[504] In its second phase, the Bank released a proposal document for consultation and held eight consultation meetings with Indigenous peoples.[505] The third phase involved a three-month consultation on a revised draft of the proposed ESF, which focused on feedback from borrower countries.[506] This process evidences the World Bank's recognition that because Indigenous peoples are especially affected by its activities and the ESF has the potential to better protect their interests, they should participate in the ESF's development. The final decision-making was done by the Development Committee of the World Bank, and the draft was approved by its Board of Executive Directors.[507]

Although this process seems promising on its face, often the notice given for consultations was short, documents were not circulated in sufficient time, translation for local languages and facilities for disabled persons were lacking, and some major Indigenous organizations were not aware of the consultations in their countries.[508] In addition, several important changes to the final ESF were made without the consultation of Indigenous peoples: for instance, the addition of the terminology of 'Sub-Saharan African Historically Underserved Traditional Local Communities'.[509] The structure of the third phase of

502 For an overview of the consultations held with Indigenous peoples, see World Bank, 'World Bank Policies Review and Update, Dialogue with Indigenous Peoples October 2013–March 2014 Summary' (World Bank, 2014) https://consultations.worldbank.org/sites/default/files/data/hub/files/consultation-template/review-and-update-world-bank-safeguard-policies/en/materials/final_summary_dialogue_with_ip_october_2013-march_2014.pdf.

503 World Bank, 'The World Bank's Safeguard Policies Proposed Review and Update: Approach Paper' (10 October 2012).

504 Ruth Houghton, 'Looking at the World Bank's Safeguard Reform through the Lens of Deliberative Democracy' (2019) 32 *Leiden Journal of International Law*, 465–482, 470. See World Bank, 'World Bank Environmental and Social Safeguard Policies Review and Update: Regional Dialogue with Indigenous Peoples, Terms of Reference' (2013) https://consultations.worldbank.org/sites/default/files/data/hub/files/safeguards_review_terms_of_reference_for_ip_regional_dialogue_2013.pdf.

505 Houghton, 'Looking at the World Bank's Safeguard Reform', 470.

506 Ibid., 470.

507 Ibid., 478.

508 Ibid., 475–476.

509 Lewis and Söderbergh, 'Some Progress but Many Gaps', 69–70.

consultation meant that borrower countries had the most input into the final outcome document, and Indigenous peoples were not able to participate to defend their rights at the point where it mattered most.

SUBSTANCE OF THE ESS The ESS requires 'stakeholder analysis and engagement planning, disclosure of information, and meaningful consultation, in a culturally appropriate and gender and inter-generationally inclusive manner'.[510] It also requires that consultation must involve Indigenous peoples' representative bodies and organizations, provide sufficient time for their decision-making processes, and allow for their effective participation in the design of project activities or mitigation measures that could potentially affect them.[511] Free, prior, and informed consent is to be established through good faith negotiation, in a mutually accepted process to be documented by the borrowing country, but does not require unanimity among an affected Indigenous people, rather 'collective support'.[512]

The ESS provides that the 'scope and scale' of consultation and participation will be 'proportionate to the scope and scale of potential project risks and impacts' that may affect Indigenous peoples.[513] Where Indigenous peoples are the sole beneficiaries of a project, it requires the borrower to 'proactively engage' to ensure their ownership and participation throughout the project cycle.[514] Where Indigenous peoples are not the sole beneficiaries, the policy requires 'meaningful consultation'.[515]

The ESS further provides that the borrowing country *must* obtain the FPIC of the affected Indigenous peoples where the project will (a) have adverse impacts on land and natural resources subject to traditional ownership or under customary use or occupation; (b) cause relocation of Indigenous peoples from such land and natural resources; or (c) have significant impacts on Indigenous peoples' cultural heritage that is material to their identity or cultural, ceremonial, or spiritual aspects of their lives.[516]

Read in conjunction, these policies require consent when the impacts on Indigenous peoples would be substantial; in cases of lesser impacts, consultation resulting in 'broad community support' will suffice. While the scope of the situations where consent is required does not precisely correspond to that

[510] Standard 7, para. 23.
[511] Ibid., para. 23. Also see para. 12.
[512] Ibid., paras. 25 and 26. Also see paras. 27 and 28.
[513] Ibid., para. 11.
[514] Ibid., para. 14.
[515] Ibid., para. 16.
[516] Ibid., para. 24.

in the UNDRIP,[517] the broad contours of the law of FPIC are reflected in the World Bank's policies.

4.3.2.8 The Green Climate Fund's Environmental and Social Policy, 2018

The Green Climate Fund (GCF) is an international financial institution established by the UNFCCC COP in 2011 with the objectives of making 'a significant and ambitious contribution' to global efforts to achieve international goals to combat climate change and to promote the shift towards low-emission and climate-resilient development, by providing funding to developing countries to mitigate and adapt to climate change.[518] While it is accountable to, and functions under, the guidance of the UNFCCC COP, it has its own international legal personality.[519] The GCF is governed by a Board of twenty-four members with equal representation from developed and developing countries that makes decisions about the Fund's policies and funding allocation.[520]

The GCF's founding document provides that the Board will develop mechanisms to promote the input and participation of Indigenous peoples, among other stakeholders, to the design, development, and implementation of activities financed by the GCF.[521]

This provision was implemented, firstly, in the 2018 Environmental and Social Policy of the GCF, which provides that, as a guiding principle, all activities it finances will 'support the full and effective participation of indigenous peoples', and the design and implementation of activities will be guided by the UNDRIP including the right to FPIC, which is noted as being 'of particular importance'.[522] Further, the GCF requires that activities are screened for potential impacts on Indigenous peoples, that borrowers facilitate the participation of Indigenous peoples in risk screening and assessment, and

[517] See the associated criticisms in María Victoria Cabrera Ormaza and Franz Christian Ebert, 'The World Bank, Human Rights, and Organizational Legitimacy Strategies: The Case of the 2016 Environmental and Social Framework' (2019) 32 *Leiden Journal of International Law*, 483–500, 492–494; Lewis and Söderbergh, 'Some Progress but Many Gaps', 67, 72–73.

[518] GCF, *Governing Instrument for the Green Climate Fund* (GCF, 2011), paras. 1–3. The Governing Instrument was approved by UNFCCC COP 17 in 2011: see UNFCCC, Decision 3/CP.17, 'Launching the Green Climate Fund' (15 March 2012) UN Doc. FCCC/CP/2011/9/Add.1, 55, Annex.

[519] GCF, *Governing Instrument*, paras. 4, 7, and 8.

[520] Ibid., paras. 5, 9, 14, 16, and 18.

[521] Ibid., para. 71.

[522] GCF, 'Environmental and Social Policy' (2018) Decision B.19/10, GCF Doc. GCF/B.19/06, para. 8(p).

that any plans will be developed with their full and effective participation 'through a process of meaningful consultation tailored to them' and ensuring their FPIC.[523]

Further to this, the GCF's 2018 Indigenous Peoples Policy, developed with the participation of a wide range of Indigenous peoples' organizations,[524] sets out requirements for participation, consultation, and FPIC that are consistent with the UNDRIP. In terms of consultation and participation, the Policy requires the GCF's accredited entities – the third parties that it delivers funds through, which include international financial institutions and UN agencies – with the participation of potentially affected Indigenous peoples, to prepare a consultation strategy and identify how the affected Indigenous peoples will participate in the design and implementation of activities and share in their benefits.[525] When the only beneficiaries of proposed activities are Indigenous peoples, the accredited entities and executing entities (the third parties who carry out projects) are further required to proactively engage with the relevant peoples 'to ensure their ownership, buy-in and participation' in the entire life cycle of the activities.[526] When Indigenous peoples are not the only beneficiaries, their concerns must be addressed through 'meaningful consultation' including a process to seek FPIC.[527] Measures to minimize, mitigate, and compensate for any adverse impacts to Indigenous peoples, as well as to mitigate environmental and social risks and impacts, must also be determined with the full and effective participation of the affected Indigenous peoples.[528] Consultations are required to be proportionate in scope and scale to the potential risks and impacts on Indigenous peoples.[529]

On FPIC, the 2018 Policy requires that GCF will 'ensure and require' evidence of 'the effective consultation and application of free, prior and informed consent' when activities are being considered that would affect Indigenous peoples' lands, territories, resources, livelihoods, and cultures or require their relocation.[530] Although this wording is ambiguous – what does it mean to "apply" FPIC? – a later provision clarifies that the GCF will require

[523] Ibid., para. 47.
[524] GCF, 'GCF Indigenous Peoples Policy' (2018) GCF Doc. GCF/B.19/05, para. 8.
[525] Ibid., para. 37.
[526] Ibid., para. 42.
[527] Ibid., para. 44. "Meaningful consultation" is defined at para. 9(m). See further requirements at paras. 51–53.
[528] Ibid., paras. 46 and 48.
[529] Ibid., para. 36.
[530] Ibid., para. 22(a).

consent.[531] The policy thereby appears to support consent in a wider range of situations than is strictly required by the UNDRIP, going over and above the spectrum-based approach. The policy further requires that consent must be given:[532]

> on the basis of indigenous peoples' own independent deliberations and decision-making process, based on adequate information to be provided in a timely manner, in a culturally appropriate manner, in a local language that is understood by them, and through a process of transparent and inclusive consultations, including with women and youth, and free of coercion or intimidation.

Recognizing that Indigenous peoples may need support to be able to participate, it provides that the Fund will support capacity-building programmes for Indigenous peoples to ensure their full and effective engagement with the GCF.[533]

The GCF's 2018 Policy stated that the organization would establish an Indigenous peoples advisory group 'to enhance coordination' between the GCF, the entities that carry out the projects and programmes it finances, states, and Indigenous peoples.[534] Constituted of one Indigenous peoples' representative from each of the four regions in which the GCF funds activities, selected by Indigenous peoples,[535] the key functions of the advisory group will be to provide advice on GCF-financed activities affecting Indigenous peoples, review the implementation of the 2018 Policy particularly on the appropriate modalities to enhance dialogue between Indigenous peoples and the GCF, and provide such other advice to the Executive Board as may be requested.[536] Further, the policy stated that the Facility would 'support the work of' such a group and ensure that its recommendations were effectively conveyed to the latter entities.[537] In 2022, the Indigenous Peoples Advisory Group was finally established, with its first term running for three years.[538] Time will tell as to whether it provides a means for the full and effective participation of Indigenous peoples in matters concerning them at the GCF.

[531] Ibid., para. 54.
[532] Ibid. The evidence that accredited entities must provide is set out at para. 55.
[533] Ibid., para. 96.
[534] Ibid., para. 81.
[535] Ibid., para. 82.
[536] Ibid., para. 81.
[537] Ibid., para. 29.
[538] GCF, 'Notification on the Indigenous Peoples Advisory Group of the Green Climate Fund' (17 February 2022) GCF Doc. GCF/notif/2022/1.

From the 2018 Policy, it can be inferred that one reason for its adoption was to contribute to the ultimate aims of the UNFCCC as well as the GCF's own mandate. The objectives of the 2018 Policy include promoting Indigenous peoples' positive contributions to climate change mitigation and adaptation and ensuring more effective, sustainable, and equitable climate change results, outcomes, and impacts,[539] objectives that align with those of the GCF and the UNFCCC. However, references to the UNDRIP in the Policy suggest that the latter was also considered necessary to align the GCF's activities with the UNDRIP's requirements.

4.3.3 *Membership on Decision-Making Committees*

Alongside FPIC policies, from 2007 onwards, some development institutions began to institute membership for Indigenous peoples on decision-making bodies. These include the World Bank in respect of its Forest Carbon Partnership Facility, the UN-REDD Programme, and the UN Indigenous Peoples Partnership. The precursor to these was the IFAD's Indigenous Peoples Assistance Facility, discussed in Chapter 3.

4.3.3.1 The World Bank Forest Carbon Partnership Facility, 2007

In December 2007, at UNFCCC COP 13, the World Bank launched the Forest Carbon Partnership Facility (FCPF) to assist its borrowing member states located in sub-tropical and tropical areas in their efforts to achieve emissions reductions from deforestation and forest degradation by providing technical and financial assistance for capacity building, and to pilot a performance-based payment system for emissions reductions from REDD+ activities.[540]

The FCPF's Charter makes express provision for Indigenous peoples' participation, including as a member of the FCPF's main functional organ, albeit not at the same level as member states. One of the FCPF's operating principles is that it shall comply with the World Bank's operational policies and procedures, 'taking into account the need for effective participation of Forest-Dependent Indigenous Peoples and Forest Dwellers in decisions that may affect them, respecting their rights under national law and applicable

539 GCF, 'Indigenous Peoples Policy', para. 11(a).

540 The FCPF's constitution has been revised several times; the most recent version is World Bank, *Charter Establishing The Forest Carbon Partnership Facility* (8 April 2020) ("FCPF Charter"), Article 2.1.

international obligations'.[541] In addition, its Charter provides that representatives of "forest-dependent indigenous peoples and forest dwellers" may be invited by the FCPF to attend its annual meetings as observers, along with representatives of relevant international organizations, NGOs, and private sector entities.[542] The Charter further provides for one seat as a non-voting observer in the Participants Committee,[543] the FCPF's main decision-making body consisting of fourteen donor state and fourteen borrower state representatives.[544]

At the FCPF's launch, the then UNPFII Chair, Victoria Tauli-Corpuz, expressed apprehension, stressing the importance of fully involving Indigenous peoples in designing, implementing, and evaluating REDD-related activities. She called for the FCPF to recognize and respect the UNDRIP, for FPIC to be obtained before any REDD initiative is pursued in their territories, and for Indigenous peoples to be represented in the FCPF's governance structure 'at the same level as governments, donors and the private sector'.[545] Notwithstanding these sentiments, the FCPF proceeded on the above basis.

4.3.3.2 The UN-REDD Programme's Policy Board, 2008–2015

From 2008 to 2015, the UN-REDD Programme was governed by a Policy Board. Four out of thirty-three seats on the Policy Board were reserved for Indigenous peoples, alongside representatives of donor countries, recipient countries, civil society, and UN agencies: one for the UNPFII Chair as a full member along with three observer seats for Indigenous peoples' representatives from the three regions in which the Programme operates.[546]

As of 2017, the governance structure of the Programme has changed so that it is now controlled by an Executive Board coupled with a Programme Assembly. The Executive Board, which is responsible for operational guidance, decision-making, and general oversight, no longer provides for full-member participation of Indigenous representatives: rather, Indigenous

[541] World Bank, *FCPF Charter*, Article 3.1(d).
[542] Ibid., Article 10.1(b).
[543] Ibid., Article 11.7(b).
[544] Ibid., Article 11.
[545] UNPFII, 'Statement on the Announcement of the World Bank Forest Carbon Partnership Facility' (11 December 2007), 1–2.
[546] UN-REDD Programme, *UN-REDD Programme Rules of Procedure and Operational Guidance* (UN-REDD Programme, 2009), para. 1.2.4. For the role of the Policy Board, see UN-REDD Programme, *Policy Board Terms of Reference* (UN-REDD Programme, 2009).

peoples have one seat as a "permanent observer."[547] Indigenous peoples do have representatives on the Programme Assembly, but this is only an advisory forum.[548]

4.3.3.3 The Dedicated Grant Mechanism for Indigenous Peoples and Local Communities, 2011

In 2009, Indigenous peoples' observers attending discussions at the Climate Investment Funds (CIF) regarding the design of the CIF's Forest Investment Program (FIP) called for dedicated resources to increase their capacity to participate in FIP implementation.[549] Following this, the CIF established a working group of Indigenous peoples and local communities, to develop the proposal for such a mechanism.[550] The working group presented its initial design at UNPFII 9, in April 2010, followed by four regional and two global meetings involving Indigenous peoples and local communities' representatives, and government counterparts from the countries in which the proposed mechanism would operate.[551] In 2011, as a result, the Dedicated Grant Mechanism for Indigenous Peoples and Local Communities (DGM) was established, intended to channel US$80 million in funding from the World Bank and other multilateral development banks under the FIP to 'enhance [Indigenous peoples' and local communities'] capacity and support initiatives to strengthen their participation in FIP and other REDD+ processes at the local, national and global levels',[552] in twelve countries in Asia, Latin America, and Africa.[553]

547 UN-REDD Programme, *Terms of Reference* (UN-REDD Programme, 2015), para. 4.2.

548 Ibid., para. 4.1.

549 Dedicated Grant Mechanism for Indigenous Peoples and Local Communities (DGM), 'Annual Report 2016' (DGM, 2016), 2 https://static1.squarespace.com/static/550abd2ce4b0c5557aa4f772/t/588f503a3a0411d31b548828/1485787204551/DGM+Annual+Report_ENG_WEB.pdf.

550 Climate Investment Funds, 'Framework Operational Guidelines' (12 September 2013) 2, https://static1.squarespace.com/static/550abd2ce4b0c5557aa4f772/t/550adcbae4b0178d56b4c7d3/1426775226201/13-09-12DGMGuidelines-website.pdf. The eventual design document is Climate Investment Funds, 'Design for the Dedicated Grant Mechanism for Indigenous Peoples and Local Communities to be Established Under the Forest Investment Program' (29 November 2011) www.climateinvestmentfunds.org/sites/cif_enc/files/meeting-documents/fip_design_proposal_dgm_for_ips_and_lc_final_november2011_0.pdf.

551 Climate Investment Funds, 'Framework Operational Guidelines', 2.

552 Ibid., iii.

553 DGM, 'About the Dedicated Grant Mechanism' (DGM, n.d.) www.dgmglobal.org/background.

The design document developed by the Indigenous peoples and local communities' working group in 2009–2010 emphasized the necessity of the 'full and effective, continuous participation of Indigenous peoples and local communities in the design and implementation of FIP investment strategies', noting this participation would be 'highly depending' on building these groups' capacity to play an informed and active role, as well as on recognizing and supporting their land tenure rights. The group recommended that the DGM should provide grants to Indigenous peoples and local communities to support their participation in the development of FIP investment strategies, programmes, and projects.[554]

The DGM has a complex architecture, including, for each country, a National Executing Agency and a National Steering Committee, as well as an overall Global Executing Agency and a Global Steering Committee.[555] Both Committees are primarily composed of representatives of Indigenous peoples and local communities, 'balanced to the extent possible by geographic area, community/ethnic group/tribe and gender' as decision-making members.[556] The National Steering Committees' membership is defined 'based on national circumstances and broad, participatory dialogues' with Indigenous peoples and local communities, which the Global Steering Committee is made up of one representative of Indigenous peoples and local communities from each project country, as well as representatives of governments and multilateral development banks as non-decision-making members.[557] These committee members are chosen by representatives of Indigenous peoples and local communities, and criteria for their selection include being from an identified group, including an Indigenous people, a forest-dependent community, 'or any other defined group that is dependent on forests for livelihood'; being a representative of an Indigenous peoples' organization (or similar) working on forestry, agriculture, or sustainable development; and being a recognized community leader actively working with communities in the field on issues relevant to the DGM and 'known for non-partisanship and transparency in their work'.[558] As such, official documents stress that Indigenous peoples are not just beneficiaries of the DGM, but 'the *proponents* of the program and the *prime movers* of its design,

554 Climate Investment Funds, 'Framework Operational Guidelines', 2.
555 Ibid., 5.
556 Ibid., 5–6.
557 Ibid., 6.
558 Ibid., 8.

and during implementation they will *preside* over the use of the grant resources'.[559]

The design document says the DGM's operations will include Indigenous peoples' full and effective participation, 'taking note of the [UNDRIP]'.[560] It also framed Indigenous peoples' participation as 'essential for achieving FIP objectives whenever there are indigenous peoples and local communities living in or near the forest'. The DGM states that '[g]reater voice and role for Indigenous Peoples and local communities would make REDD+ more effective in achieving its goals'[561] and would 'lead to better results and better development outcomes in the long term'.[562]

4.3.3.4 The UN Indigenous Peoples Partnership Policy Board, 2011

Launched in 2011 during the 10th meeting of the UNPFII, the UN Indigenous Peoples Partnership (UNIPP) is a multi-donor trust fund, set up by several UN organizations, that mobilizes and manages funding to facilitate the implementation of international standards on Indigenous peoples' rights.[563] Decisions on funding projects as well as strategic direction and governance are made by a ten-member Policy Board composed of equal representation from participating UN organizations and Indigenous peoples' representatives and experts.[564] A 2017 report of the UNIPP states that it was developed to promote Indigenous peoples' rights at the national level by, among other things, providing and supporting consultative and participatory processes and mechanisms 'based on the rights enshrined in Article 41 and 42 of UNDRIP and ILO Convention No. 169',[565] implying that the UNIPP sees its Board structure, in addition to the participatory processes it supports at the national level, as required by law.

559 Climate Investment Funds, 'Program Document for A Dedicated Grants Mechanism for Indigenous Peoples and Local Communities (DGM)' (26 January 2015), Report No. 93666-GLB, 8.

560 Climate Investment Funds, 'Design for the Dedicated Grant Mechanism', 7.

561 See, for example, Climate Investment Funds, 'Program Document', 2.

562 Ibid., 4.

563 UNDP, 'Multi-Partner Trust Fund of the UN Indigenous Peoples' Partnership: Final Programme Narrative Report 2010–2017' (UNDP, 2017), 4–5.

564 Ibid., 5–6.

565 Ibid., 5.

4.3.4 *Advisory Bodies*

4.3.4.1 GEF Indigenous Peoples Advisory Group, 2012

In its 2012 Policy, the GEF established an Indigenous Peoples Advisory Group ("IPAG") with the purpose of enhancing coordination between the Facility and Indigenous peoples.[566] The IPAG was tasked with providing advice to the GEF on the operationalization and reviewing of the 2012 Principles and Guidelines for Engagement with Indigenous Peoples, particularly on the appropriate modalities to enhance dialogue among Indigenous peoples, the GEF, and its partner agencies, and others, modalities for enhancing Indigenous peoples' capacity to engage in GEF projects and processes, resources, and tools that can be used to enhance implementation of the Guidelines, and the identification and strengthening of financial arrangements to support Indigenous peoples' efforts to protect their rights and effectively manage their resources through existing and new projects and programmes.[567]

Membership of the GEF IPAG consists of seven experts serving in their individual capacity: three Indigenous persons chosen from a pool of candidates self-selected by Indigenous peoples, with consideration for geographic balance, one chosen from the GEF NGO Network's Indigenous peoples' representatives, one independent expert, one representative from the GEF partner agencies, and the GEF Indigenous peoples focal point.[568]

A 2017 review of the IPAG found that beyond its original mandate, it had also provided a vehicle for Indigenous peoples' input into the programming strategy for the GEF's sixth cycle and had '[f]ostered the inclusion of an indigenous women's perspective in GEF's gender discussions', as well as contributing to discussions on the GEF's stakeholder engagement policy.[569] However, the review also noted that the IPAG was constrained due to its low capacity and the fact that its business was conducted in English.[570]

566 GEF, 'Principles and Guidelines', para. 45(b).

567 GEF, 'Indigenous Peoples Advisory Group to the GEF: Terms of Reference' (GEF, 2013), paras. 1 and 4.

568 Ibid., para. 10.

569 GEF, 'Review of GEF's Engagement with Indigenous Peoples' (2017) GEF Doc. GEF/ME/C.53/Inf.07, Executive Summary, para. 12, pp. 15–19.

570 Ibid., para. 13.

4.3.4.2 IFAD Indigenous Peoples Advisory Forum, 2013

In addition to its 2009 Policy discussed above, IFAD supports the participation of Indigenous peoples in matters concerning them through its Indigenous Peoples Forum ("the Forum"), a body established through a process that involved Indigenous peoples.[571] Since 2013, IFAD has convened the Indigenous Peoples Forum biennially, alongside meetings of its Governing Council.[572] It is a 'process of dialogue and consultation between representatives of Indigenous peoples, IFAD Staff and Member States' with the objectives of discussing the assessment of IFAD's engagement with Indigenous peoples, consulting on rural development and poverty reduction, and promoting the participation of Indigenous peoples' organizations in IFAD-supported activities at national, regional, and international levels.[573]

Each meeting of the Forum is preceded by a series of regional workshops with Indigenous peoples' representatives.[574] The Forum itself is guided by a steering committee composed of seven Indigenous peoples' representatives from different regions, as well as one representative each from the IPAF, the UNPFII, and the IFAD.[575] The Forum was widely welcomed by Indigenous peoples.[576]

The Forum has its limitations. Although it presents recommendations to the IFAD,[577] how these recommendations are considered and integrated into the Fund's work is not clear. A synthesis is presented to the Governing Council following each meeting of the Forum, but it does not appear that member states engage in any discussion or otherwise acknowledge the

[571] IFAD, 'Event: Workshop Establishing the Indigenous Peoples' Forum' (2011), www.ifad.org/en/web/latest/event/asset/39009688. Note: the workshop produced two documents, but these are not available.

[572] IFAD committed to establishing the Forum in its 2009 Policy on *Engagement with Indigenous Peoples*, 17.

[573] IFAD, 'Indigenous Peoples' Forum' (IFAD, n.d.), www.ifad.org/en/indigenous-peoples-forum; *Engagement with Indigenous Peoples*, 17.

[574] See, for example, IFAD, 'Proceedings of the Second Global Meeting of the Indigenous Peoples' Forum', 8.

[575] IFAD, 'IFAD's progress 2017–2018', 3.

[576] See, for example, IFAD, 'Proceedings of the First Global Meeting of the Indigenous Peoples' Forum at IFAD' (IFAD, 2013), 8.

[577] See, for example, IFAD, 'Fourth global meeting of the Indigenous Peoples' Forum at IFAD: Synthesis of Deliberations' (IFAD, 2019), 2–3; IFAD, 'Proceedings of the Third Global Meeting', 17–18; IFAD, 'Synthesis of Deliberations, Second Global Meeting, Indigenous Peoples Forum at IFAD' (IFAD, 2015), 2–3. IFAD, 'Proceedings of the First Global Meeting', 30–31.

recommendations.[578] At the conclusion of the Forum, a representative of IFAD's management responds to the recommendations and has at past Forums expressed an intention to implement them,[579] but no information is available on how the recommendations are followed up.

4.4 REGIONAL DEVELOPMENTS

It will be recalled from Chapter 3 that, beginning in the early 1990s, various organizations in the Arctic, Latin America and the Caribbean, and Europe had made moves to enable the participation of Indigenous peoples, to greater or lesser degrees, in governance processes affecting them. In the period under consideration in this chapter, some of the forms of participation examined in Chapter 3 continued – the Arctic Council and FILAC chief among these – while others sprang up or evolved from their earlier forms.

4.4.1 *Latin America and the Caribbean: The Andean Community's Consultative Council of the Indigenous Peoples, 2007*

As detailed in the previous chapter, the Andean Community established a Working Group on the Rights of Indigenous Peoples in 2001. Although the Working Group never got off the ground, political enthusiasm for Indigenous peoples' participation persisted at the highest level within the Community. On 26 September 2007, less than a fortnight after the UN General Assembly's adoption of the UNDRIP, the Andean Presidential Council passed the Declaration of Tarija. By this declaration, the Andean heads of state ratified their 'conviction that the participation and contribution of Indigenous peoples within the Andean Community allows the consolidation of democracy and the generation of conditions for the sustainability of development processes and, consequently, for regional integration projects'. They recommended that the Working Group on the Rights of Indigenous Peoples be implemented at the earliest opportunity.[580]

The Andean Council of Foreign Ministers moved quickly to implement this directive. In decision 674, adopted concurrently with the Tarija

578 See, for example, IFAD, 'Governing Council Report: Forty-second Session' (2019) IFAD Doc. GC 42, paras. 188–200; IFAD, 'Governing Council Report: Thirty-Sixth Session' (2013) IFAD Doc. GC 36, paras. 54–55; IFAD, 'Governing Council Report: Thirty-Eighth Session' (2015) IFAD Doc. GC 38, para. 90; IFAD, 'Governing Council Report: Fortieth Session', paras. 77–78.

579 See, for example, IFAD, 'Proceedings of the Third Global Meeting', 19.

580 Declaration of Tarija, XVII Andean Presidential Council (27 September 2007), para. 12.

Declaration, they established the Consultative Council of the Indigenous Peoples of the Andean Community (CCPICAN) 'as a consultative body within the framework of the Andean Integration System, to promote the active participation of indigenous peoples in matters related to subregional integration, in their spheres economic, social, cultural and political'.[581]

The CCPICAN was to primarily consist of one Indigenous delegate from each Andean member country, to be elected from among the highest level directors of the national Indigenous organizations according to procedures and modalities to be defined by each member country.[582] The member countries were each required to define these election procedures by convening the Indigenous peoples' organizations of their respective countries to first agree on the election mechanism and then elect a delegate.[583] The chosen delegate then had to be officially accredited to the Andean Community by the Ministry of Foreign Affairs of the member country.[584] The term of office for Indigenous delegates to the Council was to be one year,[585] and the role of President of the Council would rotate among the Indigenous delegates.[586] Operationally, the Consultative Council was envisaged to take decisions and opinions by consensus.[587]

The Consultative Council's membership was completed by one observer delegate from the FILAC, and one observer delegate each from three major Indigenous organizations of the wider region: the Coordinator of Indigenous Organizations of the Amazon Basin (COICA), the Andean Coordinator of Indigenous Organizations (CAOI), and the Continental Liaison of Indigenous Women of South America.[588] In practice, other national Indigenous organizations frequently attended as observers.[589]

Functionally, the mandate of the CCPICAN was fourfold.[590] First, the Council was mandated to issue opinions to the Andean Council of Foreign Ministers, the Andean Commission, or the General Secretariat of the Andean

[581] Andean Council of Ministers of Foreign Affairs, Decision 674 (26 September 2007), Article 1.
[582] Ibid., Article 2.
[583] Ibid., Article 5.
[584] Ibid., Article 5.
[585] Ibid., Article 5.
[586] Ibid., Article 6.
[587] Ibid., Article 4.
[588] Ibid., Article 2.
[589] See, for example, Andean Community, 'Minutes, 4th Ordinary Meeting of the Consultative Council of the Indigenous Peoples of the Andean Community' (23 February 2010) SG/CCPICAN/IV/ACTA, A.1.3, Annex I. As authorized in CCPICAN, 'Reglamento Interno', Article 23.
[590] Ibid., Article 3.

Community, either at their request or by its own initiative, on matters relating to the participation of Indigenous peoples in the process of subregional integration. Second, the President of the Council or their designate could attend meetings of government experts or working groups related to its activities upon invitation by the Andean member countries.[591] Third, the President of the Council or their designate could participate, with speaking rights, in the meetings of the Andean Council of Ministers of Foreign Affairs and the Andean Commission. Finally, the Council was tasked with promoting the exchange, evaluation, and dissemination of experiences and successful practices, organizational strengthening, and general cooperation between Indigenous peoples or Indigenous peoples' organizations and state entities, human rights organizations, and civil society organizations of the Andean member countries.

By August 2008, all Indigenous delegates to the CCPICAN had been elected.[592] The following month, the Council was installed.[593] The event was described by Indigenous delegates as historic, for it ended 'eight years of efforts' to create a body that represented Indigenous peoples in the Andean system.[594] The CCPICAN adopted its Internal Regulations in November that year.[595] According to those regulations, the CCPICAN's aim was 'to ensure effective participation of indigenous peoples in the subregional integration process, as established by Decision 674, [the UNDRIP], and ILO Convention 169'.[596]

Regular meetings and activities of the CCPICAN ensued. Minutes from its early meetings reveal a busy agenda, filled with meetings with officials of the Andean Community and other regional organizations, participation in

591 Ibid., Article 6 read in conjunction with Article 3.

592 Andean Community, 'Próxima instalación del Consejo Consultivo de Pueblos Indígenas de la CAN' (press release, 21 August 2008), www.comunidadandina.org/Prensa.aspx?id=2462&accion=detalle&cat=NP&title=proxima-instalacion-del-consejo-consultivo-de-pueblos-indigenas-de-la-can.

593 Andean Community, 'En reunión calificada de "histórica," instalan Consejo Consultivo que permitirá participación de pueblos indígenas en proceso andino de integración' (press reléase, 8 September 2008), www.comunidadandina.org/Prensa.aspx?id=2471&accion=detalle&cat=NP&title=en-reunion-calificada-de-historica-instalan-consejo-consultivo-que-permitira-participacion-de-pueblos-indigenas-en-proceso-andino-de-integracion.

594 Ibid.

595 CCPICAN, 'Reglamento Interno del Consejo Consultivo de los Pueblos Indígenas de la Comunidad Andina' (21 November 2008), annexed to Comunidad Andina, 'Acta: Segunda Reunión Presencial del Consejo Consultivo de los Pueblos Indígenas de la Comunidad Andina' (22 November 2008) SG/CCPICAN/II-P/ACTA.

596 Ibid., Article 1.

Andean Community meetings, the planning and execution of workplans,[597] and the planning of a CCPICAN response to the then ongoing free trade negotiations between the Andean Community and the European Union, following concerns about a lack of Indigenous representation and a dearth of attention to human rights in those negotiations.[598] The CCPICAN also proposed an official Andean Community decision recognizing ILO Convention 169 and the UNDRIP.[599]

But it was not long before the CCPICAN found itself embroiled in controversy. Even in early 2009, the CCPICAN secretary had noted a difficult political situation within the Andean Community, including bureaucratic blockages that made it difficult for the CCPICAN to move forward.[600] In June and July 2009, it held extraordinary meetings in response to the Peruvian political crisis – in which the Peruvian government sent in the military in response to Indigenous peoples' protests against oil development in the Amazon – deciding to collect testimonies from the affected Indigenous peoples, write a comprehensive report on the events, and take it to the Andean Community and international human rights bodies.[601] After the report published in February 2010, Peru promptly pushed back, alleging that the CCPICAN had acted outside its powers in publishing the report, a claim the CCPICAN disputed.[602]

Adding to the CCPICAN's difficulties, in the Internal Regulations, agreed in 2008, there had been provision for the creation of an Andean Association of Indigenous Peoples and Intercultural Communities (APICI), intended to support the CCPICAN.[603] The establishment of the APICI was subsequently

[597] See, for example, CCPICAN, 'Minutes, Second Ordinary Meeting, Consultative Council of the Indigenous Peoples of the Andean Community' (25 March 2009) SG/CCPICAN/II/ACTA, 3–4; CCPICAN, 'Minutes, Third Ordinary Meeting, Consultative Council of the Indigenous Peoples of the Andean Community' (28 May 2009) SG/CCPICAN/III/ACTA, 3.

[598] CCPICAN, 'Minutes, First Regular Meeting, Advisory Council of the Indigenous Peoples of the Andean Community' (19 December 2008) AG/CCPICAN/I/ACTA, A.1.3, 4, Agreements and Resolutions, paras. 2–3; CCPICAN, 'Minutes, Second Ordinary Meeting', Agreements and Resolutions, para. 3; CCPICAN, 'Minutes, Third Ordinary Meeting', 3, 6–8.

[599] CCPICAN, 'Minutes, Fourth Extraordinary Meeting, Consultative Council of the Indigenous Peoples of the Andean Community' (20 October 2010) SG/CCPICAN/IV-E/ACTA, Agreements and Resolutions, para. 5.

[600] CAN, 'Minutes, First Extraordinary Meeting, Consultative Council of the Indigenous Peoples of the Andean Community' (23 June 2009) SG/CCPICAN/I-E/ACTA, A.1.3, 5.

[601] CAN, 'Minutes, First Extraordinary Meeting', A.1.3, 2, Agreements and Resolutions, para. 1; CCPICAN, 'Minutes, Second Extraordinary Meeting, Consultative Council of the Indigenous Peoples of the Andean Community' (28 June 2009) SG/CCPICAN/II-E/ACTA.

[602] CAN, 'Minutes, Fourth Ordinary Meeting', Agreements and Resolutions, para. 1.

[603] CCPICAN, 'Reglamento interno', Articles 15 and 16.

discussed at the CCPICAN throughout 2009 and 2010,[604] but various procedural roadblocks meant that the APICI's establishment was delayed until June 2011.[605]

In 2010, the CCPICAN also began to have trouble with governments not granting CCPICAN members the requisite accreditation in time for meetings.[606] One of those affected was the Ecuadorean member. At the time, tensions had arisen between the Correa administration in Ecuador and Indigenous peoples in the country, a matter that the CCPICAN had discussed and communicated with the Ecuadorean government about.[607]

By the time of the Council's ninth ordinary meeting, in December 2012, frustrations were building among its members. At that meeting, the Council pointed out persistent barriers to the full performance of its functions, including a lack of resources meaning the CCPICAN could only meet once a year rather than twice as stipulated in its founding documents, the issue of governments accrediting the elected Indigenous delegates too late in the year, and the lack of a state counterpart to the CCPICAN. There was a feeling, too, that the Andean member states did not pay attention to any of the Council's recommendations. These difficulties, according to the Council, had 'generated a feeling of instability' and meant it could not carry out its mandated role.[608] To solve such issues, it called for the member countries to allocate budget for the participation of Indigenous peoples in policymaking processes across the Andean Community,[609] said that CCPICAN decisions should be binding on the Andean states,[610] and demanded the creation of an Andean Committee of Governmental Authorities on Indigenous Issues, a state

604 CCPICAN, 'Minutes, Second Ordinary Meeting', 5; CCPICAN, 'Minutes, Third Ordinary Meeting', Agreements and Resolutions, para. 5; CCPICAN, 'Minutes, Second Extraordinary Meeting', Agreements and Resolutions, para. 2; CCPICAN, 'Minutes, Fourth Ordinary Meeting', Agreements and Resolutions, para. 1; CCPICAN, 'Minutes, Third Extraordinary Meeting, Consultative Council of the Indigenous Peoples of the Andean Community' (21 April 2010) SG/CCPICAN/III-E/ACTA, 2; CCPICAN, 'Minutes, 'Fifth Ordinary Meeting, Consultative Council of the Indigenous Peoples of the Andean Community' (9 September 2010) SG/CCPICAN/V/ACTA, 2; CCPICAN, 'Minutes, Fourth Extraordinary Meeting', 3.

605 CCPICAN, 'Minutes, Seventh Meeting of the Consultative Council of Indigenous Peoples of the CAN' (21 June 2011) SG/CCPICAN/VII/ACTA, Agreements and Resolutions, para. 4.

606 CCPICAN, 'Minutes, Fourth Extraordinary Meeting', 2; CCPICAN, 'Minutes, Seventh Meeting, 3.

607 CCPICAN, 'Minutes, Fourth Extraordinary Meeting', 5, Agreements and Resolutions, para. 4.

608 CCPICAN, 'Minutes, Ninth Ordinary Meeting of the CCPICAN' (10 December 2012) Doc. SG/CCPICAN/IX/ACTA, Final Agreements, para. 1.

609 Ibid., Declaration, para. 2.

610 Ibid., Final Agreements, para. 1.

counterpart to the CCPICAN through which it was envisioned that Indigenous rights could be strengthened.[611]

The creation of such a governmental committee on Indigenous issues had already been discussed by the Andean Council of Foreign Ministers,[612] and a decision had been drafted. The draft decision envisaged that 'the institutionalization of a body for the coordination of public policies on indigenous peoples will strengthen the dialogue between the government authorities and the [CCPICAN], and will improve the effectiveness of the construction of sub-regional strategies, programs and policies and respect for the promotion and respect of the rights of Indigenous Peoples'.[613] The objective of the Committee of Governmental Authorities would be to advise the Andean Community's bodies and institutions in the development of policies, strategies, and programmes to promote the participation and rights of Indigenous peoples.[614] Made up of representatives of the state entities responsible for Indigenous affairs,[615] it would be mandated to advise and issue opinions and recommendations to Andean Community organs regarding, inter alia, the strengthening participation of Indigenous peoples in the Andean integration process; the implementation and effective application of international legal instruments on the rights of Indigenous peoples; policies, strategies, programmes, and projects to contribute to the integration and cooperation of Indigenous peoples within the Andean Community; and the generation of community norms to ensure the effective fulfilment of Indigenous peoples' rights.[616] The CCPICAN demanded the approval of this decision so as to 'formalize the dialogue between indigenous peoples and the States, with concrete and actionable agreements and obligations'.[617]

Underlying these procedural concerns was persistent social conflict in the region related to development projects on Indigenous territories. Noting common problems across the region regarding extractive industries and the persecution of Indigenous leaders, the Council decided to carry out its own documentation and analysis as to how the right of FPIC was being

[611] Ibid., para. 1.
[612] See also CAN, 'Report, First Intergovernmental Meeting of Competent National Authorities in Matters of Indigenous Peoples of the Andean Community' (13 December 2011) SG/RI. ANPI/I/INFORME.
[613] Draft Decision on Andean Committee of Government Authorities on the Rights of Indigenous Peoples, 16 January 2012, Doc. SG/dt 454, preamble, fourth recital.
[614] Ibid., Article 2.
[615] Ibid., Article 3.
[616] Ibid., Article 5(b), (e), (f), and (h).
[617] CCPICAN, 'Minutes, Ninth Ordinary Meeting', Final Agreements, para. 1.

implemented in the Andean region, envisaged to be a precursor to an eventual Andean Community decision that would standardize FPIC laws throughout the region.[618]

At first, it seemed as if the CCPICAN's strong statement of December 2012 would result in change. In May 2013, the CCPICAN had a joint meeting with Andean Community government authorities on the rights of Indigenous peoples, which resulted in agreements to negotiate a decision on the rights of Indigenous peoples in the Andean Community, based on ILO 169 and UNDRIP, to strengthen the CCPICAN's budget, to investigate how to increase the CCPICAN's participation in the Andean Community, and to hold regular meetings between the CCPICAN and government authorities responsible for Indigenous peoples' rights, among other decisions.[619]

But after that, the workings of the CCPICAN broke down, and none of these decisions appear to have been implemented. As of 2022, it has not held a meeting since December 2012. Representatives of the Bodies and Institutions of the Andean Integration System in 2019 called for the CCPICAN's immediate reactivation.[620] In March 2022, the long-awaited Andean Committee of Government Authorities on the Rights of Indigenous Peoples was finally established by the Andean Council of Ministers of Foreign Affairs.[621] As of mid-2022, it is unclear whether this heralds a return to the CCPICAN's functioning.

4.4.2 *The Arctic*

4.4.2.1 Evolutions in Indigenous Peoples' Participation in the Barents Regional Cooperation

AN INCREASED ROLE OF INDIGENOUS PEOPLES IN BARENTS COOPERATION In the post-2007 period, the level of Indigenous peoples' participation in the Barents cooperation has further evolved in response to Indigenous peoples' demands. Since 2010, the Barents Indigenous Peoples

[618] Ibid., Final Agreements, para. 3.

[619] CAN, 'Minutes, Second Joint Meeting of Government Authorities on the Rights of Indigenous Peoples and the Advisory Council of Indigenous Peoples of the Andean Community' (14 May 2013) SG/DPI.CCPICAN/II/ACTA, 1–3.

[620] Ministerio de Relaciones Exteriores de Bolivia, 'IV Reunión de representantes de órganos e instituciones del Sistema Andino de Integración' (4 October 2019) https://cancilleria.gob.bo/webmre/node/3662.

[621] Andean Council of Ministers of Foreign Affairs, 'Decision 896: Andean Committee of Government Authorities on the Rights of Indigenous Peoples' (25 March 2022).

Congress, hosted by the Working Group of Indigenous Peoples, has advocated for Indigenous peoples to have a greater role in the Barents cooperation. The declaration of the first Barents Indigenous Peoples Congress, in its preamble, recalled the establishment of the UNPFII and EMRIP, welcomed the adoption of the UNDRIP, and noted Indigenous peoples' Permanent Participant status in the Arctic Council.[622] Arguing that the Permanent Forum and the Expert Mechanism constitute affirmations that Indigenous peoples should be allowed to participate as peoples in international affairs, that the UNDRIP and the Nordic Saami Convention affirm these participatory rights in international affairs, and that the participatory role in the Arctic Council is a further reflection of this right, the preamble asserted that greater participation of Indigenous peoples in the Barents Euro-Arctic Council (BEAC) and Barents Regional Council (BRC) would 'greatly contribute' to their work.[623]

In its operative provisions, the Declaration asserted that the Nenets, Saami, and Vepsian peoples, by virtue of the right to self-determination, have 'the right to represent themselves in international affairs, which includes participatory rights in international bodies that address issues of relevance to them'.[624] At the very least, the Declaration said, this right amounts to the level of participation that Indigenous peoples have as Permanent Participants to the Arctic Council.[625] The Declaration proposed that such status should be given to Indigenous peoples relative to the BEAC and BRC, so that the Nenets, Saami, and Vepsian peoples represented by individuals chosen by them, rather than just the Chair of the Working Group of Indigenous Peoples, would be entitled to full and active participation in all meetings and activities of the BEAC and BRC including 'ample time for right to speak' at each meeting.[626]

Subsequently to this demand, the Barents Committee of Senior Officials (CSO) and BRC informally decided to allow all three Indigenous peoples to participate in their meetings directly, in addition to the Chair of the Working Group.[627] This gives the Indigenous peoples de facto largely the same level of participation in relation to the Barents regional cooperation as in relation to

[622] Barents Indigenous Peoples Congress, 'Declaration of the First Barents Indigenous Peoples Congress' (2010), third, fourth, sixth, and ninth recitals.

[623] Ibid., fifth, eighth, tenth, and twelfth recitals.

[624] Ibid., para. 2.

[625] Ibid., para. 3.

[626] Ibid., para. 4.

[627] BRC, 'Minutes, Kajaani' (BRC, 11 November 2010), pp. 10 and 18. See also Barents Regional Council, 'Barents Regional Committee, Terms of Reference' (14 November 2012), Articles 7 and 8; Barents Regional Council, 'Joint Statement of the Barents Regional Council on the Occasion of the 20th Anniversary of BEAC' (3 June 2013), para. 8.

the Arctic Council, albeit without formally bestowing upon them the title of Permanent Participant. Another improvement was made in 2013 when the BEAC invited the Chair of the Working Group as a 'permanent observer' to the BEAC.[628]

ACCEPTANCE AS A REQUIREMENT OF LAW Subsequently to the passage of the UNDRIP, in addition, Barents regional states have expressed the view that Indigenous peoples' participation in the Barents regional cooperation is required by law. In 2013, on the 20th anniversary of the Kirkenes Declaration, ministers recognized that 'indigenous peoples have the right to determine and develop priorities and strategies for their own development' as well as 'the right to participate in decision-making in matters that would affect their rights'.[629] That same year, the BEAC reaffirmed the Barents member states' commitment 'to fulfil their obligations regarding the rights of indigenous peoples, including their right to be consulted and to participate in decision-making at all levels through representatives chosen by themselves'.[630] In 2015, the BEAC again reinforced this commitment to 'protect and promote the rights of indigenous peoples and to fulfil their obligations in this regard, including by ensuring indigenous peoples' effective participation, through their own representative institutions, in decision-making at all levels on issues affecting them'.[631] In this connection, the participation of the Working Group on Indigenous Peoples at all levels of Barents cooperation was described as a right.[632] These rights-based commitments were again reaffirmed in 2017 and 2019.[633]

4.4.2.2 The Central Arctic Ocean Fisheries Agreement, 2018

Alongside the Barents regional cooperation and the Arctic Council, Indigenous peoples found their way into negotiations on Arctic fisheries in the 2010s. The roots of this involvement went back to at least 2008.

628 Barents Euro-Arctic Council, 'Joint Communique, 14th Session of the Barents Euro-Arctic Council, Tromso' (29 October 2013), para. 26.

629 Barents Euro-Arctic Council, 'Declaration on the 20th Anniversary of the Barents Euro-Arctic Cooperation, Kirkenes, Norway' (3–4 June 2013), 3.

630 Barents Euro-Arctic Council, 'Joint Communique, 14th Session', para. 25.

631 Barents Euro-Arctic Council, 'XV Session of the Barents Euro-Arctic Council, Joint Communique, Oulu' (15 October 2015), para. 24.

632 Ibid., para. 25.

633 Barents Euro-Arctic Council, 'XVI Session of the Barents Euro-Arctic Council, Joint Declaration, Arkhangelsk' (18–19 October 2017), para. 28; Resolution, 8th Barents Parliamentary Conference, Naryan-Mar (8 June 2017), 4; Umeä Declaration (3 October 2019), 1.

BACKGROUND TO INDIGENOUS PEOPLES' INVOLVEMENT IN NEGOTIATIONS In 2008, the Ilulissat Declaration was adopted by the five Arctic coastal states – the United States, Canada, Denmark (Greenland), Norway, and Russia. In that declaration, the five states recognized that the Arctic Ocean was a 'unique ecosystem' that the coastal states 'have a stewardship role in protecting'. It noted how shipping disasters and subsequent pollution of the marine environment may cause irreversible disturbance of the ecological balance and 'major harm to the livelihoods of local inhabitants and Indigenous communities'.[634]

Indigenous peoples were not included in the discussions leading to the Ilulissat Declaration, except for representatives of Greenland on the Danish delegation.[635] Nor did the Declaration reference instruments on Indigenous peoples' rights such as the UNDRIP. In response to these perceived shortcomings, in 2009 the Inuit Circumpolar Council adopted the Circumpolar Inuit Declaration on Sovereignty in the Arctic.[636] Among other things, the Circumpolar Inuit Declaration stressed the Inuit right to self-determination and other rights under the UNDRIP,[637] stated that Indigenous peoples' right to representation in intergovernmental matters is increasingly recognized,[638] and drew attention to the practical advantages to states of conducting Arctic international relations in partnership with Inuit, including the unique Inuit knowledge of Arctic ecosystems and the need for appropriate emphasis on sustainability in the weighing of resource development proposals.[639] The Declaration called for states to accept the role of Inuit as partners in the conduct of international relations in the Arctic, for reasons of sovereign rights and self-determination, and that 'Inuit consent, expertise and perspectives are critical to progress' on international issues involving the Arctic.[640] As such, the Declaration said, inclusion of Inuit would 'benefit both the Inuit community and the international community'.[641] As a follow-up to the Circumpolar Inuit Declaration, in 2014 the Inuit Circumpolar Conference adopted the

[634] Canada, Denmark, Norway, the Russian Federation, and the United States of America, Ilulissat Declaration (adopted 28 May 2008, Ilulissat, Greenland).

[635] Klaus Dodds, "Real interest'? Understanding the 2018 Agreement to Prevent Unregulated High Seas Fisheries in the Central Arctic Ocean' (2019) 10 *Global Policy*, 542–553, 549.

[636] Inuit Circumpolar Council, 'A Circumpolar Inuit Declaration on Sovereignty in the Arctic' (April 2009), https://iccalaska.org/wp-icc/wp-content/uploads/2016/01/Signed-Inuit-Sovereignty-Declaration-11x17.pdf.

[637] Ibid., para. 1.4.

[638] Ibid., para. 2.4.

[639] Ibid., para. 3.4.

[640] Ibid., paras. 3.3 and 3.5.

[641] Ibid., para. 3.6.

Kitigaaryuit Declaration, which among other things called for Inuit to be included in any commissions, committees, and councils addressing Arctic fisheries.[642]

NEGOTIATIONS TOWARDS THE CENTRAL ARCTIC OCEAN FISHERIES AGREEMENT Partly because of these Inuit declarations, when it came time to begin negotiations towards an agreement on Central Arctic fisheries, the United States, Canada, and Denmark all included representatives of Indigenous peoples on their delegations.[643] The motivation for such fisheries negotiations stemmed from the fact that melting of Arctic sea ice due to climate change means that increasing areas of the Arctic Ocean will be accessible to fishing vessels. The Central Arctic Ocean Fisheries Agreement (CAOFA), signed in 2018, was designed to respond to this material environmental change, with the objective of preventing commercial fishing from occurring at least until better scientific knowledge about the ecosystem can be gained.[644] Following the adoption of a non-binding declaration in July 2015 that established an interim ban on commercial fishing in the Central Arctic Ocean until a sound scientific basis and management regime could be put in place,[645] negotiations towards an agreement began in December 2015, and an agreement in principle was reached in November 2017. The Inuit Circumpolar Council was represented throughout, from the July 2015 discussions onwards.[646] At the first negotiation meeting in December 2015, states

642 Inuit Circumpolar Council, 'Kitigaaryuit Declaration' (24 July 2014), https://iccalaska.org/wp-icc/wp-content/uploads/2016/01/2014-Kitigaarguit-Declaration-Final-Signed.pdf.

643 Dodds, 'Real Interest', 549; Valentin Schatz, 'The Incorporation of Indigenous and Local Knowledge into Central Arctic Ocean Fisheries Management' (2019) 10 *Arctic Review on Law and Politics*, 130–134, 132; Fisheries and Oceans Canada, 'International Agreement to Prevent Unregulated High Seas Fisheries in the Central Arctic Ocean' (15 May 2019) www.dfo-mpo.gc.ca/international/arctic-arctique-eng.htm#_About_the_agreement.

644 Agreement to Prevent Unregulated High Seas Fisheries in the Central Arctic Ocean (signed 3 October 2018, not yet entered into force) OJ L 73, 3 March 2019, pp. 3–8, Article 2. On the Agreement generally, see Alexander N. Vylegzhanin, Oran R. Young, and Paul Arthur Berkman, 'The Central Arctic Ocean Fisheries Agreement as an Element in the Evolving Arctic Ocean Governance Complex' (2020) 118 *Marine Policy* 104001.

645 Canada, Denmark, Norway, the Russian Federation, and the United States of America, 'Declaration Concerning the Prevention of Unregulated High Seas Fishing in the Central Arctic Ocean' (Oslo, 16 July 2015).

646 Inuit Circumpolar Council (ICC), 'ICC Applauds Adoption of Central Arctic Ocean Fishing Moratorium' (17 July 2015) www.inuitcircumpolar.com/press-releases/icc-applauds-adoption-of-central-arctic-ocean-fishing-moratorium/; Fisheries and Oceans Canada, 'International Agreement to Prevent Unregulated High Seas Fisheries'; ICC, 'ICC Canada Applauds Canada's Recognition of the Value of Indigenous Knowledge and Encourages its Use in Climate and Fisheries Discussions' (3 December 2015) www.inuitcircumpolar.com/press-

recognized 'the interests of Arctic residents, particularly Arctic Indigenous peoples, in this topic and expressed the intention to continue to engage with them'.[647]

ONGOING PARTICIPATION OF INDIGENOUS PEOPLES IN IMPLEMENTING THE AGREEMENT The CAOFA established a moratorium on commercial fishing in the international waters of the Central Arctic Ocean for 16 years, with automatic renewals of five years unless a party to the Agreement formally objects or science-based fisheries quotas and/or rules are established.[648] It set up a Joint Program for Scientific Research and Monitoring, to improve the parties' understanding of Central Arctic Ocean ecosystems and to monitor fish stock levels with a view to determining whether fish stocks exist that could be harvested on a sustainable basis.[649]

The ongoing participation of Arctic Indigenous peoples was provided for in the Agreement. The preamble of the CAOFA recalled the UNDRIP.[650] It recognized 'the interests of Arctic residents, including Arctic indigenous peoples, in the long-term conservation and sustainable use of living marine resources and in healthy marine ecosystems in the Arctic Ocean' and underlined 'the importance of involving them and their communities'.[651] In the operative part of the Agreement, Article 5(2) provided that in the implementation of the CAOFA the states parties may form committees 'in which representatives of Arctic communities, including Arctic indigenous peoples, may participate', including with respect to the Joint Program of Scientific Research and Monitoring. According to the Canadian government, Indigenous peoples 'will continue to play an integral role in the implementation of this Agreement and their traditional knowledge will be an important source of information moving forward'.[652]

releases/icc-canada-applauds-canadas-recognition-of-the-value-of-indigenous-knowledge-and-encourages-its-use-in-climate-and-fisheries-discussions/.

[647] U.S. Department of State, 'Meeting on High Seas Fisheries in the Central Arctic Ocean' (1 December 2015) www.state.gov/remarks-and-releases-bureau-of-oceans-and-international-environmental-and-scientific-affairs/meeting-on-high-seas-fisheries-in-the-central-arctic-ocean/.

[648] Agreement to Prevent Unregulated High Seas Fisheries in the Central Arctic Ocean, Articles 3 and 13.

[649] Ibid., Article 4.

[650] Ibid., preamble, recital 10.

[651] Ibid., preamble, recital 11.

[652] Fisheries and Oceans Canada, 'Canada Signs International Agreement to Prevent Unregulated Fishing in the High Seas of the Central Arctic Ocean' (3 October 2018) www.canada.ca/en/fisheries-oceans/news/2018/10/canada-signs-international-agreement-to-prevent-unregulated-fishing-in-the-high-seas-of-the-central-arctic-ocean.html.

In this connection, the CAOFA also stressed the importance of Indigenous knowledge. The preamble notes a desire 'to promote the use of both scientific knowledge and indigenous and local knowledge' of the Arctic Ocean ecosystems as a basis for fisheries conservation and management.[653] Under Article 4 (4), the parties are obliged to ensure that the Joint Program of Scientific Research and Monitoring takes Indigenous and local knowledge into account alongside the work of relevant scientific and technical organizations, bodies, and programs. The parties, in their biennial meetings, are obliged to review 'all available scientific information' including that from Indigenous and local knowledge.[654]

4.4.3 *The European Union*

4.4.3.1 EU Arctic Dialogue Meetings

In the 1990s and early 2000s, institutions of the European Union had begun to develop policies and procedures on Indigenous peoples' participation in development cooperation.[655] Starting in 2010, the EU began to hold Arctic Dialogue meetings, annual meetings between EU officials and representatives of Arctic Indigenous peoples. The Arctic Dialogues have been criticized as lacking 'discussion on concrete problems, concerns and current EU policy developments', and having a format more akin to a conference session than a direct exchange.[656]

4.4.3.2 The European Council Conclusions on Indigenous Peoples, 2017

In the 2015–2019 EU Action Plan on Human Rights and Democracy, the European Council further undertook to develop its policy in line with the UNDRIP and the WCIP Outcome Document.[657] In response to this, a joint staff working document in 2016 laid out recommendations for EU

653 Agreement to Prevent Unregulated High Seas Fisheries in the Central Arctic Ocean, preamble, recital 12.

654 Ibid., Article 5(1)(b).

655 See Chapter 3.

656 European Commission, 'Overview of EU Actions in the Arctic and Their Impact, Final Report' (European Commission, June 2021), 35 https://eprd.pl/wp-content/uploads/2021/06/EU-Policy-Arctic-Impact-Overview-Final-Report.pdf.

657 Council of the European Union, 'Council Conclusions on the Action Plan on Human Rights and Democracy 2015–2019' (20 July 2015) 10897/15, 15.

institutions.[658] The process of preparing the joint staff working document included two consultations with Indigenous peoples' representatives – one held on the sidelines of the UNPFII's annual session – in which Indigenous peoples stressed the importance of a sustained dialogue with the EU, and the need to set up a forum at the highest level 'with a mandate to engage in policy dialogue and oversee the implementation of the EU policy, commitments and action plan on indigenous peoples'.[659] Stressing UNDRIP provisions including the right to FPIC,[660] the working document recommends conducting regular high-level EU-Indigenous Peoples dialogues 'to inform and underpin EU external action policy and its implementation on matters affecting indigenous peoples worldwide' and ensuring the participation of Indigenous peoples' representative organizations in the Policy Forum on Development, the EU's multi-stakeholder space for dialogue on development policies.[661]

Following on from this, in the 2017 Council Conclusions, among other things:[662]

> The Council underscores the crucial importance of further enhancing opportunities for dialogue and consultation with indigenous peoples at all levels of EU cooperation, including in EU funded programmes and projects under all aid modalities to secure their full participation and their free, prior and informed consent in a meaningful and systematic way, and to inform and underpin EU external action policy and its implementation worldwide. Further dialogues are important for ensuring that the EU's commitments to the UNDRIP as well as the Outcome document of the 2014 World Conference on Indigenous Peoples are taken into account also in evolving EU policy commitments and their implementation . . .

Part of the 2017 Conclusions suggests that the Council sees participation and FPIC as required by the EU's commitments to the UNDRIP and under the 2014 WCIP Outcome Document.[663] The Commission has also stated that 'building partnerships with indigenous peoples is essential to fulfil the

[658] European Commission, 'Joint Staff Working Document: Implementing EU External Policy on Indigenous Peoples' (17 October 2016) SWD(2016) 340 final.
[659] Ibid., 11.
[660] Ibid., 4–5.
[661] Ibid., 17–18.
[662] 'Council Conclusions on Indigenous Peoples' (15 May 2017), Doc. 8814/17, para. 8.
[663] Ibid., para. 2 ('The Council recalls the EU's support for adoption of the [UNDRIP] . . . and the [WCIP Outcome Document]'), para. 8. See also European Commission, 'Joint Staff Working Document', 5, 8–9 and 17–18.

objectives of poverty elimination, sustainable development, and the strengthening of respect for human rights and democracy'.[664]

In 2018, a European Parliament resolution on the violation of Indigenous peoples' rights followed up by calling for the establishment of mechanisms, at EU level, for the consultation and participation of Indigenous peoples 'with a mandate to engage in policy dialogue and monitor the implementation of EU policy, commitments and action plans relating to indigenous peoples'.[665] However, such a mechanism has not yet been established.

664 European Commission, 'Review of Progress of Working with Indigenous Peoples', 3.

665 European Parliament resolution of 3 July 2018 on violation of the rights of Indigenous peoples in the world, including land grabbing (2017/2206(INI)), para. 18.

5

Conclusion

New Epoch, Old Stones

Although the new 'epoch' foreseen by Zitkala-Ša in 1919 did not materialize during her lifetime, in that Indigenous peoples were not included among those peoples recognized by states as possessing a right to self-determination, nowadays the right of Indigenous peoples to self-determination is well established. And far from the 'stones' Deskaheh anticipated in 1923 would lie in his path to seek Haudenosaunee membership of the League of Nations in Geneva, over the intervening years, that path – towards Indigenous membership of the international community – has become well trodden. It has widened into a broad road, such that a modern-day counterpart of Deskaheh can expect to be granted a voice in many international fora. Yet, as we have seen, some stones – or barriers – remain. Let us first synthesize the content of this new epoch, at least as far as participation is concerned, before turning to consider questions arising from the remaining stones.

5.1 NEW EPOCH: A RULE OF LAW?

Spurred by sustained advocacy from the global Indigenous movement over the course of several decades, states and international organizations have established a wide-ranging practice of enabling the participation of Indigenous peoples in international law-making, policymaking, and decision-making on issues affecting them. A raft of policies and practices have existed, and currently exist, across many UN agencies and organs, regional organizations, treaty bodies, and even treaty-making processes. Negotiations and discussions towards granting Indigenous peoples enhanced participation are underway in other spaces, like the UN General Assembly and Human Rights Council. A large number and variety of states have been involved in actively pushing for these mechanisms, and even more have passively supported them – including many states that have Indigenous peoples within their borders. A small minority have opposed the creation or enhancement of mechanisms, while some, especially states in Asia and Africa, hold the position that no Indigenous peoples exist within their borders – with the implication that they perceive these mechanisms as not affecting them.

Returning to our tripartite customary international law framework discussed in Chapter 2, let us assess what this means. First, under a practice-oriented approach, this large amount of consistent practice by a representative, substantial (albeit not universal) proportion of states could lead us to the conclusion that a rule of custom exists. Here the difficulty lies in establishing the temporal nexus, the "big bang" moment, at which a rule of custom came into existence. Second, under an *opinio*-oriented approach, we might regard Articles 18, 19, and 41 of the UNDRIP as establishing a rule of custom, the content of which has further evolved and become substantiated through subsequent practice. However, this approach raises difficult questions around the proper interpretation of the substantial amount of state practice subsequent to the adoption of the UNDRIP. Third, under a two-element approach, we saw in Chapters 3 and 4 how the UNDRIP, though not customary law in itself, was itself the result of state practice, catalysed further practice, and has been a normative touchstone for the development of *opinio juris*. If we read as *opinio juris* the way that states reference the UNDRIP, particularly Articles 18, 19, and 41, in the course of justifying, supporting, or arguing for the participation of Indigenous peoples in an international governance process,[1] it is arguable that a rule of custom exists, or is at least emerging. We have seen that such sentiments have been expressed, at least, by Australia, Bolivia, Canada, Denmark, the European Union, Finland, Iceland, Israel, Mexico, New Zealand, Norway, Sweden, Turkey, and the United Kingdom. In addition, officials of UNESCO, WIPO, IFAD, FAO, UNEP, UNDP, the UN-REDD Programme, the Convention on Biological Diversity, and the Climate Investment Funds have expressed opinions to this effect. Hence under any of these approaches to the establishment of custom, it is arguable that a rule exists or is at least well into its emergence.

5.1.1 *Scope and Content of the Rule*

Let us summarize the observations of the preceding chapters, in order to outline the scope and content of the rule.

[1] The argument for this approach was made in Chapter 2.

We have seen that the meaning of "participation" varies across a spectrum: at one extreme lies Indigenous peoples' exclusive control over decision-making; close by lies co-governance or power-sharing with states; while at the other extreme Indigenous peoples might be invited to consultations, have one seat or a small minority of seats on a decision-making committee, or make up an advisory body to the decision-maker. At the former end of the spectrum are the WGIP and WGDD processes, in which states and Indigenous peoples took part on a substantially equal basis; the UNPFII, made up of experts nominated in equal proportions by states and Indigenous peoples; the EMRIP, solely consisting of experts appointed by Indigenous peoples; the World Conference on Indigenous Peoples; FILAC, where decisions are made on the basis of a majority of both Indigenous peoples and state representatives; and the IFAD Indigenous Peoples Assistance Facility; the CIF Dedicated Grant Mechanism for Indigenous Peoples and Local Communities; the UN Indigenous Peoples Partnership Policy Board; and the process of drafting the Nordic Saami Convention. In these processes, the content or implementation of the rights of Indigenous peoples are explicitly at issue. Also at the high-participation end of the spectrum lie the Arctic Council; the Barents regional cooperation; the UNFCCC Local Communities and Indigenous Peoples' Platform; the Working Group on Article 8(j) under the Convention on Biological Diversity; and the IUCN, which has a membership category for Indigenous peoples, who are granted the same procedural rights as states.

In all these processes, Indigenous peoples' organizations are permitted to attend sessions alongside states. They can make oral or written interventions, as well as draft proposals, and participate in contact groups and smaller informal groups. They are appointed as co-chairs, and as rapporteurs for drafting groups. Where the body is made up of a limited number of experts or decision-makers, Indigenous peoples nominate at least half of its composition and in some cases constitute it entirely.

In the middle of the spectrum lie the development organizations and international financial institutions that make decisions about funding projects and programmes that affect Indigenous peoples. The World Bank, UNDP, European Commission, IFAD, FAO, GEF, UNEP, UN-REDD Programme, and GCF have all passed policies for consultation with Indigenous peoples on policies and activities affecting them, as well as ensuring their free, prior, and informed consent in certain circumstances. Similarly, UNESCO has a policy to ensure Indigenous peoples' full and effective participation in matters affecting their lives and cultures.

At the other end of the spectrum lies, for instance, Indigenous peoples' participation in the FAO Committee on Food Security as one constituency of several that are deemed specially affected, and Indigenous peoples' minority share of seats on the boards of the UN-REDD Programme and the World Bank's Forest Carbon Partnership Facility. Here we can also situate Indigenous advisory boards with no formal decision-making authority, such as the Andean Community's Working Group on the Rights of Indigenous Peoples (later the Consultative Council of the Indigenous Peoples of the Andean Community); the GEF Indigenous Peoples Advisory Group; and the IFAD Indigenous Peoples Advisory Forum. These practices typically take place in organizations the activities of which affect a wide range of stakeholders, not only or primarily Indigenous peoples.

In this way, I propose that an augmented version of the "contextual-participation" approach advocated by Claire Charters plays out in practice.[2] Under Charters' approach, Indigenous peoples' participation 'should be substantial where the issue being negotiated at the international level is of considerable interest to indigenous peoples and indigenous peoples have not consented to state representation'.[3] As to the first criterion, in the processes that see higher levels of participation, the level of interest in Indigenous peoples is generally higher: the rights of Indigenous peoples are the immediate topic of discussion; decisions are being made about funding allocations to Indigenous groups; or the regional or environmental governance processes closely concern Indigenous peoples' rights. At the middle and lower ends of the spectrum lie organizations the operations of which affect Indigenous peoples to a lesser (though still important) extent. As to the second criterion, we can assume that in none of the cases studied Indigenous participants have consented to state representation (other than where we have seen states include Indigenous peoples' representatives in government delegations) by virtue of the mere fact that they find it necessary to participate separately. We may add one final criterion: the extent to which the international governance process affects other stakeholders in addition to Indigenous peoples.

Across these spectrums, we have seen that in no case have "Indigenous peoples" needed to be defined in order for mechanisms enabling their participation to effectively function. The Martinez-Cobo definition de facto remains influential, but a constructive, pragmatic approach has been followed across the board. We have also not seen any requirement for participating Indigenous peoples' organizations to demonstrate that they are representative;

2 Claire Charters, 'A Self-Determination Approach to Justifying Indigenous Peoples' Participation in International Law and Policy Making' (2010) 17 *International Journal of Minority & Group Rights*, 215–240.

3 Ibid., 240.

in this regard, if only 'indigenous peoples' representative institutions' are permitted to participate at the General Assembly, this would be out of step with past practice. Likewise, state recognition or approval of specific Indigenous peoples' organizations has not, as a rule, been required in order for those organizations to participate.[4] Indigenous peoples have chosen their delegates by themselves, in accordance with their own procedures. The accreditation of Indigenous participants, where relevant, has generally been carried out by secretariat or international organization staff, rather than states.

We have seen that limitations exist. Even at the high-participation end of the spectrum, Indigenous peoples' level of power over outcomes is observed to be ultimately limited by the state-centric structure of the international system. The text of the UNDRIP ultimately fell to be approved in the General Assembly, where Indigenous peoples are not as yet permitted to take part in votes; the Permanent Participant status in the Arctic Council does not extend to voting rights. In the WIPO IGC, Indigenous peoples' textual proposals need to be supported by at least one member state before they can be incorporated in a draft text. At a more basic level, it is still not the automatic default that Indigenous peoples will be included in an international organization or other process from the outset; most often, Indigenous peoples must struggle to be let in. The underlying colonial, state-centric structure of the international community therefore persists.

Relatedly, a second observed limitation regards the material scope of governance. Some of the participation mechanisms are ultimately limited – in terms of the material power they offer Indigenous peoples – not by the level of participation but by the scope of the mandate of the international organization or body. Where the level of participation is high and Indigenous peoples have majority control over outcomes, or work in equal partnership with states, often the stakes are limited. The FILAC, CIF DGM, and IFAD IPAF are limited by the relatively small amounts of funding they disburse. The Article 8 (j) Working Group can only provide advice on *inter alia* the implementation of Article 8(j) and has no mandate regarding other aspects of the Convention on Biological Diversity – as we saw with the negotiations towards the Nagoya Protocol. The Local Communities and Indigenous Peoples Platform under the UNFCCC effectively siloes Indigenous peoples' participation away from the rest of the Convention processes, under a mandate relating to exchanging

[4] In the Working Group on the Draft Declaration, Indigenous peoples' organizations had to apply to the Coordinator of the International Decade of the World's Indigenous People, who was then required to consult with any state concerned; but even then, the state did not have a deciding say (see further Chapter 3).

experiences on traditional knowledge, the capacity building of Indigenous peoples and local communities, and facilitating the integration of traditional knowledge in designing international and national climate action; the scope for Indigenous peoples to input into the rest of the UNFCCC via the LCIPP is limited. In the IUCN, Indigenous peoples have a distinct class of full membership, alongside states, but the IUCN is not a formal international organization, and while in some sense influential, it holds limited power. Conversely, when the stakes in decision-making are higher, the level of participation tends to be lower: witness the advisory forums to the GEF and IFAD, or the minority or non-voting seats at the Forest Carbon Partnership Facility or the UN-REDD Programme board.

5.1.2 *Reassessing the Traditional and Modern Approaches*

Let us return, for a brief moment, to the discussion that animated Chapter 2: the interminable debates about whether to apply a two-element approach, a practice-oriented approach, or an *opinio*-oriented approach to the identification of custom.

In one sense, this distinction is revealed to be not very important in the case at hand. If we apply an *opinio*-oriented approach, Articles 18, 19, and 41 of the UNDRIP are considered rule-creating in and of themselves. If we apply a practice-oriented approach, the volume of practice revealed in Chapters 4 and 5 is surely such to justify the foundation of a customary rule. If we apply a two-element approach, as I have argued, there is sufficient evidence of a practice accepted as law that we can regard a rule of customary international law as already established, or at least emerging. We do not need to rely on a practice-oriented approach, since it is clear that reasons for undertaking the practice go beyond comity or courtesy, but rather a sense of obligation. Indeed, we can see that far from being anachronistic or obsolete, as some commentators would have it, the two-element approach remains manifestly relevant.

But in another sense, the evidence has illustrated limitations associated with each approach. Under an *opinio*-oriented approach, difficult questions are raised about the proper interpretation of the large amount of state practice that has taken place subsequent to the adoption of the UNDRIP. Is this to be regarded as "subsequent practice," by analogy to a treaty? Perhaps we should view it as aiding the interpretation, or clarifying the scope, of the customary rule reflected in Articles 18 and 41 of the UNDRIP. However, because these articles of the Declaration are ambiguous as to what constitutes participation and how ways and means of ensuring it are to be established, it is strange to regard them as constituting a rule of law in and of themselves. Such a rule is necessarily indeterminate. The better approach would be to regard the development of custom as an ongoing process, in which practice subsequent to a declaration can help to add substantive content to a rule, as well as shape and direct that content.

Under a practice-oriented approach, the difficulty lies in establishing the temporal nexus, the "big bang" moment at which a rule of custom came into existence. Is it in 1982, with the establishment of the Working Group on Indigenous Populations; is it in the mid-1990s, with the foundation of the Working Group on the Draft Declaration alongside several other mechanisms in international and regional governance; is it in the late 2000s, with the adoption of the UNDRIP; or is it in the 2010s, with the further proliferation of participatory mechanisms? Perhaps this does not matter; perhaps all that should concern us is to assess the state of the international law 'on a given day'.[5] Perhaps, as is certainly the case, this problem equally exists in relation to the two-element approach. But that is not a satisfactory answer.

Finally, the two-element approach is vulnerable to the well-known problem of error: up until the big bang moment is achieved (however uncertain its precise timing), the states that believe that the practice is required by law will, by definition, be mistaken.[6] I want to here make one suggestion about the usual framing of "error": this is a convenient fiction that not only obscures process and struggle but also promotes the idea that state representatives are innocent, wholly uncalculating agents who do not attempt to shape the development of international law. In particular, it obscures the role of states, as well as non-state actors, as norm entrepreneurs[7] and proponents of specific legal norms. As we have seen, Indigenous peoples' organizations have argued since at least the 1970s that they have a legal right to participate in international governance. The "error" framing would suggest that Indigenous advocates, and their state allies, have simply been mistaken. But the better

5 James Crawford and Thomas Viles, 'International Law on a Given Day' in James Crawford, *International Law as an Open System: Selected Essays* (London: Cameron and May, 2002), 69–94.

6 For a deft handling of this problem, see Tiyanjana Maluwa, 'Custom, Authority and Law: Some Jurisprudential Perspective on the Theory of Customary International Law' (1994) 6 *African Journal of International and Comparative Law*, 387–410. For early, oft-cited statements of the problem, see Josef L. Kunz, 'The Nature of Customary International Law' (1953) 47 *American Journal of International Law*, 662–669, 667; Mark E. Villiger, *Customary International Law and Treaties: A Study of their Interactions and Interrelations with Special Consideration of the 1969 Vienna Convention on the Law of Treaties* (Dordrecht: Martinus Nijhoff, 1985), 29.

7 On norm entrepreneurs, see generally Martha Finnemore and Kathryn Sikkink, 'International Norm Dynamics and Political Change' (1998) 52 *International Organization*, 887–917, 895.

interpretation is that they are, by their statements, trying to socialize a different norm than that which previously existed; they are trying to change the international law. We might understand the statements of (at least some) "early adopter" states in the same way.[8] We cannot, of course, know this for certain. We are not mind readers. But I propose that this is one reasonable interpretation of the preceding chapters.

5.2 OLD STONES: FROM INDIGENOUS PARTICIPATION TO INDIGENOUS SOVEREIGNTY?

Now let us turn the limitations to the exercise of the right around, place them in a wider context, and view them from a different angle, as *systemic*, *institutional*, or *material* barriers to the expression of Indigenous self-determination via voice in international governance.

5.2.1 *Barriers to Self-Determination Via Voice: Systemic, Institutional, and Material*

At the *systemic* level, we can observe that all of the international organizations, treaties, and processes discussed herein relate to the environment, development, human rights, and regional governance. What the previous chapters have not discussed is Indigenous peoples' participation in international economic law-making, policymaking, and decision-making. This is because states and international organizations, on the whole, have not enabled Indigenous peoples to participate in these processes. In no publicly known case have Indigenous representatives sat at the table with states in negotiating free trade agreements, investment treaties, nor mega-regional agreements.[9] The World

8 I here follow scholars who have proposed constructive approaches to customary international law formation; see, for example, Thomas Kleinlein, 'Customary International Law and General Principles: Rethinking Their Relationship' in Brian D. Lepard (ed.), *Reexamining Customary International Law* (Cambridge: Cambridge University Press, 2017), 131–160.

9 Free trade and investment agreements are typically negotiated between states with a high level of secrecy, excluding civil society groups and Indigenous peoples. Meanwhile, international economic agreements profoundly affect Indigenous peoples' interests: Sergio Puig, 'International Indigenous Economic Law' (2019) 32 *UC Davis Law Review*, 1243–1316. At most, some states have begun to establish mechanisms for the consultation of Indigenous peoples on trade issues, for example, Te Taumata in New Zealand, established in 2019 to 'identify and understand Māori interests in relation to trade negotiations and directly affected issues … and ensure discussions to help inform New Zealand's position at the international level when those interests are affected': New Zealand Foreign Affairs and Trade, 'Memorandum of Understanding between Te Taumata and The Ministry of Foreign Affairs and Trade (MFAT)' (MFAT, 24 September 2019) www.mfat.govt.nz/assets/Uploads/MFAT-

Trade Organization (WTO) provides no status for Indigenous peoples, and *amicus* participation in international investment dispute settlement and the WTO dispute settlement mechanism provides Indigenous peoples with only a token level of participation.[10] Meanwhile, a systematic review found that of all existing treaties, only international trade and investment treaties have consistently achieved their intended objectives; by contrast, environmental, human rights, and humanitarian treaties are generally ineffective unless they include enforcement mechanisms such as financial sanctions.[11]

At the *institutional* level, we see, as noted above, that the level of Indigenous people's participation in a given body tends to be inversely proportional to the scope of that body's powers. FILAC and the FCPF have modest annual budgets in the millions, giving out grants to Indigenous groups for projects related to economic and social development and forests, respectively. In these bodies, Indigenous peoples hold a majority of voting seats. The Arctic Council, in which Indigenous peoples' Permanent Participant status places them on an equal footing with states, is ultimately limited by not being a formal international organization. Moreover, it does not have the competence to deal with some matters of great economic importance and significance to Indigenous peoples, such as fisheries, which are dealt with in separate international fora. The IUCN is similarly limited by its lack of formal international organization status. By contrast, in large international financial institutions, Indigenous peoples' participation is typically limited to a single non-voting

Te-Taumata-MOU.pdf. The Waitangi Tribunal's Report on the Trans-Pacific Partnership, in the course of finding that the Partnership's rules on e-commerce breached the Treaty of Waitangi, noted that 'until recently, the opportunity for Māori to engage in joint decision-making with the Crown and its agents [on trade agreements] has been limited or non-existent': Waitangi Tribunal, *The Report on the Comprehensive and Progressive Agreement for Trans-Pacific Partnership – Pre-Publication Version*, WAI 2522 (Waitangi Tribunal, 2020) https://waitangitribunal.govt.nz/news/tribunal-releases-report-on-electronic-commerce-chapter-in-cptpp/, p. 25. First Nations were included in Canada's consultation process post-negotiation, but prior to ratification, of the Trans-Pacific Partnership: Katya Lena Richardson, 'Finding a Duty to Consult Aboriginal Peoples During the Negotiation of Free Trade Agreements (FTAs) and Foreign Investment Promotion and Protection Agreements (FIPAs)' (2017) 7 *Western Journal of Legal Studies*, 1–17, 3. Indigenous involvement in the NAFTA renegotiations in 2017–2018 was minimal, with the National Chief of the Assembly of First Nations, Perry Bellegarde, included on the Canadian NAFTA advisory council: Leah Sarson, '"You Cannot Trade What Is Not Yours": Indigenous Governance and the NAFTA Negotiations' (2019) 49 *American Review of Canadian Studies*, 332–347, 334.

10 Natalie Jones, *Towards a Right of Peoples to Participation in Global Governance* (PhD. thesis, University of Cambridge, 2020), Chapter 7.

11 Steven J. Hoffman, Prativa Baral, and Susan Rogers Van Katwyk et al., 'International Treaties Have Mostly Failed to Produce Their Intended Effects' (2022) 119(32) *PNAS* e2122854119.

seat on an executive committee, or an advisory committee empowered only to the extent of issuing recommendations.

Here we also see that in processes intended to result in internationally legally binding agreements, like the WIPO IGC, or even persuasive "soft law" documents like the UNDRIP and the WCIP Outcome Document, even if Indigenous peoples and states are on an equal procedural footing throughout negotiations, the structure of the international institution means that the final vote remains with states. In some sense, this is but the latest manifestation of the state-centric nature of the international system that posed a barrier to Deskaheh's hearing at the League in the 1920s.

Finally, there are *material* barriers, relating, for example, to funding and other support for Indigenous peoples' participation; although funding mechanisms widely exist, they are often severely underfunded. And in some states, the kinds of retribution that Deskaheh faced have not ended.[12]

In summary, we see that while states have rhetorically welcomed Indigenous peoples' participation in international governance and taken steps to entrench it as a rule of law, at the same time they have continued to resist Indigenous peoples' demands for equal membership of the international community. When viewed holistically, processes that at face value appear to provide for inclusion might also be perceived to ultimately function to deny Indigenous sovereignty; "Indigenous" and "nation" still 'seem incommensurable'.[13]

5.2.2 *Open Questions*

With these barriers in mind, how are we then to understand international law's increasing embrace, in the form of a crystallizing customary international rule, of the right of Indigenous peoples to participation in international governance? There is an inconsistency between the formalization of this rule, coupled with states' and international organizations' outspoken

[12] See, for example, Russian attempts to prevent Koola Sami from attending the World Conference on Indigenous Peoples: President of the Republic of Finland, 'Statement by President of the Republic of Finland Sauli Niinistö at the World Conference on Indigenous Peoples (WCIP) United Nations, New York 22 September 2014' (22 September 2014) www.presidentti.fi/en/speeches/statement-by-president-of-the-republic-of-finland-sauli-niinisto-at-the-world-conference-on-indigenous-peoples-wcip-united-nations-new-york-22-september-2014/.

[13] Language borrowed from Audra Simpson, *Mohawk Interruptus* (Durham, NC.: Duke University Press, 2014), 7.

rhetoric in favour of Indigenous peoples' participation, and the systematic, institutional, and material barriers to such participation that remain.

One way to understand the contradiction is to view it in the light of international law's colonial origins, its ongoing implication in imperialism, its tendency to align with the interests of capital, and its capacity to enable exploitation by powerful actors.[14] Sundhya Pahuja has identified that international law has 'a dual quality … both an imperial and counter-imperial dimension'.[15] In other words, it can be used by powerful actors to exploit and extract, but it can also be used to 'challenge established relations of power and exploitation'.[16] Such challenges, however, face difficulties. In Pahuja's study, attempts by Third World actors to use international law for emancipatory purposes were consistently undermined and constrained by being 'subsumed within a pervasive rationality that successfully made a claim for the universality of a particular … set of values originating in and congenial to the North'.[17]

In this book, the impetus has come not from the Third World, but from the Fourth World,[18] to challenge ongoing colonial power relations and assert Indigenous sovereignty via seeking membership of the international community. Could it be that a subsumption, or even co-optation, of Indigenous participation has occurred, similar to that described by Pahuja?

Writing about the self-determination of Indigenous peoples in relation to Canada, Glen Coulthard drew on the work of Frantz Fanon to suggest that the Canadian state's move, from the 1960s onwards, to a politics of recognition of Indigenous peoples has not fundamentally transformed the underlying

[14] There is a vast and ever-growing literature chronicling these tendencies. To mention just a few volumes: Antony Anghie, *Imperialism, Sovereignty, and the Making of International Law* (Cambridge: Cambridge University Press, 2005); Sundhya Pahuja, *Decolonising International Law: Development, Economic Growth and the Politics of Universality* (Cambridge: Cambridge University Press, 2011); Bhupinder S. Chimni, *International Law and World Order: A Critique of Contemporary Approaches*, 2nd ed. (Cambridge: Cambridge University Press, 2017); Martti Koskenniemi, Walter Rech, and Manuel Jiménez Fonseca (eds.), *International Law and Empire – Historical Explorations* (Oxford: Oxford University Press, 2017); Rose Parfitt, *The Process of International Legal Reproduction: Inequality, Historiography, Resistance* (Cambridge: Cambridge University Press, 2019); Ntina Tzouvala, *Capitalism As Civilisation: A History of International Law* (Cambridge: Cambridge University Press, 2020); David Schneiderman, *Investment Law's Alibi's: Colonialism, Imperialism, Debt and Development* (Cambridge: Cambridge University Press, 2022).

[15] Pahuja, *Decolonising International Law*, 1.

[16] Ibid., 2.

[17] Ibid., 2.

[18] George Manuel and Michael Posluns, *The Fourth World: An Indian Reality* (Minneapolis: University of Minnesota Press, 2019 [1974]).

colonial relationship.[19] Despite the shift from a politics of explicit exclusion or assimilation of Indigenous peoples to one of accommodation and conciliation, as Coulthard has it, 'the relationship between Indigenous peoples and the state has remained *colonial* to its foundation'.[20] In other words, 'colonial relations of power are no longer reproduced primarily through overtly coercive means, but rather through the asymmetrical exchange of mediated forms of state recognition and accommodation',[21] and these hierarchical relations continue to facilitate the dispossession of Indigenous land and self-determining authority.[22]

As part of this, Coulthard points out how the Canadian state and industry have appropriated the discourse of "sustainability" 'to push their shared vision of economic development', under which the land and resource base of Indigenous communities remain 'open for exploitation and capitalist development'.[23] In this connection, Audra Simpson notes how political recognition can appear 'as a transcendent and universal human desire that becomes a political antidote to historical wrongdoing'.[24]

By analogy, then, we must at least consider the possibility that mechanisms for Indigenous peoples' participation in international governance may function in part to legitimize and protect (neo)colonial global structures, as 'the field of power through which colonial relations are produced and maintained'.[25]

Let us return to the arguments made by state delegates and international organization officials to justify policies for Indigenous peoples' participation. We have seen how although sometimes these are justified on moral grounds of affectedness, more often an appeal is made to purportedly "universal," or at least shared, goals or ideals: the protection of the environment, the achievement of sustainable development objectives, and the very future of human survival on Earth.[26] We might also recall how states and international organizations have also openly, repeatedly acknowledged the benefits bestowed by

19 Glen Sean Coulthard, *Red Skin, White Masks: Rejecting the Colonial Politics of Recognition* (Minneapolis: University of Minnesota Press, 2014).

20 Coulthard, *Red Skin, White Masks*, 6 (emphasis in original).

21 Ibid., 15.

22 Ibid., 6–7.

23 Ibid., 77.

24 Audra Simpson, *Mohawk Interruptus*, p. 20.

25 Coulthard, *Red Skin, White Masks*, 17.

26 George Manuel has pointed out how '[t]he colonial system is always a way of gaining control over another people for the sake of what the colonial power has determined to be 'the common good.' People can only become convinced of the common good when their own capacity to imagine ways in which they can govern themselves has been destroyed': Manuel and Posluns, *The Fourth World*, p. 60.

Indigenous participation in terms of the credibility and legitimacy of the international organizations and governance processes concerned. But in reality, these goals are not universal; Indigenous peoples and states can and do occupy opposing structural positions in the global economy.[27] Meanwhile, these discourses function to obscure the fact that in the international processes that structure the material economy – the making and implementation of trade and investment treaties – Indigenous peoples are almost entirely excluded. And the crystallization of a rule of customary international law might function to allow states to offload any further responsibility to address structural injustices that continue to inform our settler-colonial present.

The idea that Indigenous participation in international governance may have been co-opted for ends materially opposed to Indigenous interests is not new. Jeff Corntassel in 2007 argued that during the first UN Indigenous Decade, from 1995 to 2004, Indigenous communities' efforts had sometimes been overly focused on representation in global forums, rather than pursuing other forms of political mobilization including grassroots resistance.[28] Corntassel drew attention to the risks to Indigenous communities posed by overly relying on global forums for emancipation, utilizing Michael Lacy's account of co-optation,[29] under which 'powerful entities promote their own legitimacy through processes of blunting and channeling'.[30] States might blunt an Indigenous political agenda by shifting and altering it to fit the dominant norms of existing institutional structures, while under channelling effects 'Indigenous communities are dissuaded from engaging in grassroots mobilization and/or directly confronting corporate/state practices'.[31] In this way, as Taiaiake Alfred warned, '[t]he complexity of Indigenous-state relations gives agents of the state many opportunities and mechanisms to move Indigenous leaders away from their communities, politically and ideologically, and towards the state'.[32]

[27] See, for one example of how international law negotiates these positions, Julia Dehm, *Reconsidering REDD+: Authority, Power and Law in the Green Economy* (Cambridge: Cambridge University Press, 2021).

[28] Jeff Corntassel, 'Partnership in Action? Indigenous Political Mobilization and Co-optation during the First UN Indigenous Decade (1995–2004)' (2007) 29 *Human Rights Quarterly*, 137–166, 140. See also Jeff Corntassel, 'Towards Sustainable Self-Determination: Rethinking the Contemporary Indigenous-Rights Discourse' (2008) 33 *Alternatives*, 105–132.

[29] '[C]ooptation occurs if, in a system of power, the power holder intentionally extends some form of political participation to actors who pose a threat': Michael G. Lacy, 'The United States and American Indians: Political Relations', in Vine Deloria, Jr. (ed.), *American Indian Policy in the Twentieth Century* (Norman, O.K.: University of Oklahoma Press, 1985), 83.

[30] Corntassel, 'Partnership in Action', 140.

[31] Ibid.

[32] Taiaiake Alfred, *Peace, Power, Righteousness: An Indigenous Manifesto* (Oxford: Oxford University Press, 1999), 74.

A decade and a half since Corntassel wrote, the issues he raised remain pertinent. This is not to say that Indigenous peoples ought not to keep looking to international law and international organizations for emancipation. Nor is it necessarily to suggest that efforts to secure an enhanced status for Indigenous peoples in the General Assembly are entirely misplaced. That suggestion would be nihilistic, at odds with the reality that people are capable of remaking human-created institutions and shifting power. On the contrary, a category of membership for Indigenous peoples at the General Assembly, if designed in a way that preserves and promotes Indigenous self-determination and sovereignty, could indeed prove transformative. And international institutions remain a vital component of any project of Indigenous worldmaking.[33] Ongoing Indigenous peoples' struggles and mobilization in the intergovernmental sphere – including but not limited to the General Assembly, the Human Rights Council, the ECOSOC, as well as the Andean Community, and the UNESCO World Heritage Committee – will no doubt continue.

However, the work of scholars like Coulthard, Simpson, Alfred, and Corntassel might suggest that such strategies should form only one part of a worldmaking project. In other words, a 'radical Indigenous internationalism'[34] might extend far beyond the halls of the United Nations, to 'on-the-ground struggles of freedom'[35] – a struggle that dates back to the beginning of colonial conquest.[36] Local and regional regeneration and resurgence of Indigenous economies and cultures are, in this analysis, vital, in addition to internationalism vis-à-vis fellow Indigenous nations, other subaltern peoples, and the more-than-human world. These strategies could even be mutually reinforcing with the project of global representation.[37]

In addition, the option of refusal might be kept in mind. Audra Simpson outlines how refusal, as an alternative to the politics of recognition, 'comes

[33] After Adom Getachew, *Worldmaking after Empire: The Rise and Fall of Self-Determination* (Princeton: Princeton University Press, 2019).

[34] *Our History Is the Future: Standing Rock versus the Dakota Access Pipeline* (London: Verso, 2019), Chapter 6.

[35] Coulthard, *Red Skin, White Masks*, 48, 165–170.

[36] Documented extensively; for just a few examples, see Manuel and Posluns, *The Fourth World*; Nick Estes, *Our History Is the Future*; See also Taiaiake Alfred and Jeff Corntassel, 'Being Indigenous: Resurgences against Contemporary Colonialism' (2005) 40 *Government and Opposition*, 597–614.

[37] As Amar Bhatia has noted, 'if the spectrum of participants at international law is widened to include Indigenous peoples and poor migrants, potentially both the Fourth and Third Worlds, then the possibility for effective action and resistance, including material gains on the ground, should increase': Amar Bhatia, 'The South of the North: Building on Critical Approaches to International Law with Lessons from the Fourth World' (2012) 14 *Oregon Review of International Law*, 131–175, 172.

with the requirement of having one's *political* sovereignty acknowledged and upheld, and raises the question of legitimacy for those who are usually in the position of recognizing: What is their authority to do so? Where does it come from? Who are they to do so?'[38] In this respect, George Manuel's call for shared power continues to resonate:[39]

> We cannot become equal members in *your* society. We *can* become a member of a new society in which everyone chooses to share. But that cannot happen until you begin to reconsider and reformulate your understanding, and your view of the world, as we have begun to reformulate ours.

At a planetary conjuncture characterized by a fundamental conflict between capital and life, this urgent task of worldmaking is not solely of concern to Indigenous peoples. Ultimately, the Indigenous experience of participation in international governance might inform the questions asked by other peoples and marginalized groups when seeking access to, or justice from, international institutions and the wider international community. This might include questioning the ways in which international law is already complicit in the co-optation of Indigenous, and other, movements to legitimize its institutions and its underlying economic relations. Beyond international governance, perhaps the demand for Indigenous self-determination on Indigenous terms, and associated Indigenous worldbuilding processes, can be learned from in broader movements to build global solidarity and resistance from below.

[38] Simpson, *Mohawk Interruptus*, 11 (emphasis in original).
[39] Manuel and Posluns, *The Fourth World*, 261 (emphasis in original).

Bibliography

ALL INTERNET MATERIALS WERE LAST ACCESSED 20 JULY 2022.

Adkisson, Richard V., 'The Andean Group: Institutional Evolution, Intraregional Trade, and Economic Development' (2003) 37(2) *Journal of Economic Issues* 371–379.

'African Declaration on the World Conference on Indigenous Peoples 2014' (21 November 2012), http://cendoc.docip.org/collect/cendocdo/index/assoc/HASH0176/0f3c47ed.dir/WCIP_Afridecl_en.pdf.

Agon, Sivan Shlomo, and Eyal Benvenisti, 'The Law of Strangers: The Form and Substance of Other-Regarding International Adjudication' (2018) 68(4) *University of Toronto Law Journal* 598–660.

Aguilar, Soledad, Xenya Cherny, Elisa Morgera, Nicole Schabus, and Elsa Tsioumani, 'Summary of the Fourth Meeting of the Working Group on Article 8(j) of the Convention on Biological Diversity' (2006) 9(339) *Earth Negotiations Bulletin*, https://enb.iisd.org/events/4th-meeting-cbd-ad-hoc-open-ended-working-group-article-8j/summary-report-23-27-january-2006.

Ahmad Khan, Sabaa, 'Rebalancing State and Indigenous Sovereignties in International Law: An Arctic Lens on Trajectories for Global Governance' (2019) 32 *Leiden Journal of International Law* 675–693.

Åhren, Mattias, *Indigenous Peoples' Status in the International Legal System* (Oxford: Oxford University Press, 2016).

Aikio, Pekka, and Martin Scheinin (eds.), *Operationalizing the Right of Indigenous Peoples to Self-Determination* (Turko, Finland: Institute for Human Rights, Åbo Akademi University, 2000).

Akehurst, Michael, 'Custom as a Source of International Law' (1974–1975) 47(1) *British Yearbook of International Law* 1–53.

Alfred, Taiaiake, *Peace, Power, Righteousness: An Indigenous Manifesto* (Oxford: Oxford University Press, 1999).

Alfred, Taiaiake, and Jeff Corntassel, 'Being Indigenous: Resurgences against Contemporary Colonialism' (2005) 40 *Government and Opposition* 597–614.

Alfredsson, Gudmundur, 'Fourth Session of the Working Group on Indigenous Populations' (1986) 55 *Nordic Journal of International Law* 22–30.

Allen, Stephen, and Alexandra Xanthaki (eds.), *Reflections on the UN Declaration on the Rights of Indigenous Peoples* (London: Hart, 2011).

Alston, Philip (ed.), *Peoples' Rights* (Oxford: Oxford University Press, 2002).

Alvarez, José E., *International Organizations as Law-Makers* (Oxford: Oxford University Press, 2006).

'International Organizations and the Rule of Law' (2016) 14 *New Zealand Journal of Public and International Law* 3–46.

Anaya, S. James, 'A Contemporary Definition of the International Norm of Self-Determination' (1993) 3 *Transnational Law and Contemporary Problems* 131–164.

Indigenous Peoples in International Law (2nd ed., Oxford: Oxford University Press, 2004).

'International Human Rights and Indigenous Peoples: The Move toward the Multicultural State' (2004) 21 *Arizona Journal of International & Comparative Law* 13–61.

'The Right of Indigenous Peoples to Self-Determination in the Post-Declaration Era' in Claire Charters and Rodolfo Stavenhagen (eds.), *Making the Declaration Work: The United Nations Declaration on the Rights of Indigenous Peoples* (Copenhagen: IWGIA, 2009) 184–199.

Anaya, S. James, and Luis Rodríguez-Piñero, 'The Making of the UNDRIP' in Jessie Hohmann and Marc Weller (eds.), *The UN Declaration on the Rights of Indigenous People: A Commentary* (Oxford: Oxford University Press, 2018) 38–62.

Anderson, K., 'The Ottawa Convention Banning Landmines, the Role of International Non-Governmental Organizations, and the Idea of International Civil Society' (2000) 11(1) *European Journal of International Law* 91–120.

Anghie, Antony, *Imperialism, Sovereignty and the Making of International Law* (Cambridge: Cambridge University Press, 2004).

Arajärvi, Noora, 'From State-Centricism to Where? The Formation of Customary International Law and Non-State Actors' (3 May 2010), http://ssrn.com/abstract=1599679.

'From the "Demands of Humanity": The Formulation of *Opinio Juris* in Decisions of International Criminal Tribunals and the Need for a Renewed Emphasis on State Practice' in Brian D. Lepard (ed.), *Reexamining Customary International Law* (Cambridge: Cambridge University Press, 2017) 189–230.

Arangio Ruiz, Gaetano, 'The Normative Role of the General Assembly of the United Nations and the Declaration of Principles of Friendly Relations' (1972) 137 *Recueil des Cours* 419–742.

Baldwin, Clive, and Cynthia Morel, 'Using the United Nations Declaration on the Rights of Indigenous Peoples in Litigation' in Stephen Allen and Alexandra Xanthaki (eds.), *Reflections on the UN Declaration on the Rights of Indigenous Peoples* (London: Hart, 2011) 121–144.

Bankes, Nigel, and Timo Koivurova, 'Introduction' in Nigel Bankes and Timo Koivurova (eds.), *The Proposed Nordic Saami Convention: National and International Dimensions of Indigenous Property Rights* (Oxford: Hart, 2013) 1–18.

Barelli, Mauro, 'The Role of Soft Law in the International Legal System: The Case of the United Nations Declaration on the Rights of Indigenous Peoples' (2009) 58(4) *International & Comparative Law Quarterly* 957–983.

Seeking Justice in International Law: The Significance and Implications of the UN Declaration on the Rights of Indigenous Peoples (London: Routledge, 2016).
Barsh, Russel Lawrence, 'United Nations Seminar on Indigenous Peoples and States' (1989) 83 *American Journal of International Law* 599–604.
'An Advocate's Guide to the Convention on Indigenous and Tribal Peoples' (1990) 15 *Oklahoma City University Law Review* 209–236.
'Indigenous Peoples in the 1990s: From Object to Subject of International Law' (1994) 7 *Harvard Human Rights Journal* 33–86.
'Indigenous Peoples and the UN Commission on Human Rights: A Case of the Immovable Object and the Irresistible Force' (1996) 18(4) *Human Rights Quarterly* 782–813.
Baxter, Robert R., 'Treaties and Custom' (1970) 129 *Recueil des cours* 25–106.
Becker Lorca, Arnulf, *Mestizo International Law: A Global Intellectual History 1842–1933* (Cambridge: Cambridge University Press, 2014).
Bederman, David J., *Custom as a Source of Law* (Cambridge: Cambridge University Press, 2010).
Benvenisti, Eyal, 'Margin of Appreciation, Consensus, and Universal Standards' (1999) 31(4) *New York University Journal of International Law and Politics* 843–854.
The Law of Global Governance (Leiden: Brill Nijhoff 2014).
'Upholding Democracy Amid the Challenges of New Technology: What Role for the Law of Global Governance?' (2018) 29(1) *European Journal of International Law* 9–82.
Bhatia, Amar, 'The South of the North: Building on Critical Approaches to International Law with Lessons from the Fourth World' (2012) 14 *Oregon Review of International Law* 131–175.
Blokker, Niels, 'International Organizations and Customary International Law: Is the International Law Commission Taking International Organizations Seriously?' (2017) 14(1) *International Organizations Law Review* 1–12.
Bloom, Evan T., 'Current Developments: Establishment of the Arctic Council' (1999) 93 *American Journal of International Law* 712–722.
Bluemel, Erik B., 'Separating Instrumental from Intrinsic Rights: Towards an Understanding of Indigenous Participation in International Rule Making' (2005) 30(1) *American Indian Law Review* 55–132.
Bodansky, Daniel, 'Customary (And Not So Customary) International Environmental Law' (1995) 3(1) *Indiana Journal of Global Legal Studies* 105–119.
Boehme, Franziska, Lindsay Burt, Patricia Goff and Audie Klotz, 'Cultural Diversity and the Politics of Recognition in International Organizations' (2018) 9 *Journal of International Organizations Studies* 27–41.
von Bogdandy, Armin, Rüdiger Wolfrum, Jochen von Bernstorff, Philip Dann and Matthias Goldmann (eds.), *The Exercise of Public Authority by International Institutions: Advancing International Institutional Law* (Heidelberg: Springer, 2010).
von Bogdandy, Armin, Matthias Goldmann and Ingo Venzke, 'From Public International to International Public Law: Translating World Public Opinion into International Public Authority' (2017) 28(1) *European Journal of International Law* 115–145.
Bokor-Szegö, Hanna, *The Role of the United Nations in International Legislation* (Amsterdam: North-Holland Publishing Company, 1978).

Bonnin, Gertrude (Zitkala-Ša), 'Editorial Comment' (1919) 6(4) *American Indian Magazine* 161–162.

Boyle, Alan, 'Soft Law in International Law-Making' in Malcolm D. Evans (ed.), *International Law* (4th ed., Oxford: Oxford University Press, 2014) 118–135.

Boyle, Alan and Christine Chinkin, *The Making of International Law* (Oxford: Oxford University Press, 2007).

Brölmann, Catherine, 'Capturing the Juridical Will of International Organizations' in Sufjan Droubi and Jean d'Aspremont (eds.), International Organizations and Non-State Actors in the Formation of Customary International Law (Manchester: Manchester University Press, 2020) 42–61.

Brosius, J. Peter, 'Indigenous Peoples and Protected Areas at the World Parks Congress' (2004) 18 *Conservation Biology* 609–612.

Buccini, John Anthony, 'The Long and Winding Road to Stockholm: The View from the Chair' in David Leonard Downie and Terry Fenge (eds.), *Northern Lights against POPs: Combatting Toxic Threats in the Arctic* (Montreal: McGill-Queen's University Press, 2003) 224–255.

Burger, Julian, 'United Nations Working Group on Indigenous Populations: The United Nations and Indigenous Peoples' in Lydia van de Fliert (ed.), *Indigenous Peoples and International Organizations* (Nottingham: Russel Press, 1994) 90.

Byers, Michael, *Custom, Power and the Power of Rules: International Relations and Customary International Law* (Cambridge: Cambridge University Press, 1999.

Cabrera Ormaza, María Victoria, and Franz Christian Ebert, 'The World Bank, Human Rights, and Organizational Legitimacy Strategies: The Case of the 2016 Environmental and Social Framework' (2019) 32 *Leiden Journal of International Law* 483–500.

Cambou, Dorotheé, 'Enhancing the Participation of Indigenous Peoples at the Intergovernmental Level to Strengthen Self-Determination: Lessons from the Arctic' (2018) 87 *Nordic Journal of International Law* 26–55.

Campbell, Richard, Jonathan Krueger, Leila Mead, and Tiffany Prather, 'POPS INC-1 Highlights Monday, 29 June 1998' (29 June 1998) 15(6) *Earth Negotiations Bulletin*, https://enb.iisd.org/events/1st-session-inc-international-legally-binding-instrument-implementing-international-action-1.

Carmen, Andrea, 'International Indian Treaty Council Report from the Battle Field – The Struggle for the Declaration' in Claire Charters and Rodolfo Stavenhagen (eds.), *Making the Declaration Work: The United Nations Declaration on the Rights of Indigenous Peoples* (Copenhagen: IWGIA, 2009) 86–95.

Carpenter, David O., 'Polychlorinated Biphenyls (PCBs): Routes of Exposure and Effects on Human Health' (2006) 21(1) *Reviews on Environmental Health* 1–23.

Cassese, Antonio, *Self-Determination of Peoples: A Legal Reappraisal* (Cambridge: Cambridge University Press, 1995).

Cassese, Sabino, Bruno Carotti, Lorenzo Casini, Eleonora Cavalieri, and Euan MacDonald, *Global Administrative Law: The Casebook* (3rd ed., Rome: Irpa, 2012).

Castellino, Joshua, *International Law and Self-Determination: The Interplay of the Politics of Territorial Possession with Formulations of Post-colonial National Identity* (The Hague, Boston: Martinus Nijhoff, 2000).

Castellino, Joshua and Doyle, Cathal, 'Who Are 'Indigenous Peoples'? An Examination of Concepts Concerning Group Membership in the UNDRIP' in Jessie Hohmann and Marc Weller (eds.), *The UN Declaration on the Rights of Indigenous People: A Commentary* (Oxford: Oxford University Press, 2018) 7–37.

Charnovitz, Steve, 'The Illegitimacy of Preventing NGO Participation' (2011) 36(3) *Brooklyn Journal of International Law* 891–910.

Charters, Claire, 'A Self-Determination Approach to Justifying Indigenous Peoples' Participation in International Law and Policy Making' (2010) 17 *International Journal of Minority & Group Rights* 215–240.

Charters, Claire and Rodolfo Stavenhagen (eds.), *Making the Declaration Work: The United Nations Declaration on the Rights of Indigenous Peoples* (Copenhagen: IWGIA, 2009).

Chávez, Luis Enrique, 'The Declaration on the Rights of Indigenous Peoples Breaking the *Impasse*: The Middle Ground' in Claire Charters and Rodolfo Stavenhagen (eds.), *Making the Declaration Work: The United Nations Declaration on the Rights of Indigenous Peoples* (Copenhagen: IWGIA, 2009) 96–107.

Cheng, Bin, 'Epilogue' in Bin Cheng (ed.), *International Law: Teaching Practice* (London: Stevens & Sons, 1982) 203–233.

Chimni, B.S., *International Law and World Order: A Critique of Contemporary Approaches*, 2nd ed. (Cambridge: Cambridge University Press, 2017).

'Customary International Law: A Third World Perspective' (2018) 112(1) *American Journal of International Law* 1–46.

Chinkin, Christine, 'The Challenge of Soft Law: Development and Change in International Law' (1989) 28 *International and Comparative Law Quarterly* 850–866.

Clavero, Bartolomé, 'The Indigenous Rights of Participation and International Development Policies' (2005) 22 *Arizona Journal of International & Comparative Law* 41–51.

Corntassel, Jeff, 'Partnership in Action? Indigenous Political Mobilization and Co-optation during the First UN Indigenous Decade (1995–2004)' (2007) 29 *Human Rights Quarterly* 137–166.

'Toward Sustainable Self-Determination: Rethinking the Contemporary Indigenous-Rights Discourse' (2008) 33 *Alternatives* 103–132.

Coulthard, Glen Sean, *Red Skin, White Masks: Rejecting the Colonial Politics of Recognition* (Minneapolis: University of Minnesota Press, 2014).

Crawford, James R., *The Creation of States in International Law* (2nd ed, Oxford: Oxford University Press, 2007).

Chance, Order, Change: The Course of International Law (Leiden: Martinus Nijhoff, 2014).

Crawford, James, and Thomas Viles, 'International Law on a Given Day' in James Crawford, *International Law as an Open System: Selected Essays* (London: Cameron and May, 2002) 69–94.

Cullen, Holly and Karen Morrow, 'International Civil Society in International Law: The Growth of NGO Participation' (2001) 1(1) *Non-State Actors & International Law* 7–39.

D'Amato, Anthony, 'The Concept of Special Custom in International Law' (1969) 63 *American Journal of International Law* 211–223.

'Trashing Customary International Law' (1987) 81(1) *American Journal of International Law* 101–105.

'Customary International Law: A Reformulation' (1998) 4 *International Legal Theory* 1–6.

Daes, Erica-Irene A., 'The Contribution of the Working Group on Indigenous Populations to the Genesis and Evolution of the UN Declaration on the Rights of Indigenous Peoples' in Claire Charters and Rodolfo Stavenhagen (eds.), *Making the Declaration Work: The United Nations Declaration on the Rights of Indigenous Peoples* (Copenhagen: IWGIA, 2009) 48–77.

Damstra, Terri, 'Potential Effects of Certain Persistent Organic Pollutants and Endocrine Disrupting Chemicals on the Health of Children' (2002) 40 *Clinical Toxicology* 457–465.

Danilenko, Gennady M., 'The Theory of Customary International Law' (1988) 31 *German Yearbook of International Law* 9–47.

Law-Making in the International Community (Leiden: Nijhoff, 1993).

Daugirdas, Kristina, 'How and Why International Law Binds International Organizations' (2016) 57(2) *Harvard International Law Journal* 325–381.

Davis, Kevin, Angela Fisher, Benedict Kingsbury, and Sally Engle Merry (eds.), *Governance by Indicators: Global Power through Classification and Rankings* (Oxford: Oxford University Press, 2012).

Davis, Shelton H., 'The World Bank and Operational Directive 2.0', in Lydia van de Fliert (ed.), *Indigenous Peoples and International Organizations* (Nottingham: Russell Press, 1994) 75.

Dehm, Julia, *Reconsidering REDD+: Authority, Power and Law in the Green Economy* (Cambridge: Cambridge University Press, 2021).

Dehm, Sara, 'Passport' in Jessie Hohmann and Daniel Joyce (eds.), *International Law's Objects* (Oxford: Oxford University Press, 2018) 342–356.

Deplano, Rossana, 'Assessing the Role of Resolutions in the ILC Draft Conclusions on Identification of Customary International Law' (2017) 14 *International Organizations Law Review* 227–253.

Depledge, Joanna, *The Organization of Environmental Negotiations: Constructing the Climate Change Regime* (London: Earthscan, 2005).

Deshman, Abigail C., 'International Organizations and Horizontal Review: The World Health Organisation, the Parliamentary Council of Europe, and the H1N1 Pandemic' in Cassese et al, *Global Administrative Law*, ch I.E.9.

Dewailly, Eric, and Christopher Furgal, 'POPs, the Environment, and Public Health' in David Leonard Downie and Terry Fenge (eds.), *Northern Lights against POPs: Combatting Toxic Threats in the Arctic* (Montreal: McGill-Queen's University Press, 2003) 3–21.

Disko, Stefan, Helen Tugendhat and Lola García-Alix, 'World Heritage Sites and Indigenous Peoples' Rights: An Introduction' in Stefan Disko and Helen Tugendhat (eds.), *World Heritage Sites and Indigenous Peoples' Rights* (Copenhagen: IWGIA, 2014) 3–38.

Dodds, Klaus, "Real Interest'? Understanding the 2018 Agreement to Prevent Unregulated High Seas Fisheries in the Central Arctic Ocean' (2019) 10 *Global Policy* 542–553.

Dorough, Dalee S., 'The Rights, Interests and Role of the Arctic Council Permanent Participants' in Robert C. Beckman, Tore Henriksen, Kristine Dalaker Kraabel, Erik J. Molenaar and J. Ashley Roach (eds.), *Governance of Arctic Shipping: Balancing Rights and Interests of Arctic States and User States* (Leiden: Brill Nijhoff, 2017) 68–10.

Droubi, Sufjan, 'Institutionalisation of Emerging Norms of Customary International Law through Resolutions and Operational Activities of the Political and Subsidiary Organs of the United Nations' (2017) 14(2) *International Organizations Law Review* 254–290.

Duyck, Sébastien, 'Participation of Non State Actors in Arctic Environmental Governance' (2012) 40 *Nordia Geographical Publications* 99–110.

Eide, Asbjørn, 'The Indigenous Peoples, the Working Group on Indigenous Populations and the Adoption of the UN Declaration on the Rights of Indigenous Peoples' in Claire Charters and Rodolfo Stavenhagen (eds.), *Making the Declaration Work: The United Nations Declaration on the Rights of Indigenous Peoples* (Copenhagen: IWGIA, 2009) 32–47.

Endorois Welfare Council et al, 'Joint Statement on Continuous Violations of the Principle of Free, Prior and Informed Consent in the Context of UNESCO's World Heritage Convention' (Statement to the PFII, New York, 17 May 2011) https://aippnet.org/joint-statement-on-continuous-violations-of-the-principle-of-free-prior-and-informed-consent-in-the-context-of-unescos-world-heritage-convention/.

Engström, Viljam, *Understanding Powers of International Organizations: A Study of the Doctrines of Attributed Powers, Implied Powers and Constitutionalism* (Åbo, Finland: Åbo Akademi University Press, 2009).

Errico, Stefania, 'The World Bank and Indigenous Peoples: The Operational Policy on Indigenous Peoples (O.P. 4.10) between Indigenous Peoples' Rights to Traditional Lands and to Free, Prior, and Informed Consent' (2006) 13 *International Journal on Minority and Group Rights* 367–390.

Erueti, Andrew, 'The International Labour Organization and the Internationalisation of the Concept of Indigenous Peoples' in Stephen Allen and Alexandra Xanthaki (eds.), *Reflections on the UN Declaration on the Rights of Indigenous Peoples* (London: Hart, 2011) 93–120.

Estes, Nick, *Our History Is the Future: Standing Rock versus the Dakota Access Pipeline* (London: Verso, 2019).

Fenge, Terry, 'POPs and Inuit: Influencing the Global Agenda' in David Leonard Downie and Terry Fenge (eds.), *Northern Lights against POPs: Combatting Toxic Threats in the Arctic* (Montreal: McGill-Queen's University Press, 2003) 192–213.

Finnemore, Martha, and Kathryn Sikkink, 'International Norm Dynamics and Political Change' (1998) 52 *International Organization* 887–917.

First International Conference on the Cultural and Intellectual Property Rights of Indigenous Peoples, *The Mataatua Declaration on Cultural and Intellectual Property Rights of Indigenous Peoples* (June 1993).

Fisheries and Oceans Canada, 'Canada Signs International Agreement to Prevent Unregulated Fishing in the High Seas of the Central Arctic Ocean' (3 October 2018) www.canada.ca/en/fisheries-oceans/news/2018/10/canada-signs-international-agreement-to-prevent-unregulated-fishing-in-the-high-seas-of-the-central-arctic-ocean.html.

'International Agreement to Prevent Unregulated High Seas Fisheries in the Central Arctic Ocean' (15 May 2019) www.dfo-mpo.gc.ca/international/arctic-arctique-eng.htm#_About_the_agreement.

Fitzmaurice, Gerald, 'The Law and Procedure of the International Court of Justice, 1951–54: General Principles and Sources of Law' (1953) 30 *British Yearbook of International Law* 1–70.

Fitzmaurice, Malgosia, 'The 2007 United Nations Declaration on the Rights of Indigenous Peoples' (2012) 17 *Austrian Review of International and European Law* 139–266.

Foro Indígena de Abya Yala, 'Declaration of the Indigenous Forum of Abya Yala' (13 April 2013) http://cendoc.docip.org/collect/cendocdo/index/assoc/HASH017a/6014b4a5.dir/WCIP_AbyaYaladecl_en.pdf.

Foster, Caroline E., 'Articulating Self-Determination in the Draft Declaration on the Rights of Indigenous Peoples' (2001) 12(1) *European Journal of International Law* 141–157.

Fox, Gregory H., 'The Right to Political Participation in International Law' (1992) 17 *Yale Journal of International Law* 539–607.

Franck, Thomas M., 'Post-Modern Tribalism and the Right to Secession' in Catherine Brölmann, René Lefeber and Marjoleine Zieck (eds.), *Peoples and Minorities in International Law* (Leiden: Martinus Nijhoff, 1993) 3–27.

French, Duncan, *Statehood and Self-Determination: Reconciling Tradition and Modernity* (Cambridge: Cambridge University Press, 2013).

Friedrich, Jürgen, 'Legal Challenges of Non-Binding Instruments: The Case of the FAO Code of Conduct for Responsible Fisheries' in von Bogdandy et al (eds.), *Exercise of Public Authority*, 511–540.

Fromherz, Christopher J., '"Indigenous Peoples" Courts: Egalitarian Juridical Pluralism, Self-Determination, and the United Nations Declaration on the Rights of Indigenous Peoples' (2008) 156(5) *University of Pennsylvania Law Review* 1341–1381.

Fry, James D., 'Formation of Customary International Law through Consensus in International Organizations' (2015) 17(1) *Austrian Review of International and European Law Online* 49–82.

García-Alix, Lola, *The Permanent Forum on Indigenous Issues* (Copenhagen: IWGIA, 2003).

General, Levi (Deskaheh), 'I Am Going to Geneva' in Daniel M. Cobb (ed.) *Say We Are Nations: Documents of Politics and Protest in Indigenous America since 1887* (Chapel Hill: University of North Carolina Press, [1923] 2015) 48.

'To the League of Nations; The Redman's Appeal for Justice' (1923), accessed at www.docip.org.

Getachew, Adom, *Worldmaking after Empire: The Rise and Fall of Self-Determination* (Princeton: Princeton University Press, 2019).

Gihl, Torsten, 'The Legal Character of Sources of International Law' (1957) 1 *Scandinavian Studies in Law* 53–92.

Gilbert, Jérémie and Cathal Doyle, 'A New Dawn over the Land: Shedding Light on Collective Ownership and Consent' in Stephen Allen and Alexandra Xanthaki (eds.), *Reflections on the UN Declaration on the Rights of Indigenous Peoples* (London: Hart, 2011) 290.

Global Indigenous Women's Caucus, 'Recommendations for Outcome of UNGA High Level Plenary Also to Be Called the World Conference on Indigenous Peoples' (30 March 2013) http://cendoc.docip.org/collect/cendocdo/index/assoc/HASH01f5/8707c3a9.dir/WCIP_Women_Declaration_ENG.pdf.

Global Indigenous Youth Caucus, 'Global Indigenous Youth Caucus Declaration on the World Conference on Indigenous Peoples 2014' (2013) http://cendoc.docip.org/collect/cendocdo/index/assoc/HASH0106/75023a4a.dir/WCIP_Youth_Declaration_ENGa.pdf.

Gordon, Veronica, 'Appropriation without Representation? The Limited Role of Indigenous Groups in WIPO's Intergovernmental Committee on Intellectual Property and Genetic Resources, Traditional Knowledge, and Folklore' (2014) 16 *Vanderbilt Journal of Entertainment and Technology Law* 629–667.

Grand Council of the Crees, Letter to Claire Charters (2012), accessible at www.ohchr.org/EN/Issues/IPeoples/Pages/ConsultationonIPparticipationintheUN.aspx.

Griffiths, Tom, 'Indigenous Peoples and the World Bank: Experiences with Participation' (Forest Peoples Programme, July 2005).

Guibernau, Montserrat, 'Nations without States: Political Communities in the Global Age' (2004) 25(4) *Michigan Journal of International Law* 1251–1282.

Gunning, Isabelle R., 'Modernizing Customary International Law: The Challenge of Human Rights' (1991) 31 *Virginia Journal of International Law* 211–247.

Habermas, Jürgen, 'Three Normative Models of Democracy' (1994) 1 *Constellations* 1–10.

Hannum, Hurst, *Autonomy, Sovereignty and Self-Determination: The Accommodation of Conflicting Rights* (rev. ed., Philadelphia: University of Pennsylvania Press, 1996).

Heath, J. Benton, 'SARS, the 'Swine Flu' Crisis and Emergency Procedures in the WHO' in Cassese et al., *Global Administrative Law*, ch I.B.10.

Heinämäki, Leena, 'Towards an Equal Partnership between Indigenous Peoples and States: Learning from Arctic Experiences' (2011) 3 *Yearbook of Polar Law* 193–246.

Henriksen, John B., 'The UN Declaration on the Rights of Indigenous Peoples: Some Key Issues and Events in the Process' in Claire Charters and Rodolfo Stavenhagen (eds.), *Making the Declaration Work: The United Nations Declaration on the Rights of Indigenous Peoples* (Copenhagen: IWGIA, 2009) 78–85.

John Henriksen for the Indigenous Global Coordinating Group, 'Second Round of Consultations Organized by the President of the General Assembly, Opening Intervention' (16 July 2014) http://cendoc.docip.org/collect/cendocdo/index/assoc/HASH2d41/e4092f25.dir/WCIP_2nd160714_GCGOpening_en.pdf.

Higgins, Rosalyn, *The Development of International Law by the Political Organs of the United Nations* (Oxford: Oxford University Press, 1963).

'The United Nations and Lawmaking: The Political Organs' (1970) 64 *ASIL* 37–47.

Problems and Process: International Law and How We Use It (Oxford: Oxford University Press, 1995).

Hofbauer, Jane A., *Sovereignty in the Exercise of the Right to Self-Determination* (Leiden; Boston: Brill, 2017).

Hoffman, Steven J., Prativa Baral, and Susan Rogers Van Katwyk, et al., 'International Treaties Have Mostly Failed to Produce Their Intended Effects' (2022) 119(32) *PNAS* e2122854119.

Houghton, Ruth, 'Looking at the World Bank's Safeguard Reform through the Lens of Deliberative Democracy' (2019) 32 *Leiden Journal of International Law* 465–482.

Hovell, Devika, 'Due Process in the United Nations' (2016) 110(2) *American Journal of International Law* 1–48.

Hunter, Julie, Pradeep Singh and Julion Aguon, 'Broadening Common Heritage: Addressing Gaps in the Deep Sea Mining Regulatory Regime' (2018) *Harvard Environmental Law Review* (online), <https://harvardelr.com/2018/04/16/broadening-common-heritage/.

Hurrell, Andrew, 'Power, Institutions, and the Production of Inequality' in Michael Barnett and Raymond Duvall (eds.), *Power in Global Governance* (Cambridge: Cambridge University Press 2005) 33–58.

'ICC Applauds Adoption of Central Arctic Ocean Fishing Moratorium (17 July 2015) www.inuitcircumpolar.com/press-releases/icc-applauds-adoption-of-central-arctic-ocean-fishing-moratorium/.

'ICC Canada Applauds Canada's Recognition of the Value of Indigenous Knowledge and Encourages Its Use in Climate and Fisheries Discussions' (3 December 2015) www.inuitcircumpolar.com/press-releases/icc-canada-applauds-canadas-recognition-of-the-value-of-indigenous-knowledge-and-encourages-its-use-in-climate-and-fisheries-discussions/.

'IIPFCC Proposals for the Indigenous Peoples Knowledge-Sharing Platform' (10 November 2016), http://cendoc.docip.org/collect/cendocdo/index/assoc/HASH9abd/808d79dd.dir/IIPFCC%20propIndPeoplesknowledgeplatform_EN.pdf.

Indigenous Peoples of the North, Siberia and the Far East, 'Salekhard Declaration' (29 March 2013) http://cendoc.docip.org/collect/cendocdo/index/assoc/HASHf411/953b9d0d.dir/WCIP_RussiaDecl_en.pdf.

Indigenous Peoples of the North, Siberia and the Far East, *The Indigenous World – 2014* (Copenhagen: IWGIA, 2014).

The Indigenous World – 2019 (Copenhagen: IWGIA, 2019).

The Indigenous World – 2020 (Copenhagen: IWGIA, 2020).

International Alliance of the Indigenous Peoples of the Tropical Rainforest, 'Submission of the International Alliance to the CBD Secretariat: The Biodiversity Convention – The Concerns of Indigenous Peoples', reproduced in International Alliance of Indigenous-Tribal Peoples of the Tropical Forest, *Indigenous Peoples, Forest, and Biodiversity* (Copenhagen: IWGIA, 1996) 105–122.

International Indigenous Forum on Biodiversity and Ecosystem Services (IIFBES), 'Report of the Task Force on Indigenous and Local Knowledge' (12 January 2015), www.asianindigenouswomen.org/index.php/component/k2/item/118-statement-by-the-international-indigenous-forum-on-biodiversity-and-ecosystem-services-iifbes.

International Indigenous Peoples' Forum on Climate Change (IIPFCC), 'Executive Summary of Indigenous Peoples' Proposals to the UNFCCC COP 20 and COP21' (30 November 2014), www.iipfcc.org/resources.

International Indigenous Peoples' Forum on World Heritage (IIPFWH), 'International Indigenous Peoples' Forum on World Heritage' (n.d.), www.iipfwh.org.

International Work Group for Indigenous Affairs, *International Expert Workshop on the World Heritage Convention and Indigenous Peoples* (Copenhagen: IWGIA, 2012).

Inuit Circumpolar Council, 'A Circumpolar Inuit Declaration on Sovereignty in the Arctic' (April 2009), https://iccalaska.org/wp-icc/wp-content/uploads/2016/01/Signed-Inuit-Sovereignty-Declaration-11x17.pdf.

Israel, Brian R., 'International Law and Governance in a Changing Arctic' (2014) 108 *American Journal of International Law* 348–359.

Jennings, Robert Y., 'The Identification of International Law' in Bin Cheng (ed.), *International Law, Teaching and Practice* (London: Stevens & Sons, 1982) 3–9.

Johansen, Bruce E., 'The Inuit's Struggle with Dioxins and Other Organic Pollutants' (2002) 26 *American Indian Quarterly* 479–490.

Jones, Natalie, *Towards a Right of Peoples to Participation in Global Governance* (PhD thesis, University of Cambridge, 2020).

Kaufmann, Eric, and Oded Haklai, 'Dominant Ethnicity: From Minority to Majority' (2008) 14 *Nations and Nationalism* 743–767.

Kelly, J. Patrick, 'The Twilight of Customary International Law' (2000) 40 *Virginia Journal of International Law* 449–543.

Kelsen, Hans, 'Théorie du droit international coutumier' (1939) 1(4) *Revue international de la théorie du droit* 253–274.

Keohane, Robert O., Stephen Macedo and Andrew Moravcsik, 'Democracy Enhancing Multilateralism' (2009) 63(1) *International Organization* 1–31.

Kingsbury, Benedict, 'Reconciling Five Competing Conceptual Structures of Indigenous Claims in International and Comparative Law' (2001) 34 *NYU Journal of International Law & Politics* 189–250.

Kingsbury, Benedict, David M. Malone, Paul Mertenskötter, Richard B. Stewart, Thomas Streinz, and Atsushi Sunami, *Megaregulation Contested: Global Economic Ordering after TPP* (Oxford: Oxford University Press 2019).

'Kitigaaryuit Declaration' (24 July 2014), https://iccalaska.org/wp-icc/wp-content/uploads/2016/01/2014-Kitigaarguit-Declaration-Final-Signed.pdf.

Klabbers, Jan, 'International Organizations in the Formation of Customary International Law' in Enzo Cannizzaro and Paolo Palchetti (eds.), *Customary International Law on the Use of Force: A Methodological Approach* (Leiden: Martinus Nijhoff 2005) 179–195.

'The Right to Be Taken Seriously: Self-Determination in International Law' (2006) 28 *Human Rights Quarterly* 186–206.

'The Transformation of International Organizations Law' (2015) 26(1) *European Journal of International Law* 9–82.

'Sources of International Organizations Law: Reflections on Accountability' in Jean D'Aspremont and Samantha Besson (eds.), *The Oxford Handbook of the Sources of International Law* (Oxford: Oxford University Press 2017) 987–1006.

Kleinlein, Thomas, 'Customary International Law and General Principles: Rethinking Their Relationship' in Brian D. Lepard (ed.), *Reexamining Customary International Law* (Cambridge: Cambridge University Press, 2017) 131–160.

Knop, Karen, *Diversity and Self-Determination in International Law* (Cambridge: Cambridge University Press, 2008).

Koivurova, Timo, 'The Draft Nordic Saami Convention: Nations Working Together' (2008) 10 *International Community Law Review* 279–293.

'Sovereign States and Self-Determining Peoples: Carving Out a Place for Transnational Indigenous Peoples in a World of Sovereign States' (2010) 12(2) *International Community Law Review* 191–212.

'The Status and Role of Indigenous Peoples in Arctic International Governance' (2011) 3 *Yearbook of Polar Law* 169–192.

'Can Saami Transnational Indigenous Peoples Exercise Their Self-Determination in a World of Sovereign States?' in Nigel Bankes and Timo Koivurova (eds.), *The Proposed Nordic Saami Convention: National and International Dimensions of Indigenous Property Rights* (Oxford: Hart, 2013) 105–124.

Koivurova, Timo and Leena Heinämäki, 'The Participation of Indigenous Peoples in International Norm-Making in the Arctic' (2006) 42 *Polar Record* 101–109.

Kopelmanas, Lazare, 'Custom as a Means of the Creation of International Law' (1937) *British Yearbook of International Law* 127–151.

Koskenniemi, Martti, *The Gentle Civilizer of Nations: The Rise and Fall of International Law 1870–1960* (Cambridge: Cambridge University Press, 2001).

Koskenniemi, Martti, Walter Rech, and Manuel Jiménez Fonseca (eds.), *International Law and Empire – Historical Explorations* (Oxford: Oxford University Press, 2017).

Krisch, Nico and Benedict Kingsbury, 'Introduction: Global Governance and Global Administrative Law in the International Legal Order' (2006) 17(1) *European Journal of International Law* 1–13.

Kuhnlein, Harriet V., Laurie Hing Man Chan, Grace Egeland and Olivier Receveur, 'Canadian Arctic Indigenous Peoples, Traditional Food Systems, and POPs' in David Leonard Downie and Terry Fenge (eds.), *Northern Lights against POPs: Combatting Toxic Threats in the Arctic* (Montreal: McGill-Queen's University Press, 2003) 22–40.

Kunz, Josef L., 'The Nature of Customary International Law' (1953) 47 *American Journal of International Law* 662–669.

Kymlicka, Will, *Multicultural Citizenship: A Liberal Theory of Minority Rights* (Oxford: Clarendon, 1995).

Lacy, Michael G., 'The United States and American Indians: Political Relations' in Vine Deloria, Jr. (ed.), *American Indian Policy in the Twentieth Century* (Norman, O.K.: University of Oklahoma Press, 1985) 83.

Lagoutte, Stephanie, Thomas Gammeltoft-Hansen and John Cerone (eds.), *Tracing the Roles of Soft Law in Human Rights* (Cambridge: Cambridge University Press, 2016).

Lallas, Peter L., 'The Stockholm Convention on Persistent Organic Pollutants' (2001) 95 *American Journal of International Law* 692–708.

Lang, Sabine, *NGOs, Civil Society, and the Public Sphere* (Cambridge: Cambridge University Press, 2013).

Lauterpacht, Hersch, *The Development of International Law by the International Court* (London: Stevens & Sons, 1957).

Lawson, Charles, Edwin Bikundo and Kieran Tranter, 'The Perils of Parliamentarism: The World Intellectual Property Organization and Indigenous Peoples' (2019) 39 (2) *Oxford Journal of Legal Studies* 285–315.

Lemarchand, René, 'Consociationalism and Power Sharing in Africa: Rwanda, Burundi, and the Democratic Republic of the Congo' (2006) 106(422) *African Affairs* 1–20.
Lepard, Brian D., *Customary International Law: A New Theory with Practical Applications* (Cambridge: Cambridge University Press, 2016).
'Toward a New Theory of Customary International Human Rights Law' in Brian D. Lepard (ed.), *Reexamining Customary International Law* (Cambridge: Cambridge University Press, 2017) 233–265.
Lewis, Corinne, and Carl Söderbergh, 'The World Bank's New Environmental and Social Framework: Some Progress but Many Gaps Regarding the Rights of Indigenous Peoples' (2019) 23 *International Journal of Human Rights* 63–86.
Lightfoot, Sheryl R, *Global Indigenous Politics: A Subtle Revolution* (New York: Routledge, 2016).
'Decolonizing Self-Determination: Haudenosaunee Passports and Negotiated Sovereignty' (2021) 27 *European Journal of International Relations*, 971–994.
Lijphart, Arend, *Democracy in Plural Societies: A Comparative Exploration* (New Haven: Yale University Press, 1977).
Lindroth, Marjo, 'Indigenous-State Relations in the UN: Establishing the Indigenous Forum' (2006) 42 *Polar Record*, 239–428.
Loukacheva, Natalia, '"Arctic Indigenous Peoples" Internationalism: In Search of a Legal Justification' (2009) 45 *Polar Record* 51–58.
Macedo, Stephen and Allen Buchanan (eds.), *Secession and Self-Determination* (New York: New York University Press, 2003).
MacKay, Fergus, 'The Draft World Bank Operational Policy 4.10 on Indigenous Peoples: Progress or More of the Same?' (2005) 22 *Arizona Journal of International & Comparative Law* 65–98.
Macklem, Patrick, 'Indigenous Recognition in International Law: Theoretical Observations' (2008) 30 *Michigan Journal of International Law* 177–210.
'Self-Determination in Three Movements' in Fernando R. Tesón (ed.), *The Theory of Self-Determination* (Cambridge: Cambridge University Press, 2016) 94–119.
Maisley, Nahuel, 'The International Right of Rights? Article 25(a) of the ICCPR as a Human Right to Take Part in International Law-Making' (2017) 28(1) *European Journal on International Law* 89–113.
Maluwa, Tiyanjana, 'Custom, Authority and Law: Some Jurisprudential Perspective on the Theory of Customary International Law' (1994) 6 *African Journal of International and Comparative Law* 387–410.
Manuel, George and Michael Posluns, *The Fourth World: An Indian Reality* (Minneapolis: University of Minnesota Press, [1974] 2018).
Marine Mammal Commission, *The Marine Mammal Commission Compendium of Selected Treaties, International Agreements, and Other Relevant Documents on Marine Resources, Wildlife, and the Environment*, First Update (Washington, DC.: The Marine Mammal Commission, 1994).
Martínez, Miguel Alfonso, 'Study on Treaties, Agreements and Other Constructive Arrangements between States and Indigenous Populations: Final Report' (22 June 1999) UN Doc. E/CN.4/Sub.2/1999/20.

Martínez Cobo, José R., 'Study of the Problem of Discrimination against Indigenous Populations, Volume V, Conclusions, Proposals and Recommendations' (1986) UN Doc. E/CN.4/Sub.2/1986/7.

Mathias, Stephen, 'The Work of the International Law Commission on Identification of Customary International Law: A View from the Perspective of the Office of Legal Affairs' (2016) 15(1) *Chinese Journal of International Law* 17–31.

McMillan and Sophie Rigney, 'The Place of the First Peoples in the International Sphere: A Logical Starting Point for the Demand for Justice by Indigenous Peoples' (2016) 39(3) *Melbourne University Law Review* 981–1002.

McCorquodale, Robert, 'Self-Determination: A Human Rights Approach' (1994) 43(4) *International & Comparative Law Quarterly* 857–885.

Mégret, Frédéric and Florian F. Hoffman, 'The UN as a Human Rights Violator? Some Reflections on the United Nations Changing Human Rights Responsibilities' (2003) 23 *Human Rights Quarterly* 314–342.

Meijers, H., 'On International Customary Law in the Netherlands' in Ige F. Dekker and Harry H.G. Post (eds.), *On the Foundations and Sources of International Law* (Utrecht: TMC Asser Press, 2003) 77.

Mendelson, Maurice H., *The Formation of Customary International Law* (Brill, 1998).

Meskell, Lynn, 'UNESCO and the Fate of the World Heritage Indigenous Peoples Council of Experts (WHIPCOE)' (2013) 20 *International Journal of Cultural Property* 155–174.

Minde, Henry, 'Sami Land Rights in Norway: A Test Case for Indigenous Peoples' (2001) 8 *International Journal on Minority and Group Rights* 107–125.

Ministerio de Relaciones Exteriores de Bolivia, 'IV Reunión de Representantes de Órganos e Instituciones del Sistema Andino de Integración' (4 October 2019) https://cancilleria.gob.bo/webmre/node/3662.

Morgera, Elisa, 'Dawn of a New Day? The Evolving Relationship between the Convention on Biological Diversity and International Human Rights Law' (2018) 53 *Wake Forest Law Review* 691–712.

Muehlebach, Andrea, '"Making Place" at the United Nations: Indigenous Cultural Politics at the U.N. Working Group on Indigenous Populations' (2001) 16 *Cultural Anthropology* 415–448.

Narr, Henrike, 'Nothing about Us without Us: Access for Indigenous Peoples to the United Nations and Perceptions of Legitimacy' (PhD thesis, University of Tübingen, 2019).

Natural Justice, 'WCIP Concludes in New York with Adoption of Outcome Document' (Natural Justice, 2 October 2014, https://naturaljustice.org/wcip-concludes-in-new-york-with-adoption-of-outcome-document/).

Navajo Nation Council, *Adopting and Recommending Position Statements Regarding the United Nations Recognition for the Navajo Nation* (22 July 2009) NNHRC/Report 03/2009.

New Zealand Foreign Affairs and Trade, 'Memorandum of Understanding Between Te Taumata and The Ministry of Foreign Affairs and Trade (MFAT)' (MFAT, 24 September 2019) www.mfat.govt.nz/assets/Uploads/MFAT-Te-Taumata-MOU.pdf.

Niezen, Ronald, *The Origins of Indigenism: Human Rights and the Politics of Identity* (Berkeley: University of California Press, 2003).

North American Indigenous Peoples' Caucus, 'Decisions and Recommendations of the North American Indigenous Peoples' Caucus Regarding the UN High-Level Plenary Meeting to Be Called a World Conference on Indigenous Peoples' (3 March 2013) http://cendoc.docip.org/collect/cendocdo/index/assoc/HASH01f5/624f3354.dir/WCIP_NAIPC_Declaration_ENG.pdf.

Nunatsiaq News, 'Indigenous Peoples Meet in Arctic Norway to Prepare 2014 UN Conference' (Nunatsiaq News, 10 June 2013, https://nunatsiaq.com/stories/article/65674indigenous_peoples_meet_in_arctic_norway_to_prepare_un_conference/).

Öberg, Marko Divac, 'The Legal Effects of Resolutions of the UN Security Council and General Assembly in the Jurisprudence of the ICJ' (2015) 16(5) *European Journal of International Law* 879–906.

Oguamanam, Chidi, *Intellectual Property in Global Governance: A Development Question* (New York: Routledge 2012).

Orakhelashvili, Alexander, *Peremptory Norms in International Law* (Oxford: Oxford University Press, 2006).

'The Pacific Declaration of the Preparatory Meeting for Pacific Indigenous Peoples on the World Conference on Indigenous Peoples 2014' (21 March 2013) http://cendoc.docip.org/collect/cendocdo/index/assoc/HASH01f3/69157d75.dir/WCIP_Pacifidecl_en.pdf.

'Our Proposals to Governments' (27 November 2015), 3, www.iipfcc.org/resources.

Pacholska, Magdalena, 'New Kids on the Block: International Organizations as Customary Rules Creators' (2019) 21(3–4) *International Community Law Review* 325–343.

Pahuja, Sundhya, *Decolonising International Law: Development, Economic Growth and the Politics of Universality* (Cambridge: Cambridge University Press, 2011).

Parfitt, Rose, *The Process of International Legal Reproduction: Inequality, Historiography, Resistance* (Cambridge: Cambridge University Press, 2019).

Paulson, Nels, Ann Laudati, Amity Doolittle, Meredith Welsh-Devine, and Pablo Pena, 'Indigenous Peoples' Participation in Global Conservation: Looking beyond Headdresses and Face Paint' (2012) 21 *Environmental Values* 255–276.

Pavkovic, Aleksandar and Peter Radan (eds.), *On the Way to Statehood: Secession and Globalisation* (Aldershot: Ashgate, 2008).

Pearson, Zoe, 'Non-Governmental Organizations and the international Criminal Court: Changing Landscapes of International Law' (2006) 39(2) *Cornell International Law Journal* 243–284.

Peters, Anne, 'International Organizations in International Law' in Jacob Katz Cogan, Ian Hurd and Ian Johnstone (eds.), *The Oxford Handbook of International Organizations* (Oxford: Oxford University Press, 2016) 33–59.

Piiparinen, Touko, 'Secretariats' in Jacob Katz Cogan, Ian Hurd and Ian Johnstone (eds.), *The Oxford Handbook of International Organizations* (Oxford: Oxford University Press, 2016) 839–858.

Pomerance, Michla, *Self-Determination in Law and Practice – The New Doctrine in the United Nations* (The Hague: Martinus Nijhoff, 1982).

Poto, Margherita Paola, 'Participatory Rights of Indigenous Peoples: The Virtuous Example of the Arctic Region' (2016) 28 *Environmental Law & Management* 81–89.

'Participatory Engagement and the Empowerment of the Arctic Indigenous Peoples' (2017) 19 *Environmental Law Review* 30–47.

President of the Republic of Finland, 'Statement by President of the Republic of Finland Sauli Niinistö at the World Conference on Indigenous Peoples (WCIP) United Nations, New York 22 September 2014' (22 September 2014) www.presidentti.fi/en/speeches/statement-by-president-of-the-republic-of-finland-sauli-niinisto-at-the-world-conference-on-indigenous-peoples-wcip-united-nations-new-york-22-september-2014/.

Price Cohen, Cynthia, 'The Role of Nongovernmental Organizations in the Drafting of the Convention on the Rights of the Child' (1990) 12 *Human Rights Quarterly* 137–147.

Puig, Sergio, 'International Indigenous Economic Law' (2019) 32 *UC Davis Law Review* 1243–1316.

Pulitano, Elvira, *Indigenous Rights in the Age of the UN Declaration* (Cambridge: Cambridge University Press, 2014).

Quane, Helen, 'The United Nations and the Evolving Right to Self-Determination' (1998) 47(3) *International & Comparative Law Quarterly* 537–572.

Raustiala, Kal, 'States, NGOs, and International Environmental Institutions' (1997) 41 (4) *International Studies Quarterly* 719–740.

Rehman, Javaid, 'Between the Devil and the Deep Blue Sea: Indigenous Peoples as the Pawns in the US "War on Terror" and the Jihad of Osama Bin Laden' in Stephen Allen and Alexandra Xanthaki (eds.), *Reflections on the UN Declaration on the Rights of Indigenous Peoples* (Oxford: Hart 2011) 561–584.

Reinisch, August, 'Securing the Accountability of International Organizations' (2001) 7(2) *Global Governance* 131–149.

'Sources of International Organizations' Law: Why Custom and General Principles Are Crucial', in Jean D'Aspremont and Samantha Besson (eds.), *The Oxford Handbook of the Sources of International Law* (Oxford: Oxford University Press, 2017) 1007–1024.

Reinisch, August and Christina Irgel, 'The Participation of Non-Governmental Organisations (NGOs) in the WTO Dispute Settlement System' (2001) 1(2) *Non-State Actors & International Law* 127–151.

Representatives of Inuit and Sami peoples, 'Arctic Declaration on the World Conference on Indigenous Peoples 2014: The Arctic Preparatory Meeting in Nuuk, Greenland' (24 October 2012) http://cendoc.docip.org/collect/cendocdo/index/assoc/HASH1e2e/4e5c63dc.dir/WCIP_Nuuk_ENG.pdf

Reynolds, Andrew, 'Reserved Seats in National Legislatures: A Research Note' (2005) 30(2) *Legislative Studies Quarterly* 301–310.

Richardson, Katya Lena, 'Finding a Duty to Consult Aboriginal Peoples During the Negotiation of Free Trade Agreements (FTAs) and Foreign Investment Promotion and Protection Agreements (FIPAs)' (2017) 7 *Western Journal of Legal Studies* 1–17.

Rigney, Sophie 'On Hearing Well and Being Well Heard: Indigenous International Law at the League of Nations' (2021) 34(2) *Third World Approaches to International Law Review* 122–153.

Rigo Sureda, Andrés, *The Evolution of the Right of Self-Determination: A Study of United Nations Practice* (Leiden: AW Sijthoff, 1973).

Roberts, Anthea, 'Traditional and Modern Approaches to Customary International Law: A Reconciliation' (2001) 95(4) *American Journal of International Law* 757–791.

Is International Law International? (Oxford: Oxford University Press, 2018).

Robinson, Daniel F., Pedro Roffe and Ahmed Abdel-Latif, 'Introduction: Mapping the Evolution, State-of-Play and Future of the WIPO IGC' in Daniel F. Robinson, Ahmed Abdel-Latif, and Pedro Roffe (eds.), *Protecting Traditional Knowledge: The WIPO Intergovernmental Committee on Intellectual Property and Genetic Resources, Traditional Knowledge and Folklore* (New York: Routledge, 2017) 3–9.

Rodríguez-Piñero, Luis, *Indigenous Peoples, Postcolonialism, and International Law: The ILO Regime (1919–1989)* (Oxford: Oxford University Press, 2005).

Rosas, Allan, 'Internal Self-Determination' in Christian Tomuschat (ed.), *Modern Law of Self-Determination* (Dordrecht: Martinus Nijhoff, 1993) 225–252.

Rottem, Svein Vigeland, 'A Note on the Arctic Council Agreements' (2015) 46 *Ocean Development and International Law* 50–59.

Saami Council, 'Saami Council Position Paper' (11 October 2015), 2, www.iipfcc.org/resources.

Sanders, Douglas, 'The UN Working Group on Indigenous Populations' (1989) 11 *Human Rights Quarterly* 406–433.

'The Legacy of Deskaheh: Indigenous Peoples as International Actors', in Cynthia Price Cohen (ed.), *Human Rights of Indigenous Peoples* (Ardsley, NY: Transnational Publishers, 1998) 73–88.

Sarson, Leah, '"You Cannot Trade What Is Not Yours": Indigenous Governance and the NAFTA Negotiations' (2019) 49 *American Review of Canadian Studies* 332–34.

Saul, Matthew, 'The Normative Status of Self-Determination in International Law: A Formula for Uncertainty in the Scope and Content of the Right' (2011) 11(4) *Human Rights Law Review* 609–644.

Scarpa, Federica, 'The EU, the Arctic, and Arctic Indigenous Peoples' (2014) 6(1) *The Yearbook of Polar Law Online* 427–465.

Schachter, Oscar, 'New Custom: Power, *Opinio Juris* and Contrary Practice' in Jerzy Makarczyk (ed.), *Theory of International Law at the Threshold of the Twenty-First Century: Essays in Honour of Krzysztof Skubiszewski* (The Hague: Kluwer, 1996) 531–540.

Scharf, Michael P., 'Seizing the 'Grotian Moment': Accelerated Formation of Customary International Law in Times of Fundamental Change' (2010) 43(3) *Cornell International Law Journal* 439–469.

Schatz, Valentin, 'The Incorporation of Indigenous and Local Knowledge into Central Arctic Ocean Fisheries Management' (2019) 10 *Arctic Review on Law and Politics* 130–134.

Scheinin, Martin and Mattias Åhren, 'Relationship to Human Rights, and Related International Instruments' in Jessie Hohmann and Marc Weller (eds.), *The UN Declaration on the Rights of Indigenous People: A Commentary* (Oxford: Oxford University Press, 2018) 63–86.

Schermers, Henry G., and Niels M. Blokker, *International Institutional Law: Unity within Diversity* (Leiden: Martinus Nijhoff, 2011).

Schöndorf-Haubold, Bettina, 'The Administration of Information in International Administrative Law – The Example of Interpol', in von Bogdandy et al (eds.), *Exercise of Public Authority*, 229–268.

Schramm, Annette, and Jan Sändig, 'Affectedness Alliances: Affected People at the Centre of Transnational Advocacy' (2018) 3(5–6) *Third World Thematics* 664–683.

Scrivener, David, 'Arctic Environmental Cooperation in Transition' (1999) 35 *Polar Record* 51–58.

Selin, Henrik, and Noelle Eckley Selin, 'Indigenous Peoples in International Environmental Cooperation: Arctic Management of Hazardous Substances' (2008) 17 *Review of European Community & International Environmental Law* 72–83.

Shelton, Dina, *Remedies in International Human Rights Law*, 3rd ed., (Oxford: Oxford University Press, 2015).

Shraga, Daphna, 'ILC Articles on Responsibility of International Organizations: The Interplay between the Practice and the Rule (A View from the United Nations' in Maurizio Ragazzi (ed.), *Responsibility of International Organizations: Essays in Memory of Sir Ian Brownlie* (Leiden: Martinus Nijhoff, 2013) 201.

Simma, Bruno and Philip Alston, 'The Sources of Human Rights Law: Custom, *Jus Cogens* and General Principles' (1989) 12 *Australian Year Book of International Law* 82–108.

Simpson, Audra, *Mohawk Interruptus* (Durham, N.C.: Duke University Press, 2014).

Sinclair, Guy Fiti, 'State Formation, Liberal Reform and the Growth of International Organizations' (2015) 26 *European Journal of International Law* 445–469.

Skubiszewski, Krzysztof, 'Resolutions of the U.N. General Assembly and Evidence of Custom', in *Le droit international a l'heure de sa codification, éudes en l'honneur de Roberto Ago* (Vol. I) (1987) 503.

Smith, Jackie and Dawn West, 'The Uneven Geography of Global Civil Society: National and Global Influences on Transnational Association' (2005) 84(2) *Social Forces* 621–652.

Smrkolj, Maja, 'International Institutions and Individualized Decision-Making: An Example of UNHCR's Refugee Status Determination' in von Bogdandy et al (eds.), *Exercise of Public Authority*, 165–194.

Solomon, Maui, 'An Indigenous Perspective on the WIPO IGC' in Daniel F. Robinson, Ahmed Abdel-Latif, and Pedro Roffe, *Protecting Traditional Knowledge: The WIPO Intergovernmental Committee on Intellectual Property and Genetic Resources, Traditional Knowledge and Folklore* (Oxford: Routledge, 2017) 219–229.

Solonec, Tammy 'UN Mechanisms for Indigenous Peoples: A Personal Account of Participation in 2010' (2010) 7 *Indigenous Law Bulletin* 8–12.

Stamatopolou, Elsa, 'Indigenous Peoples and the United Nations: Human Rights as a Developing Dynamic' (1994) 16 *Human Rights Quarterly* 58–81.

'Statement of the International Indigenous Peoples' Forum on World Heritage, Item 7B – State of Conservation of Properties Inscribed on the World Heritage List' (July 2021), https://iipfwh.org/publications/.

Stavenhagen, Rodolfo, 'Making the Declaration on the Rights of Indigenous Peoples Work: The Challenge Ahead', in Stephen Allen and Alexandra Xanthaki (eds.),

Reflections on the UN Declaration on the Rights of Indigenous Peoples (London: Hart, 2011) 147–170.

Stewart Richard B., 'Remedying Disregard in Global Regulatory Governance: Accountability, Participation, and Responsiveness' (2014) 108(2) *American Journal of International Law* 211–270.

Stewart, Richard B. and Michelle Ratton Sanchez-Badin, 'The World Trade Organization: Multiple Dimensions of Global Administrative Law' (2011) 9(3–4) *International Journal of Constitutional Law* 556–586.

Storr, Cait, *International Status in the Shadow of Empire: Nauru and the Histories of International Law* (Cambridge: Cambridge University Press, 2020).

Subbiah, Sumathi, 'Reaping What They Sow: The Basmati Rice Controversy and Strategies for Protecting Traditional Knowledge' (2004) 27(2) *Boston College International & Comparative Law Review* 529–559.

Summers, James, *Peoples and International Law* (2nd ed., Leiden: Martinus Nijhoff, 2014).

Swepston, Lee, 'A New Step in the International Law on Indigenous and Tribal Peoples: ILO Convention No 169 of 1989' (1990) 15 *Oklahoma City University Law Review* 677–752.

Taki, Hiroshi, '*Opinio Juris* and the Formation of Customary International Law: A Theoretical Analysis' (2008) 51 *German Yearbook of International Law* 447–466.

Talmon, Stefan, 'Determining Customary International Law: The ICJ's Methodology between Induction, Deduction and Assertion' (2015) 26 *European Journal of International Law* 417–443.

Tesón, Fernando R. (ed.), *The Theory of Self-Determination* (Cambridge: Cambridge University Press, 2016).

'Fake Custom' in Brian D. Lepard (ed.), *Reexamining Customary International Law* (Cambridge: Cambridge University Press, 2017) 86–110.

Thew, Harriet, 'Youth Participation and Agency in the United Nations Framework Convention on Climate Change' (2018) 18 *International Environmental Agreements* 369–389.

Thirlway, Hugh, *International Customary Law and Codification: An Examination of the Continuing Role of Custom in the Present Period of Codification of International law* (Leiden: Sijthoff, 1972).

Thornberry, Patrick, *Indigenous Peoples and Human Rights* (Manchester: Manchester University Press, 2002).

Tomaselli, Alexandra, 'The Right to Political Participation of Indigenous Peoples: A Holistic Approach' (2014) 24 *International Journal on Minority and Group Rights* 390–427.

Tomuschat, Christian (ed.), *Modern Law of Self-Determination* (Dordrecht: Martinus Nijhoff, 1993).

Trinidad, Jamie, *Self-Determination in Disputed Colonial Territories* (Cambridge: Cambridge University Press, 2018).

Tunkin, Grigory I., 'Remarks on the Juridical Nature of Customary Norms of International Law' (1961) 49(3) *California Law Review* 419–430.

'The Role of Resolutions of International Organizations in Creating Norms of International Law' (1987) 230 *Coexistence* 5.

Tzouvala, Ntina, *Capitalism As Civilisation: A History of International Law* (Cambridge: Cambridge University Press, 2020).

U.S. Department of State, 'Meeting on High Seas Fisheries in the Central Arctic Ocean' (1 December 2015) www.state.gov/remarks-and-releases-bureau-of-oceans-and-international-environmental-and-scientific-affairs/meeting-on-high-seas-fisheries-in-the-central-arctic-ocean/.

Umozurike, U.O., *Self-Determination in International Law* (Hamden, Connecticut: Archon Books, 1972).

Van den Bossche, Peter, 'NGO Involvement in the WTO: A Comparative Perspective' (2008) 11(4) *Journal of International Economic Law* 717–749.

Van Dyke, Vernon, 'Human Rights and the Rights of Groups' (1974) 28(4) *American Journal of Political Science* 725–741.

Veatch, Richard, *Canada and the League of Nations* (Toronto: University of Toronto Press, 1975).

Vested, Anne, Aleksander Giwercman, Jens Peter Bonde, and Gunnar Toft, 'Persistent Organic Pollutants and Male Reproductive Health' (2014) 16(1) *Asian Journal of Andrology* 71–80.

Vigil, Kiara M., 'Who Was Henry Standing Bear? Remembering Lakota Activism from the Early Twentieth Century' (2017) 37(3) *Great Plains Quarterly* 157–182.

Villiger, Mark E., *Customary International Law and Treaties: A Study of Their Interactions and Interrelations with Special Consideration of the 1969 Vienna Convention on the Law of Treaties* (Dordrecht: Martinus Nijhoff, 1985).

Vizcaino, Esther, Joan O. Grimalt, Ana Fernández-Somoano, and Adonina Tardon, 'Transport of Persistent Organic Pollutants across the Human Placenta' (2014) 65 *Environment International* 107–115.

Vrdoljak, Ana Filipa, 'Indigenous Peoples, World Heritage, and Human Rights' (2018) 25 *International Journal of Cultural Property* 245–281.

Vylegzhanin, Alexander N., Oran R. Young, and Paul Arthur Berkman, 'The Central Arctic Ocean Fisheries Agreement as an Element in the Evolving Arctic Ocean Governance Complex' (2020) 118 *Marine Policy* 104001.

Ward, Tara, 'The Right to Free, Prior, and Informed Consent: Indigenous Peoples' Participation Rights within International Law' (2011) 10 *Northwestern University Journal of International Human Rights* 54–84.

Watt-Cloutier, Sheila, *The Right to Be Cold* (Minneapolis, University of Minnesota Press 2018).

'WCIP – Asia Declaration' (9 November 2012) http://cendoc.docip.org/collect/cendocdo/index/assoc/HASH0176/8f7023dd.dir/WCIP_asiedecl_en.pdf.

Weil, Prosper, 'Towards Relative Normativity in International Law' (1983) 77 *American Journal of International Law* 413–442.

Weller, Marc, 'Self-Determination of Indigenous Peoples: Articles 3, 4, 5, 18, 23, and 46(1)' in Jessie Hohmann and Marc Weller (eds.), *The UN Declaration on the Rights of Indigenous People: A Commentary* (Oxford: Oxford University Press, 2018) 115–149.

Wessel, Ramses A., 'Executive Boards and Councils' in Jacob Katz Cogan, Ian Hurd, and Ian Johnstone (eds.), *The Oxford Handbook of International Organizations* (Oxford: Oxford University Press, 2016) 802–821.

West, Paige, James Igoe and Dan Brockington, 'Parks and Peoples: The Social Impact of Protected Areas' (2005) 35 *Annual Review of Anthropology* 251–277.
Whare, Tracey, 'Reflective Piece on Māori and the ILO' (2020) 24 *International Journal of Human Rights* 303–306.
Wiessner, Siegfried, 'Rights and Status of Indigenous Peoples: A Global Comparative and International Legal Analysis' (1999) 12 *Harvard Human Rights Journal* 58–128.
'Indigenous Sovereignty: A Reassessment in Light of the UN Declaration on the Rights of Indigenous Peoples' (2008) 41 *Vanderbilt Journal of Transnational Law* 1141–1176.
Willemsen Diaz, Augusto, 'How Indigenous Peoples' Rights Reached the UN' in Claire Charters and Rodolfo Stavenhagen (eds.), *Making the Declaration Work: The United Nations Declaration on the Rights of Indigenous Peoples* (Copenhagen: IWGIA, 2009) 16–31.
Woo, Grace Li Xiu, 'Canada's Forgotten Founders: The Modern Significance of the Haudenosaunee (Iroquois) Application for Membership in the League of Nations' [2003] (1) *Law, Social Justice & Global Development Journal* 1.
Wood, Michael, 'Do International Organizations Enjoy Immunity under Customary International Law?' (2013) 10(2) *International Organizations Law Review* 287–318.
'International Organizations and Customary International Law' (2015) 48(3) *Vanderbilt Journal of Transnational Law* 609–620.
'Customary International Law and Human Rights' (European University Institute Working Paper AEL 2016/03).
Xanthaki, Alexandra, *Indigenous Rights and United Nations Standards* (Cambridge: Cambridge University Press, 2007).
'Indigenous Rights in International Law over the Last Ten Years and Future Developments' (2009) 10 *Melbourne JIL* 27–37.
Young, Iris Marion, *Inclusion and Democracy* (Oxford: Oxford University Press, 2000).

INTERNATIONAL DOCUMENTS

AFRICAN COMMISSION ON HUMAN AND PEOPLES' RIGHTS

'Resolution on the Protection of Indigenous Peoples' Rights in the Context of the World Heritage Convention and the Designation of Lake Bogoria as a World Heritage Site' (5 November 2011) ACHPR res.197 (L)2011

ANDEAN COMMUNITY

Additional Protocol to the Cartagena Agreement (signed 10 June 2000, not yet in force)
Decision 524 (9 July 2002) Official Gazette of the Cartagena Agreement, No. 814
Declaration of Machu Picchu on Democracy, the Rights of Indigenous Peoples and the Fight against Poverty (2001)
Declaration of Tarija, XVII Andean Presidential Council (27 September 2007)

Draft Decision on Andean Committee of Government Authorities on the Rights of Indigenous Peoples (16 January 2012) Doc. SG/dt 454

Draft Internal Regulation on the Working Group on the Rights of Indigenous Peoples (17 May 2003) Doc. No. SG/dt 215

Draft Internal Regulation on the Working Group on the Rights of Indigenous Peoples (second version) (8 March 2006) Doc. No. SG/dt 215/Rev.1

'En reunión calificada de "histórica," instalan Consejo Consultivo que permitirá participación de pueblos indígenas en proceso andino de integración' (press reléase, 8 September 2008), www.comunidadandina.org/Prensa.aspx?id=2471&accion=detalle&cat=NP&title=en-reunion-calificada-de-historica-instalan-consejo-consultivo-que-permitira-participacion-de-pueblos-indigenas-en-proceso-andino-de-integracion

'Minutes, Second Joint Meeting of Government Authorities on the Rights of Indigenous Peoples and the Advisory Council of Indigenous Peoples of the Andean Community' (14 May 2013) SG/DPI.CCPICAN/II/ACTA

Protocol of Amendment Establishing the Andean Community and the Andean Integration System (signed 10 March 1996 and entered into force 3 June 1997)

Protocol of Sucre (signed 25 June 1997 and entered into force 14 April 2003)

'Próxima instalación del Consejo Consultivo de Pueblos Indígenas de la CAN' (press release, 21 August 2008), www.comunidadandina.org/Prensa.aspx?id=2462&accion=detalle&cat=NP&title=proxima-instalacion-del-consejo-consultivo-de-pueblos-indigenas-de-la-can

'Report, First Intergovernmental Meeting of Competent National Authorities in Matters of Indigenous Peoples of the Andean Community' (13 December 2011) SG/RI.ANPI/I/INFORME

Andean Council of Ministers of Foreign Affairs

Decision 674 (26 September 2007)

Decision 896: Andean Committee of Government Authorities on the Rights of Indigenous Peoples (25 March 2022)

Consultative Council of the Indigenous Peoples of the Andean Community

'Minutes, Fifth Ordinary Meeting, Consultative Council of the Indigenous Peoples of the Andean Community' (9 September 2010) SG/CCPICAN/V/ACT

'Minutes, First Extraordinary Meeting, Consultative Council of the Indigenous Peoples of the Andean Community' (23 June 2009) SG/CCPICAN/I-E/ACTA

'Minutes, First Regular Meeting, Advisory Council of the Indigenous Peoples of the Andean Community' (19 December 2008) AG/CCPICAN/I/ACTA

'Minutes, Fourth Extraordinary Meeting, Consultative Council of the Indigenous Peoples of the Andean Community' (20 October 2010) SG/CCPICAN/IV-E/ACTA

'Minutes, Fourth Ordinary Meeting of the Consultative Council of the Indigenous Peoples of the Andean Community' (23 February 2010) SG/CCPICAN/IV/ACTA

'Minutes, Ninth Ordinary Meeting of the CCPICAN' (10 December 2012) SG/CCPICAN/IX/ACTA

'Minutes, Second Extraordinary Meeting, Consultative Council of the Indigenous Peoples of the Andean Community' (28 June 2009) SG/CCPICAN/II-E/ACTA
'Minutes, Second Ordinary Meeting, Consultative Council of the Indigenous Peoples of the Andean Community' (25 March 2009) SG/CCPICAN/II/ACTA
'Minutes, Seventh Meeting of the Consultative Council of Indigenous Peoples of the CAN' (21 June 2011) SG/CCPICAN/VII/ACTA
'Minutes, Third Extraordinary Meeting, Consultative Council of the Indigenous Peoples of the Andean Community' (21 April 2010) SG/CCPICAN/III-E/ACTA
'Minutes, Third Ordinary Meeting, Consultative Council of the Indigenous Peoples of the Andean Community' (28 May 2009) SG/CCPICAN/III/ACTA
'Reglamento interno del Consejo Consultivo de los Pueblos Indígenas de la Comunidad Andina' (21 November 2008), annexed to Comunidad Andina, 'Acta: Segunda Reunión Presencial del Consejo Consultivo de los Pueblos Indígenas de la Comunidad Andina' (22 November 2008) SG/CCPICAN/II-P/ACTA

ARCTIC COUNCIL

Arctic Council Rules of Procedure (revised version, 2013)
Arctic Environmental Protection Strategy (14 June 1991)
Barrow Declaration (13 October 2000), accessible at https://oaarchive.arctic-council.org/handle/11374/87
Declaration on the Establishment of the Arctic Council (1996) 35 ILM 1387
Inuvik Declaration (21 March 1996)
Nuuk Declaration on Environment and Development in the Arctic (16 September 1993)

BARENTS EURO-ARCTIC COOPERATION

'Second Barents Parliamentary Conference, Conclusions of the Chair, CSO Information document' (22 August 2005) Doc.BEAC.CSO.2005.25
'About Us' (n.d.) www.barentscooperation.org/en/About
Agreement on the Establishment of an International Barents Secretariat for the Cooperation in the Barents Euro-Arctic Region, 15 November 2007
Conference Resolution, 6th Barents Parliamentary Conference, 23–24 April in Harstad, Norway
Declaration on Cooperation in the Barents Euro-Arctic Region, Conference of Foreign Ministers in Kirkenes (11 January 1993)
'Declaration on the Twentieth Anniversary of the Barents Euro-Arctic Cooperation, Kirkenes, Norway, 3–4 June 2013' (2013)
Resolution of the Fifth Parliamentary Barents Conference, Lulea (20 May 2011)
Resolution, Eighth Barents Parliamentary Conference, Naryan-Mar (8 June 2017)
Umeä Declaration (3 October 2019)

Barents Euro-Arctic Council

'Ninth Session of the Barents Euro-Arctic Council (BEAC), Joint Communique' (3 October 2003)

'Twelfth Session of the Barents Euro-Arctic Council, Joint Communique, Murmansk' (15 October 2009)
'Thirteenth Session, 12 October 2011, Speeches and Statements' (2011)
'Declaration on the Twentieth Anniversary of the Barents Euro-Arctic Cooperation, Kirkenes, Norway' (3–4 June 2013)
'Joint Communique, Fourteenth Session of the Barents Euro-Arctic Council, Tromso' (29 October 2013)
'Joint Statement, Barents Euro-Arctic Council, Second Session, 14th–15th September 1994, Tromso, Norway' (1994), accessible at www.barentsinfo.fi/beac/docs/499_doc_Tromsocommunique_1994_e.pdf
'Joint Statement of the Fourth Session of the Council of the Barents Euro-Arctic Region, 5–6 November 1996, Petrozavodsk' (1996)
Seventh Meeting of Environment Ministers, Declaration, 19 October 2005
Statement of Minister Timo Soini to the XV Session of the BEAC, 15 October 2015, www.barentsinfo.fi/beac/docs/Soini-BEAC-kokouspuhe-2015.pdf
'Third Session, October 9–10, 1995, Rovaniemi, Joint Statement' (1995)
'XIII Session of the Barents Euro-Arctic Council, Joint Communique, Kiruna' (12 October 2011)
'XV Session of the Barents Euro-Arctic Council, Joint Communique, Oulu' (15 October 2015)
'XVI Session of the Barents Euro-Arctic Council, Joint Declaration, Arkhangelsk' (18–19 October 2017)

Barents Regional Council

'Barents Regional Committee, Terms of Reference' (14 November 2012)
'Joint Statement of the Barents Regional Council on the Occasion of the Twentieth Anniversary of BEAC' (3 June 2013)
'Joint Statement of the Barents Regional Council on the XIV Session of the Barents Euro-Arctic Council, 29 October 2013, Tromso, Norway' (2013)
'Minutes, Kajaani' (BRC, 11 November 2010)
'The Barents Regional Council' (n.d.) www.barentscooperation.org/en/Barents-Regional-Council
'The Protocol Agreement from the Statutory Meeting of the Regional Council of the Barents Region (the Euro-Arctic Region) adopted by the Regional Council of the Barents Region, Kirkenes, 11 January 1993'

Working Group of Indigenous Peoples

'Annual Report 2008', www.barentsinfo.fi/beac/docs/BEAC_Working_Groups_Annual_Reports_2008.pdf
'Annual Report 2019', www.barentsinfo.fi/beac/docs/WGIP_Annual_Report_2019.pdf
Terms of Reference for the Working Group of Indigenous Peoples in the Barents Euro-Arctic Region (15 December 2010)
'Working Group of Indigenous Peoples' (n.d.) www.barentscooperation.org/en/Working-Groups/Working-Group-of-Indigenous-Peoples
'Working Group of Indigenous Peoples in the Barents Euro-Arctic Region, Action Plan for Indigenous Peoples in the Barents Euro-Arctic Region, 2013–2016' (2012)

Barents Indigenous Peoples Congress

'Declaration of the first Barents Indigenous Peoples Congress' (2010)
Resolution from the 3rd Barents Indigenous Peoples' Congress (14 April 2015)

CLIMATE INVESTMENT FUNDS

Dedicated Grant Mechanism for Indigenous Peoples and Local Communities

'About the Dedicated Grant Mechanism' (DGM, n.d.) www.dgmglobal.org/background

'Annual Report 2016' (DGM, 2016), https://static1.squarespace.com/static/550abd2ce4b0c5557aa4f772/t/588f503a3a0411d31b548828/1485787204551/DGM+Annual+Report_ENG_WEB.pdf

'Design for the Dedicated Grant Mechanism for Indigenous Peoples and Local Communities to be established under the Forest Investment Program' (29 November 2011) www.climateinvestmentfunds.org/sites/cif_enc/files/meeting-documents/fip_design_proposal_dgm_for_ips_and_lc_final_november2011_0.pdf

'Framework Operational Guidelines' (12 September 2013), https://static1.squarespace.com/static/550abd2ce4b0c5557aa4f772/t/550adcbae4b0178d56b4c7d3/1426775226201/13-09-12DGMGuidelines-website.pdf

'Program Document for A Dedicated Grants Mechanism for Indigenous Peoples and Local Communities (DGM)' (26 January 2015), Report No. 93666-GLB

CONVENTION ON BIOLOGICAL DIVERSITY

Conference of the Parties

Rules of Procedure for Meetings of the Conference of the Parties to the Convention on Biological Diversity, Annex to Decision I/1 and Decision V/20

'List of Participants' (8 December 1994) UN Doc. UNEP/CBD/COP/1/Inf.11

'List of Participants' (30 November 1995) UN Doc. UNEP/CBD/COP/2/Inf.16

'List of Participants' (31 March 2006) UN Doc. UNEP/CBD/COP/8/INF/48

Decision IV/9 (1998) UN Doc. UNEP/CBD/COP/DEC/IV/9

Decision V/16 (26 May 2000) UN Doc. UNEP/CBD/COP/DEC/V/16

Decision V/26 (26 May 2000) UN Doc. UNEP/CBD/COP/DEC/V/26

Decision VI/10 (2002) UN Doc. UNEP/CBD/COP/6/20, Annex I

Decision VII/16 (13 April 2004) UN Doc. UNEP/CBD/COP/DEC/VII/16

Decision VII/19 (13 April 2004) UN Doc. UNEP/CBD/COP/DEC/VII/19

Decision VII/28 (2004) UN Doc. UNEP/CBD/COP/DEC/VII/28

Decision VIII/5 (15 June 2006) UN Doc. UNEP/CBD/COP/DEC/VIII/5

Decision IX/8 (9 October 2018) UN Doc. UNEP/CBD/COP/DEC/IX/8

Decision IX/13 (9 October 2008) UN Doc. UNEP/CBD/COP/DEC/IX/13

Decision X/40 (29 October 2010) UN Doc. UNEP/CBD/COP/DEC/X/40
Decision XI/14 (5 December 2012) UN Doc. UNEP/CBD/COP/DEC/XI/14
Decision XII/12 (13 October 2014) UN Doc. UNEP/CBD/COP/DEC/XII/12

Subsidiary Body on Scientific, Technical and Technological Advice

Consolidated *Modus Operandi* of the Subsidiary Body on Scientific, Technical and Technological Advice, decision VIII/10, Annex III

Working Group on Article 8(J)

'Report of the Working Group on the Implementation of Article 8(j) and Related Provisions, Report of the First Meeting' (12 April 2000) UN Doc. UNEP/CBD/COP/5/5
'Participatory Mechanisms for Indigenous and Local Communities: Note by the Executive Secretary' (27 November 2001) UN Doc. UNEP/CBD/WG8J/2/4
'Report of the Ad Hoc Open-Ended Inter-sessional Working Group on Article 8(j) and Related Provisions of the Convention on Biological Diversity on the Work of its Second Meeting' (14 February 2002) UN Doc. UNEP/CBD/COP/6/7
'Mechanisms to Promote the Effective Participation of Indigenous and Local Communities in Matters Related to the Objectives of Article 8(j) and Related Provisions: Note by the Executive Secretary' (28 September 2003) UN Doc. UNEP/CBD/WG8J/3/6
'Report of the Fifth Meeting of the Ad Hoc Open-Ended Working Group on Article 8(j) and Related Provisions of the Convention on Biological Diversity' (13 November 2007) UN Doc. UNEP/CBD/COP/9/7
'Participatory Mechanisms for Indigenous and Local Communities in the Work of the Convention: Note by the Executive Secretary' (20 May 2009) UN Doc. UNEP/CBD/WG8J/6/3
'Report of the Seventh Meeting of the Ad Hoc Open-Ended Working Group on Article 8(j) and Related Provisions of the Convention on Biological Diversity' (24 November 2011) UN Doc. UNEP/CBD/COP/11/7
'Progress Report on Capacity-building and Development and Participation of Indigenous Peoples and Local Communities in the Work of the Convention' (1 February 2016) UN Doc. UNEP/CBD/SBI/1/INF/1

Nagoya Protocol

'Decision NP-1/4: Cooperative Procedures and Institutional Mechanisms to Promote Compliance with the Nagoya Protocol and to Address Cases of non-compliance' (20 October 2014) UN Doc. UNEP/CBD/NP/COP-MOP/DEC/1/4

Other

'Statement by Dr. Ahmed Djohlaf, Executive Secretary, Convention on Biological Diversity, to the United Nations Permanent Forum on Indigenous Issues at its Sixth Session' (17 May 2007), www.cbd.int/doc/speech/2007/sp-2007-05-17-unpfii-en.pdf
'Statement by Mr. Ahmed Djoghlaf, Executive Secretary of the Convention on Biological Diversity, on the Occasion of the Opening of the Ninth Session of the

United Nations Permanent Forum on Indigenous Issues: "Indigenous Peoples; Development with Culture and Identity"'(19 April 2010) 4–5, www.cbd.int/doc/speech/2010/sp-2010-04-19-UNPFII-en.pdf
'Statement by Dr. Ahmed Djoghlaf, Executive Secretary of the Convention on Biological Diversity, to the International Indigenous and Local Community Consultation on Access and Benefit-Sharing and the Development of an International Regime' (19 September 2007), www.cbd.int/kb/record/statement/38752?RecordType=statement&Subject=TKIP
'Press Release: The Executive Secretary of the Convention on Biological Diversity Welcomes the Adoption of the Declaration on the Rights of Indigenous Peoples' (30 June 2006) www.cbd.int/doc/press/2006/pr-2006-07-06-drip-en.pdf
'Report of the CBD to the UNPFII 2017' (2017) www.un.org/development/desa/indigenouspeoples/wp-content/uploads/sites/19/2018/02/SCBD_UNPFII-QUESTIONNAIRE-SCBD-Response-27-December-2017_vf_JSc-2.pdf

EUROPEAN UNION

Commission

'Commission Working Document on support for indigenous peoples in the development co-operation of the Community and the Member States' (11 May 1998) SEC(1998) 773 final
'Communication from the Commission to the European Parliament, the Council, the European Economic and Social Committee and the Committee of the Regions: 2016 Report on the Application of the EU Charter of Fundamental Rights' (18 May 2017) SWD(2017) 162 final
'Joint Staff Working Document: Implementing EU External Policy on Indigenous Peoples' (17 October 2016) SWD(2016) 340 final
'Overview of EU Actions in the Arctic and Their Impact, Final Report' (European Commission, June 2021), https://eprd.pl/wp-content/uploads/2021/06/EU-Policy-Arctic-Impact-Overview-Final-Report.pdf
'Report from the Commission to the Council – Review of Progress of Working with Indigenous Peoples' COM(2002) 291 final

Council

2002 Council Conclusions on Indigenous Peoples, General Affairs and External Relations, 2463rd Council meeting, document 13466/02 (18 November 2002)
'Council Conclusions on Indigenous Peoples' (15 May 2017) Doc. 8814/17
'Council Conclusions on the Action Plan on Human Rights and Democracy 2015–2019' (20 July 2015) 10897/15
Council Regulation (EC) No. 1007/2009 of the European Parliament and of the Council of 16 September 2009 on Trade in Seal Products [2009] OJ L 286/36
Council Resolution 'Indigenous Peoples within the Framework of the Development Cooperation of the Community and the Member States' (30 November 1998) C/98/421

Parliament

European Parliament Resolution of 3 July 2018 on Violation of the Rights of Indigenous Peoples in the World, Including Land Grabbing (2017/2206(INI))

FUND FOR THE DEVELOPMENT OF INDIGENOUS PEOPLES OF LATIN AMERICA AND THE CARIBBEAN

XIII Asemblea General – Sesión Extraordinaria: Minuta de Resoluciones (FILAC, 2016)

Acta de la Primera Asamblea General Ordinaria del Fondo para el Desarrollo de los Pueblos Indigenas de America Latina y el Caribe, Santa Cruz de la Sierra, Bolivia, 22 a 25 de mayo de 1995 (FILAC 1995)

Normatividad Institucional (n.d.) www.filac.org/wp/wp-content/uploads/2017/10/Jerarquia-Normativa.pdf.

GLOBAL ENVIRONMENT FACILITY

'GEF Policy on Agency Minimum Standards on Environmental and Social Safeguards' (2011) GEF Doc. GEF/C.41/Rev.1

'Indigenous Peoples Advisory Group to the GEF: Terms of Reference' (GEF, 2013)

Instrument for the Establishment of the Restructured Global Environment Facility (GEF, 2015)

'Partnering with Indigenous Peoples to Conserve the Global Environment' (8 August 2014) www.thegef.org/news/partnering-indigenous-peoples-conserve-global-environment

'Principles and Guidelines for Engagement with Indigenous Peoples' (2012) GEF Doc. GEF/C.42/Inf.03/Rev.1

'Review of GEF's Engagement with Indigenous Peoples' (2017) GEF Doc. GEF/ME/C.53/Inf.07

User Guide: Indigenous Peoples and GEF Project Financing (GEF, 2016)

GREEN CLIMATE FUND

'Environmental and Social Policy' (2018) Decision B.19/10, GCF Doc. GCF/B.19/06

'GCF Indigenous Peoples Policy' (2018) GCF Doc. GCF/B.19/05

Governing Instrument for the Green Climate Fund (GCF, 2011)

'Notification on the Indigenous Peoples Advisory Group of the Green Climate Fund' (17 February 2022) Doc. GCF/notif/2022/1

INTERGOVERNMENTAL SCIENCE-POLICY PLATFORM ON BIODIVERSITY AND ECOSYSTEM SERVICES

Global Assessment Report on Biodiversity and Ecosystem Services of the Intergovernmental Science-Policy Platform on Biodiversity and Ecosystem Services (Bonn: IPBES Secretariat, 2019)

'Indigenous and Local Knowledge in IPBES' (n.d.) https://ipbes.net/indigenous-local-knowledge

'IPBES administrative and institutional arrangements' (2013) Decision IPBES/1/4
'Participation of IPLC in IPBES' (n.d.) https://ipbes.net/participation-iplc-ipbes/
'Report of the Plenary of the Intergovernmental Science-Policy Platform on Biodiversity and Ecosystem Services on the Work of its Fifth Session' (11 April 2017) UN Doc. IPBES/5/15
'Report of the Plenary of the Intergovernmental Science-Policy Platform on Biodiversity and Ecosystem Services on the Work of its Seventh Session' (22 May 2019) UN Doc. IPBES/7/10
Resolution on the Intergovernmental Science-Policy Platform on Biodiversity and Ecosystem Services (second session of the plenary meeting to determine the modalities and institutional arrangements for IPBES, 21 April 2012)

INTERNATIONAL FUND FOR AGRICULTURAL DEVELOPMENT

Governing Council

'Governing Council Report, Fortieth Session' (2017) IFAD Doc. GC 40
'Governing Council Report: Forty-Second Session' (2019) IFAD Doc. GC 42
'Governing Council Report: Thirty-Eighth Session' (2015) IFAD Doc. GC 38
'Governing Council Report: Thirty-Sixth Session' (2013) IFAD Doc. GC 36

Other

'Closing Remarks by IFAD President at the Indigenous People's International Conference on Sustainable Development and Self-determination' (19 June 2012) www.ifad.org/en/web/latest/speech/asset/39034628
Engagement with Indigenous Peoples: Policy (IFAD, 2009)
'Event: Workshop Establishing the Indigenous Peoples' Forum' (2011), www.ifad.org/en/web/latest/event/asset/39009688
'Fourth Global Meeting of the Indigenous Peoples' Forum at IFAD: Synthesis of Deliberations' (IFAD, 2019)
'Good Practices in IFAD's Engagement with Indigenous Peoples' (IFAD 2021), www.ifad.org/documents/38714170/44358796/IPs_engagement_Good_Practices.pdf/deaa1849-6518-e223-8274-d672f1081499?t=1651742225818
'How to Do Seeking Free, Prior and Informed Consent in IFAD Investment Projects'
'IFAD's Progress in its Engagement with Indigenous Peoples in the Biennium 2017–2018' (IFAD, 2018)
'IFAD's Statement by Mattia Prayer Galleti Lead Technical Specialist at UNPFII' (26 April 2019), www.ifad.org/en/web/latest/speech/asset/41123449
'India: Country Strategic Opportunities Programme 2018–2024' (21 August 2018) IFAD Doc. EB 2018/124/R.19
'Indigenous Peoples Assistance Facility' (IFAD, n.d.) www.ifad.org/en/ipaf
'Indigenous Peoples' Forum' (IFAD, n.d.), www.ifad.org/en/indigenous-peoples-forum
'Operational Procedures and Guidelines for Country Strategies' (IFAD, n.d.)
'Policy on Environment and Natural Resource Management' (IFAD, 2011)
'Policy on Improving Access to Land and Tenure Security' (IFAD, 2008)
'Proceedings of the First Global Meeting of the Indigenous Peoples' Forum at IFAD' (IFAD, 2013)

'Proceedings of the Second Global Meeting of the Indigenous Peoples Forum at IFAD' (IFAD, 2015)
'Proceedings of the Third Global Meeting of the Indigenous Peoples Forum at IFAD' (IFAD, 2017)
'Social, Environmental and Climate Assessment Procedures' (IFAD, 2017)
'Statement by IFAD President to Roundtable at the World Conference on Indigenous Peoples' (22 September 2014), www.ifad.org/en/web/latest/speech/asset/39030687
Strategic Framework 2016–2024 (IFAD, 2015)
'Synthesis of Deliberations, Second Global Meeting, Indigenous Peoples Forum at IFAD' (IFAD, 2015)
'The Traditional Knowledge Advantage: Indigenous Peoples' Knowledge in Climate Change Adaptation and Mitigation Strategies' (IFAD, 2016)
'Welcoming Remarks by Gilbert Houngbo, President of IFAD at the Fourth Indigenous Peoples' Forum' (12 February 2019) www.ifad.org/en/web/latest/speech/asset/41016256

Executive Board

'Executive Board: Minutes of the Ninety-Seventh Session' (2009) IFAD Doc. EB 2009/97/R.3/Rev.1
'IFAD's Engagement with Indigenous Peoples' (2 August 2006) IFAD Doc. EB 2006/88/R.34
'Letter Agreement Between IFAD and the International Bank for Reconstruction and Development for the Transfer of the Grants Facility for Indigenous Peoples' (2 August 2006) IFAD Doc. EB 2006/88/R.40

INTERNATIONAL LABOUR ORGANIZATION

'Ratifications of C169 – Indigenous and Tribal Peoples Convention, 1989 (No. 169)' www.ilo.org/dyn/normlex/en/f?p=NORMLEXPUB:11300:0::NO:11300:P11300_INSTRUMENT_ID:312314:NO.
Partial Revision of the Indigenous and Tribal Populations Convention, 1957 (No. 107), Report VI(1)

Governing Body

'Minutes of the 234th Session' (November 1986) ILO Doc. GB.234/PV (Rev.) I/8

INTERNATIONAL LAW COMMISSION

'Draft Articles on the Law of Treaties with Commentaries' (1966) Yearbook of the International Law Commission, vol. II, 187
'Draft Articles on the Responsibility of International Organizations' (3 June 2011) UN Doc. A/CN.4/L.778
'Draft Conclusions on Identification of Customary International Law, with Commentaries' (2018) UN Doc. A/73/10

'Formation and Evidence of Customary International Law, First Report on Formation and Evidence of Customary International Law, by Sir Michael Wood, Special Rapporteur' (17 May 2013) UN Doc. A/CN.4/663

'Identification of Customary International law, Second Report on Identification of Customary International Law, by Sir Michael Wood, Special Rapporteur' (22 May 2014) UN Doc. A/CN.4/672

'Identification of Customary International Law, Third Report on Identification of Customary International Law, by Sir Michael Wood, Special Rapporteur' (27 March 2015) UN Doc. A/CN.4/682

'Report of the International Law Commission on the Work of its Sixty-third Session (2011): Topical Summary of the Discussion Held in the Sixth Committee of the General Assembly During its Sixty-sixth Session, Prepared by the Secretariat' (2012) UN Doc. A/CN.4/650/Add.1

'Responsibility of International Organizations, Comments and Observations Received from International Organizations' (2011) UN Doc. A/CN.4/637

INTERNATIONAL MARITIME ORGANIZATION

International Maritime Organization, 'Marine Environment Protection Committee, 70th Session, Agenda Item 17, Any Other Business, Arctic Indigenous Food Security and Shipping, Submitted by FOEI, WWF and Pacific Environment' (19 August 2016) IMO Doc. MEPC 70/17/10

INTERNATIONAL SEABED ASSOCIATION

International Seabed Association, Regulations on Prospecting and Exploration for Polymetallic Nodules in the Area (22 July 2013) ISA Doc. ISBA/19/C/17

INTERNATIONAL UNION FOR CONSERVATION OF NATURE

'IUCN Members' (n.d.) www.iucn.org/about/members/iucn-members.

IUCN Statutes (adopted 5 October 1948 and last amended 27 September 2016), in IUCN, *Statutes, including Rules of Procedure of the World Conservation Congress, and Regulations* (Switzerland: IUCN, 2022)

Resolutions

'Including Indigenous Peoples' Organisations in the Structure of the Union' (2016) WCC-2016-Res-004

'Strengthened Institutional Inclusion Concerning Indigenous Peoples' (2020) WCC-2020-Res-002

'Establishment of an Elected Indigenous Councillor Position' (2020) WCC-2020-Dec-140

LEAGUE OF NATIONS

The Aaland Islands Question: Report Submitted to the Council of the League of Nations by the Commission of Rapporteurs (April 1921) League of Nations Doc. B7 [C] 21/68/106

OFFICE OF THE UN HIGH COMMISSIONER ON HUMAN RIGHTS

'About the Mandate of the Expert Mechanism on the Rights of Indigenous Peoples' (n.d.) www.ohchr.org/EN/Issues/IPeoples/EMRIP/Pages/Reviewofthemandate.aspx
'Current Experts in the Expert Mechanism on the Rights of Indigenous Peoples' (n.d.) www.ohchr.org/EN/Issues/IPeoples/EMRIP/Pages/Membership.aspx.
'Fact Sheet No. 9 (Rev.1), The Rights of Indigenous Peoples' (1997)
'Promotion and Protection of the Rights of Indigenous Peoples with Respect to Their Cultural Heritage: Report' (19 August 2015) www.ohchr.org/EN/Issues/IPeoples/EMRIP/Pages/Studyonculturalheritage.aspx.
'Summary of responses to the questionnaire on the review of the mandate of the Expert Mechanism on the Rights of Indigenous Peoples' (April 2016), www.ohchr.org/EN/Issues/IPeoples/EMRIP/Pages/Reviewofthemandate.aspx

ORGANIZATION OF AMERICAN STATES

American Declaration on the Rights of Indigenous Peoples (15 June 2016) OAS Doc. AG/RES.2888 (XLVI-O/16)

UNITED NATIONS

Rules of Procedure of the General Assembly (2021) UN Doc. A/520/Rev.19

UN COLLABORATIVE PROGRAMME ON REDUCING EMISSIONS FROM DEFORESTATION AND FOREST DEGRADATION IN DEVELOPING COUNTRIES

Framework Document (UN-REDD Programme, 2008)
Guidelines on Free, Prior and Informed Consent (UN-REDD Programme, 2013)
Policy Board Terms of Reference (UN-REDD Programme, 2009)
'UN-REDD Programme Operational Guidance: Engagement of Indigenous Peoples & Other Forest Dependent Communities' (UN-REDD Programme, 2009)
UN-REDD Programme Rules of Procedure and Operational Guidance (UN-REDD Programme, 2009)

UN COMMISSION ON HUMAN RIGHTS

Resolutions

Commission on Human Rights Res. 1982/19 (10 March 1982)
Commission on Human Rights Res. 1990/62 (7 March 1990)
Commission on Human Rights Res. 1994/28 (4 March 1994)
Commission on Human Rights Res. 1995/30 (3 March 1995).
Commission on Human Rights Res. 1995/32 (3 March 1995)
Commission on Human Rights Res. 2000/87 (28 April 2000)

Other

'Report of the Eighteenth Session' (1962) UN Doc. E/CN.4/832/Rev.1

'Study of the Problem of Discrimination Against Indigenous Populations, Final Report (Supplementary Part) submitted by the Special Rapporteur Mr. Jose R. Martinez Cobo' (20 June 1982) UN Doc. E/CN.4/Sub.2/1982/2/Add.6

'Report on the United Nations Seminar on the Effects of Racism and Racial Discrimination on the Social and Economic Relations Between Indigenous Peoples and States' (1989) UN Doc. E/CN.4/1989/22

'Report of the Meeting of Experts to Review the Experience of Countries in the Operation of Schemes of Internal Self-government for Indigenous Peoples' (1992) UN Doc. E/CN.4/1992/42

'Report of the United Nations Technical Conference on Practical Experience in the Realization of Sustainable and Environmentally Sound Self-Development of Indigenous Peoples' (1992) UN Doc. E/CN.4/Sub.2/1992/31 and Add.1

'Technical Meeting on the International Year for the World's Indigenous People Convened in Accordance with General Assembly Resolution 48/128' (1992) UN Doc. E/CN.4/1992/AC.4/TM/8

'Reconvened Technical Meeting on the International Year for the World's Indigenous People Held in Accordance with General Assembly Resolution 46/128: Proposal Submitted by the Mikmaq Grand Council' (1992) UN Doc. E/CN.4/1992/AC.4/TM.2/CRP.1

'Future Role of the Working Group: Note by the Chairperson-Rapporteur of the Working Group on Indigenous Populations' (15 July 1993) UN Doc. E/CN.4/Sub.2/AC.4/1993/8

'Study on the Protection of the Cultural and Intellectual Property of Indigenous Peoples' (28 July 1993) UN Doc. E/CN.4/Sub.2/1993/28

'Consideration of a Permanent Forum for Indigenous People: Report of the Workshop Held in Accordance with Commission Resolution 1995/30' (1995) UN Doc. E/CN.4/Sub.2/AC.4/1995/7

'Report of the Expert Seminar on Practical Experience Regarding Indigenous Land Rights and Claims' (25 May 1996) UN Doc. E/CN.4/Sub.2/AC.4/1996/6

Commission on Human Rights, 'Report of the Seminar on the Draft Principles and Guidelines for the Protection of the Heritage of Indigenous People' (19 June 2000) UN Doc. E/CN.4/Sub.2/2000/26

'Report on the Second Workshop on Multiculturalism in Africa: Peaceful and Constructive Group Accommodation in Situations Involving Minorities and Indigenous Peoples' (2 April 2001) UN Doc. E/CN.4/Sub.2/AC.5/2001/3

'Report on the Third Workshop on Multiculturalism in Africa: Peaceful and Constructive Group Accommodation in Situations Involving Minorities and Indigenous Peoples' (17 June 2002) UN Doc. E/CN.4/Sub.2/AC.4/2002/4

'Report of the Workshop on Data Collection and Disaggregation for Indigenous Peoples' (10 February 2004) UN Doc. E/C.19/2004/2

'Report on the Expert Seminar on Indigenous Peoples and the Administration of Justice', November 2003, Madrid (10 June 2004) UN Doc. E/CN.4/Sub.2/AC.4/2004/6

'Report of the Seminar on Treaties, Agreements and Other Constructive Arrangements Between States and Indigenous Peoples', Dec 2003, Geneva (1 June 2004) UN Doc. E/CN.4/Sub.2/AC.4/2004/7
'Report on the Expert Seminar on Indigenous Peoples' Permanent Sovereignty Over Natural Resources and Their Relationship to Land' (5 May 2006) UN Doc. E/CN.4/Sub.2/AC.4/2006/3

UN COMMITTEE ON ECONOMIC, SOCIAL AND CULTURAL RIGHTS

Concluding Observations

Committee on Economic, Social and Cultural Rights, 'Concluding Observations on the Fifth Periodic report of Costa Rica' (21 October 2016) UN Doc. E/C.12/CRI/CO/5
Committee on Economic, Social and Cultural Rights, 'Concluding Observations on the Second Periodic Report of Honduras' (11 July 2016) UN Doc. E/C.12/HND/CO/2

General Comments

'General Comment No. 21, Right of Everyone to Take Part in Cultural Life' (21 December 2009) UN Doc. E/C.12/GC/21

UN COMMITTEE ON THE ELIMINATION OF RACIAL DISCRIMINATION

General Recommendation 21: The Right to Self-determination (1996) UN Doc. A/52/18

UN DEVELOPMENT PROGRAMME

Guidance Note: UNDP Social and Environmental Standards, Standard 6: Indigenous Peoples (UNDP, 2017)
'Multi-Partner Trust Fund of the UN Indigenous Peoples' Partnership: Final Programme Narrative Report 2010–2017' (UNDP, 2017)
'Rebecca Grynspan: Remarks at UN Permanent Forum on Indigenous Issues' (16 May 2011) (speech delivered to UNPFII) www.undp.org/content/undp/en/home/presscenter/speeches/2011/05/16/rebeca-grynspan-remarks-at-un-permanent-forum-on-indigenous-issues-.html
Social and Environmental Standards (UNDP, 2014)
UNDP and Indigenous People: A Policy of Engagement (UNDP 2001)

UN ECONOMIC AND SOCIAL COUNCIL

Resolutions

ECOSOC Res. 1296 (XLIV) (23 May 1968)
ECOSOC Res. 1982/34 (7 May 1982)
ECOSOC Res. 1989/77 (24 May 1989)
ECOSOC Res. 1990/238 (25 May 1990)
ECOSOC Res. 1995/32 (25 July 1995)

ECOSOC Res. 1996/31 (25 July 1996)
ECOSOC Res. 2000/22 (28 July 2000)

Decisions

ECOSOC decision 1988/134 (27 May 1988)
ECOSOC decision 1992/256 (20 July 1992)

Other

'Working Group on Indigenous Populations: Consideration of a Permanent Forum for Indigenous People' (6 July 1995) UN Doc. E/CN.4/Sub.2/AC.4/1995/7/Add.2
'Report of the Committee on Non-Governmental Organizations on the First Part of its 1998 Session' (19 June 1998) UN Doc. E/1998/72
'Report of the Open-Ended Inter-Sessional Ad Hoc Working Group on a Permanent Forum for Indigenous Peoples in the United Nations System' (1999) UN Doc. E/CN.4/1999/83

UN EDUCATIONAL, SCIENTIFIC AND CULTURAL ORGANIZATION

2014–2021 Medium-Term Strategy (2014) UNESCO Doc. 37 C/4
'2017 Report to the UNPFII' (2018), www.un.org/development/desa/indigenouspeoples/wp-content/uploads/sites/19/2018/02/UNESCO_03012018Questionnaire-to-Agencies-Nov-2017.pdf
'2018 Report to the UNPFII' (2019), p. 13, www.un.org/development/desa/indigenouspeoples/wp-content/uploads/sites/19/2019/01/PFII-Questionnaire-to-Agencies-UNESCO.pdf
'Address by Irina Bokova, Director-General of UNESCO on the Occasion of the Closing of the Conference "Resilience in a Time of Uncertainty: Indigenous Peoples and Climate Change"' (27 November 2015) UNESCO Doc. DG/2015/235
'Consultation on a UNESCO Policy on Engaging with Indigenous Peoples' (12 July 2017) www.unesco.org/new/fileadmin/MULTIMEDIA/HQ/SC/pdf/170712-UNESCO-IPP-MSConsultation-Compilation-comments.pdf
'Decisions Adopted by the Executive Board at Its 202nd Session' (2017) UNESCO Doc. No. 202 EX/DECISIONS
'Indigenous Peoples and UNESCO 2020: Outcomes of Questionnaire for the UN Permanent Forum on Indigenous Issues' (2020), www.un.org/development/desa/indigenouspeoples/wp-content/uploads/sites/19/2021/04/UNESCO_Consolidated-SWAP-Report-UNPFII-20-final-clean.pdf
'Indigenous Peoples and UNESCO 2021: Outcomes of the Questionnaire for 22nd Session of the UN Permanent Forum on Indigenous Issues' (31 December 2021), www.un.org/development/desa/indigenouspeoples/wp-content/uploads/sites/19/2022/03/UNESCO-Consolidated-Report-UNPFII-22_final.pdf
'Message From Mr Koïchiro Matsuura, Director-General of UNESCO on the Occasion of the International day of the World's Indigenous People' (9 August 2008) UNESCO Doc. DG/ME/ID/2008/011 REV

'Message from Mr Koïchiro Matsuura, Director-General of UNESCO on the Occasion of the International Day of the World's Indigenous People' (9 August 2009) UNESCO Doc. DG/ME/ID/2009/12

'Message from Ms Audrey Azoulay, Director-General of UNESCO, on the Occasion of International Day of the World's Indigenous Peoples – *Migration and Movement*' (9 August 2018) UNESCO Doc. DG/ME/ID/2018/26

'Message from Ms Audrey Azoulay, Director-General of UNESCO on the Occasion of the International Day of the World's Indigenous Peoples' (9 August 2019) UNESCO Doc. DG/ME/ID/2019/26

'Message from Ms Irina Bokova, Director-General of UNESCO on the Occasion of the International Day of the World's Indigenous People' (9 August 2012) UNESCO Doc. DG/ME/ID/2012/015

'Open Call for Nominations Addressed to the Indigenous Peoples and Indigenous Peoples' Organizations' (14 October 2020) https://iyil.ph/documents/61/Open_Call_For_Nomination_Indigenous_Peoples_Document.pdf

'Policy on Engaging with Indigenous Peoples' (9 August 2017) UNESCO Doc. 202 EX/9

'UNESCO Launches the Global Task Force for Making a Decade of Action for Indigenous Languages' (22 March 2021) https://en.unesco.org/news/unesco-launches-global-task-force-making-decade-action-indigenous-languages

'UNESCO Policy on Engaging with Indigenous Peoples' (2018) UNESCO Doc. No. 201 EX/6

World Heritage Committee

'Decisions Adopted During the 43rd Session of the World Heritage Committee' (2019) UNESCO Doc. WHC/19/43.COM/18

'Operational Guidelines for the Implementation of the World Heritage Convention' (2015) UNESCO Doc. WHC.15/01

'Progress Report on World Heritage Indigenous Peoples Council of Experts (WHIPCOE)' (2001) UNESCO Doc. WHC-2001/CONF.208/13

'Report of the Twenty-fifth Session' (2002) UNESCO Doc. WHC-2001/CONF.205/WEB.3

'Report on the Proposed World Heritage Indigenous Peoples Council of Experts (WHIPCOE)' (2001) UNESCO Doc. WHC-01/CONF.208.24

'State of Conservation of the Properties Inscribed on the World Heritage List' (2017) Decision 41 COM 7

'Supporting Paper to the Submission of the Indigenous Peoples Forum Presented to the 24th Session of the World Heritage Committee' (28 November 2000) UNESCO Doc. WHC-2001/CONF.205/WEB.3

UN ENVIRONMENT PROGRAMME

Intergovernmental Negotiating Committee for an International Legally Binding Instrument for Implementing International Action on Certain Persistent Organic Pollutants

'List of Participants' (10 August 1998) UN Doc. UNEP/POPS/INC.1/INF/15

'List of Participants' (11 September 1999) UN Doc. UNEP/POPS/INC.3/INF/17

'Provisional List of Delegations' (24 March 2000) UN Doc. UNEP/POPS/INC.4/INF/11/Rev.1

'Provisional List of Participants' (9 December 2000) UN Doc. UNEP/POPS/INC.5/INF/11/Rev.1

'List of Participants' (26 June 2001) UN Doc. UNEP/POPS/CONF/INF/4/Rev.1

Stockholm Convention on Persistent Organic Pollutants

Basel, Rotterdam and Stockholm Conventions, 'Guidelines for the Participation of Representatives of Observers at Meetings of the Conferences of the Parties to the Basel, Rotterdam and Stockholm Conventions (BRS) and their Subsidiary Bodies' (July 2016)

'Report of the Conference of the Parties of the Stockholm Convention on Persistent Organic Pollutants on the Work of its First Meeting' (6 May 2005) UN Doc. UNEP/POPS/COP.1/31

OTHER

'UNEP and Indigenous Peoples: A Partnership in Caring for the Environment: Policy Guidance' (UNEP, 2012) https://wedocs.unep.org/bitstream/handle/20.500.11822/11202/UNEP_Indigenous_Peoples_Policy_Guidance_endorsed_by_SMT_26_11_12.pdf?sequence=1&isAllowed=y.

UNEP Environmental, Social and Economic Sustainability Framework (UNEP, 2015)

UN EXPERT MECHANISM ON THE RIGHTS OF INDIGENOUS PEOPLES

'Thirteenth session / Regional Meetings of the Expert Mechanism on the Rights of Indigenous Peoples' (2020) (OHCHR, www.ohchr.org/EN/Issues/IPeoples/EMRIP/Pages/Session13.aspx)

'Advice No 2 (2011): Indigenous Peoples and the Right to Participate in Decision-Making' (2011) UN Doc. A/HRC/18/42

'Advice No 8 (2015): Promotion and Protection of the Rights of Indigenous Peoples with Respect to their Cultural Heritage' (2015) UN Doc. A/HRC/30/53

'Annual Report of the Expert Mechanism on the Rights of Indigenous Peoples' (8 August 2017) UN Doc. A/HRC/36/57

'COVID-19 Yet Another Challenge for Indigenous Peoples' (6 April 2020), www.un.org/development/desa/indigenouspeoples/wp-content/uploads/sites/19/2020/04/EMPRIP-English.pdf.

'Efforts to Implement the United Nations Declaration on the Rights of Indigenous Peoples: Indigenous Peoples and the Right to Self-Determination' (2021) UN Doc. A/HRC/48/75

'Final Report of the Study on Indigenous Peoples and the Right to Participate in Decision-Making' (17 August 2011) UN Doc. A/HRC/18/42

'Joint Submission of Grand Council of the Crees, et al.: Nagoya Protocol on Access and Benefit Sharing: Substantive and Procedural Injustices Relating to Indigenous Peoples Human Rights' (2011)

'Proposals for the Human Rights Council' (July 2020) www.ohchr.org/sites/default/files/ProposalsHRCChairsProposal.pdf

'Report of the Expert Mechanism on the Rights of Indigenous Peoples on its Fourth Session' (19 August 2011) A/HRC/18/43

'Report of the Expert Mechanism on the Rights of Indigenous Peoples on its Fifth Session' (17 August 2012) UN Doc. A/HRC/21/52

'Report of the Expert Mechanism on the Rights of Indigenous Peoples on its Sixth Session' (31 July 2013) UN Doc. A/HRC/24/49

'Report of the Expert Mechanism on the Rights of Indigenous Peoples on its Seventh Session' (8 August 2014) UN Doc. A/HRC/27/64

'Report of the Expert Mechanism on the Rights of Indigenous Peoples on its Ninth Session, Geneva, 11–15 July 2016' (8 August 2016) UN Doc. A/HRC/33/56

'Report of the Open-ended Meeting of Indigenous Peoples on the Follow-up to the World Conference of Indigenous Peoples' (10 July 2015) UN Doc. A/HRC/EMRIP/2015/CRP.2

UN Web TV, 'Item 7: Indigenous Peoples' Participation - Fifth Meeting, Tenth Session Expert Mechanism on Rights of Indigenous Peoples' https://media.un.org/en/asset/k1d/k1d8z1yoa6

UN FOOD AND AGRICULTURE ORGANIZATION

'2017 Report to the UNPFII' (2018), www.un.org/development/desa/indigenouspeoples/wp-content/uploads/sites/19/2018/02/FAO-Questionnaire-to-Agencies-UNFPII-2017.pdf

Basic Texts of the Food and Agriculture Organization of the United Nations (FAO 2017)

Environmental and Social Management Guidelines (FAO, 2015)

'FAO Activities 2018' (2018), www.un.org/development/desa/indigenouspeoples/wp-content/uploads/sites/19/2018/12/2018-FAO-UNPFII-Questionnaire.pdf

FAO Policy on Indigenous and Tribal Peoples (FAO, 2010)

'Free Prior and Informed Consent: An Indigenous Peoples' Right and a Good Practice for Local Communities: Manual for Project Practitioners' (FAO, 2016)

'Report of the Council of FAO, Hundred and Forty-sixth Session' (2013) FAO Doc. CL 146/REP, Appendix F, FAO Strategy for Partnerships with Civil Society Organizations

'Respecting Free, Prior and Informed Consent: Practical Guidance for Governments, Companies, NGOs, Indigenous Peoples and Local Communities in Relation to Land Acquisition' (FAO, 2014)

Committee on Food Security

'Reform of the Committee on World Food Security' (2009) FAO Doc. CFS:2009/2 Rev.2

'Report of the Thirty-Fifth Session of the Committee on World Food Security' (2009) FAO Doc. C 2009/21-Rev.1

UN FRAMEWORK CONVENTION ON CLIMATE CHANGE

Conference of the Parties

Decision 3/CP.17, 'Launching the Green Climate Fund' (15 March 2012) UN Doc. FCCC/CP/2011/9/Add.1

Decision 2/CP.23, 'Report of the Conference of the Parties on its Twenty-Third Session, Addendum: Decisions Adopted by the Conference of the Parties' (8 February 2018) UN Doc. FCCC/CP/2017/11/Add.1

Decision 2/CP.24, 'Local Communities and Indigenous Peoples Platform: Draft Conclusions Proposed by the Chair' (7 December 2018) UN Doc. FCCC/SBSTA/2018/L.18

Decision 16/CP.26, 'Local Communities and Indigenous Peoples Platform', in UNFCCC, 'Part two: Action taken by the Conference of the Parties at its Twenty-sixth Session' (8 March 2022) UN Doc. FCCC/CP/2021/12/Add.2

'List of Participants' (9 December 1997) UN Doc. FCCC/CP/1997/INF.5

'List of Participants' (4 November 1999) UN Doc. FCCC/CP/1999/INF.3

'List of Participants' (24 November 2000) UN Doc. FCCC/CP/2000/INF.2

'List of Participants' (26 July 2001) UN Doc. FCCC/CP/2001/INF.2

'List of Participants' (8 November 2001) UN Doc. FCCC/CP/2001/INF.4

'List of Participants' (1 November 2002) UN Doc. FCCC/CP/2002/INF.2

'List of Participants' (11 December 2003) UN Doc. FCCC/CP/2003/INF.1

'List of Participants' (17 December 2004) UN Doc. FCCC/CP/2004/INF.3

'List of Participants' (9 December 2005) UN Doc. FCCC/CP/2005/INF.2

'List of Participants' (16 November 2006) UN Doc. FCCC/CP/2006/INF.1

Subsidiary Body for Implementation

'Report of the Subsidiary Body for Implementation on its Twentieth session' (2004) UN Doc. FCCC/SBI/2004/10

'Report of the Subsidiary Body for Implementation on its Forty-Fifth session' (2017) UN Doc. FCCC/CP/2016/20

Subsidiary Body for Scientific and Technological Advice

'Local Communities and Indigenous Peoples Platform: Draft Conclusions Proposed by the Chair' (5 December 2019) UN Doc. FCCC/SBSTA/2019/L.13

'Local Communities and Indigenous Peoples Platform: Proposals on Operationalization Based on the Open Multi-stakeholder Dialogue and Submissions: Report by the Secretariat' (2017) UN Doc. FCCC/SBSTA/2017/6

'Report of the Subsidiary Body for Scientific and Technological Advice on its Forty-Sixth session' (30 June 2017) UN Doc. FCCC/SBSTA/2017/4

Facilitative Working Group

'The First meeting of the Facilitative Working Group of the Local Communities and Indigenous Peoples Platform' (18 September 2019) UN Doc. FCCC/SBSTA/2019/4

'Report of the Facilitative Working Group of the Local Communities and Indigenous Peoples Platform' (20 August 2021) UN Doc. FCCC/SBSTA/2021/1

Other

'2019 report to the UNPFII' (8 January 2019), www.un.org/development/desa/indigenouspeoples/wp-content/uploads/sites/19/2019/01/Questionnaire-to-Agencies-Nov-2018_UNFCCC-input-v-8-Jan.pdf

'Draft Paris Outcome' (9 December 2015) https://unfccc.int/sites/default/files/resource/docs/2015/cop21/eng/da01.pdf
'Draft Paris Outcome' (10 December 2015) https://unfccc.int/sites/default/files/resource/docs/2015/cop21/eng/da02.pdf
'How to Obtain Observer Status' (n.d.) https://unfccc.int/process-and-meetings/parties-non-party-stakeholders/non-party-stakeholders/overview/how-to-obtain-observer-status
'Submission Portal' (n.d.), https://www4.unfccc.int/sites/submissionsstaging/Pages/Home.aspx

UN GENERAL ASSEMBLY

Resolutions

UNGA Res. 1514 (XV) (14 December 1960)
UNGA Res. 1541 (XV) (15 December 1960)
UNGA Res. 2625(XXV) (24 October 1970)
UNGA Res. 3485 (12 December 1975)
UNGA Res. 37/30 (23 November 1982)
UNGA Res. 40/131 (13 December 1985)
UNGA Res. 42/15 (10 November 1987)
UNGA Res. 42/47 (30 November 1987)
UNGA Res. 45/164 (18 December 1990)
UNGA Res. 46/128 (17 December 1991)
UNGA Res. 48/163 (21 December 1993)
UNGA Res. 56/140 (19 December 2001)
UNGA Res. 61/295 (2 October 2007)
UNGA Res. 63/161 (18 December 2008)
UNGA Res. 65/162 (20 December 2010)
UNGA Res. 65/198 (21 December 2010)
UNGA Res. 66/296 (17 September 2012)
UNGA Res. 67/153 (20 December 2012)
UNGA Res. 68/149 (18 December 2013)
UNGA Res. 70/232 (23 December 2015)
UNGA Res. 71/231 (8 September 2017)
UNGA Res. 72/155 (19 December 2017)
UNGA Res. 73/156 (17 December 2018)
UNGA Res. 75/475 (16 December 2020)
UNGA Res. 76/459 (16 December 2021)

Draft Resolutions

'Draft Resolution by the General Assembly on Enabling the Participation of Indigenous Peoples' Representatives and Institutions in Meetings of Relevant United Nations Bodies on Issues Affecting Them' (21 April 2017) www.un.org/development/desa/indigenouspeoples/wp-content/uploads/sites/19/2016/02/

CLEAN-FINAL-ZERO-DRAFT-21-APRIL-2017-RESOLUTION-ON-IP-PARTICIPATION.pdf
'Draft Resolution by the General Assembly on Enabling the Participation of Indigenous Peoples' Representative Institutions in Meetings of Relevant United Nations Bodies on Issues Affecting Them (REV 1)' (19 May 2017) www.un.org/pga/71/wp-content/uploads/sites/40/2015/08/Participation-of-indigenous-peoples.pdf
'Draft Resolution by the General Assembly on Enabling the Participation of Indigenous Peoples' Representative Institutions in Meetings of Relevant United Nations Bodies on Issues Affecting Them (REV 2)' (6 June 2017) www.un.org/pga/71/wp-content/uploads/sites/40/2015/08/Indigenous-peoples-6-June-2017.pdf
'Draft Resolution by the General Assembly on Enabling the Participation of Indigenous Peoples' Representative Institutions in Meetings of Relevant United Nations Bodies on Issues Affecting Them (REV 2, Technical Update)' (16 June 2017) www.un.org/pga/71/wp-content/uploads/sites/40/2015/08/Indigenous-peoples-16-June-2017.pdf
'Draft Resolution on Enhancing the Participation of Indigenous Peoples' Representatives and Institutions in Meetings of Relevant United Nations Bodies on Issues Affecting Them' (10 August 2017) www.un.org/pga/71/wp-content/uploads/sites/40/2015/08/Indigenous-peoples.pdf
'Draft Resolution Submitted by the President of the General Assembly: Enhancing the Participation of Indigenous Peoples' Representatives and Institutions in Meetings of Relevant United Nations Bodies on Issues Affecting Them' (15 August 2017) UN Doc. A/71/L.82

Decisions

UNGA decision 74/565 of 12 August 2020, in General Assembly, 'Resolutions and Decisions adopted by the General Assembly During its Seventy-Fourth Session, Volume III', GAOR 74 Supp. 49 (2020) UN Doc. A/74/49 (vol. III)
UNGA decision 75/561 of 16 April 2021, in General Assembly, 'Resolutions and Decisions adopted by the General Assembly During its Seventy-Fifth session, Volume III', GAOR 75 Supp. 49 (2021) UN Doc. A/75/49 (vol. III)

Verbatim Records

UNGAOR, 47th session, 82nd plenary meeting, UN Doc. A/47/PV.82
UNGAOR, 61st session, 107th plenary meeting, UN Doc. A/61/PV.107
UNGAOR, 61st session, 108th plenary meeting, UN Doc. A/61/PV.108
UNGAOR, 69th session, 4th plenary meeting, UN Doc. A/69/PV.4
UNGAOR, 69th session, 5th plenary meeting, UN Doc. A/69/PV.5

Summary Records

UNGAOR, 67th session, 3rd Committee, 18th meeting, UN Doc. A/C.3/67/SR.18

Third Committee

'Indigenous Issues: Draft Resolution' (18 October 2010) UN Doc. A/C.3/65/L.22
'Indigenous Issues: Revised Draft Resolution' (12 November 2010) UN Doc. A/C.3/65/L.22/Rev.1

President of the General Assembly

'Letter Appointing the Four Advisers Who Will Assist Him in Conducting Consultations on the Participation of Indigenous Peoples at the United Nations' (18 February 2016), www.un.org/development/desa/indigenouspeoples/participation-of-indigenous-peoples-at-the-united-nations.html.

'Letter by the President of the General Assembly Re-appointing the Four Advisors and Convening a Meeting on the Issue of Participation of Indigenous Peoples at the United Nations' (28 September 2016) www.un.org/esa/socdev/unpfii/documents/2016/Docs-updates/PGA-Letter-Invitation-IP-Consultation-October-2016.pdf

'Letter Dated 5 April 2012 to all Permanent Missions and Permanent Observer Missions to the United Nations Appointing Co-chairs to Lead the Informal Consultations for the High Level Meeting on Indigenous Issues', http://cendoc.docip.org/collect/cendocdo/index/assoc/HASH9ea4/2914b6ff.dir/Informalmeeting_Indigissues_letten1.pdf.

'Letter Dated 30 May 2014 to Representatives of Indigenous Peoples' (30 May 2014), http://cendoc.docip.org/collect/cendocdo/index/assoc/HASH4a77/6cf01eaa.dir/PGALetter_toIP_wcip_300514.pdf

'Letter Enclosing the Communication From the Advisers on the Way Forward on the Consultations on the Participation of Indigenous Peoples at the United Nations' (9 March 2016), www.un.org/development/desa/indigenouspeoples/participation-of-indigenous-peoples-at-the-united-nations.html

Advisors to the President of the General Assembly, 'Elements for Discussion During the Seventy-First Session of the General Assembly' (December 2016), www.un.org/esa/socdev/unpfii/documents/2016/Docs-updates/PGA_Elements_for_further_discussion_22_Dec_final.pdf

Advisors to the President of the General Assembly, 'Elements for Discussion During the Seventy-first Session of the General Assembly' (February 2017), www.un.org/esa/socdev/unpfii/documents/2017/PGA_Consultations/Clean_Elements_paper_February_2017.pdf

World Conference on Indigenous Peoples

Asia Indigenous Peoples Caucus and Asia Indigenous Peoples Pact, 'Statement of the Asia Indigenous Peoples Caucus and the Asia Indigenous Peoples Pact' (22 September 2014), http://cendoc.docip.org/collect/cendocdo/index/assoc/HASH01be/440d5885.dir/WCIP14R1AIPP007.pdf

Estonia, 'President Ilves at the United Nations World Conference on Indigenous Peoples, 22 September 2014' (22 September 2014), http://cendoc.docip.org/collect/cendocdo/index/assoc/HASHbcba/63c4d6c5.dir/WCIP14PMilvesEstonia006.pdf

Guatemala, 'Intervención de la Delegación de Guatemala, Connie Taracena – Ministra Consejera, dialogo interactivo organizado por el Presidente de la Asamblea General sobre la Conferencia Mundial sobre los Pueblos Indigena' (17 June 2014), http://cendoc.docip.org/collect/cendocdo/index/assoc/HASH012d/279f0c00.dir/IIH_WCIP170614_connieguatemala1.pdf

'Informal Interactive Hearing in preparation for the World Conference on Indigenous Peoples, 17–18 June, United Nations Headquarters, New York, Summary Report', www.un.org/en/ga/69/meetings/indigenous/consultations.shtml

Mexico, 'Palabras del Presidente de Los Estados Unidos Mexicanos, Licenciado Enrique Peña Nieto, durante la Sesión Plenaria de La Conferencia Mundial de Los Pueblos Indígenas' (22 September 2014), http://cendoc.docip.org/collect/cendocdo/index/assoc/HASH01d0/c7a5b270.dir/WCIP14PMenriqueMexico007.pdf.

Norway, 'GA: Informal on the Outcome of the High-Level Meeting Indigenous Peoples, Statement Held by Iselin Hebbert Larsen on Behalf of Norway' (3 June 2014), http://cendoc.docip.org/collect/cendocdo/index/assoc/HASH0174/1f5036d0.dir/WCIP_infcons03042014_iselinnorway.pdf

'Outcome Document of the High-level Plenary Meeting of the General Assembly Known as the World Conference on Indigenous Peoples' (15 September 2014) UN Doc. A/69/L.1

Peru, 'Intervención del Señor Gabriel Quijandría, Viceministro de Desarrollo Estratégico de los Recursos Naturales en la mesa redonda tierras, territorios y recursos de los pueblos indígenas' (23 September 2014), http://cendoc.docip.org/collect/cendocdo/index/assoc/HASH0183/31ca808c.dir/WCIP14R3gabrielPeru005.pdf

President of the Sami Parliament of Norway, 'Remarks by Aili Keskitalo, President of the Sami Parliament of Norway, 22 Sep. 2014, World Conference on Indigenous Peoples' (22 September 2014), http://cendoc.docip.org/collect/cendocdo/index/assoc/HASHabe4/9acd9dab.dir/WCIP14PMailiSaami009.pdf

'Press Release: UN Member States Reaffirm Commitment to the Rights of Indigenous Peoples at First World Conference on Indigenous Peoples' (United Nations, 22 September 2014), www.un.org/en/ga/69/meetings/indigenous/pdf/Press-Release_final.pdf

The President of the Republic of Finland, 'Statement by President of the Republic of Finland Sauli Niinistö at the World Conference on Indigenous Peoples (WCIP) United Nations, New York 22 September 2014' (22 September 2014), http://cendoc.docip.org/collect/cendocdo/index/assoc/HASH018a/44a49367.dir/WCIP14PMniistoFinland004.pdf.

'The World Conference on Indigenous Peoples: Consultations' (n.d.) www.un.org/en/ga/69/meetings/indigenous/consultations.shtml

United States, 'WCIP Roundtable 1: "UN System Action for the Implementation of the Rights of Indigenous Peoples," United States Statement by Ambassador Keith Harper' (22 September 2014), http://cendoc.docip.org/collect/cendocdo/index/assoc/HASH013e/1a524365.dir/WCIP14R1keithUSA023.pdf

United States, 'U.S. Statement at Informal Consultation on the World Conference on Indigenous Peoples, June 3 2014' (3 June 2014), http://cendoc.docip.org/collect/cendocdo/index/assoc/HASH05e5/4e03feba.dir/WCIP_infcons03042014_terryus.pdf

'World Conference on Indigenous Peoples – Documents' (n.d.) www.un.org/en/ga/69/meetings/indigenous/documents.shtml

Other

'Compilation of Submissions to IP Advisers Email Address' (20 May 2016), www.un.org/esa/socdev/unpfii/documents/2016/Docs-updates/Compilation_of_submission_to_GAConsultation_08_07_2016-rev3.pdf

'Compilation of Views on Possible Measures Necessary to Enable the Participation of Indigenous Peoples' Representatives and Institutions in Relevant United Nations Meetings on Issues Affecting Them, and of Good Practices Within the United Nations Regarding Indigenous Peoples' Participation' (25 July 2016) UN Doc. A/70/990
'Enhancing the Participation of Indigenous Peoples' Representatives and Institutions in Meetings of Relevant United Nations Bodies on Issues Affecting them: Report of the Secretary-General' (27 July 2020) UN Doc. A/75/255
'First Informal Interactive Hearing with Indigenous Peoples, President's Summary' (31 May 2018), www.un.org/development/desa/indigenouspeoples/wp-content/uploads/sites/19/2019/06/Informal-interactive-hearing-Letter-to-Indigenous-Peoples-31-May.pdf
'Letter Dated 10 September 2013 from the Permanent Representatives of the Plurinational State of Bolivia, Denmark, Finland, Guatemala, Mexico, New Zealand, Nicaragua, Norway and Peru to the United Nations addressed to the Secretary-General' (13 September 2013) UN Doc. A/67/994
Preparatory Committee for the United Nations Conference on Environment and Development, 'Report of the Preparatory Committee for the United Nations Conference on Environment and Development on the Work of its Fourth Session' (12 May 1992) UN Doc. A/CONF.151/PC/128
'Programme of Action for the Second International Decade of the World's Indigenous People' (2005) UN Doc. A/60/270
Report of the Preparatory Committee for the United Nations Conference on Environment and Development (21 June 1991) UN Doc. A/46/48
Report of the Special Rapporteur on the Rights of Indigenous Peoples to the General Assembly (2012) UN Doc. A/67/301
Rio Declaration on Environment and Development (13 June 1992) UN Doc. A/CONF.151/26
'Second Informal Interactive Hearing with Indigenous Peoples on Indigenous Peoples Enhanced Participation in the United Nations, President's Summary' (20 May 2019), www.un.org/pga/73/wp-content/uploads/sites/53/2019/05/Summary-of-the-Informal-interactive-hearing-with-indigenous-peoples.pdf
Vienna Declaration and Programme of Action (25 June 1993) UN Doc. A/CONF.157/23

UN HUMAN RIGHTS COMMITTEE

Communications

Angela Poma Poma v. Peru, Communication No. 1457/2006, UN Doc. CCPR/C/95/D/1457/2006 (2009)
Länsman et al. v. Finland, Communication No. 511/1992, UN Doc. CCPR/C/52/D/511/1992 (1994)

General Comments

Concluding Observations

'Concluding Observations: Mexico' (27 July 1999) UN Doc. CCPR/C/79/Add.109
'Concluding Observations: Norway' (1 November 1999) UN Doc. CCPR/C/79/Add.112

'Concluding Observations: Sweden' (24 April 2002) UN Doc. CCPR/CO/74/SW
'Concluding Observations on the Sixth Periodic Report of Morocco' (1 December 2016) UN Doc. CCPR/C/MAR/CO/6
'Concluding Observations on the Second Periodic Report of Honduras' (24 July 2017) UN Doc. CCPR/C/HND/CO/2
'Concluding Observations on the Seventh Periodic Report of Norway' (25 April 2018) UN Doc. CCPR/C/NOR/CO/7

Other

'Report of the Human Rights Committee, Volume I' (2000) UN Doc. A/55/40

UN HUMAN RIGHTS COUNCIL

'Expert Workshop to Review the Mandate of the Expert Mechanism on the Rights of Indigenous Peoples: Report' (10 May 2016) UN Doc. A/HRC/32/26
'Final Report of the Study on Indigenous Peoples and the Right to Participate in Decision-making: Report of the Expert Mechanism on the Rights of Indigenous Peoples' (17 August 2011) UN Doc. A/HRC/18/42
'Half-day Panel Discussion on the World Conference on Indigenous Peoples: Human Rights as a Cross-cutting Theme in the World Conference on Indigenous Peoples' (24th session, 17 September 2013)
'Intersessional Round Table on Ways to Enhance the Participation of Indigenous Peoples' Representatives and Institutions in Meetings of the Human Rights Council on Issues Affecting Them' (11 January 2022) UN Doc. A/HRC/49/69
'Report of the Special Rapporteur on the Rights of Indigenous Peoples' (2012) UN Doc. A/HRC/21/47
'Report of the Special Rapporteur on the Situation of Human Rights and Fundamental Freedoms of Indigenous People, James Anaya' (15 July 2009) UN Doc. A/HRC/12/34
'Practical Implications of a Change in the Mandate of the Voluntary Fund for Indigenous Populations' (5 July 2010) UN Doc. A/HRC/15/38
'Progress Report on the Study on Indigenous Peoples and the Right to Participate in Decision-Making: Report of the Expert Mechanism on the Rights of Indigenous Peoples' (23 August 2010) UN Doc. A/HRC/15/35
'Ways and Means of Promoting Participation at the United Nations of Indigenous Peoples' Representatives on Issues Affecting them' (2012) UN Doc. A/HRC/21/24

Resolutions

Human Rights Council Res. 2006/2 (29 June 2006)
Human Rights Council Res. 5/1 (18 June 2007)
Human Rights Council Res. 6/36 (14 December 2007)
Human Rights Council Res. 18/8 (13 October 2011)
Human Rights Council Res. 21/24 (11 October 2012)
Human Rights Council Res. 30/11 (11 October 2015)
Human Rights Council Res. 33/25 (5 October 2016)
Human Rights Council Res. 39/13 (28 September 2018)
Human Rights Council Res. 42/19 (26 September 2019)
Human Rights Council Res. 45/12 (6 October 2020)
Human Rights Council Res. 48/11 (8 October 2021)

UN PERMANENT FORUM ON INDIGENOUS ISSUES

Reports

'Report of the Second Session' (2003) UN Doc. E/C.19/2003/22
'Report of the Third Session' (2004) UN Doc. E/C.19/2004/23
'Report of the Seventh Session' (2008) UN Doc. E/C.19/2008/13
'Report on the Tenth Session' (2011) UN Doc. E/C.19/2011/14
'Report on the Eleventh Session' (2012) UN Doc. E/C.19/2012/13
'Report on the Twelfth Session' (2013) UN Doc. E/C.19/2013/25
'Report on the Fourteenth Session' (2015) UN Doc. E/2015/43-E/C.19/2015/10
'Report on the Seventeenth Session' (2018) UN Doc. E/2018/43*-E/C.19/2018/11*
'Report on the Eighteenth Session' (2019) UN Doc. E/2019/43-E/C.19/2019/10

International Expert Group Meetings

'Report of the International Expert Group Meeting on Indigenous Languages' (21 January 2008) UN Doc. E/C.19/2008/3
'Report of the International Expert Group Meeting on Indigenous Peoples and Forests' (11 February 2011) UN Doc. E/C.19/2011/5
'Report of the International Expert Group Meeting on the International Regime on Access and Benefit-sharing and Indigenous Peoples' Human Rights of the Convention on Biological Diversity' (14 March 2007) UN Doc. E/C.19/2007/8

Other

'Political Position Document and Plan of Action of the World's Indigenous Women Adopted in the World Conference of Indigenous Women' (2014) UN Doc. E/C.19/2014/CRP.1
'Statement of O. Lorde on Behalf of the UNPFII at the World Heritage Committee', 39th Session (29 June 2015)
'Statement on the Announcement of the World Bank Forest Carbon Partnership Facility' (11 December 2007)

UN SECURITY COUNCIL

UNSC Res. 384 (22 December 1975) UN Doc. S/RES/384
UNSC Res. 389 (22 April 1976) UN Doc. S/RES/389
UNSC Res. 581 (13 February 1986) UN Doc. S/RES/581

UN SUB-COMMISSION ON PREVENTION OF DISCRIMINATION AND PROTECTION OF MINORITIES

Resolutions

Sub-Commission on Prevention of Discrimination and Protection of Minorities Res. 1982/31 (29 September 1982) UN Doc. E/CN.4/Sub.2/RES/1982/31
Sub-Commission on Prevention of Discrimination and Protection of Minorities Res. 1985/22 (29 August 1985) UN Doc. E/CN.4/Sub.2/1985/22

Sub-Commission on Prevention of Discrimination and Protection of Minorities Res. 1990/29 (31 August 1990)
Sub-Commission on Prevention of Discrimination and Protection of Minorities Res. 1994/45 (26 August 1994)
Sub-Commission on Prevention of Discrimination and Protection of Minorities Res. 1994/50 (26 August 1994)

Other

'Study of the Problem of Discrimination against Indigenous Populations' (1986) UN Doc. E/CN.4/Sub.2/1986/7 & Adds.1–4, 1987
'Universal Declaration on Indigenous Rights: A Set of Preambular Paragraphs and Principles' (1988) UN Doc. E/CN.4/Sub.2/1988/25
'First Revised Text of the Draft Universal Declaration on the Rights of Indigenous Peoples' (1989) UN Doc. E/CN.4/Sub.2/1989/33
'Report on its Forty-Sixthth session' (1994) UN Doc. E/CN.4/Sub.2/1994/5

UN WORKING GROUP ON INDIGENOUS POPULATIONS

Draft Declaration on the Rights of Indigenous Peoples (1994) UN Doc. E/CN.4/Sub.2/1994/2/Add.1
'Annotations to the Provisional Agenda' (8 June 1994) UN Doc. E/CN.4/Sub.2/AC.4/1994/1/Add.1
'Working Group on Indigenous Populations: Consideration of a Permanent Forum for Indigenous People' (6 July 1995) UN Doc. E/CN.4/Sub.2/AC.4/1995/7/Add.2

Reports

'Report of the Working Group on Indigenous Populations on its Fifth Session' (24 August 1997) UN Doc. E/CN.4/Sub.2/1987/22
'Report of the WGIP on its Sixth Session' (24 August 1988) UN Doc. E/CN.4/Sub.2/1988/24
'Report of the Working Group on Indigenous Populations on its Seventh Session' (25 August 1989) UN Doc. E/CN.4/Sub.2/1989/36
'Report of the Working Group on Indigenous Populations on its Eighth Session' (27 August 1990) UN Doc. E/CN.4/Sub.2/1990/42
'Report of the Working Group on Indigenous Populations on its Ninth Session (3 October 1991) UN Doc. E/CN.4/Sub.2/1991/40/Rev.1
'Report of the Working Group on Indigenous Populations on its Eleventh Session', UN Doc. E/CN.4/Sub.2/1993/29
'Report of the Working Group on Indigenous Populations on its Fifteenth Session' (13 August 1997) UN Doc. E/CN.4/Sub.2/1997/14

WORLD BANK

'About the Grants Facility for Indigenous Peoples' (World Bank, 2004), http://web.worldbank.org/archive/website00524/WEB/OTHER/GLOBAL-3.HTM

Bank Procedure 4.10 on Indigenous Peoples (World Bank 2005)
Charter Establishing the Forest Carbon Partnership Facility (8 April 2020)
Operational Directive 4.20, Indigenous Peoples (World Bank 1991)
Operational Manual: OP 4.10 – Indigenous Peoples (World Bank 2005)
Operational Manual Statement, 'Tribal People in Bank financed Projects', OMS 2.34 (1982)
Office of Environmental and Scientific Affairs, 'A Five-Year Implementation Review of OMS 2.34 (1982–1986)' (June 1987)
The World Bank Environmental and Social Framework (World Bank, 2017)
'The World Bank's Safeguard Policies Proposed Review and Update: Approach Paper' (10 October 2012)
'World Bank Environmental and Social Safeguard Policies Review and Update: Regional Dialogue with Indigenous Peoples, Terms of Reference' (2013), https://consultations.worldbank.org/sites/default/files/data/hub/files/safeguards_review_terms_of_reference_for_ip_regional_dialogue_2013.pdf
'World Bank Policies Review and Update, Dialogue with Indigenous Peoples October 2013–March 2014 Summary' (World Bank, 2014), https://consultations.worldbank.org/sites/default/files/data/hub/files/consultation-template/review-and-update-world-bank-safeguard-policies/en/materials/final_summary_dialogue_with_ip_october_2013-march_2014.pdf
World Bank Country Evaluation and Regional Relations Operations Evaluation Department, *Implementation of Operational Directive 4.20 on Indigenous Peoples: An Evaluation of Results* (10 April 2003) Report No. 23754
World Bank Operations Evaluation Department, *Implementation of Operational Directive 4.20 on Indigenous Peoples: An Independent Desk Review* (10 January 2003) Report No. 25332

Consultations

'Summary of Consultations with External Stakeholders regarding the World Bank Draft Indigenous Peoples Policy, Draft OP/BP 4.10' (18 April 2002)

WORLD INTELLECTUAL PROPERTY ORGANIZATION

'Assemblies of the Member States of WIPO, Thirty-Seventh Series of Meetings, General Report' (2002) WIPO Doc. A/37/14
'Assemblies of the Member States of WIPO, Fifty-Seventh Series of Meetings, October 2 to 11, 2017, Summary Report, Addendum, Item 18 of the Consolidated Agenda' (11 October 2017) WIPO Doc. A/57/11/Add.6
'Draft Study on the Participation of Observers in the Work of the Intergovernmental Committee on Intellectual Property and Genetic Resources, Traditional Knowledge and Folklore' (2012) WIPO Doc. WIPO/GRTKF/IC/20/7
General Rules of Procedure, No. 399 (FE) Rev. 3, 1998 (adopted 28 September 1970; amended 27 November 1973, 5 October 1976, and 2 October 1979)
'Intergovernmental Committee IGC' https://wipo.int/tk/en/igc/
'Presentations on Indigenous and Local Community Experiences', www.wipo.int/tk/en/igc/panels.html

Secretariat

'Note on Existing Mechanisms for Participation of Observers in the Work of the WIPO Intergovernmental Committee on Intellectual Property and Genetic Resources, Traditional Knowledge and Folklore' (10 October 2011)

WIPO General Assembly

'Establishment of the WIPO Voluntary Fund for Accredited Indigenous and Local Communities' (2005) WIPO Doc. WO/GA/32/6

'WIPO General Assembly, Twenty-Sixth (12th Extraordinary) Session, Report' (3 October 2000) WIPO Doc. WO/GA/26/10

'WIPO General Assembly, Thirtieth (16th Ordinary) Session, Report' (1 October 2003) WIPO Doc. WO/GA/30/8

'WIPO General Assembly, Thirty-First (15th Extraordinary) Session, Report' (5 October 2004) WIPO Doc. WO/GA/31/15

'WIPO General Assembly, Thirty-Second (17th Ordinary) Session, Report' (5 October 2005) WIPO Doc. WO/GA/32/13

'WIPO General Assembly, Thirty-Third (16th Extraordinary) Session, Report' (3 October 2006) WIPO Doc. WO/GA/33/10

'WIPO General Assembly, Thirty-Fourth (18th Ordinary) Session, Report' (12 November 2007) WIPO Doc. WO/GA/34/16

Intergovernmental Committee on Intellectual Property, Genetic Resources, Traditional Knowledge and Folklore

'Draft Report on the Twenty-Fifth Session' (18 October 2013) WIPO Doc. WIPO WIPO/GRTKF/IC/25/8 PROV.2

'Draft Report on the Fortieth Session' (30 September 2019) WIPO Doc. WIPO/GRTKF/IC/40/20 PROV.2

'Draft Study on the Participation of Observers in the Work of the Intergovernmental Committee on Intellectual Property and Genetic Resources, Traditional Knowledge and Folklore', WIPO Doc. WIPO/GRTKF/IC/20/7

'Intersessional Working Group (IWG) 2, March 2011' (2011) WIPO Doc. WIPO/GRTKF/IWG/2/3

'Participation of Local and Indigenous Communities in the Work of the Committee' (2002) WIPO Doc. WIPO/GRTKF/IC/4/12

'New Zealand Proposal – Practical Participation of Indigenous and Local Communities' (2005) WIPO Doc. WIPO/GRTKF/IC/7/14

'Practical Guide for Observers' (n.d.), www.wipo.int/export/sites/www/tk/en/igc/pdf/observers_practical_guide.pdf.

'Report on the First Session' (2001) WIPO/GRTKF/IC/1/13

'Report on the Second Session' (14 December 2001) WIPO/GRTKF/IC/2/16

'Report on the Third Session' (21 June 2022) WIPO/GRTKF/IC/3/17

'Report on the Fourth Session' (17 December 2002) WIPO/GRTKF/IC/4/15

'Report on the Fifth Session' (2003) WIPO/GRTKF/IC/5/15

'Report on the Seventh Session' (2005) WIPO/GRTKF/IC/7/15

'Report on the Thirteenth Session' (30 April 2009) WIPO/GRTKF/IC/13/11

'Report on the Fourteenth Session' (1 October 2009) WIPO/GRTKF/IC/14/12

'Report on the Fifteenth Session' (14 May 2010) WIPO/GRTKF/IC/15/7

'Report on the Sixteenth Session' (10 December 2010) WIPO/GRTKF/IC/16/8
'Report on the Eighteenth Session' (29 July 2011) WIPO/GRTKF/IC/18/11
'Report on the Nineteenth Session' (23 February 2012) WIPO/GRTKF/IC/19/12
'Report on the Twentieth Session' (13 July 2012) WIPO/GRTKF/IC/20/10
'Report on the Twenty-Seventh Session' (2 July 2014) WIPO/GRTKF/IC/27/10
'Report on the Twenty-Eight Session' (2014) WIPO/GRTKF/IC/28
'Report on the Thirty-Third Session' (12 June 2017) WIPO/GRTKF/IC/33/7
'Report on the Thirty-Fifth Session' (2018) WIPO/GRTKF/IC/35/10
'Report on the Thirty-Sixth Session' (2018) WIPO/GRTKF/IC/36/11
'Report on the Thirty-Seventh Session' (2019) WIPO/GRTKF/IC/37/17
'Report on the Thirty-Eighth Session' (2019) WIPO/GRTKF/IC/38/16
'Report on the Thirty-Ninth Session' (2019) WIPO/GRRTKF/IC/39/18
'Rules of Procedure' (2001) WIPO/GRTKF/IC/1/2

Budget Committee

WIPO Budget Committee, 'Draft Program and Budget 1998–1999' (1998) WIPO Doc. WO/BC/18/2—A/32/2

OTHER

Canada, Denmark, Norway, the Russian Federation, and the United States of America, 'Ilulissat Declaration' (adopted 28 May 2008, Ilulissat, Greenland)
Canada, Denmark, Norway, the Russian Federation, and the United States of America, 'Declaration Concerning the Prevention of Unregulated High Seas Fishing in the Central Arctic Ocean' (Oslo, 16 July 2015)
Helsinki Final Act (1975) 14 ILM 1293–1325
'List of Non-governmental Organizations Recommended for Accreditation by the Secretary-General of the Conference: United Nations Conference on Environment and Development' (19 March 1991) UN Doc. A/CONF.151/PC/L.28/Add.9
Report of the United Nations Conference on Environment and Development, Annex I: Rio Declaration on Environment and Development (12 August 1992) UN Doc. A/CONF.151/26 and Rev.1
UN Conference on Environment and Development, *Agenda 21* (1992)
UN Conference on Environment and Development, 'Report of the United Nations Conference on Environment and Development, Volume II: Proceedings of the Conference' (1993) UN Doc. A/CONF.151/26/Rev.1 (Vol. II)
UN Development Group, *Guidelines on Indigenous Peoples' Issues* (UN 2008) https://unsdg.un.org/sites/default/files/UNDG_guidelines_EN.pdf
World Commission on Environment and Development, *Our Common Future* (1987)

Index

For EU product safety concerns, contact us at Calle de José Abascal, 56–1°, 28003 Madrid, Spain or eugpsr@cambridge.org.

www.ingramcontent.com/pod-product-compliance
Lightning Source LLC
LaVergne TN
LVHW011703200926
848484LV00004B/1059
9781009406314